THE CORRESPONDENCE OF H.G. WELLS

Volume 1

THE CORRESPONDENCE OF H.G. WELLS

THE CORRESPONDENCE OF H.G. WELLS

Volume 1 1880–1903

Edited by
DAVID C. SMITH

LONDON AND NEW YORK

First published in 1998 by Pickering & Chatto (Publishers) Limited

This edition first published in 2021
by Routledge
2 Park Square, Milton Park, Abingdon, Oxon OX14 4RN

and by Routledge
52 Vanderbilt Avenue, New York, NY 10017

Routledge is an imprint of the Taylor & Francis Group, an informa business

© 1998 Letters of H.G. Wells by the Literary Executors of the Estate of H.G. Wells
© 1998 Introduction, notes, editorial apparatus and selection by David C. Smith
© 1998 Introductory essay 'Wells in his Letters' by Patrick Parrinder

All rights reserved. No part of this book may be reprinted or reproduced or utilised in any form or by any electronic, mechanical, or other means, now known or hereafter invented, including photocopying and recording, or in any information storage or retrieval system, without permission in writing from the publishers.

Trademark notice: Product or corporate names may be trademarks or registered trademarks, and are used only for identification and explanation without intent to infringe.

British Library Cataloguing in Publication Data
A catalogue record for this book is available from the British Library

ISBN: 978-0-367-76553-8 (Set)
ISBN: 978-1-00-316751-8 (Set) (ebk)
ISBN: 978-0-367-76512-5 (Volume 1) (hbk)
ISBN: 978-1-00-316741-9 (Volume 1) (ebk)

Publisher's Note
The publisher has gone to great lengths to ensure the quality of this reprint but points out that some imperfections in the original copies may be apparent.

Disclaimer
The publisher has made every effort to trace copyright holders and would welcome correspondence from those they have been unable to trace.

THE CORRESPONDENCE OF
H. G. WELLS

Volume 1 1880–1903

An enthusiastic reader at an early age – Bertie Wells aged 10 (*H G Wells Papers, University of Illinois Library*).

THE CORRESPONDENCE OF
H. G. WELLS

VOLUME 1
1880–1903

Edited by
DAVID C. SMITH

Consulting Editor
Patrick Parrinder

LONDON AND NEW YORK

First published 1998 by Pickering & Chatto (Publishers) Limited

Published 2016 by Routledge
2 Park Square, Milton Park, Abingdon, Oxon OX14 4RN
711 Third Avenue, New York, NY 10017, USA

Routledge is an imprint of the Taylor & Francis Group, an informa business

© Letters of H. G. Wells by The Literary Executors of the Estate of H. G. Wells 1998

© Introduction, notes, editorial apparatus and selection by David C. Smith 1998

© Introductory essay 'Wells in his letters' by Patrick Parrinder 1998

All rights reserved. No part of this book may be reprinted or reproduced or utilised in any form or by any electronic, mechanical, or other means, now known or hereafter invented, including photocopying and recording, or in any information storage or retrieval system, without permission in writing from the publishers.

Notice:
Product or corporate names may be trademarks or registered trademarks, and are used only for identificationand explanation without intent to infringe.

BRITISH LIBRARY CATALOGUING IN PUBLICATION DATA
Wells, H. G. (Herbert George), 1866–1946
  The correspondence of H. G. Wells. – (The Pickering masters)
  1. Wells, H. G. (Herbert George), 1866–1946 – Correspondence
  2. Novelists, English – 20th century – Correspondence
  I. Title II. Smith, David
  823.9′12
  ISBN 13: 978-1-85196-1-733 (set)
  ISBN 13 : 978-1-13875-9-015 (hbk) (volume 1)

LIBRARY OF CONGRESS CATALOGING-IN-PUBLICATION DATA
Wells, H. G. (Herbert George), 1866–1946
  (Correspondence)
  The correspondence of H. G. Wells / edited by David Clayton Smith.
  p.   cm.
  Includes index.
  Contents: v. 1. 1880–1903 – – v. 2. 1904–1918 – – v. 3. 1919–1934 – – v. 4. 1935–1946.
    ISBN 1-85196-173-9 (set : alk. paper). – – ISBN 1-85196-170-4 (v. 1 : alk. paper). – – ISBN 1-85196-171-2 (v. 2 : alk. paper). – – ISBN 1-85196-172-0 (v. 3 : alk. paper). – – ISBN 1-85196-158-5 (v. 4 : alk. paper).
    Wells, H. G. (Herbert George), 1866–1946 – – Correspondence. 2. Novelists. English – – 20th century – – Correspondence. 3. Journalists – – Great Britain – – Correspondence.   I. Smith, David C. (David Clayton), 1929-   . II. Title.
PR5776.A4   1996
823′.912 – – dc20
  [B]   96-31086
                                                                                                          CIP

Typeset by Waveney Typesetters
Wymondham, Norwich

CONTENTS

VOLUME 1

Frontispiece	ii
Wells in his Letters, by Patrick Parrinder	vii
The Wells Correspondence	xvii
Selecting and Editing the Letters	xxi
Types of Letter	xxii
Acronyms Used	xxvi
Rules of Transcription	xxvii
Editorial Apparatus	xxix
Archives and Other Sources Consulted	xxx
A Biographical Outline	xxxiv
Chronology	xliv
Acknowledgements	li
THE CORRESPONDENCE OF H. G. WELLS 1880–1903	1
Appendix	453

VOLUME 2

Frontispiece	ii
Chronology	vi
THE CORRESPONDENCE OF H. G. WELLS 1904–1918	1

VOLUME 3

Frontispiece	ii
Chronology	vi
THE CORRESPONDENCE OF H. G. WELLS 1919–1934	1

VOLUME 4

Frontispiece	ii
Chronology	vi
THE CORRESPONDENCE OF H. G. WELLS 1935–1946	1
Indexes: i) Recipient ii) Subject	537

WELLS IN HIS LETTERS
by Patrick Parrinder

H. G. Wells was a novelist, journalist, teacher and prophet, and a man of prodigious energies. These energies were manifest not only in his writing but in his love-life, his political and business activities, his family relationships, and in his letters. The present edition is the first general collection of his correspondence, and it is the first, in terms of its scope and variety, to do this immensely prolific author justice. To his output of 150 books and pamphlets and over 4,200 published items we may now add some 2,800 selected letters. The statistics alone are impressive enough, but the letters offer a unique record of the intellectual vitality, the sense of mission, the candour and the personal warmth that Wells sustained throughout his long life.

Wells's finest creative work as a novelist and scientific romancer was mostly confined to a relatively brief period, roughly between 1895 and 1910. He was essentially a writer of the newspaper age, before the rise of radio and television, and his visionary novels and speculative essays brought him what was even then an exceptional degree of fame and influence. Much of his later correspondence reflects this. He received, and answered, hundreds of letters from ordinary readers, from would-be writers, from editors and fundraisers, and from some of the leading political figures of the twentieth century who became his friends and interlocutors. At the same time, Wells's letters give a sense of the pattern of his life and work that is subtly different from the conventional accounts put forward by his biographers. Many of the most scintillating letters in this collection were written in adolescence, revealing the verbal inventiveness, the self-possession and the gift of irrepressible fantasy displayed by the young Wells. Some of the most admirable letters are found in the final volume, where he confesses past mistakes and defiantly faces up to disappointment, infirmity and approaching death. Taken as a whole, the letters constitute a very rich archive, on which no biographer – not even David C. Smith himself – has yet drawn fully.

This does not mean that they offer sensational revelations of the sort that are prized chiefly for their capacity to discredit the person who wrote them. Wells was nothing if not a controversialist: he had his enemies and detractors during his lifetime, and it is a sign of his continuing importance that he still irritates the same sort of people today. Certainly the letters disclose aspects of his private life that were previously unknown to us, including friendships, love-affairs, intellectual enthusiasms, and a host of small domestic details. But Wells's correspondence also confirms that, once he had become an established writer, his private face was not significantly different from his public face. He was a pioneer of the open discussion of social prejudices and sexual emotions in his novels and autobiographies (including the posthumous volume *H. G. Wells in Love*). When he observed the conventional reticences of his day it was usually to protect the other people in his life, rather than to protect himself. His candour is part of his greatness as a writer. It gives these letters their representative quality, as expressions of the developing 'persona' that he memorably analysed at the beginning of *Experiment in Autobiography* (1934), but it also suggests some limitations.

The letters contain few secrets. Except when he is writing to his brothers and his fellow-students in youth, or at the height of one of his love-affairs, they do not constitute a secret journal. Usually they are ancillary to his other activities as a writer and human being. He writes love-letters when the beloved is unavoidably absent, business letters when business arrangements have to be made and recorded, and so on. Often he gives new friends his telephone number. His wife, Catherine Wells, and later on his secretaries helped him to deal with many of his letters. His private correspondence runs into his public correspondence: this is the prime justification for David C. Smith's decision to print the personal letters and the letters to the press together, as part of the same sequence. Inevitably, parts of his life are missing from the letters, and many letters are themselves missing (while others must be sought elsewhere, for reasons that will be explained below). They are not invariably a reliable guide to whatever was uppermost in his work and thoughts.

Wells wrote to an unknown correspondent in 1916 that 'I am a novelist & I want to get back to novel writing' (volume 2, p. 482). Only a small proportion of these letters casts any direct light on Wells the writer of novels. His intellectual and artistic formation as a young man is richly revealed, and a handful of letters present his often disparaging afterthoughts about what he had written: he describes *The War of the Worlds*, for example, as a 'clotted mass of fine things spoilt' (volume 1, p. 333), indicating that from time to time he was his own harshest critic. The letters confirm that he took almost ten years to develop and refine the basic idea of his early masterpiece *The Time Machine*; on the other hand, he speaks of the 'feverish time' when, anxious to consolidate his initial breakthrough, he was writing *The Island of Doctor Moreau* and *The Wonderful Visit* at the rate of 7,000 words a day (volume 1, p. 284).

Later on when he complained of overwork it was most often the result of his political and educational campaigns. The letters convey a strong sense of his ceaseless political activities, as well as setting out his views on socialism, feminism, racism, totalitarianism, nationalism, eugenics, anti-Semitism, and much else. Doubtless, as he said of himself in a 1932 letter published in T. S. Eliot's *Criterion*, he was a 'sufficiently copious and careless writer to furnish material for hostile criticisms' (volume 3, p. 416), but with the publication of these letters there is no longer any excuse for ill-informed criticisms. Nor can any reader overlook Wells's abiding concerns for world citizenship, for a socialism at once 'liberal' and 'revolutionary', for equality of opportunity and, above all, for intellectual freedom. He was, as he said, a 'thorn in the side of Toryism' (volume 4, p. 288) and a lifelong opponent of British and other imperialisms; and some people have never forgiven him for it.

Wells was a controversialist in an age of journalistic controversy, when contemporaries such as George Bernard Shaw, G. K. Chesterton and Hilaire Belloc raised the stinging riposte and the letter to the editor to a fine art. There is ample evidence – see for example his wonderful demolition of Shaw's views on Russia (and on everything else) in 1914 (volume 2, pp. 406–13) – that Wells gave as good as he got in these arguments. In Vincent Brome's *Six Studies in Quarrelling* (London: Cresset, 1958) he is shown at loggerheads with Shaw, Belloc, Churchill, and Henry Arthur Jones. The present edition adds new material on these debates, as well as on his role in many other battles private and public, including the 'war against socialism' of 1906–7 in which the Tory press made him a prime target. Some of the quarrels reflect his testiness and irascibility in later life, while others reveal his opponents' eccentricities. Notable among the latter is his short-lived patronage of Ford Madox Hueffer's *English Review*, culminating in a 1909 letter in which he all too plausibly accuses Hueffer, who would later change his name to Ford Madox Ford, of disguising his voice and pretending to be someone else when answering the telephone (volume 2, p. 238).

Previous collections of letters
Wells's letters to the press were not the only aspect of his correspondence to be made public during his lifetime. Numerous brief excerpts from letters to his family and friends were included by Geoffrey West in his biography *H. G. Wells: A Sketch for a Portrait* (London: Gerald Howe, 1930). Perhaps stimulated by West's researches, Wells himself reprinted many of the family letters in facsimile in *Experiment in Autobiography* four years later. It was in this way that the characteristic Wellsian 'picshuas', or pen-and-ink cartoons, became known to a wider readership. Other letters appeared with his permission in memoirs by his contemporaries. After his death, the huge archive of incoming

letters, draft replies and carbon copies created by his wife and daughter-in-law was purchased by the University of Illinois at Urbana. Their collection has been supplemented, wherever possible, by original copies and xeroxes of Wells's own letters. The first director of the Wells Collection was Gordon N. Ray, at that time a professor of English at the University of Illinois. Under his supervision the letters were transcribed and catalogued, and a series of individual volumes of correspondence appeared. Ray was principally interested in Wells as a novelist, so the series had an exclusively literary bias. He jointly edited the first and best-known volume, *Henry James and H. G. Wells* (London: Hart-Davis, 1958), with the great James scholar Leon Edel. Thanks to this volume the Wells–James quarrel has remained a byword for the conflict between the demands of artistic integrity and political and social engagement in the twentieth century.

Henry James was in the habit of destroying most of the letters that he received, so that of the 70 items reprinted by Edel and Ray only eleven were letters from Wells. There is a very similar pattern in the Wells–George Gissing letters, edited by Royal A. Gettmann (London: Hart-Davis, 1961), which includes thirteen Wells letters. *Arnold Bennett and H. G. Wells*, edited by Harris Wilson (London: Hart-Davis, 1960) and the much more recent *Bernard Shaw and H. G. Wells*, edited by J. Percy Smith (Toronto: University of Toronto Press, 1995) offer a far more balanced representation of both sides. Gordon N. Ray also wrote a biographical study of *H. G. Wells and Rebecca West* (London: Macmillan, 1974), every word of which was vetted by Rebecca West (much to the fury of her and Wells's son Anthony West). Ray claimed to have read more than 800 Wells letters in Dame Rebecca's possession, and more than 50 of these are quoted in his book, though very few are given in full.

H. G. Wells: His Turbulent Life and Times (London: Macmillan, 1969), a biography by Lovat Dickson, included extensive quotations from Wells's letters to the publisher Frederick Macmillan. Other Wells letters have appeared in the secondary literature on his friends and acquaintances such as Joseph Conrad, Sir Richard Gregory and Olaf Stapledon. In the present edition David C. Smith has reprinted a small number of already published letters, always with due acknowledgment, but the bulk of the material in his four volumes has never been collected before. This is therefore both a major work of scholarship and one that should be supplemented by the sources mentioned above in order for a complete picture of Wells's known correspondence to emerge. In addition, there are further categories of Wells letters that may become available to researchers in the future, and there is one crucial and as yet unpublished archive. Wells's letters to Rebecca West are on deposit in the Beineke Library at Yale, where they were embargoed until after the deaths of Rebecca and

Anthony West. If Ray's report of their extent is correct, they would suffice, together with the other known letters not published here, to fill a fifth volume on the same scale as the ones in the present edition.

Volume 1: 1880–1903
'The literary life', Wells wrote in 1911, 'is one of the modern forms of adventure'. His sense of his own life as a modern adventure is recorded in his autobiographies and autobiographical novels, especially in *Tono-Bungay* where the hero not only rises in society but becomes a sociologist and social anthropologist. True adventure implies hardship and danger, and demands a sensibility capable of fully registering the fear and exhilaration that marks the adventurer's progress through life. Wells's early letters meet these requirements. Letter 3, outlining his daily routine as a draper's apprentice at the age of thirteen, expresses the sense of enslavement that thousands of young people in late Victorian England must have felt at their first entry into the world of work. Wells revolted against the discipline of a twelve-hour day behind the counter and got himself sacked from his first job, but he was forced to return to the drapery trade, where his period of servitude lasted several years. His intelligence and scholastic promise were manifest, and the letters he wrote to his parents in 1883 begging to be allowed to take up an unpaid teaching post show his gathering desperation.

The prevailing tone of the early letters is not one of anger or bitterness but of courage, high spirits, and a precocious comic talent. When we find him addressing his brother Frank (for example) as 'his most sublime Majesty' (p. 14), or parodying the language of invoices, business letters or the Sunday sermon, we are witnessing the deliberate or inadvertent literary apprenticeship of a great entertainer. His letters to his mother are more formal and punctilious than those to his brothers, yet he produces his most amusing 'picshuas' for her benefit. Letter 33, which begins by recording that 'I have passed all my Science Exams' and ends with 'HOORAY!' and the signature 'Your affectionate Goodfornaught/ H. G. Wells/ Now an independent/ Gentleman' (pp. 34–5) is a classic of its kind, precisely marking the transition to our modern meritocratic society from the classbound world of Balzac and Dickens.

Reading such a letter in the pages of a nineteenth-century novel, we might fear the worst; and Wells's path to independence and respectability remained a chequered one. The fruit of his examination successes was a trainee teacher's scholarship to the Normal School (later the Royal College) of Science in South Kensington, but after a heady first year under T. H. Huxley he neglected his studies and eventually failed his Finals. Meanwhile, he wrote and published his first stories and made some steadfast friends, including his lifelong correspondents 'Rags' (later Sir Richard) Gregory and Elizabeth Healey. He continued to delight in facetious forms of address – 'Dear Geezer', 'Dear Hats', 'Incarnato Devilspit', and so on – and left his friends in no doubt of his lack of respect for the 'Abnormal Science School' (p. 49) and its teaching. In the summer of 1887 he was back on the job market, taking an obscure teaching post at Holt Academy for a few weeks and then, on August 29th, suffering the footballing accident whose grim consequences are set out in Letter 57 to his mother. His life was briefly in danger, and for years afterwards he would be in frail health, with frequent relapses. 'My only chance now for a living is literature. ... Yours/ Truly/ A Wreck', he wrote to his fellow-student A. Morley Davies (p. 66).

Some of the most fascinating letters date from his period of convalescence with William Burton, another student contemporary, at Stoke-on-Trent ('Stoik' or 'Stuck', in Wellsian jargon) the following year. He read Emerson and Whitman, wrote copiously, and described himself as the 'Prophet of the Undelivered Spell' (pp. 102–3). He completed 'The Chronic Argonauts', the first version of *The Time Machine*, and began to plan a sequel. But it was not until 1894, when he had established himself as a biology teacher and educational journalist and suffered a further severe breakdown, that he could write to Elizabeth Healey that 'our ancient Chronic Argonauts' had at last become a complete story. 'It's my trump card & if it does not come off very much I shall know my place for the rest of my career', he added (p. 226). As the world knows, *The Time Machine* did come off, and Wells, always restless, never learnt his place. Nevertheless, as his fame and prosperity grew and the circle of his correspondents widened he continued to write to the members of his family and his earliest friends with affection and gratitude. 'If I have done anything in this world', he told R. A. Gregory in 1925, 'it is largely because you and [Tommy] Simmons did so much in the crucial years to make me believe in myself' (volume 3, p. 203).

Wells lived through the eighteen-nineties, and wrote his finest science fiction, in a state of chronic invalidism. Some, though not all, of his doctors thought he was consumptive. There was a marked change in the direction of his work after 1900, when he shook off the cosmic pessimism of the early scientific romances and turned to politics and social prophecy. The letters reveal that his change of outlook was accompanied, if not exactly prompted, by an extraordinary onset of physical vigour. His house at Sandgate had been designed by C. F. A. Voysey in 1899 to accommodate a client who, it was feared, might soon be confined to a wheelchair. Instead, Wells took up mountain walking, went on punishing bicycle rides, challenged his house-guests to games of hockey, and played energetically with his two sons, who were born in 1901 and 1903.

Volume 2: 1904–1918, and Volume 3: 1919–1934
Wells's new-found physical energy was accompanied by a manifest enlargement of his sexual needs. In 1893 he had left his first wife, Isabel, for Amy Catherine Robbins, whom he married in 1895. They remained together until her death in 1927. 'My inmost heart is yours', he wrote to Catherine when he first received the news of her terminal cancer (volume 3, p. 235). Readers must judge the proportions of self-knowledge and self-deception in that statement, but we may be sure that Catherine herself accepted and was comforted by it. He invariably returned to her from his numerous love-affairs and, on at least one occasion, he wrote her a letter of self-justification, describing his need for other women as a matter of simple physical appetite, of 'sexual exasperation' which he would normally 'get pacified in London' (volume 2, p. 372). Many of his women friends shared his sexual opportunism, and usually they remained on friendly terms with him long after the physical relationship had ceased. His correspondence with Violet Hunt, Ella Hepworth Dixon, Margaret Sanger, and Constance Coolidge is representative of these relationships. Amber Reeves and Rebecca West had children by him and regarded him as a desirable long-term companion and potential husband, though each had to accept her subordinate place in his life. The quality, though not the number and complexity, of his sexual relationships necessarily changed after Catherine Wells's death in 1927. Some of his most affecting love-letters were written to Moura Budberg, the 'trusty Girl Guide' (volume 3, p. 56) whom he had got to know at Maxim Gorky's house in Moscow in 1920. Moura was to become the companion of his old age, though, distressingly for Wells, she maintained an intricate life of her own. 'She is always flitting off. I scream with rage when I am left alone, like a bad child', Wells was to tell Constance Coolidge (volume 4, p. 11).

Around 1904 Wells asked his closest friends to return his letters, and then destroyed a few that he had written at the time of his desertion of Isabel. There is no evidence of any later suppressions on his part. He was on good terms with Isabel after her remarriage and only one of his major relationships, that with Odette Keun, ended in mutual recriminations. One of the most surprising accusations brought against Wells in recent years – that of misogyny – is amply refuted not only by his affection and generosity towards his former lovers but by his platonic friendships with many other remarkable women, including Elizabeth Healey, Violet Paget ('Vernon Lee') and Eileen Power.

Just as the letters record his return to rude health at the beginning of the century, they also map the first signs of loss of vigour and physical decline. Undernourished and skeletal as a young man, we find him complaining in his late thirties of a 'slight tendency to embonpoint' (volume 2, p. 83) which would become more pronounced later. He was prone to influenza and bronchitis, and after the First World War, when he was newly wealthy from the profits of *The Outline of History*, he began like many of his upper-class contemporaries to spend his winters by the Mediterranean. This habit was already established by the time that he built a house at Lou Pidou near Grasse with Odette Keun. In his sixties he began to suffer from diabetes and, characteristically, he wrote about his illness in a 1933 letter to *The Times* (volume 3, pp. 479–80) which led to the foundation of the Diabetic Association.

As he devoted more of his time to social and political propaganda after 1900, Wells seems to have doubted whether he was best placed as a professional writer forced to live by his pen. He took an interest in the newly-formed Sociological Society, debated eugenics with Francis Galton – though his dismissal of eugenics as a 'sham science' (volume 2, p. 437) more or less represents his considered view – and wrote to the Conservative Prime Minister Arthur Balfour about the possibility of a public endowment (volume 2, p. 71). It is tempting to wonder how long Wells would have lasted as (say) a professor at the London School of Economics, another new institution which he observed with some interest. In the long run he accepted that, whatever else he might do, he would always remain a novelist. His pleasure in reading up about radioactivity in preparation for his atomic bomb novel *The World Set Free* (1914) is quite infectious (volume 2, p. 346). Any other signs of enthusiasm for science fiction are extremely rare in his correspondence, however. He preferred to be known as an encyclopaedist, educator and political journalist, though in the nineteen-thirties he also turned to radio and the cinema. The letters reveal some unexpected literary friendships, for example with Henry Newbolt, Robert Ross, Thomas Hardy and Siegfried Sassoon. He played an important, and hitherto mostly unsuspected, part in the revival of Oscar Wilde's reputation. He was invariably generous to younger writers, going out of his way to express admiration for James Joyce, Katherine Mansfield and Wyndham Lewis, and striking up intimate friendships with J. B. Priestley and Frank Swinnerton. In the early nineteen-thirties he took up a new public campaign. He succeeded John Galsworthy as International President of PEN, and gave up much of his time to defending free speech and protesting against the suppression of thought under totalitarian regimes.

Volume 4: 1935–1946
Many of Wells's later public activities could be traced back to 1918, when he joined Lord Northcliffe's government propaganda unit at Crewe House and tried to get agreement on a statement of Allied war aims. The immediate outcome was Wells's bitter disillusionment with the Treaty of Versailles and the League of Nations; but in the long term his experiences at Crewe House led to

his project for an 'Open Conspiracy' of liberal revolutionaries, and to the Human Rights campaign that he launched at the beginning of the Second World War. This campaign arose naturally from his perception that the fight against Hitler demanded a statement of positive war aims just as the war against the Kaiser had done. From the letters in Volume 4 we can appreciate for the first time Wells's almost fanatical persistence in getting agreement on a declaration of rights, in subjecting the declaration to constant redrafting to remove its Eurocentric bias, and in circulating the various documents to influential people in as many different countries as possible. Usually he refused to take personal credit for what may well be regarded as his most significant political achievement. Wells's critique of the League of Nations helped to prepare for the setting up of the United Nations, while his work on human rights led more directly to the Universal Declaration of Human Rights adopted by the UN in December 1948. James Dilloway has told this story in his pamphlet *Human Rights and World Order* (London: The H. G. Wells Society, 1983). Wells said that he had expended on the Human Rights campaign 'a vast amount of toil and some hundreds of pounds' (p. 473). Among much other evidence, David C. Smith prints a 1945 letter to Wells from Eduard Beneš, the head of the Czechoslovak Government in exile who was on the point of returning to his homeland. Beneš, who would be forced to resign by the Communist coup of 1948, spoke of his admiration for Wells's 'vigorous fight for ideals which we both embrace', and looked to the building of a new nation based upon the 'democratic principles to which [we] are both pledged' (p. 520).

Fundamental to any modern declaration of rights are the equal rights of all races. Wells was a fervent anti-racist, but throughout the nineteen-thirties and forties he had to confront his ambivalence towards the Jews. He repeatedly condemned Nazi persecution, but he denounced Zionism as a form of outmoded nationalism and (as a 1943 letter to Chaim Weizmann makes clear) he opposed the creation of the state of Israel. Moreover, he had an exasperating tendency to hold separatist Jews responsible for their own persecution. He claimed to be defending progressive and cosmopolitan Jewry against the 'reactionary elements still disagreeably active in the Jewish tradition' (p. 88), but by 1943 he had to admit that he had gone much too far. '*Mea culpa*; I have girded at Jews as Johnson used to gird at Scotchmen', he wrote to Weizmann, blaming his own 'ready irritability and tactlessness' (pp. 424–5). What he felt about the revelations of the Nazi death camps or, indeed, about other aspects of the immediate post-war world can only be surmised. 'I get more and more anarchistic and ultra left as I grow older', he told Bertrand Russell (p. 524), and defiantly voted Communist in the 1945 election. But for most of the remaining fifteen months of his life he was too ill to write letters.

Volume 4 begins with a fleeting and evidently delightful love-affair with Constance Coolidge and, throughout, it has its lighter side. Faced with Marie Stopes's manuscript on *The Change of Life*, he told the great birth-control campaigner that he could detect no lunar periodicity in himself, although he had kept a 'very careful private diary for two or three years' (p. 82). He admonished his fellow-residents in Hanover Terrace, Regent's Park, about the noise of persistently barking dogs and the nuisance posed by a large Salvation Army hoarding. He threatened to sue for defamation and loss of earnings when a reviewer in the *Methodist Recorder* opined that the quality of his books had deteriorated. He saw out both the Blitz and the flying-bomb attacks in Hanover Terrace, even though most of his windows were shattered. A well-known photograph of him as an old man shaking his fist, later to be captioned in a book on Wells by the Russian critic J. Kagarlitski as 'H. G. Wells demonstrating his hatred of capitalism', in fact expresses his hatred of the sycamore tree in the next-door garden.[1]

Wells had written to Enid Bagnold in 1932 that 'I keep well & I work. What more can one desire?' (volume 3, p. 409). He had plenty of other desires but, as his body failed, he found most solace in the idea of work. Suffering from gout in early 1944, he declared that 'Apparently I am going to die from the toes upward, so that I shall be able to keep on writing until the end' (p. 486). He nearly did. There were six books in 1942, including a doctoral thesis and his last novel; one each in 1943 and 1944, including his denunciation of Roman Catholicism, *Crux Ansata*; and two in 1945. In one of his last letters he angrily denied a newspaper report that he was plunged into the depths of despair. 'Stoicism has been my refuge all my life', he wrote to his old friend Elizabeth Healey. 'Take what comes to you & help the weaker brethren to endure' (p. 532). It was a sad conclusion for a man of Wells's energies, but a good epitaph all the same.

University of Reading   PATRICK PARRINDER
1997

NOTE

[1] J. Kagarlitzki, *The Life and Thought of H. G. Wells*, trans. Moura Budberg (London: Sidgwick & Jackson, 1966), facing p. 130.

THE WELLS CORRESPONDENCE

Herbert George Wells, H.G, as he was universally known, was an astonishingly prolific writer. He produced about 160 books and pamphlets in a writing career which extended from 1886 to his death in 1946. During that time, his total published output amounted to more than 4,000 individual items. Several of his books have never been out of print since their first publication. His name is still well known fifty years after his death. He was a literary and political force throughout the world during his lifetime and after. There has not been, prior to this edition, any wholesale effort to collect his correspondence in one place, even though as one reads memoirs of the time, it is not unusual to find quotations from his letters to one or another of his colleagues and friends.

Wells was also a remarkably prolific letter writer. Although he was active in a time when the telephone came to be as commonplace as the post box, he seldom used the instrument. He had a telephone installed in his home very early on , but it was mainly for use by his secretaries, or servants. He used the telephone directory to obtain addresses for those persons to whom he wrote letters. He conducted some business by telephone from France in the late 1920s and early 1930s, but not much.

During his lifetime, postal delivery was reliable and quick. He and others in his time depended on two home deliveries a day: same day delivery in London for mail posted before noon, and next day delivery throughout the British Isles. Next or second day delivery was available throughout the continent of Europe, and mail to America was routinely delivered within a week after posting. Even when he lived abroad, although he used the telephone to talk with his secretary in London, this was done primarily to ensure that the post was answered, and that his letters went out on time.

The researcher into Wells's life and thought is faced with a monumental task. In addition to the books, pamphlets, magazine articles and other published material, there is a mountain of correspondence to sift through. I would estimate that there are now approximately 5,000 letters which can be attributed to H.G. Wells and which are available for consultation by researchers. About half of these can be classed as business letters. They provide a window into Wells's negotiations with publishers and agents. These letters allow the researcher to follow the sales of his work, observe marketing methods used or discarded and witness the different demands of serial and book production.

They also give an insight into his radio broadcasts and his forays into film production. In these letters are proposals for books and articles which were never finished, and for works which later emerged in totally different form. The business correspondence is fascinating correspondence in itself, for through it we are able to follow a great writer throughout his productive career. A few such letters are provided in this collection, but they are confined to sample specimens in the main.

The other half of Wells's correspondence, which forms the main body of this collection, is more personal. It constitutes about 3,000 or more letters. Although some of these letters are typewritten by a secretary in their final form (Wells bought his first typewriter in the spring of 1898) the majority of these letters are in holograph.

Wells's personal correspondence extends from letters to great statesmen such as President Franklin D. Roosevelt and Prime Ministers Winston Churchill and A. J. Balfour, to humbler figures such as George Meek, who made his living by pushing a bath chair along the beaches and promenades of England's southern coasts, and 'Mark Benney', a novelist who wrote of his life in the slums and his time in prison. There is a less extensive, but nevertheless fascinating correspondence with his various women friends and lovers. He wrote love letters to Catherine Wells, to Rebecca West, to Odette Keun, to Moura Budberg, to Margaret Sanger, to Constance Coolidge, and to others. Few men of his time, or later, have had as wide an acquaintance with persons of the opposite sex. He was a staunch feminist, and a supporter of equality for women. This side of the man, and those times when he slipped from the highest standards, form a significant part of these volumes.

Wells responded to virtually everyone who wrote to him. He read manuscripts from aspirant novelists, and commented on their efforts. He conducted political campaigns, both in the Fabian Society and when he stood for Parliament. He tried to effect political, social and economic reform on a world scale. He addressed letters to the press (about 300 were published), and he made engagements to meet and dine with significant parties to discuss all these matters.

Over the last few years, one or two critics of Wells have depicted him as an anti-Semite and racist. There has been a strong reaction to these remarks, and the vast majority of Wells scholars have found little, if anything, of this sort in his work. These comments appear to be based on incorrect readings of a few paragraphs in his 1901 book of social commentary, *Anticipations*, reprinted in 1914. The passages concerned are clearly ironic and do not reflect racism and anti-Semitism; instead, they call attention to the need for a stronger and better analysis of these phenomena.

As time went by, Wells became increasingly opposed to nationalism in all its forms. He felt that it was nationalism which had helped destroy the League of Nations and which had prevented an international order from being constructed with world peace at its centre. This led him to oppose Zionism in some of its manifestations. He did not become an anti-Semite, but he was an anti-Zionist.

Early in the 1930s a brief exchange about anti-Semitism took place in *The Jewish Chronicle* and *Liberty Magazine*. Wells's secretary wrote to the papers pointing out that Wells had been misquoted in these articles. The editors of both magazines apologised to him, but at least one critic of Wells has failed ever to report this.

Anti-Zionist comments from Wells continued to appear in several newspapers in the 1930s and his anti-nationalist remarks reached their apex in a talk (later printed) given to the Australian and New Zealand Association for the Advancement of Science, in Canberra, in January 1939. This talk, titled 'The Poison of History', received wide acclaim, but also heavy attacks.

If there were to be any evidence that Wells harboured racist views one would expect it to occur in his private correspondence. Little, however, if anything of this sort appears. Moreover, his lengthy correspondence with Israel Zangwill, Chaim Weizmann and other Jewish and Zionist leaders, where he debates such issues, provide a more accurate analysis. If one were to look back at Wells's review essay of 1907, titled 'Race Prejudice', which appeared in the *Daily Chronicle* (12 February 1907) and in America in *The Independent Review* (14 February 1907) one would find more evidence to refute the charge of racism. Reviewing Jean Finot's book *Race Prejudice* and the first edition of Sydney Olivier's *White Capital and Coloured Labour*, Wells remarks: 'If one could slay just one dragon, it would be that of racial prejudice'.

Any person who wrote in such detail and with such stamina as Wells could do so only within a remarkably well organised life and home. Those persons who formed his entourage did so because they believed that what he did was important for them, and for the world in general. A successful filing system was in place almost from the beginning of his writing career, and virtually any incoming piece of paper, along with its response, became part of it.

Wells's first secretary, later his wife, was Amy Catherine Robbins, known by most in the world as 'Jane' (although she generally signed her own correspondence as 'Catherine', or occasionally 'Amy'). When she fell ill, a young Scotswoman, Marjorie Craig, who was already employed to manage various administrative affairs, took over the role. Craig married Wells's eldest son, Gip, and even with a family of her own, became indispensable to Wells's writing career. At the height of Wells's success, the household also used another efficient secretary, Lucienne Southgate. These people expanded the filing system, organised the paper flow even more efficiently, and made it possible for H. G. Wells to be the world figure he became.

After Wells's death in 1946, Marjorie Craig Wells continued to organise the estate's business. However, it increasingly made sense for the paper collection to be located in a central place where it could be made available to scholars. The University of Illinois Library, under the leadership of Professor Gordon N. Ray, approached the Wells estate about the possibility of organising a Wells archive. Although there was some protestation against moving such a literary treasure trove to the United States, the cost of acquiring and housing such a volume of material was so great that no U.K. library offered an alternative. The transfer of materials was completed in 1954.

The librarians at the University of Illinois have fulfilled their responsibilities admirably. The collection has grown steadily as new acquisitions have been added. A detailed finding guide and catalogue has been prepared, and it is constantly updated to show the latest acquisitions. In addition, a mammoth amount of labour has been expended in dating the correspondence. I have relied on this detailed work, even though I occasionally differ from it, for dating much of the correspondence in this collection.

The other archives which are especially important to the study of H. G. Wells include the Public Library at the London Borough of Bromley. Here, the librarian, the late A. H. Watkins, created a library of Wells publications, and many reviews of his books. Some letters are found here as well. The scholar working in this busy building can think of the young Wells, so anxious to leave the town. The Twentieth Century Authors collection in the Mugar Library at Boston University made a very strong effort to purchase Wells materials when they were offered for sale. Howard Gotlib, founder of this collection, is a Wellsian by nature and this collection is very valuable. A third collection is housed at Hofstra University in New York. It is especially rich in materials which were once in the possession of an earlier Wells Society. The fourth large collection forms part of the Harry Ransom Archives at the University of Texas. Many other good smaller H. G. Wells holdings have been a source of materials for this work.

This collection of letters is both *prolegomena* and *appendix* to Wells's great *Experiment in Autobiography*. Here is Bertie Wells, the Busswhacker, Bits, Jaguar, Aigee, Poudoulsky, and H.G. – all the bits, pieces, simulacra, and ghost versions of Mr. Lewisham, Artie Kipps, George Ponderevo, William Clissold, the Camford Visitor – and even Mr. Morley, T. H. Huxley, and R. A. Gregory. This complex individual, who educated two or three generations of humans on how to live and behave, is a figure always larger and more vibrant than life. His letters speak for themselves, and his message – in all its forms – may yet help us through a tight place or two as we face the future.

Selecting and Editing the Letters

The method of selection of these letters is related to the principle of analysis by saturation. Thus, I have attempted to provide as many of the letters written by H.G. Wells as possible, excluding only letters earlier Wells scholars and biographers have made readily available in print. This decision has been taken in order to allow more space for the inclusion of letters which have never previously been published, nor collected.

Where it has not been possible to include the whole body of correspondence of a particular type – business letters, for example, or letters to the press – selections have been made. Business letters have been selected mainly from the earlier period of Wells's life, to show him establishing himself as a professional author. Correspondence with the organisation PEN (Poets, Essayists, Novelists), of which Wells was President from 1933 until the war, and a member of its governing council until his death, is also represented in samples. From the vast amount of correspondence from Wells to Hermon Ould, the General Secretary, and other members of the group, the letters chosen deal mainly with censorship and the rising tide of totalitarianism. Some, although not all letters to one-time correspondents have been included. Letters to anonymous recipients, unless especially enlightening, have usually not.

Only a few letters to Henry James, George Gissing, and George Bernard Shaw are included. I have included several letters from Wells's early life which appear in his *Experiment in Autobiography*. That work, which appeared in one volume in the United States and two volumes in England has different pagination, although identical otherwise. I have noted my use of such letters with the remark, 'This letter appears in *ExA*'. A third volume of the *Autobiography*, originally held back as persons were still alive, was published only in 1984 in England.

Most of the letters to Arnold Bennett which were located some years ago by John Huntington and do not appear in the Wells/Bennett collection have been included. Details of the location of these letters appear in the bibliographical material. I have also chosen to include parts of three letters to Rebecca West and a few to Olaf Stapledon. Where the letters to other correspondents are available only in out of print or scarce editions, I have included them in this work, with locations of alternate printings indicated.

I have not printed many of the letters in the Macmillan files, although I have read virtually all of them. Lovat Dickson, who worked for Macmillan, and who wrote *H. G. Wells: His Turbulent Life and Times* (London: Macmillan, 1969) used these letters to great advantage and they can be studied in his book. Geoffrey West had access to much Wells correspondence when working on his book *H.G. Wells: A Sketch for a Portrait*, (London: Gerald Howe, 1930). He used the correspondence, but rarely prints complete letters. I have used some of these where I was able to view the originals. Several of these letters which West quotes in part are apparently no longer extant, so I have chosen to eschew their use, unsure as to the correct readings. They include letters to Dr. Collins, one to Elizabeth Healey, and several to J. V. Milne.

Every known letter to Catherine Wells appears in the collection. After 1910 or so, most of them are post cards. I have included, as an appendix in volume one, five letters written by Catherine Wells to her husband between 1900 to 1906. These provide a context for several of Wells's letters to her in this period. This appendix also contains three letters from Wells to Winston Churchill.

All in all, letters from nearly sixty archives and private collections have provided material for this collection. Notices in the literary press have brought in some fifty letters from around the world, a dozen of which have proved to be of importance. More, I am sure, still exist. For a fuller account of sources consulted and material included or excluded in this collection see 'Archives and Other Sources Consulted' below.

Types of Letter

There are seven different types of letter in the correspondence. Some letters are extant in two or even three of these states. The editor has worked with the best state available, i.e., the cleanest or latest state, but where possible he has checked and scanned earlier states of the correspondence. Where there are two or more states of an individual document, the earlier versions of the document are frequently located in the Wells collection at the University of Illinois Library, Urbana, Illinois. However, many of the documents which appear in this collection, as well as others not included, occur there in a typed carbon copy form of a letter which may or may not exist elsewhere. The ancillary holdings at Illinois allow researchers to track down useful information about little-known correspondents with whom Wells had a useful or important exchange. The best efforts of the editor have been given to tracing such persons, but success did not occur in every case.

TYPES OF LETTER

The seven different types of Wells's letters are as follows:

1. *Handwritten draft directions to secretaries as to how a letter should be answered*

These tend to be responses to business ventures, requests for talks, or for Wells to read a manuscript. In the case of well-known publishers or agents, these letters are written in a more or less standard way, but are composed by the secretary for Wells's signature. If this is the case, the words 'I sign' appear with the notes, or if the letter is for the secretary's signature, 'You sign' appears. Wells was not above distancing himself from unpleasant conflicts or people he disliked by having his secretaries sign letters which he composed. Many of these directions appear on the original incoming letter as marginalia. In the latter half dozen years of his life, they may also appear on small (2" by 3") pieces of paper, and are frequently in pencil and difficult to read. I have included a transcript of this version when it was unavailable in any other way.

2. *Draft letters in Wells's hand*

More frequent than handwritten draft directions are draft letters in Wells's hand. These are occasionally very long. His habit was to write out notes for such letters, and then rework the notes, with marginalia, suggested interjections with location indicated by an arrow and a caret, and sometimes by a large balloon of new materials with a long arrow of direction. This method of writing closely followed his general method of composition, in which he wrote drafts, reworked them, and then had them presented in typed fair copies for second and third reworkings. My decision, when it is necessary to use a draft document of this type, is to put the interjections, interpolations, and new material in the text where he indicated.

3. *Typed copies of drafts*

A third and more frequent state would ordinarily be a typed copy of the second state reworked to meet his demands. There may still be interpolations, interjections and new materials, but usually not many. Again, if such materials appear, I have added them to the document according to Wells's directions. He had a typewriter available after 1898, and although it was primarily used for business at first, still some typewritten materials date from that time.

4. *Typewritten letters*

The fourth state is the typewritten (very occasionally handwritten) copy, which is usually a carbon copy after the mid-1920s. Occasionally a signature appears. More often, the signature is typed in. Some have no indication of the signature. Addressees of these documents are sometimes very difficult to identify, for a salutation such as, "My dear Smith," is not very revealing. The location where the letters were written is also often missing. I have added 'London' where I am sure of that much, and other places such as 'Lou Pidou' when that location is apparent from context. Most of the letters marked 'London' after 1936 were actually written from 13, Hanover Terrace, Regent's Park, N.W. 1. From the late twenties to the mid thirties, Wells mailed his draft correspondence back to his secretary, so some materials marked 'Lou Pidou' were actually sent from London. Wells and his daughter-in-law, Marjorie Craig Wells, talked virtually every day on the telephone about the business correspondence. If Majorie was unable to be present, Lucienne Southgate, played this role until the mid-1930s.

Other indications of location of the letter or the date it was composed are given from the editor's detective work, aided by early workers at Bertrand Rota (the antiquarian bookseller which handled the transfer of the Wells archive to Illinois) and at the University of Illinois in the late 1940s and early fifties. Guesses and deductions always appear in square brackets.

5. *Correspondence cards, postcards, etc*
Wells wrote an amazing amount of correspondence cards, short notes, postal cards, and other brief communications. Most are in his holograph, although some are typed. Many fewer real dates occur on these, and providing some clue as to dating has been a prominent part of the editing of these letters. Postal cards more often than not have illustrations of his houses, 'Spade House', 'Easton Glebe' and 'Lou Pidou'. I have not identified these, but I have given some details of other post cards and their illustrations. I have used available and legible postmarks wherever possible to date correspondence when the date is otherwise unknown.

6. *Personal correspondence*
Wells continued to conduct his personal, family and private correspondence mainly in holograph until the day he died. Many such letters exist in Illinois as they were returned to the estate by their recipients, and ever since the collection was founded efforts have been made to locate and obtain materials of this sort. Other collections are rich in these documents as well. This edition has examples from and often extensive coverage of this correspondence with the exception of that with a few individuals, for which my search has been futile.

It is believed that Joseph Conrad – or perhaps Jessie Conrad after she wrote her version of his life – destroyed all incoming letters to himself. Two Wells letters to Conrad do exist however: one, an undated expression of thanks for

Conrad's response to a review in 1896, and the other, a note concerning a forthcoming visit, which contains some literary commentary. Both occur in this collection at the proper place. Conrad's correspondence with Wells is unusually rich, and I was able to take great advantage of it in my biography of Wells. I have provided a few examples of these letters, some in extract, to give a flavour of what we may be missing.

Another individual whose letters from Wells have not been located is Eileen Power, with whom Wells had a strong academic and political friendship from 1928 to her death in 1940. Nothing but a few notes of these survive, but several of Power's letters to Wells, illustrating the various aspects of their friendship, are included in this collection. Yet another person is E. Ray Lankester. Wells and Lankester were very good friends from 1904 to Lankester's death. Their friendship was not often expressed in letters, but one or two letters from Lankester to Wells are provided because of their content.

Others to whom Wells almost certainly wrote include Gabriel Tarde (a few letters exist in France, but in private hands), C. P. Snow and Konni Zilliacus (possibly), A. A. Milne (almost certainly, for there is a large Milne to Wells correspondence), Dorothy Richardson (correspondence destroyed in 1948), Sidney Olivier and Cynthia Asquith. No letters to Reginald Turner have emerged from my searches and there is a hiatus in the letters to Violet Paget from 1914 to 1922. There are relatively few letters to Odette Keun prior to 1935 and to Moura Budberg from the 1920s. There is one other area where letters written by H. G. Wells may exist. This is correspondence to his children. A very few letters to Anna-Jane Blanco-White and a few to G. P. Wells in his role as collaborator with Julian Huxley and H. G. Wells on *The Science of Life* also appear in this collection. There must have been non-business letters to G. P. Wells, and probably others to Frank Wells and Anthony West, but if these exist, they must be in private hands.

7. Letters to the press
Wells wrote well over 300 letters to the press in his lifetime. Many of them, of course, concerned his published writing: they corrected mistakes, explained meanings in other words, defended positions. Others were the almost obligatory letters denouncing censorship, calling for a greater openness of discussion, opposing taxes on books, and similar matters. Examples of all these sorts of letters are printed in this edition. In other letters, Wells engaged in public controversy, and, taking a particular stand on a major issue, attempted to persuade the country, or world, to adopt his stance. He defended democracy against totalitarianism, attempted to secure a post-war world free of violence and anger (in both world wars), and supported the struggle for equality in all

matters for women. Although Wells often used the device of a letter to put his views before the public, it was a form of writing for which newspaper editors rarely paid. Those letters to the press which are not included here are mainly repetitions, or deal with technical matters – punctuation, printer's errors – in the presentation of Wells's work.

Acronyms Used in this Edition

The following acronyms are used to identify the original form in which the letters were read. Although it is worth mentioning again that some letters were seen in two or three different forms, the highest form in the hierarchy described above is the one chosen for printing. There is no indication of the other versions unless they are quite different. Wells, like many in his time, cancelled words or phrases, but sent the letters anyway. This had more to do with the price and availability of paper than some hidden psychological reason. We have dealt with these matters by assuming that a cancel indicates words in draft or error, and the version printed in this edition, therefore, follows the final words written or typed, not the cancels. In only one or two cases have we deviated from this, when it was felt that the cancels were particularly revealing, and some doubt remained as to which form the letter was to be sent in. In these cases, the cancels have been retained. Where the acronym ends with a capital 'S', this indicates that Wells signed the correspondence.

AL – autograph letter
AN – autograph note
APC – autograph postcard
ACC – autograph correspondence cards
ADL – autograph draft letter
PL – published letter
TCC – typed carbon copy letter
TCCD – typed carbon copy draft letter
TDL – typed draft letter
TL – typed letter
TN – typed note
TTY – telegram, cablegram
Extract – for the few cases in which the entire letter is not provided
Transcription
Typed Transcription

These last three descriptions deserve an additional word of explanation. In the early days after the Wells archive moved to Illinois, a strong effort was made to obtain copies and transcriptions of letters located in other archives. Where I know the origin of such transcriptions or copies, I indicate this, but the provenance of some Wells letters remains unknown. Some copies which occur today appear both on an almost unreadable microfilm, and in typed transcription, without provenance. I have used these when necessary, but recognise the problems of third generation transcriptions, and so have limited my choice of such letters. Unfortunately, some of these transcriptions, usually made outside of Illinois, and by persons with little knowledge of either Wells or his era, contain a number of risible errors. By reference to the original, I have silently corrected these as often as possible. In many cases, even though the original document is untraceable, a draft or copy exists in Illinois. Such letters with their problems of provenance and transcription form a very small part of this collection.

Rules of Transcription

In this compilation of the letters of H. G. Wells there is as little editorial intrusion as is possible, although the editor has attempted to identify proper names and to elucidate unusual names and usages. The following rules are used throughout the collected letters.

1. **Spelling**. Wells was a naturally accurate speller. The very rare misspellings encountered in the edition are left as they appear but have been footnoted. Only a dozen or so cases occur. The intrusive 'sic' has not been used. Other misspellings are a result of Wells's jokey or juvenile use of words where he creates nonsensical language. American spelling occurs in some places.

2. **Capitalisation and Punctuation**. Wells's manuscripts are followed exactly, except in the following:

a) Question marks and full stops are supplied to incomplete sentences. Wells also frequently used a dash to indicate a break in his thinking. The dash is retained, but when a sentence is ending, a full stop is added as well.

b) Wells's writing provides examples of the changing rules of punctuation. For this reason, we have produced his letters *ad litteram*. Single and double inverted commas appear intermittently throughout. Single inverted commas are used in editorial comments.

c) Wells was addicted to the use of the ampersand. In order to give the most complete effect of reading his original letters, this usage is retained. Where he uses 'and' this is retained.

3. **Cancellations.** Editorial usage differs as to whether cancelled material should or should not be retained in edited collections. In this edition, it has been assumed that a cancel indicates words in draft or error, and the version printed here therefore follows the final words written or typed, not the cancels. The few exceptions occur only where we felt the cancels were particularly revealing or it is unclear as to the state in which the letter was to be sent.

4. **Interlineations and marginalia.** These are silently transferred into the text when they occur.

5. **Abbreviations and contractions** are retained where there is no possible error of interpretation. Wells used contractions frequently in all his correspondence except the strictest business correspondence. If the contraction and/or abbreviation appear to be misleading, they are corrected, inside editorial square brackets.

6. **Underlining.** Words underlined by Wells retain the underlining. On occasion he uses a double underline for emphasis. These too are retained.

7. **Correspondence in languages other than English** is immediately followed by a translation, after the original letter. Unusual foreign words or phrases are also translated, either following the phrase and placed in square brackets or in a footnote. Commonly used interchangeable words are not translated.

8. **Addresses** follow the format, printed or written, of the original. Addresses in square brackets are supplied by the editor, where known.

9. **Dates** are given as they appear. Many of Wells's letters are not dated, but the editor has tried to provide as much information as is possible. Letters with little or no information are placed at the ends of months and years as is discernible by the editor's deductive reasoning. Conjectural identification is in square brackets, so [July 1883] indicates that the exact day is uncertain, [2? July 1883] indicates that the supplied day is uncertain, [February? 1880] indicates that the month is uncertain, and [February 1880?] indicates that the year is uncertain.

10. **Signatures and closings.** Wells normally signed his letters as 'H. G. Wells', and 'H. G.'.Letters to friends and family are often signed with pet names. These are glossed the first time they appear. He adopted a method of

closing his letters which may be mystifying to the first time reader of manuscripts. What appears to be Y____r in large scrawl is 'Yours ever,' only used with close friends. The editor has attempted in these cases to render his original intention.

11. **Postscripts, or nota benes.** Wells occasionally uses the abbreviations P.S., or N.B. Such usage is retained. More often than not however, these addenda to his letters simply appear in available space. They appear in this edition immediately after the signature.

12. **Letters signed by a group of writers.** These appear as they appeared in the original. For those letters with less than twenty signatories, names are listed as they appeared. For the very few letters with more than twenty signatures, a note is appended with the number of subscribers. These latter letters are tribute letters, to Edward Carpenter and Robbie Ross, or letters commenting on censorship, which mainly come from *The Times*.

Editorial Apparatus

1. **Letters are presented** in the strict chronological order of writing, with only a few exceptions, where understanding is difficult unless placement is consecutive. Letters are numbered in sequence throughout the edition.

2. **Headings** of letters consist of the number of the letter, the name of the recipient and a short identification of provenance. Also indicated is the state of the letter at the time of reading (see acronyms above).

3. **Spacing.** There has been no attempt to reproduce spacing irregularities, although if they appear to be important, a footnote is supplied.

4. **Illustrations.** Wells frequently illustrated his letters with sketches. These are described in square brackets at the approximate location in the letter. In the case where comprehension might be difficult, we have supplied a facsimile. Other examples of Wells's letter sketches, which he called 'picshuas', are given as illustrations.

5. **Torn or mutilated manuscripts.** Letters are given in the whole, wherever possible. Missing portions or mutilations are described where they occur.

6. **Proper names** are given in complete form on first appearance. If a nickname is used thereafter, it is glossed at the first appearance.

7. **Conjectural Readings.** Wells's handwriting is distinctive. Under stress or in later life, it is also frequently tiny. Where the editor's readings are conjectural, information is supplied in square brackets as to the conjecture. Defeat is indicated by [*illegible word*]. Some letters, originally in pencil, or more time worn than others, are very difficult to read. A footnote may indicate this so that readers may provide their own conjectures.

8. **Editorial comment.** Square brackets are also used for editorial comment. These emendations are designed for easier reading and use, and strong efforts have been undertaken to limit these intrusions.

Archives and other Sources Consulted for this Edition

i) *Archives*
Below is a list of archives consulted for this edition. Where a short title is used it appears in brackets. It is employed as a statement of provenance in the setting of letters themselves.

1. University of Arkansas (Arkansas)
2. Bancroft Library (Bancroft)
3. Boston University (Boston)
4. BBC Written Archives (BBC)
5. British Library
6. British Newspaper Library, Colindale (Colindale)
7. British Theatre Museum
8. Bromley Public Library (Bromley)
9. Cambridge University Library (Cambridge)
10. Central Zionist Archives, Jerusalem (Central Zionist Archives)
11. Colby College (Colby)
12. Cornell University (Cornell)
13. Churchill College, Cambridge (Churchill)
14. Dorset County Museum and Archives, Dorchester (Dorchester)
15. Harvard University (Harvard)
16. Hofstra University (Hofstra)
17. Central Library, Kingston Upon Hull
18. University of Hull (Hull)
19. Huntington Library (Huntington)
20. Lilly Library, Indiana University (Indiana)
21. University of Illinois (Illinois)
22. Imperial College of Science and Technology (Imperial College)

23. Brotherton Collection, Leeds University (Leeds)
24. Library of Congress
25. Liverpool University (Liverpool)
26. London School of Economics (LSE)
27. McMaster University (McMaster)
28. University of Maine (Maine)
29. Manchester Central Library (Manchester)
30. Massachusetts State Archives (Massachusetts)
31. Milwaukee Public Library (Milwaukee)
32. National Library of Scotland, Edinburgh (Scotland)
33. New York Public Library (NYPL)
34. Reading University Library (Reading)
35. Smith College (Smith)
36. Somerville College, Oxford (Somerville)
37. Syracuse University (Syracuse)
38. Harry Ransom Center, University of Texas (Texas)
39. Trinity College, Cambridge (Trinity)
40. University of Victoria, B.C. (Victoria)
41. Modern Records Centre, Warwick University (Warwick)
42. Wellcome Institute, London (Wellcome)
43. Yale University (Yale)

ii) *Private Collections*
The following individuals and institutions allowed me to copy and use Wells letters which are in their possession:

1. Richard Curle
2. Ferret Fantasy
3. Patrick Gardiner (Gardiner)
4. John Green
5. John Hammond
6. Adrian Hogben (Hogben)
7. Eric Korn (Korn)
8. Elmer Larson
9. George Locke (Locke)
10. Donald Malcolm
11. Patrick Parrinder
12. Sotheby's
14. Leon Stover
15. Nigel Williams

Most of these last consist of a single or perhaps two letters. Only those who were major contributors to the collection are listed with a short title. It is also appropriate to thank at least a dozen other archives who searched their holdings for me, or allowed me to look and see possible Wells items. Their helpful suggestions were much appreciated.

iii) *Published letters*
There are a number of Wells letters which appear in books which had limited circulation or which are long out of print. It was felt that they should be made available again, and they will be found in their appropriate place in these volumes. Fewer than fifty such letters are used, however. This edition does not print many letters from standard collections. A list of those collections, as well as a brief account of other available letters, not printed here, is given below:

Robert Crossley, 'The Letters of Olaf Stapledon and H. G. Wells, 1931–1942,' in Gary Wolfe, ed., *Science Fiction Dialogues*, (Chicago: Academy Chicago, 1982)

Leon Edel and Gordon N. Ray, eds., *Henry James and H.G. Wells*, (Urbana: University of Illinois Press, and London: Rupert Hart-Davis, 1958)

Royal A. Gettman, ed., *George Gissing and H. G. Wells*, (Urbana: University of Illinois Press, and London: Rupert Hart-Davis, 1961)

Gordon N. Ray, *H. G. Wells and Rebecca West*, (New Haven: Yale University Press, and London: Macmillan, 1974).

J. Percy Smith, ed., *Bernard Shaw and H. G. Wells*, (Toronto and London: University of Toronto Press, 1995)

Harris Wilson, ed., *Arnold Bennett and H. G. Wells*, (Urbana: University of Illinois Press, and London: Rupert Hart-Davis, 1960)

Lovat Dickson, *H. G. Wells: His Turbulent Life and Times* (New York: Atheneum, and London: Macmillan, 1969)

iv) *Sales and Auctions*
Letters written by Wells appear at antiquarian book sales and auctions from time to time, but usually as single items. In fact, most major Wells collections are already deposited in libraries and archives, and usually are not for sale. In the mid 1970s, a cache of Wells letters, supposedly located in Florence, was, however, offered for sale to London antiquarian book dealers. Bids were tendered by at least one dealer, but the lot was withdrawn by the anonymous owner or agent.

In December 1972, Sotheby's auctioned a small Wells collection, thirty-one items, of about sixty pages. Where they are located at the time of publication of this collection is not known. The letters and other materials extend from 1899 to 1905, with one item from 1939. All of the materials were sent to A. F. and Florence Popham, and to Doris Popham, their daughter. Florence Popham was a writer, one of whose characters was named Peacock. The materials, which date from the earliest time, refer obliquely to a character in Thomas Peacock's novel, *Melincourt*, one Sir Oran Haut-ton, who is, in fact, an orang-utan. The Pophams were neighbours of the Wellses in the 1890s.

A BIOGRAPHICAL OUTLINE

Herbert George Wells was born 21 September 1866 at home in Bromley, Kent. He was the fourth child and the third son of Joseph Wells, previously a gardener, but at that time a professional cricketer and shopkeeper, and of Sarah Wells, a former ladies' maid. When Wells was eleven Joseph Wells fell and broke a leg while pruning a tree and thereafter was unable to undertake strenuous work for the remainder of his life. As the income from the shop was quite small, Sarah Wells was forced to return to work as a housekeeper with her former employer who lived at Uppark near Petersfield.

Wells's sister, Fanny, died before H.G. Wells was born. His two older brothers, Fred and Frank, eventually left home, apprenticed out as drapers. Wells spent his earliest years as a rather isolated child in near poverty, although he would have been regarded as being part of the lowest edge of the middle class. He lived for much of this time in underground rooms, which he remembered as dark damp enclosures. He was a short, slight child, due, he thought, to his limited diet of bread, cheese and dripping. His mother taught him to read, and by the age of four he was eager for every piece of printed matter he could get his hands on.

Wells attended a dame school in Bromley, and then became a pupil at a local institution called Morley's Academy. He was an avid student. This trait was enhanced when, at the age of seven, he suffered a broken leg and was confined to his bed for a long period. During his convalescence, he and his father walked long distances together, where he learned to observe the small details of nature. During this period his reading broadened substantially, as the local subscription library was ransacked to meet his insatiable appetite for knowledge.

Wells left school at the age of thirteen and became successively a draper, a pupil teacher, and an assistant in a chemist's shop, before being finally bound apprentice to a second draper. He hated most of these jobs and did not flourish in them. Between his periods of work he returned to Uppark, where he was able to use the fine library, made up mainly of editions of the classics. He also used a telescope to look at the moon and the stars, which whetted his imagination for unknown worlds. His trial month as a chemist was in Midhurst where he was spotted as a very bright boy by Horace Byatt, headmaster of the Midhurst Grammar School. Two years later Byatt offered Wells a position as an usher, a pupil teacher. After much discussion with his parents he left the draper's life to which he had been condemned.

While a student at Midhurst, Wells won a series of intellectual prize contests, which provided a small income for the school. 'Cramming' for these examinations meant that he absorbed an incredible amount and variety of information. In 1884 Wells won a place in the newly developed teacher training programme at the Normal School of Science in South Kensington, London. While a student at South Kensington he helped found a student magazine, continued to read widely, participated in a debating club, and generally expanded his world view. He did very well in his formal subjects, scoring either firsts or seconds in all but one, geology, in which he failed his final examination.

Wells's friends from his undergraduate days such as R. A. Gregory, A. T. Simmons and Elizabeth Healey remained close to him and provided a supportive background for his activities for the remainder of his life. Their correspondence was very significant to him. A rather distant, but extremely important mentor, T. H. Huxley, taught the biology class in his first year. Few persons could have benefited more from their undergraduate training than H. G. Wells.

In 1887 Wells obtained a teaching position at Holt Academy, near Wrexham on the Welsh border. Shortly afterwards he suffered a severe injury when he was fouled in a football match. His kidneys were acutely damaged, and he was forced to leave teaching for a time. He recuperated first at Uppark, and then for a time at Stoke-on-Trent. His letters from this period are revealing documents of growth, ambition, and his sense of the need for social change.

He obtained his degree from the University of London, and was elected to a Fellowship of the Zoological Society in 1890. During this period he taught at Henley House School in Kilburn, served as a demonstrator in Zoology at the Royal College for a brief time, and also taught for the University Correspondence College in Cambridge. The proprietor, William Briggs, encouraged Wells to write and he began work on a biology textbook.

At his lodging near Primrose Hill, where he lived with a distant aunt, he fell in love with his cousin, Isabel Wells. They were married in 1891. Within two years Wells had published his first two books, *Honours Physiography*, written with his friend R. A. Gregory, and *Textbook of Biology*, a major work in two volumes.The latter became a standard textbook in the fields of Botany and Zoology. It remained in print, undergoing a number of revisions, most of which Wells had little to do with, until about 1937.

Wells continued to suffer from periodic bouts of illness, which have been diagnosed retrospectively as possibly being incipient tuberculosis, kidney disease, or even psychosomatic stress. These illnesses meant that he was ordered at different times to stop work in order to recuperate. Eventually he was forced to give up teaching altogether. His vacations from teaching seemed to have acted as intellectual as well as physical forces of rejuvenation. He read voraciously during these periods.

He met his second wife, Amy Catherine Robbins, in one of the demonstration laboratories in which he taught. Teacher and student fell in love, and began a life together late in 1893. In 1894 he divorced Isabel, and in 1895 he and Amy Catherine Robbins were married.

During this tumultuous personal time, he did an immense amount of writing for both the educational and popular press. By 1896 he had published over 400 such items of journalism. He served as a book reviewer for the *Saturday Review*, wrote drama criticism for the *Pall Mall Gazette*, and was well enough known to get a byline for a series of dramatic short stories. This 'fiction of the future' as he later termed it, captured English readers with its vibrancy, unusual settings, and the interplay of science and life. Several volumes of his short pieces were collected over the next half dozen years, including *Select Conversations With An Uncle* (1895), *The Stolen Bacillus* (1895), *Certain Personal Matters* (1897), *The Plattner Story* (1897) and *Tales of Space and Time* (1899).

While undertaking this writing, and undergoing still further bouts of illness, the young writer also began to produce a collection of novels which gave him great prestige and ultimately changed the face of literature. In rapid succession he published *The Time Machine* (1895), *The Wonderful Visit* (1895), *The Island of Doctor Moreau* (1896), *The Wheels of Chance* (1896), *The Invisible Man* (1897), *The War of the Worlds* (1898) and *When The Sleeper Wakes* (1899). Thanks to his prodigious output he not only found his life work, but also income enough to secure his future rather than fear it.

With these works he became the primary creator of the genre now called science fiction. In 1898, however, Wells's health broke down again. His physician prescribed sea air and Wells and Catherine moved to the Channel coast, to a house designed by C. F. A. Voysey, built on the cliffs in the village of Sandgate.

During the first decade of the twentieth century, Wells and Amy Catherine (now usually known at home as 'Jane') began their family: two sons, G. P. (known as Gip) and Frank, were born. Wells also extended his acquaintance to include many other literary figures such as Joseph Conrad, George Gissing, Henry James, Arnold Bennett, Ford Madox Ford, E. Nesbit, Violet Paget ('Vernon Lee'), Edmund Gosse, Henry Newbolt, Graham Wallas and Stephen Crane. He was a brilliant conversationalist, even though he spoke with a high and somewhat atonal voice. Wherever he was to be found, a circle of admirers and friends were to be found also.

A BIOGRAPHICAL OUTLINE

He became involved in several extra-marital love affairs, the most important being with Elizabeth von Arnim, Dorothy Richardson (who gave birth to his still-born child) and Amber Reeves, who gave birth to his daughter, Anna-Jane. Reeves, during her pregnancy, married a New Zealander, Rivers Blanco-White, and Anna-Jane became the couple's legal daughter.

Wells extended his writing range substantially during this period. In addition to fiction, he began to experiment with books of social commentary which earned him a very large audience throughout the English-speaking world. His work also began to be translated into German, French, Italian, Spanish, Russian, and Swedish. Many of his books were also made available in paperback editions. He began to give public addresses on his general subjects, the best known of this period being his 1902 address to the Royal Institution, entitled *The Discovery of the Future*.

His primary cycle of books of socio-political commentary included *Anticipations* (1901), which was an effort to predict the general social and technological course of the twentieth century; *Mankind in the Making* (1903), an effort to establish a scientific road toward a better society; *A Modern Utopia* (1905), which used a fictional format to describe a possible utopia, and *New Worlds For Old* (1908), which offered more discussion of the implications of his thinking. In this same year he also wrote *First and Last Things*, a personal statement of beliefs and a description of his social ethics and creed.

He continued to write science fiction, producing *The First Men in the Moon* (1901), *The Sea Lady* (1902), *Twelve Stories and A Dream* (1903) and *The Food of the Gods* (1904). These works attempted to explore the possible impact of science and technology on humans, and as time went on, his fiction became more closely intertwined with his work of social commentary. For the rest of his life he was in constant demand from the editors of newspapers and popular magazines to provide shorter views of his thinking.

Wells also began to experiment with more personal fiction, often dealing with the details of his love affairs, only lightly disguised. He became a member of the Fabian Society, where he met and became good friends with Beatrice and Sidney Webb, Bernard Shaw, and many less well-known Fabian supporters. A number of people would play a significant part in his world and his correspondence for the remainder of his life. He developed an active club life in London, commuting to the capital for four days a week, while spending the weekend in Sandgate. He was introduced into the upper echelons of society in particular by Lady Elcho (later Countess Wemyss) who befriended and guided him in this new world. He became a fixture at the Reform Club, which at this time formed an intellectual centre for the left of the Liberal party.

From 1902 to 1906 Wells was a prominent member of the Co-efficients, a non-party discussion group which met monthly to discuss world issues. Here he met Lord Haldane, Leo Amery, Sir Edward Grey, James Garvin, Lord Milner, Bertrand Russell, Pember Reeves, and Sydney Olivier. He also met Ray Lankester, Gilbert Murray and Winston Churchill at this time. Eventually he broke with the Fabian Society having attempted and failed to make them adopt a more vigorous political programme. Alfred Harmsworth, Lord Northcliffe, provided a newspaper outlet for his ideas, along with others during this period of high turmoil.

Attacks on the political content of his writing and especially on his unorthodox sexual ideas, mainly issuing from the right, formed part of a nationwide campaign against socialism and its supposed collateral idea, free love, during 1906 and 1907. Wells fought back strongly with letters to the press. Even if not accepted, his ideas were debated in very wide circles.

Few prominent men or women in this period were unaware of his work, and many knew him personally as well. At Sandgate, and later at Church Row in Hampstead and Easton Glebe in Essex, the Wells family entertained a wide circle of guests virtually every weekend. These times, filled with games, charades, amateur theatricals, good food and great talk were the intellectual bases for much writing and discussion from 1900 to 1927, when Catherine Wells died. After that, Wells's social relationships tended to take place on the French Riviera, at his clubs, or occasionally in more formal dinner parties. Throughout his life he was surrounded by the intellectual elite as his world stature continued to grow.

Wells at his best was arguably the leading novelist of the Edwardian twilight just before the Great War. His fiction explored class relationship, social change, and the impact of science and it was, to a considerable extent, autobiographical. These books include *Kipps* (1905), *In The Days of the Comet* (1906), *The War in the Air* (1908), perhaps his greatest novel *Tono-Bungay* (1909), *The History of Mr Polly* (1910), and *The New Machiavelli* (1911). During this time he also published several novels dealing with the changing relationships of men and women. Among them are *Love and Mr Lewisham* (1900) and *Ann Veronica* (1909). *Ann Veronica* especially was adopted as an exemplary text by the increasing number of young feminists who were demanding an equal status in the world. Wells was one of the strongest male supporters of equality for women in his time, and he wrote widely in defence of birth control and governmental support for mothers and small children. He began a tumultuous relationship with Rebecca West, and she bore his child, Anthony Panther West, during the weekend the first world war began.

When the war broke out, in August 1914, Wells immediately began to write a series of newspaper columns on its meaning and significance. He told his readers that this could be 'the war that would end war', but only if the peace settlement dealt with the causes of the war, which he described as the uneven distribution of the fruits of capitalism and rampant nationalism. The principal lesson that he drew from the war was the need for a world government, designed to promote social welfare, as well as to regulate such matters as international trade and commerce and the manufacture of munitions.

Wells worked for a time at a government agency for propaganda, Crewe House, where he developed a set of war aims for the Allies which were designed to establish the controlling principles of a peace settlement. In these statements of aims he focused on the treatment of Russia, then going through its convulsive revolutionary period; the necessity for involvement on the part of the United States; and the need for a League of Nations. Documents in which he laid out his ideas on these subjects were delivered to Woodrow Wilson and other world leaders by his new friends, Walter Lippmann and Bainbridge Colby.

His influence on the thinking of the time was very great, and the novels he produced during this period, notably *Mr Britling Sees It Through* (1916), and *Joan and Peter* (1918), were widely read. He visited the battle fronts as a war correspondent, and was personally involved in developing new methods of warfare. He took an interest in the impact of aircraft on war, and watched the development of the tank, an invention foreshadowed in his earlier short story, 'The Land Ironclads'. He also advocated the movement of supplies to the front lines by means of portable transport mechanisms.

When, very soon after its founding, the League of Nations began to be perceived as a failure, Wells drew the conclusion that part of the problem was the poor education of humans. He began an effort to improve this situation by writing, over the decade of the 1920s, three huge textbooks through which he hoped every person could provide their own education. With the aid of teams of researchers, he produced *The Outline of History* (1920), *The Science of Life* (1930), and *The Work, Wealth and Happiness of Mankind* (1931). These books were money spinners. Wells became wealthy and never worried about financial matters again. This position, inevitably, gave him great freedom to experiment in his fiction, and to act as a teacher and prophet, commenting on world affairs.

He covered the Washington Disarmament Conference as a newspaper reporter in 1921, and gave invited lectures at the Sorbonne, before the Reichstag, in Madrid and throughout the United States. He travelled widely, often by aircraft, before such travel was commonplace. In all he made six significant trips to America. In the early 1930s he interviewed Franklin D. Roosevelt and Joseph Stalin, and published the results of their conversations. He conducted two year-long weekly newspaper columns dealing with world affairs, both of which were collected in book form.

Increasingly he began to call attention to the potential problems of fascism and totalitarianism. He was one of the first persons in the West to focus on the threat posed by Mussolini and Hitler. To counteract the movement towards totalitarianism which he observed, he called for international control of the air, of trade, and of commerce, while urging a high standard of modern education for all people. His blueprint for world government, *The Open Conspiracy* (1928) went through three versions in the next decade. He twice stood unsuccessfully for Parliament, in the Labour interest, for the London University seat.

He continued to write fiction, often in experimental forms and much of it putting forward his views on world peace and government. He was still widely read, and the best of his novels of this interwar period remain very good reading. These include *Men Like Gods* (1923), *The Dream* (1924), *The World of William Clissold* (3 volumes, 1926), and *Meanwhile* (1927), the latter a frontal attack on fascism. In this period he also published novels dealing with his personal life, especially *The Secret Places of the Heart* (1922), based on his relationships with Rebecca West and Margaret Sanger – a successor to his earlier novels of love and passion *Marriage* (1912), *The Passionate Friends* (1913), and *The Wife of Sir Isaac Harman* (1914). In this latter year he also produced a *tour de force* of science fiction, *The World Set Free*, which predicted the fission process in atomic energy.

In 1925 he published *Christina Alberta's Father* which he described as a modern version of *Ann Veronica*. The audience for his writing continued to consist primarily of young persons, feminist thinkers, socialists, and those interested in a new and better world. All of his books were translated into other languages, and the translations now included Czech, Hungarian, Dutch, and Turkish. He formed his last two major personal relationships during this period with Odette Keun, with whom he built a home on the French Riviera in Grasse, and Moura Budberg, whom he had met on visits to Russia in 1914 and 1920. Both women were significant partners for him, especially after Catherine Wells died in 1927. The Keun relationship broke up badly in a stormy finale, in the early 1930s, which is reflected in his novel, *Apropos of Dolores* (1938).

Wells was active in the formation of PEN, an organisation originally developed as a loose world federation of writers. During the 1930s, he served as its international president and the organisation became active in support of oppressed artists and in opposition to increasingly powerful totalitarian regimes. PEN, under Wells's leadership, took strong stands against censorship at world congresses convened in Edinburgh, Dubrovnik and Buenos Aires. Wells continued to speak widely on many topics, and was the first person to give an uncensored talk on the BBC, speaking on 'World Peace' in 1927. He continued to be heard on the wireless until 1943, usually speaking on topical subjects.

Wells became very interested in film as a device for disseminating knowledge. Several of his novels were filmed, and under the guidance of producer Alexander Korda, he wrote two important scripts, *Things to Come*, (1936), and *The Man Who Could Work Miracles* (1937). The first of these is still regarded as a classic, often being listed among the top twenty films of all time. In it Wells predicted the horrors of modern warfare, especially the bombing of civilians.

Now in his late sixties, Wells continued to write widely for the press and in other print media. He produced one of the great autobiographies of this century, *Experiment in Autobiography* (1934). He also wrote a statement of his beliefs which was heavily influenced by the teaching of C. G. Jung, *The Anatomy of Frustration* (1936). As the second world war drew closer he produced a clutch of shorter novels warning of the future for humans in the advent of war. These books included *The Croquet Player* (1936), *Star Begotten* (1937), *The Camford Visitation* (1937), *The Brothers* (1938), *The Holy Terror* (1939), and *All Aboard For Ararat* (1940). His books on world affairs, such as *After Democracy* (1932) and *World Brain* (1938), continued to be widely read.

In addition to these works, Wells worked on the idea of a new world encyclopaedia. He made an extensive visit to Australia in 1938-9 at the request of the centenary committee of the Australian and New Zealand Association for the Advancement of Science (ANZAAS). He was one of five such special delegates from England. He also travelled to America in 1937 and 1940. He chaired Section L of the British Association for the Advancement of Science, which studied educational theory and pedagogy, especially in consequence of the rather overwhelming new scientific discoveries which were appearing. In his address to the Section L meeting in Nottingham he provided a blueprint for modern education. Eighteen months later, his talk, 'The Poison of History', (discussed on p. xix above), given to the centennial convocation of the ANZAAS, called for an end to nationalist histories. It was widely reprinted and discussed in the months prior to the onset of the Second World War.

He remained at home in London throughout the war, with the exception of his last trip to the United States in late 1940. During this time he oversaw a new campaign to develop a set of war aims, a major enterprise which finally led to 'A Declaration of Human Rights' (1943). This document, in a revised form, introduced to the United Nations by Eleanor Roosevelt in 1948, was adopted as part of the UN Charter. It was circulated all over the world, and was translated into over thirty languages. The commentary from readers of its various drafts was used to revise and refine the document to achieve the widest possible measure of agreement.

During these last years Wells wrote one more novel, *You Can't Be Too Careful* (1941), as well as several guides to the pathways leading to the new world he envisaged. He also delivered a slashing attack on Roman Catholicism, *Crux Ansata* (1943). He was awarded the D.Sc by the University of London for his doctoral thesis, *On the Quality of Illusion in the Continuity of Individual Life of the Higher Metazoa, with Particular Reference to the Species Homo Sapiens* (1942). Here, as he had done throughout his life, he argued that although humans might think of the individual as being more important, this belief was illusory, and only the group – the species – mattered. Humans, as a species, he believed, were the first of the great dominating animals who could control much of the future. However, as he always remarked, this venture would take hard work, and much thought. The twentieth century, to use his words, was 'a race between education and catastrophe'.

He continued to write up to the end of his life, and although unable to go out, except to vote in the 1945 election, he entertained his old friends and new acquaintances at tea and occasionally at dinner. Many of his illnesses in later life were believed to spring from the incipient tuberculosis of his youth. He was a victim of diabetes for the last fifteen years of his life, but characteristically enough, took advantage of this problem to found the Diabetic Association, raising much money for research into its causes, and establishing homes for diabetic children. He died on 13 August 1946. His body was cremated and the ashes scattered over the English Channel. A memorial service took place in October, 1946.

One of the last books Wells wrote, *Mind at The End of Its Tether* (1945), has been widely regarded as demonstrating that he had finally given up the prospect of a better future. Even in this work, however, he urged his readers, 'Adapt or Perish'. He also told them that he 'had warmed his hands at the fire of life ... and now, he awaited his end, watching mankind, ...'. He continued to observe mankind, which he described at its best as 'curious, teachable and experimental from the cradle to the grave'. But without leadership, which did not appear to be forthcoming, he felt that what might ensue was 'the darkest shadow upon the hopes of mankind.'

Wells was not a pessimist, but a realist. He had not given up on the human species, but he was not sanguine that it would meet the challenge. Nothing in the half century since his death would have caused him to revise this verdict.

As the *Sydney Morning Herald* remarked in their obituary column commemorating his life:

> ... with the death of Wells, we shall pass into a blackness we can only imagine. Without men like Wells, we should be much poorer. While they are alive to make themselves heard, men of good-will feel comparatively safe. When they are dead, the world is left to the mercy of the bookburners, the Communists, the Fascists, the Ku Klux Klan, the extremists of all kinds, the frightened little men with big whips. That is why one says, with the death of Wells, the lights are going out....

CHRONOLOGY

1866	Born 21 September, Atlas House, 47 High Street, Bromley, Kent, third son of Joseph and Sarah Wells.
1874	Breaks leg, semi-invalid for some months, much reading.
c.1871–8	Student at dame school, then at Morley's Commercial Academy, Bromley.
1880–82	Writes *The Desert Daisy*, published 1957. Various apprenticeships. Sarah Wells at Uppark after 1880.
1881	Moves to Hyde's Drapery Emporium, 13 King's Road, Southsea.
1883–4	Pupil, and later pupil teacher at Midhurst Grammar School. Now living at North Street, Midhurst followed by brief stays at 181 Euston Road, and 46 Fitzroy Road, London.
1884–7	At Normal School (later Royal College) of Science. Helps found, and edits, *Science Schools Journal*; begins *The Time Machine*.
1887–8	Moves to Holt Academy, Nr Wrexham, Denbighshire, where he teaches until September 1887. Injured in football accident. Recuperates at Uppark, Petersfield and 18 Victoria Street, Basford, Stoke-on-Trent. Continues work on *The Time Machine*. An early version, 'The Chronic Argonauts', appears in *Science Schools Journal*.
1888	Returns to London to Theobald's Road, then 12 and then 46 Fitzroy Road.
1888–91	Teaches at Henley House School, Kilburn. Receives B.Sc. and elected Fellow of the Zoological Society (FZS) and Fellow of the College of Preceptors (FCP) in 1890. Tutor at University Correspondence College. Marries his cousin, Isabel Wells and moves to 28 Haldon Road, Wandsworth. Begins publishing educational and scientific journalism, and writes for the *Educational Times*. 'Rediscovery of the Unique' appears in the *Fortnightly Review*.
1892–3	Publishes *Honours Physiography* with Richard Gregory, and *Text-*

book of Biology (two volumes). Works briefly as a demonstrator in Royal College laboratories. Health deteriorates. Much journalism, and is eventually forced to full time writing. Journalism, short stories, book reviews in *Pall Mall Gazette*. Meets, as student, Amy Catherine Robbins.

1893 Moves to 4 Cumnor Place, Sutton.

1894 Returns to London, living at 7 and then 12 Mornington Road.

1894–5 Divorces Isabel, marries Amy Catherine. Moves to Tusculum Villa, Eardley Road, Sevenoaks, and then to Lynton, Maybury Road, Woking. Writes *Select Conversations with an Uncle, The Time Machine, The Wonderful Visit, The Stolen Bacillus and Other Incidents*. All published in 1895.

1896 Moves to Heatherlea, Worcester Park, Surrey. Meets George Gissing and many other authors of the time. Writes *The Island of Doctor Moreau, The Wheels of Chance*.

1897 Meets Arnold Bennett. Publishes *The Plattner Story and Others, The Invisible Man*, and a collection of journalism, *Certain Personal Matters*.

1898 Falls seriously ill. Recuperates at several Channel sites in and near Folkestone. Publishes *The War of the Worlds*. Meets Joseph Conrad, Henry James, Ford Madox Hueffer, and travels abroad for first time to Italy.

1899 Publishes *When the Sleeper Wakes, Tales of Space and Time*. Still rather unwell, and in recuperation.

1900 Publishes *Love and Mr. Lewisham*. Builds Spade House, Sandgate, Kent, designed by C. F. A. Voysey.

1901 First child, G. P. (Gip) Wells is born. Meets Beatrice and Sidney Webb. Joins Fabian Society. Publishes *The First Men in the Moon* and his first sociological-political commentary, *Anticipations*. His audience grows substantially, and he begins to be regarded as a savant in many quarters. His friendships are extended as well. Adopts a life style of living in town, at Reform Club, from Tuesday through Friday, and in Sandgate otherwise.

1902 Publishes *The Sea Lady*. Gives public address at the Royal Insti-

	tution, *The Discovery of the Future*. This piece is widely reprinted and discussed.
1903–4	Second son, Frank Wells born. Gissing dies. Publishes *Twelve Stories and a Dream* and his second political work, *Mankind in the Making*. Close friendship with Graham Wallas. Member of discussion group, The Co-efficients. Other friends include G. B. Shaw, E. Ray Lankester, Violet Paget ('Vernon Lee'), E. Nesbit, Henry Newbolt. *The Food of the Gods* appears.

END OF VOLUME 1

1905	Writing steadily. Wide correspondence, growing circle of both literary and political friends. *Kipps* and *A Modern Utopia* appear.
1906	[Letters 612–655] Visits USA, and writes *The Future in America*. Publishes *In the Days of the Comet*. Falls in love with Amber Reeves. Publishes *Socialism and the Family*.
1907	Becomes centre of a political storm over future government of England and place of Socialism, throughout much of 1907. Breaks with Fabians. Publishes *This Misery of Boots*.
1908	Third major political statement, *New Worlds for Old*, is published as is his personal philosophical statement, *First and Last Things*. *The War in the Air* also published.
1909–10	Anna-Jane, daughter of Wells and Amber Reeves Blanco-White is born. Great period of literary production. *Ann Veronica*, *The History of Mr. Polly* and *Tono-Bungay* are published. Moves to 17 Church Row, Hampstead.
1911	Spends from June to September in France at Maison du Canal, Pont de l'Arche, Eure.
1911–13	His collection of short fiction, *The Country of the Blind* appears. Begins Friendship with Frank Swinnerton. Moves to Little Easton Rectory, Dunmow, Essex. Publishes *Floor Games*, for children, *The New Machiavelli*, for adults. His talk, 'The Contemporary Novel', published. Brief love affair with Elizabeth von Arnim. Meets Rebecca West. Publishes *Marriage*, *Little Wars* and *The Passionate Friends*.

1914   First visit to Russia (January 1914). Rebecca West's son, Anthony, born in August 1914. First World War breaks out. Publishes *The World Set Free, An Englishman Looks at the World* and *The Wife of Sir Isaac Harman*. His collection of newspaper pieces from the beginning of the war, *The War That Will End War*, has strong impact on public opinion. When in London he lives at 52 St James's Court, Buckingham Gate.

1915   Publishes *Bealby, The Research Magnificent* and *Boon*. This last leads to a break with Henry James, and with many pursuers of 'Art for Art's Sake'. Little Easton Rectory now renamed Easton Glebe after remodelling.

1916–17   Publishes *Mr Britling Sees it Through* and *The Elements of Reconstruction* and *What is Coming?*. Tours battle fronts in France and Italy in August 1916, and writes *War and the Future*. Publishes a statement of unitarian-like belief, later renounced, *God the Invisible King*, with related novel, *The Soul of a Bishop*.

1918   Works at Crewe House on war propaganda. Secretary to League of Nations committee, a private group. Strong friendships with Americans, especially Walter Lippmann. *Joan and Peter* and *In the Fourth Year* appear.

END OF VOLUME 2

1919   Publishes *The Undying Fire*; begins work on *The Outline of History*, reflecting his sense of failure of both the League of Nations and modern education.

1920   *The Outline of History* appears. Visits Russia, interviews Lenin and Gorki. Meets Moura Budberg. *Russia in the Shadows* published.

1921–2   Covers world disarmament conference in Washington for US and English press; publishes *Washington and the Hope of Peace* and *The Salvaging of Civilisation*. Love affair with Margaret Sanger begins. *The Secret Places of the Heart* appears. Stands for Parliament in 1922 and 1923, loses both times. Publishes *A Short History of the World*. When in London he lives at 4 Whitehall Court, Whitehall Mansions, often referred to as Flat 120 or simply Whitehall Court.

1923–4   Intimate relations with Rebecca West end. Publishes *Men Like Gods, The Dream A Year of Prophesying* and *The Story of a Great Schoolmaster*. Begins practice of wintering on the French Riviera at Lou Bastidon, Quartier St Jean, Grasse, and meets Odette Keun.

1925–6   *The World of William Clissold* is published. Conducts public discussion with Hilaire Belloc as to the authenticity of *The Outline of History. Christina Alberta's Father* is published.

1927   He and Keun build house in Grasse, 'Lou Pidou', where he lives in winter from 1927–32. *Meanwhile* appears and results in his banishment from Italy by Mussolini. Speaks at Sorbonne. *Collected Short Stories* published and the final volumes of his collected edition, *The Atlantic Edition* (1924–7) also appear. Catherine Wells dies. His London address is now 614 St Ermin's, Westminster.

1928   *The Book of Catherine Wells*, a tribute volume and collection of some of her writing. Marjorie Craig Wells, his daughter-in-law, assumes post as secretary/manager. Begins his campaign for world peace with series of public addresses and is active in PEN, a world affiliation of authors. Publishes *The Way the World is Going, The Open Conspiracy, Mr Blettsworthy on Rampole Island*. When in Paris he lives at 124 Quai d'Auteuil, XVIth.

1929–30   Gives talk on 'World Peace' on BBC, first non-censored talk on this medium. Speaks in Reichstag. Moves to 47 Chiltern Court, Clarence Gate, London. Publishes *The Science of Life* with Julian Huxley and G. P. Wells. Has trouble over collaborator with a third textbook which is delayed. Close friendships with Enid Bagnold, Christabel Aberconway, and Eileen Power. Ernest Barker, Ritchie Calder, C. P. Snow, J. B. S. Haldane become part of his circle. Publishes *The Autocracy of Mr. Parham, The King who was King*, and many pamphlets and short pieces in the cause of world peace.

1931–2   First wife Isabel and Arnold Bennett die. Breaks up with Odette Keun. Publishes *After Democracy, The Work, Wealth and Happiness of Mankind*, and *The Bulpington of Blup*.

1933–4   Establishes liaison with Moura Budberg. Publishes *The Shape of Things to Come*. Is elected International President of PEN. Visits USSR and interviews Stalin. Publishes *Experiment in Autobiography*.

END OF VOLUME 3

CHRONOLOGY

1935 Visits USA and meets Franklin D. Roosevelt. Moves to final home, 13 Hanover Terrace, Regent's Park. Collaborates with Alexander Korda on the film, *Things to Come*. Writes *The New America: The New World*.

1936 Publishes *The Anatomy of Frustration* and *The Croquet Player*. His seventieth birthday is occasion of a public dinner in his honour given by PEN. Writes film script of *The Man Who Could Work Miracles*.

1937 Publishes *Star Begotten*, *The Camford Visitation* and *Brynhild*. Chairs Section L of the British Association and publishes 'The Informative Content of Education'.

1938-9 Publishes *The Brothers*, *Apropos of Dolores*, *The Fate of Homo Sapiens*, *The New World Order* and *World Brain*. Visits Australia, gives series of talks, including one at ANZ Association for Advancement of Science, 'The Poison of History'. Publishes *The Holy Terror* and *Travels of a Republican Radical in Search of Hot Water*. When war breaks out, is in Stockholm for PEN meeting, subsequently cancelled.

1940 Remains in Hanover Terrace throughout the war except for a speaking tour in the US in autumn of 1940. Begins campaign for a statement of war aims, which leads to 'A Declaration of the Rights of Man' (later to be called, 'A Declaration of Human Rights'). Publishes *The Rights of Man*, *All Aboard for Ararat*, *Common Sense of War and Peace* and *Babes in The Darkling Wood*. At British Association conference in London with statement on 'Science and the World Mind' and 'A Charter of Scientific Fellowship'.

1941-2 His last novel, *You Can't Be Too Careful* published; also *Guide to The New World*, *Phoenix*, *The Conquest of Time* and *The Outlook for Homo Sapiens* which is an amalgamation of *The Fate of Homo Sapiens* and *The New World Order*, both published in 1939. Receives D. Sc. from the University of London, and published his thesis, *On the Quality of Illusion in the Continuity of Individual Life*.

1943-4 Continues to write polemical journalism, some of which is reprinted in *'42 to '44*. His attack on Roman Catholicism, *Crux Ansata*, appears.

1944–5   Publishes two last books, *The Happy Turning*, and *Mind at the End of Its Tether*, and 'The Betterave Papers', a last literary statement. Becoming quite ill.

1946   Grows steadily more feeble. Continues to entertain friends at tea. Dies 13 August 1946. Cremated, with ashes scattered over the English Channel. Memorial service held in October.

ACKNOWLEDGEMENTS

For work which has been so long in completion (namely, from the time when I first began to seriously think about H.G. Wells, nearly forty years ago), the temptation is to say thank you to a generic 'everyone' and hope that is sufficient. But many people have suffered in their relationships with me, and for that they deserve solace, comfort, and thanks. Should I miss anyone out, please put this down to frailty of mind and spirit, not a lack of appreciation.

The first group of persons I would like to thank are members of the H. G. Wells Society. They include the late Peter Hunot, and the late A. H. 'Bob' Watkins. Others in England who form part of the Society circle are Sylvia Hardy, George Hay, John Hammond, Chris Rolfe, Brian Aldiss, Alan Mayne, Rose Tilly, Peter Lonsdale, Mary Mayer, James Dilloway and John Green. I want to thank Catherine Stoye for her encouragement of my work on her grandfather and grandmother. Special thanks go to Michael Sherborne, who read this edition in proof and made many valuable comments and suggestions. It is not possible to thank Patrick Parrinder enough for his guidance as consulting editor, which has been invaluable. We have shared our interests in Wellsian matters for more than twenty years and I have gained new insights during our meetings and correspondence throughout that time.

Others in England who have been of inestimable aid and support include Robert Baldock of Yale University Press, the indomitable and delightful Michael Foot, the late Michael Katanka, Jenny Taylor, George Locke of Ferret Fantasy, Anne Barrett of the Imperial College Library, Janet Smith of the Haldane Collection, Angela Raspin, the nonpareil of the LSE library and archives, Michael Bott of the Reading University library, and C. Lingard of the Manchester Central Library. Special thanks and much affection go to Eric Korn, who read part of volume one in manuscript, Tom and Nancy Sharpe, Piers and Vivien Brendon, and the staff of the Tavistock Hotel, Tavistock Square, London. The staffs at the British Library, the LSE library and the Colindale Newspaper Library have been wonderful to me and diligent in locating my requests. The current staff at the Bromley Public Library have been most accommodating, in the tradition of Bob Watkins, and Miss H. Plinke.

Pickering & Chatto have been a wonderful company to work for: stresses and strains were alleviated, questions answered promptly, and fax machines hummed day and night. Bridget Frost, Rebecca Saraceno, Jane Mahony, and

James Powell, have all been very pleasant to work with on this project. Copy-editors Margaret Deith and Stephen Easton queried me properly and have been able to cure me of many Americanisms. Suzanne Moulton read my copy against the copy texts and her sharp eyes have saved me from many infelicities and errors. Philip Aslet has compiled two excellent indexes.

Thanks go to Linda Shaughnessy of AP Watt, literary executors of the Wells Estate, and the Wells Estate itself for allowing us to publish this collection of letters. Thanks also to those organisations and individuals who have made pictures available for inclusion in this edition. Every effort has been made to trace copyright holders in all cases.

From the Netherlands, Monique Reintjes has provided me with information concerning Odette Keun. In the USA, Leon and Takeko Stover have been wonderful and supportive friends, as have Gene Rinkel, Fred Nash and Mary Ceibert at the University of Illinois Library. Andrea Lynn of the University of Illinois has been extremely helpful. Librarians at McMaster, Texas, Milwaukee, Arkansas, Boston and Colby, as well as a dozen other places have cheerfully provided me with copies of material. Howard Gotlib of the Mugar Library is owed many thanks for several kind gestures. Kelly Bridgewater at Illinois did some emergency copying for me for which I thank him especially. Adrian Hogben allowed me to use his father's unpublished memoir, and made copies for me of his father's and mother's correspondence with H. G. Wells as well as a few other Wells letters not in Illinois. In France I would like to mention Annie Escuret, Pierre Coustillas, Bernard Loing and the late J. P. Vernier who have been extremely accommodating in their gifts of knowledge to me. Julius Kagarlitski of Moscow is a faithful Wellsian and an intrepid translator. In Canada, C. J. Fox was helpful in providing leads to Wyndham Lewis materials. Special thanks to Rochelle Rubinstein of the Central Zionist Archive in Jerusalem.

In Maine, I wish to thank Bill Baker, Jerry Nadelhaft, Dick Blanke, the late E.O. Schriver, Jacques Ferland, Carole Gardner, Kathy Moring, Debby Grant, Howard Segal, the late Howard Schonberger, C. Stewart Doty, the late John Nolde, the late Robert Thomson, Jay Bregman, Margaret Nagle, the late Jack Walas, Steve and Tabitha King, Clyde MacDonald, Charles Scontras, Mel Johnson, Muriel Sanford, Sam Garwood, Dawn Lacadie, Frank Wihbey, Frank Eggert, Sharon Jackiu, Hal Borns, George Jacobson, George Denton, Dan Belknap, Ron Davis, Scott Anderson, Diane D'Angelo, David Demeritt and Patrick Kirby who first introduced me to the Potteries. Elsewhere in the U.S. Judy Austin, Judy Barrett Litoff, Larry Malley, W. R. Baron, and Jim Crouthamel have provided the scholarly support and friendship which is supposed to characterise our profession.

ACKNOWLEDGEMENTS

For helping in my university education, I wish to extend special thanks to the wonderful scholars I encountered, such as Edward W. Fox and Paul W. Gates of Cornell University, and Gwilym Roberts and the late Myron Starbird, of the University of Maine, Farmington. Still another debt needs to be paid to the wonderful school teachers who first fostered and fanned the enthusiasm they saw in a small boy so many years ago.

Finally, I could never have done the work I have been able to do without the help of Sylvia, my wife and companion of more than forty years, our children Clayton and Kit, Kit's husband, Jamie, and their son, Joshua. My parents and Sylvia's parents gave the greatest possible help and support when it was most needed. As my mother-in-law used to say when money and time were tight, and resignation tempting, "You only go this way once!".

Bangor and Topsfield, Maine DAVID C. SMITH
1997

The

Correspondence

of

H. G. Wells
1880–1903

H. G. Wells did not always date his correspondence. My dating of his letters is somewhat conjectural, and I have occasionally had to alter my thinking after the volume was set in page proof. Where this has happened, I have indicated it as clearly as possible. The letters which were written before 1885 or so and which survive are the letters of a teenaged boy, although a very precocious one. Their importance is not in their precise date, but rather in the vocabulary, ideas and attitudes of this young man. Many years later when writing to 'Mark Benney' (a pseudonym of Harry Degras, see volume 4), Wells remarked that he wrote 'babu' English[1] until he was about seventeen.

About the same time that the first letter we have was written, Wells also produced his first 'book', which looked something like a strip cartoon with a running story text. This little book, of 96 pages, was published in a facsimile edition in 1957.[2] Two other manuscripts of the same kind were shown at a centenary exhibition at the Bromley Public Library in 1966. Their whereabouts is not known. In addition, many of the early letters which Wells wrote contain sketches, 'picshuas', as he called them. We have reproduced some of these sketches to give the flavour of the original letters, but otherwise a simple description of the sketch is provided.

---

[1] This phrase was widely used in Victorian times to denote the excessively formal English often used by clerks in India.
[2] *The Desert Daisy*, with an introduction by Gordon N. Ray (Urbana: Beta Phi Mu, 1957).

1. To Sarah Wells

Illinois, ALS

[Bromley, Kent] [1880]

My dear Mother,

I hope you are well & will forgive my not writing before.

No news. No excitement of any description in Bromley & the "rain it raineth every day" so we are living in a state of nothing to do indoors.

My much beloved Cousins do not favour me with a letter & so I am without a subject of any kind to spin a letter out of.

Therefore, I will eke it out with illustration.

Here goes!

Here you observe me trying to think of something to tell you.

Here you observe me going out into the streets to find something to tell you.

Here you see me trying to get across to Shortlands[1] & being prevented by the flood.

Here you see me caught in a grievous hail storm & hurricane.

THE LETTERS: 1880–1903

Here you see me after the storm.

Here you observe my joy at discovering an idea how to fill this letter.

Here you see me following up the idea by illustrating this letter.

Here you see the Postman about to deliver this letter.

THE CORRESPONDENCE OF H. G. WELLS: VOLUME 1

& Here is a fancy sketch (anything but complimentary) of Mrs Wells of Up Park reading this letter from,
>Yours affectionately
>>Bertie

---
[1] Shortlands is an area in Bromley near where the Wells family lived.

2. To Frank Wells

Illinois, ALS

Windsor[1]   [February 1880]

Ah, my brother. When the Valentines come tumbling in from all the heiresses in Godalming addressed to 'F.G. Wells Esq. alias the young man with a face smooth as a girl. 41 High St. Godalming' you will see amongst them the form of 'the DREADED DUTCH DOLL'.[2] & you will remember (alas for you too late).
>Your long forgotten! Your neglected! Your forlorn! your ill used! and cetera Brother.
>>BUSS !!!!

---
[1] Undated piece of notepaper, with a sketch of Frank Wells as a walking Dutch doll at the bottom of the page.
[2] The Dutch doll appears to be a jointed set of wooden dolls used as a scare toy, perhaps. Frank was living and working in Godalming.

3. To Sarah Wells

Illinois, ALS

Rodgers & Denyers[1]
25 High Street
Windsor

Sunday, July 4th 1880

My dear Mother,

Here I am sitting in my bed room after the fatigues of the day etc. Cough slightly better & I am tolerably comfortable.

I give you an account of one days work to give you an idea of what I have to do.

- Morning

We sleep 4 together viz 3 apprentices & 1 of the hands in one room (of course in separate beds).
We lay in bed until 7:30 when a bell rings & we jump up & put trousers slippers socks & jacket on over nightgown & hurry down & dust the shop etc.
About 8:15 we hurry upstairs & dress & wash for breakfast.
At 8:30 we go into a sort of vault underground (lit by gas) & have breakfast.

After breakfast I am in the shop & desk till dinner at 1 (we have dinner underground as well as breakfast) & then work till tea (which we have in the same place) & then go on to supper at 8:30 at which time work is done & we may then go out until 10:30 at which hour the apprentices are obliged to be in the house. I don't like the place much, for it is not at all like home.

Give love to Dad & give the cats my best respects. I'm rather tired of being indoors but this morning I went to Clewer Church & then on to Surly[2] which I found much better than I used to think it in fact it's a perfect heaven to R&D's.

I'm rather tired so excuse further writing
    Yours
      H. G. Wells
N.B. My washing will be 12/- a quarter.

---

[1] This letter, written from the first firm with which Wells was placed, is a useful document as it describes the actual working day of such an apprentice.

[2] Surly Hall was an inn, on the Thames, two miles from Windsor, managed by his uncle Tom Pennicott, Sarah Wells's second cousin. Several cousins, who were important figures in his adolescence, lived here. This letter also appears in *Experiment in Autobiography* (London: Victor Gollancz and The Cresset Press, 1934), ch. 3 §4.

4. To Frank Wells

Illinois, ALS

Rodgers & Denyers
25 High Street
Windsor [late Summer 1880]

My dear Brother[1]

Being rather hard up for paper I just write on one of our billheads to let you know I am alive. Excuse my writing as we go into shop at 7:30 & do not get [out] till past 8 in the evening so you see I have no home except on Sundays & as I spend my Sundays chiefly at the Surly Hall I have hardly any time even then. I write this in the desk as we are rather slack this afternoon.

When I first arrived here I was put in there, but now another takes my place.
    [*missing corner*]
but at the same time I don't like it at all. I hope you and Fred[2] are well and enjoying yourselves. Tomorrow we have a grand review here & as we are going to close early I shall try & go. If I do I [shall] write a long letter giving a full & (of course) true account of it if I have time.

Excuse my writing any more as Mr R is wandering up and down the shop like the Wandering Jew & I am not sure but he may light on me writing this.
    I rem.
        Your angelic brother
            Bussy[3]

[*A small sketch of a woman's head appears at the bottom of the letter. The bottom right corner of this letter is torn away so that a few words are missing, as well as the caption to the sketch.*]

---

[1] Relatively few letters survive from Wells to his brother Frank and to his father, Joseph. He certainly saw them more often than his other brother, Fred, who lived and worked first at Bromley, then at Wokingham before migrating to South Africa. Such letters to Frank as do exist tend to be rather jokey. They also appear to be spur-of-the-moment compositions. Several items of verse from the mid-1880s appear in these compositions. As few of them are dated, except very generally, errors in dating are very possible. The family relations are nevertheless interesting, and the few, occasionally cryptic, letters to Frank are important.

[2] Frederick J. Wells, H.G.'s elder brother

[3] Wells uses intimate and personal nicknames throughout his life for his family, and close companions. His own family referred to him as Buss, Buzz, Busswhacker, The Buzzwhacker, Busswuss and other similar terms. Where the names came from is not known.

5. To Frank Wells

Illinois, ALS

[Address unknown] [1880?]

Dear Brother,

Do ask the G.V.[1] soon about me & answer my last letter & save me from another visit home. I can fancy it.

The Old Man carefully telling all the confounded old gossips in the Beastly Old Town[2] what boys he has got & what a disgrace they are to him.

Mustard Seed[3] sympathetic[?][4] & guying him for marrying below him.

Huxleys Davis and co like the birds of the air as you justly call them jublibant[?].[5] J. Wells Esq. offering to give me a chance as his errand boy. & all the rest of the seed of the _____ you know rejoicing to see the fall of Wells jun. The Clods with my rival artist in ecstasys.

The Wells of Greenwich & the Wells of Gloucester. The Wells of Bromley & the Wells of Tunbridge will praise the Lord for the Downfall of the sinful Wells who rejected them

& so on.
But serious please book it up & ask old B or I shall have to undergo the ordeal. Unless an untimely death by my own hand terminates a well spent life.

I feel in good spirits at the prospect of getting down to Godalming where I hope fresh places scenes faces & air will serve to liven up your greatly dispirited Brother

                    Buss

NB Ask the G.V. & answer at once.[6]

---

[1] The nickname given to Joseph Wells within the family. It may mean Governor, or be another form of *Deo volente*. Wells's own children often referred to their father, when he was not about, as 'God'.

[2] Bromley

[3] Mustard Seed must have been a friend of Joseph Wells, if my transcription of Wells's handwriting is correct.

[4] My reading of the sense of these paragraphs would be 'presenting a false sympathy' for Joseph Wells in what is an ironic letter.

[5] Probably a misspelling for 'jubilant'

[6] The anxieties and hatred of the apprentice life come through this letter with considerable force, even though it is ironically cryptic at times. Joseph Wells was a good cricketer, but injury had ended his cricketing life. His shop was a failure. His marriage appears to have been failing, and the sterility of life in the Bromley home must also have seemed like another prison to Wells.

His brothers were sympathetic, but they had been apprenticed when they were young and there seemed few other prospects of advancement in the England of this period.

6. To Frank Wells [?]

Illinois, AL

[Address unknown] [1 September 1880]

My dear Brother,

Pray forgive me the sin that I have committed & write to me & tell me so.

It's too bad not to write. When I lived at home in the light of maternal admiration didst thou not write to me once a fortnight at least & now I live abroad amidst the heathen thou dost not write once a month.

Since August the first have I waited & Lo! there is no letter & it is Sep 1. By Gum if thou writest not soon I would send you a —

[remainder of letter missing]

7. To Frank Wells

Illinois, ALS

(ent. Stationer's Hall)[1] [c. September 1880]

My dear Brother.

I just write you a line to let you know that (er) I (er) - haven't got anything to write about. Thanks for remembering my birthday. Next time Sep 21 comes around just write and let me know you remember it & don't remember it in silence.

I did remember Freddy's birthday & I'll promise you that I won't forget yours!

Yea! O Frank!! Remember the Rattle!!! Think of the Coming Dutch Doll !!!! & - Tremble! !!!!!!!!!!etc.
    DUTCH DOLL
    I am my dear Brother
    Your affectionate Son
        Busswuss
NB Sep 21, is my birthday & if I don't receive a letter before then if I don't send a dozen dutch dolls all tied together by the legs.[2]
        I are,
            Buss

---

[1] This letter was probably written from his apprenticeship lodging in Windsor, at Denyers & Rogers, but the sheets only carry this statement and a printed abstract figure as a letter head.
[2] Four apparently jointed wooden dolls connected together occur in a sketch at the foot of this page. Page 4 of this letter is a large face of a man who is pictured with a rather stern visage. The caption reads:

> Here is the Windsor Postmaster when he
> saw that rattle, Only time he ever smiled in his life.

8. To Sarah Wells

Illinois, ALS

[Atlas House
47 High Street
Bromley, Kent]　　　　　　　　　　　　　　　　　　　[Autumn 1880]

Dear Mother,

    Please forgive my [not] writing before as all my spare time for the last week has been occupied in looking up what I have forgotten since I left school so that if I do go to Chichester or Wells I shall be ready for work.

Before putting me at Chichester be careful to ask whether the Profession of a School Master is at all a paying one, etc. etc.

Bromley is very quiet & there is hardly any news.

Of course you know Mr. Morley is going to retire at Xmas.[1]

I have not heard from Windsors for some weeks.

I received the coat, etc. from Frank & am much pleased with them.

The coat has a large[?] hood & when I have it over my head I look like a

Roumanian infantry man or a 'Friar of Orders Grey & Brown'. Saw the Woodhouse people² on Sunday & stayed to tea with Dad.

      I am your affection Son
        Buss

---

¹ Morley had owned and run a school in Bromley for many years, which all three of the Wells children attended. Morley was a positive force in Wells's life, and when he wrote of his teachers in later years, occasionally with some venom, Morley was never treated in this way. Wells, in fact, became quite angry with persons who thought he was caricaturing Morley in some of his writing.

² Probably Bromley acquaintances. The letterhead of this stationery is the same abstract figure as in letter 7; however I believe the letter was written from Bromley.

9. To Sarah Wells

Illinois, ALS

[Midhurst]   [1880-1?]

My dear Mother,

  I recd your letter this morning & I am just going to write to Bowkett.¹
  The place here is very jolly.² The hours are moderate, the fare good & not much hard work to do. I am getting on pretty well. I have just been to church. The church I go to is an old fashioned place, where the clergyman wears a black gown and the pews are so high that you can indulge in a quiet doze without any conspicuousness.
  I got hat & tie from Frank this morning and all I want now is a towel.

      I am my dear Mum
        Bussy

---

¹ Two Bowkett brothers, Sidney and Maurice, were classmates of Wells at Mr Morley's Academy. He continued to see and hear from them until about 1910. Maurice emerged as a recipient of Wells's charity in the mid-1930s.

² Wells was apprenticed to a Midhurst chemist for a short time. This was a fortuitous placement as he was noticed there by Horace Byatt, who was to offer him his first opportunity to become a teacher.

10. To Fred Wells

Illinois, ALS

13 Kings Road
[Southsea] [1881?]

Dear Fred,

To still the uneasy palpitations of your anxious & loving heart, I write. Since I last saw you I have substituted Southsea for Harting as my environment & abandoned the habitual use of smut & blaspheming.
Excuse verbosity & accept my blessing.
H.G. Wells

11. To Frank Wells

Illinois, ALS

[Bromley] [1881-2?]

Unto
My dear Frank and much beloved brother, greeting and good wishes

My dear Brother,

This letter send I unto you hoping thereby to improve your mental and moral state and also to improve the evil and wicked, who surround you on all sides.
My dear Brother
It grieveth me sorely to see thy manifold great sins and thy small weaknesses in number as the sands of the sea or the sands in a grocer's sugar.
With fasting weeping sackcloth & ashes have I seen them, as also with my own eyes.
And lo I saw that thou hadest not that most blessed gift of charity which as our beloved & departed (thank the lord) brother Paul saith 'covereth a multitude of sins' as also said the old millionaire's wife when she bought two 3/11 blankets & gave them away to the poor.

Now my brother it occurreth unto me that I should feel great joy in coming unto thee at Godalming this Sunday which is to come and if thou canst send unto me the money I will come unto thee & with thee will I spend the two nights and one day (which providence hath ordained unto me) in grave & serious discourses.

Now my brother will I cease this letter for the night cometh when no <u>man</u> can work much more write letters to damned brothers who ain't a going to write back. A greeting unto thee and all thy friends and a hope that thou mayest not overeat thyself with the succulent gooseberry or the acrid apple for a brother with the guts ache is not an agreeable person to call on.

  I hereunto witness my hand
     H G WELLS
of ye church at <u>Portsmouth</u>

12. To Frank Wells [?]

Illinois, AL

[Bromley]   [1881–2?]

To his most sublime Majesty
  Charles (O18 zy) Emperor of Godalming.
    (<u>Please quote number when ordering</u>)

My dear Brother in love & Good Works.
  It beseemeth me well to indite unto you this epistle, inasmuch as, a barometric depression in this district hath culminated in meterological disturbances, & accompanied by a decrease in atmospheric caloric, hath caused hitherto invisible aqueus vapour to condense into minute drops, which have descended in no small quantities in these last few hours.
  I received a consignment of goods in good order this morning & hope to be able to acknowledge completion of order before this little planet of ours hath performed many more diurnal rotations.
  In the packet was a roll of unclean note paper whereon was a number of streaks of some black substance which on analysis proved to be graphite in a rather impure form. I am about to offer a prize

[remainder of letter missing]

THE LETTERS: 1880-1903

13. To Frederick Wells

Illinois, ALS

The High Place
Bromley   Kal Sext [c. Spring 1882]

Wretch![1]

Your daring attempt to extort money was foredoomed to failure.

The invoice you sent was on the face of it obviously a whiz, a catch a hare, a gebat,[2] an execrable effort to extort: You charge me for sauce; when did I have it, show me my order, get me the young man who served me, the walker who saw me have it, the porter who delivered it. (Bring your clerks, your day books, your ledgers, your false witnesses, liars, rogues & vagabonds and prove it if You Can.) No Sir! Your bill is a list of items I have never had and I refuse to pay it and should you send it in again I shall prosecute you and expose your system of blackmail to the astonished Universe. I am only deterred from this course now by consideration for the feelings of my friend your father. So mind your eye.

Frederick Wells
        Write, if yet the power remains, by return and tell me, whither you intend to betake that shattered hulk of yours for your holidays. There are many in Bromley that would be pleased to sun themselves in the light of your upper end (front part of head).

My father & myself place our poor but honest residence at your disposal should you deign to honour this Stony Desert with your honoured & refreshing presence. The shattered relics of the Wells family would greet your advent with tumultuous rejoicing and the Brooke House population would receive you with stately yet frugal hospitality. The Harem you once maintained here is a still diffused through the town. To be continually subject to encounters with female persons who persist in regarding you as your brother, although perhaps in the long run likely to shake the certainty of your knowledge of your own identity, is not in the first instance an unpleasant occurrence, that is to say, if the meeting is not both effusive & public.

Frank is supposed to be dead, but no certain information has reached us from Shrewsbury for some time.

I think of going down there for a week or so soon and wandering round after relics of him.

>Believe me, Fred
>>Your very Affct Brother
>>>Herbert Geo. Wells

---

[1] The family often used humorous forms of address when they dealt with each other, and this appears to be an example. It is, however, written at about the time the china shop-cum-sports store was going under. The date of this letter is very tentative. If I am right, Wells was aged about fifteen, nearly sixteen. The letter could have been written slightly earlier than the Spring of 1882, but probably not later.
[2] An obsolete form of gibbet

14. To Fred Wells

Illinois, ALS

47 High Street
Bromley, Kent [1882–3?]

My dear Brother,

'Satan finds some mischief still for idle hands to do.' How truly this remarkable line of the Psalmist applies to the present case. The whole cause and occasion of writing is explained if we add that Joseph W. finds the pens & paper & stamps.

Regarded in a strictly technical sense the statement that "Bromley is a desert" savours of mendacity, but considered as a poetical expression approximates to the unimpeachably veracious. There is nothing to do. No one to talk at except my dear Parent & the Bourgessi for the Wellode[1] are out of town and the former occasionally requires intervals for rest, refreshment or meditation (in which term all included under the phrase 'paying a visit' is included) while the latter, also, cannot always be at command - visiting them more than twice a day, appearing as a somewhat excessive proceeding. In this dire extremity it may be allowed that giving vent to my feelings by the penny post (Heaven bless Sir Rowland Hill)[2] is, in moderation, a justifiable proceeding to which the objection that there is absolutely nothing to put in my letters fails to present an impediment of sufficient magnitude to arrest.

What have I said? Nothing to put in my letters. Preserve me Heaven! from an indignant father's wrath!! Have I not a photograph of that respected relative to enclose!!! Forgive me, if, in my loquacity, I have thus previously sinned. Let me rather say, "Saving such photograph is nothing", worthy of thine eyes or ears.

I am between the horns of a dilemma. Before me lie two objectionable courses. Either I must write to you a curt communication, which the Lord forbid, or, I must descend to trivial details with which to employ my pen, details equally unworthy of you and myself.

Which shall I do? How shall I decide? More than human agency shall answer. Bring hither the oracular ha'p'ny. Let us place the decision in the hands of the Gods. - ting - the coin of destiny ascends - heads for shortness - tails for frivolity - ding - tails! The ha'penny is cast. Frivolity hath it. My brother. Let me frivol.

I and my father are eating apples. They are very nice. Hopton's. Two peniworth. - for tuppence.

* * * * * * * * * *

These stars indicate mental exhaustion. It is over now - a thing of the past. The apples also are gone. Pleasure ever is evanescent. Apples, I often think, are as the poet says, 'things of beauty that "like the snowflakes in a river, gleam awhile, then fade forever". Vanish without a trace save in some few cases, when abdominous pains and agitation for a while supervene. I visited Frank's shanty last week. I think he illustrates very forcibly a favourite theory of mine. Every mortal child, old or young, requires a certain amount of play with a doll's house - must have it in fact when young, like the measles, the affection appears at a more advanced age with much greater intensity & more danger to the system. It appears to have been a defect in Frank's early education that he never had a doll's house to play wiv. Had ships, cannons, tin soldiers, but no doll's house. Hence the shanty.

Trusting that the enclosed fotograf will meet with your approval.

With best wishes believe me my dear
    brother to remain
Your own affect. H. G. Wells

---

[1] The Burgess family are cousins. Wells wrote letters to them announcing the death of his parents; see volume 2. The Wellodes may be his brothers.

[2] Rowland Hill (1795–1879) originated the Penny Post. His pamphlet, *Post Office Reform* (1837) was instrumental in developing the stamp, low cost postage, and other reforms. He served for many years as Secretary to the Post Office.

15. To Fred Wells

Illinois, AL

13 Kings Rd.
[Southsea]   [late Spring 1883]

My dear Fred.

    I was deeply shocked to receive a letter from you this morning. Such an event, so much out of the usual course of events, gave me considerable nervous agitation for some time & you cannot imagine my deep thankfulness on finding nothing serious had occurred.
    I find that you was rather out of your way to Southhampton in being at Romsey you should have come by the old road through Aldersbury & Landford whereas you turned to the left before you reached Landford & went through White Parish to Romsey.
    The distance from Salisbury to Southhampton is 20 miles & from Southhampton here 17 if you come via Titchfield & Gosport.
    Tell that fellow that Miss Wallace is still bkper, & Key shopwalker, but is not allowed to buy for the fancy as he accumulated too much job stock. A Mr. Ostkoff is in the silks, Archon[?] in the dresses Chambers still in the office & Markham in the millinery.[1]

[letter breaks off here]

---

[1] Wells is a good natural speller normally. In this letter his spelling and grammar are retained as he wrote them; he was, after all, only fifteen when this letter was written. The persons named are shop assistants in the drapery where Wells was indentured.

16. To Frank Wells

Illinois, ALS

13 King's Road
Southsea [1883?]

My dear Brother,

[A small sketch of a head of a hen entitled <u>Eggs</u>trodinary <u>Hen</u>fatuation at top of page one.]

 The profound respect that I once bore you as an Elder Brother, the regard that I once had toward you as a good intentioned though extremely stupid young man has been almost entirely destroyed by information that has been conveyed to me though Authentic & Original Sources of Information.

 I have been informed by persons of unimpeachable Veracity (and I may say that Circumstances were noticed by me during my brief soujourn with you that now being remembered tend to confirm their witness).

 That you have so far forgotten your self & the Venerated Name of the poor but Honourable Family of which you are such an extremely unappreciative member that you have shamelessly displayed & freely abandoned yourself to the promptings of a wild & groundless affection for a brown & white female common English fowl.

 You have built with your own infatuated hands this creature a sumptuous residence & have further allowed yourself to be detected in close conversations with this creature (on one occasion with such portions of your dress disarrayed as should have been most carefully adjusted).

 Now I put it to you for your own good & for the sake of the High Immaculate Reputation of the Very Ancient Honourable but somewhat Indigent Family of which you unappreciably bear membership whether such conduct is not of itself calculated to lower this hitherto high & immaculate Name to a profound depth of Ignoble Shame & to so weigh down the Same as to prevent its unfortunate Members from entertaining even the embers of a hope that it Rise again during these saddened times.?

 Would it not be much better to endeavour either to punish & put away this creature or to, if your affection be really & sincerely attached to her marry her or settle down quickly in some rising town where fresh eggs are regularly urgently & largely required? I place this consideration before you in no spirit of mocking levity but with a sincere regard to your present & future welfare.

Nothing is more calculated to advance a young man in business than a good Reputation. Nothing more likely to injure this great desideratum than an incestuous amour or rumour of incestuous amour with a creature as far below you in moral intellect & spiritual development as an English domestic hen.
With this.
    I beg to conclude I subscribe myself
        Your very anxious
           Brother
             H G Wells

17. To Sarah Wells

Illinois, ALS

[Address unknown]   [1883?]

[...] I see you have been conducting a correspondence with the eminent draper and esteemed man J Key. I had to cut patterns of chintz some time back for you and I considered that they supplied the requirements of our correspondence and was somewhat surprised to find you did not take them unto consideration.[1]
    In conclusion
        Believe me
            My dear Mother
                H.G. Wells

---

[1] This half page may be a remnant of another letter, or an enclosure. At the foot of the page is a rather grotesque sketch with a caption, 'Ever the same RV'

18. To Sarah Wells

Illinois, ALS

[Address unknown] [c. 1883]

Dear Mater,[1]

Letter arrived this morning.

Shall be home next Sunday.

Have just been for an invigorator on the Beach. Above

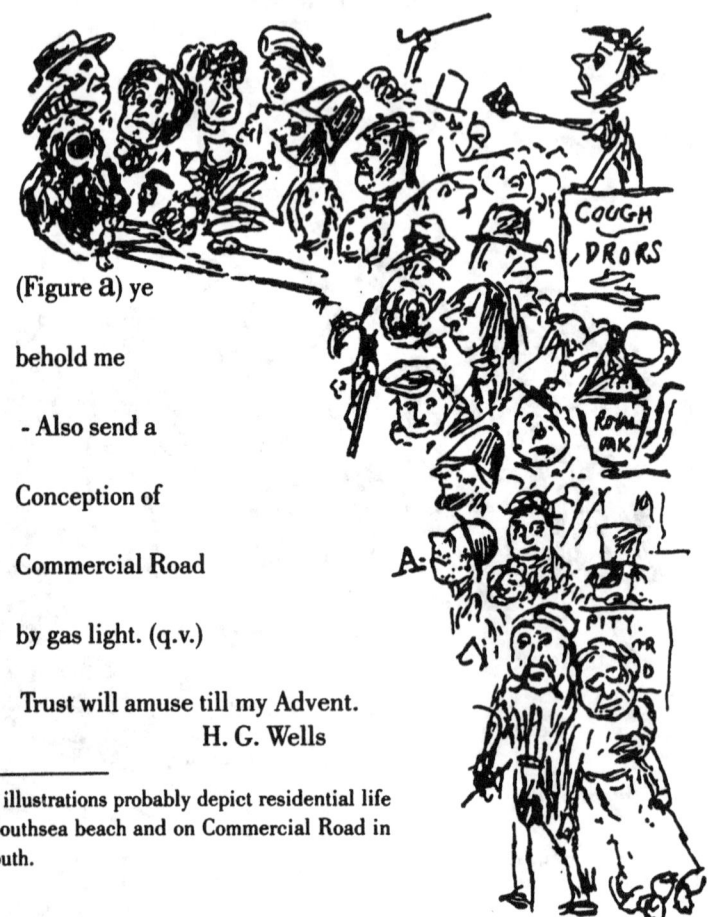

(Figure a) ye

behold me

- Also send a

Conception of

Commercial Road

by gas light. (q.v.)

Trust will amuse till my Advent.
H. G. Wells

---

[1] These illustrations probably depict residential life at the Southsea beach and on Commercial Road in Portsmouth.

19. To Sarah Wells

Illinois, ALS

13 Kings Road [*date obliterated*:
Southsea c. mid-July 1883]

My dear Mother,

By borrowing some money I was enabled to go to Midhurst on Saturday. Mr Byatt[1] received me very kindly & gave me a dinner & took me over his new house.

He informs me that I am too old to enter the teaching profession in the ordinary way as a pupil teacher in an elementary school and that my only method would be to obtain a position as an assistant teacher in a middle class school. In any case, for about nine or ten months I should have to maintain myself.

He offers to take me in his own school after the next holidays in September. I should have more instruction to receive than work to do for a little while and he could therefore give me no wages, and I should have to keep myself.

There is an assistant master there and he informs me that he pays an old lady 3/- a week for a bedroom, share in her sitting room and to do his cooking and he estimates his total expenses (including this 3/-) washing & food to be under 10/- a week. (Of course the cost of clothes for a schoolmaster is half that of a draper).

Now I had a talk with this assistant master and he informs me that if I chose to come I can share his room <u>& old lady</u> for 2/6 a week.

This in other words means that for a little while you would have to pay about 10/- a week for me or estimating clothes to cost £10 a year you would have to pay for me about £35 in the year for one year more.

But then when the start is made there is every prospect of rising to a good position in the world while in my present trade I am a draper's assistant throughout life.

But I must begin at once. If I start at all I must start next September. Which would you prefer?

I leave the matter in your hands.
    & remain
    Your aff. Son
        H.G. Wells

[*on the next line, upside down, '4 weeks course'*]

N.B. Have you written to the GV about the holidays.[2]

---

[1] Mr Byatt was the Headmaster of Midhurst School and Wells's benefactor.
[2] This letter appears in facsimile in *ExA*, ch. 4 §2.

20. To Sarah Wells

Illinois, ALS

13 Kings Road
Southsea   [July 1883]

My dear Mother,

    I am very sorry to hear of our loss in Mr. Woodhouse & for his daughter who will be left alone in that solitary house.

I proposed that I should leave here soon, not only from a desire to study but because I believe that it would in the End prove most economical by far to do so.

I shall live more inexpensively at Midhurst unless you have made other arrangements which I trust you may not have done. While here I am wearing nice clothes shabby, working very hard (for the sale is coming on & two of our elder men may soon be leaving) & above all things

Wasting Time.

Mr. Byatt cannot know all the little expenses for clothes the wearing out of shoes etc etc that are going on here or perhaps he might not be so ready to advise me to stay here until September.

Loaders of Southsea sell good sized boxes for 12/6 there is my fare to Midhurst to pay & (at the utmost) 10/- a week to keep me there.

Box	12. 6
Fare to Midhurst	3. 0
4 times 10/-	<u>2. 0.0.</u>
	£2. 15. 6

£2. 15. 6 that is the expenses of my journey & one month's keep & a suit of clothes would cost more.

I put the case just as it is before you but I do not wish to put you to any inconvenience.

Do as you wish & I shall be happy in the execution of your wishes but if you wish me to go to Midhurst I shall be happy in a superlative degree.

H.G. Wells

NB You have forgotten your shawl. Shall I send it on to you or bring it with me in August or September?

21. To Sarah Wells

Illinois, ALS

13 Kings Road
Southsea [c. July 1883]

My Dear Mother,

I fail to see how Mr. Byatt could be offended by my pursuing say a month in preparation for my Engagement with him. I should be at my lodgings during that time engaged in study. I might not even see him until the commencement of the term.

Time here is wasted. I can not study here in a room crowded with a set of noisy lads after twelve hours misery.

There is a sale coming rapidly on. Hands are leaving and there is every probability of our being shorthanded and overworked.

Had you read my letter carefully you would have seen the Economy of my leaving, at the latest early in August. This would be a direct and immediate saving to begin with.

And you do not imagine that I shall be able to pass examinations without study? I shall not leave Midhurst & cease to be an expense to you until I have matriculated. A month lost absolutely lost now only means another month added on to the time I am to be a clog around your neck.

You chose to bargain with Mr. Hide[1] behind my back and you have inflicted the misery on me of seeing you swindled by that little hound. You have paid another lot of money for him to board me in this vile hole until September & you are letting him profit by my labour & me fritter away my life here.

I have been so foolish as to waste the greater part of 17 years, more than 1/4 of my life already. I have a fearful lot of lee way to make up & I must set to work at once if you will let me.

I shall set a small value on my life the fag end of my life. I shall not enjoy it very much if I have [to] look back not on success & well earned rewards but on so much time spent in half hearted work at school, 6 months at Rogers & Denyer, 2 at home 1 at Woking 3 at Midhurst 28 at Southsea & so on.

June is lost. July is being spent in letter writing. Will you try & save August? Remember what Mr. Morley used to say, 'A Moment lost can never be regained'.

You will not trust me. You ask Mr. Hide or Mr. Byatt and do as they advise you & they have other interests to consult than yours or mine. I know these two men better than you do & I implore you as earnestly as I can to trust me a little more than you do either.

I am your son but you let Mr. Hide try to put distrust between myself & yourself & between myself & Mr. Byatt.

It would be the kindest & wisest thing you could do now to let me leave here very soon.

To explain all about these examinations would take too long now, but it requires no lengthy arguments to see that if it requires 10 months to study up to pass an examination if those ten months begin now they would end before they would if they began in September. I have written a lot of letters & repeated all these arguments over & over again. I shall not do so again. This is the last of that disruption I shall write.[2]

You could write to Mr. Hide when you wished me to leave or if you thought I could not be trusted to buy a box & take my ticket you might come to see him yourself.

I remain
  hoping that
You will believe me to be,
    Your affectionate Son
      H. G. Wells [3]

---

[1] Hide is an incorrect spelling for Hyde, who was the owner of the draper's shop from which Wells was departing to begin his formal education.

[2] A paragraph follows which is crossed out. It says, 'As you do not seem inclined to trust me to buy a box on the assumption that I should I suppose steal the money & get tipsy on it'.

[3] Wells used two similar styles of handwriting at this time. One is very clear, and may be a result of a 'fair copy'. The other, and this letter is an example of the type, tends to be freer in its calligraphy. Wells always used spaces freely in his correspondence, but the many spaces in this letter (not reproduced in this transcription) are an indication of his distraught state of mind. This letter clearly marks the first significant intellectual crossroads in his life.

22. To Sarah Wells

Illinois, ALS

13 Kings Rd.
[Southsea]   [July 1883]

My dear Mother,

    Hope that my remissions[?] in correspondence (a most unusual thing for me to be guilty of) may not have alarmed you.

I have had a very kind letter from Dad & also one from Mr. Byatt in which he half promises me a crib[1] when I leave here if I pass a very stiff exam. It will require hard work & time but I can give that if I can but obtain books.

I spoke to you about the books at home when I was at Up Park. The French & Latin books, geographies & grammar would be most valuable to me. The books that you have of mine with you my Midhurst school books would help me also greatly if you could manage to drop a few this way.

I will get the O clo'[?] sent off soon & should consider a few books as a generous return.

Believe me,
My dear Mother
Your very affecte Son
H.G. Wells

---

[1] Used here in the sense of a place, a position

23. To Sarah Wells

Illinois, ALS

13 Kings Rd
Southsea   [22? July 1883]

My dear Mother,

I am afraid Father is fully determined not to sign the agreement but it would be perhaps better to write once more to him before you proceed to act without him & tell him that my apartments are engaged & even most of my goods sent on to Midhurst & reminding him of all that he has received from you in the last few years. Ask him to sign the agreement or expect no more.

He is now blocking my path in life & he will be a continual threat for the next two years unless he signs.

Believe me to be
Your very aff. Son,
H.G. Wells

24. To Sarah Wells

Illinois, ALS

13 Kings Road
Southsea   [24? July 1883]

My dear Mother,

I have purchased a box and am about to send it on to Midhurst.

I have also had my portmanteau repaired & shall be able to take the remainder of my luggage on in that.

Your shawl I will forward to Petersfield station in a few days.

Unless you have made other arrangements I had already agreed to lodge with another of the masters and it is only necessary for me to write & tell him the date of my departure from this place, in order to have accommodations prepared.

So that if it would be a trouble to you the journey you contemplate to Midhurst could be avoided.

Believe me, my dear Mother
   Your very affte Son, HGW

25. To Sarah Wells

Illinois, ALS

13 Kings Rd,
Southsea   [late July 1883]

My dear Mother,

Mr Hyde has informed me of the date of my departure & I have signed the agreement cancelling the indentures.

With a portion of the money you sent me I have bought a rough box and am just about to send it to Mrs. Walton my landlady. As there are many books in it, it is very heavy & I think it will take up the remainder of my money to send it to Midhurst.

Mr. Harris the companion with whom I share the room has written to inform me that on Mr. Byatt's informing the boys of my advent [?] as a tutor among them they seemed all very much pleased so I hope to find my new circle very much more pleasant than the one in which I now move.

I share your hope that this may be the last movement I shall make & promise to do all in my power that it shall be so.

 Believe me
  My dear Mother
   to be
    Your very affte son,
     H.G. Wells

26. To Sarah Wells

Illinois, ALS

13 Kings Road
[Southsea]   [July 1883]

My dear Mother,

 I felt sorry for my unsympathetic & cold hearted letter almost immediately after I had despatched it & I hope that you will forgive me sending it. But there are many circumstances to irritate me, many little temptations to sharp speaking and unjust thinking at this place and you must not set too much value on the evil little snarls in some of my letters.

To write to Father & to tell him that Mr. Hide having informed you that he did not consider me to be well fitted for a business man you had taken me away and that I had obtained a situation as a teacher at the Grammar School Midhurst would be the next thing I would advise you to do. He cannot refuse to cancel my indentures & you are not obliged to mention to him that at present I receive no salary.

If you could forward the box I do not think there would be any necessity for another tiresome journey hither.

You might write to Mr. Hide & say you wished me to leave on July 30th or August 1st or any date before Sept. that would best suit you & I could go direct to Midhurst & commence study.

 Believe me, Mother
  Your very affectionate son
   H.G. Wells

N.B As I purchase my own food at Midhurst & pay for my room by the week, I should have to have some ready money with me. For there will be no heavy bills necessary up there.

27. To Sarah Wells

Illinois, ALS

13 Kings Road
Southsea [July 1883]

My Dear Mother.

Now it is all over I almost feel ashamed of myself for my very cowardly action of again throwing myself on your hands but I trust & I will do all in my power to ensure that it shall not be long that I shall be dependent on you.

You must remember that all depends now on myself. My future does not now lie at the mercy of Mr. Hide whether he chooses to lie or tell truth. All I have to do now is pass examinations not to flatter employers shopwalkers & heads of departments.

And I believe it would be for my own good and for yours if I could pass the time between now & the commencement of my duties in September not here in work but at Midhurst[1] in study. I wish to pass certain examinations as quickly as possible for when they are passed I shall be able to earn some money entitled in fact to demand some.

It is very painful for me each night to reflect on the one day more that has gone to add to the bulk that has already accumulated of time wasted. It is very painful to be here an inferior of those to whom I cannot but feel myself in some respects superior. I am wearing out good clothes wasting valuable time fretting away myself - here and I ask you to grant me one more kindness shorten my stay here at the Vile Sinful town & this Unhappy shop.

Remember that it will shorten the time that I shall be a clog around your neck.

& will render me
Still More Your Grateful Son HGW

---

[1] Midhurst Grammar School, where Wells was about to become a student, acting as an usher (pupil-teacher) in the small establishment.

28. To Sarah Wells

Illinois, ALS

North Street
Midhurst   [2? August 1883]

My dear Mother,

    I arrived safe here about an hour ago & am quite delighted & proud of my new nest.

    Mrs. Walton boards lodges & washes for me at 12/- a week which she will not object to your paying quarterly.

    I am very comfortable & should be pleased to see you any time you can find it convenient to call & inspect my arrangements.

    I left Mr Hide in a very friendly spirit & am now about to report myself to Mr Byatt so

              Believe me to be
                    Your very affte Son
                        H.G. Wells

29. To Fred Wells

Illinois, ALS

3 George Street
Godalming [*address crossed out*]

Midhurst   Spt. 4. 83

Mr. Fred,

    Sir.

    Mr. Frank is composing a number of applications for ye Farnham cribbe[1] and he being very violent causeth me to write with a shaky hand & quaking heart & to spell words wrong with great velocity & contentment.

    He will write first as from George St. Godalming, then yelling violently hurl the innocent sheet to the other end of the room & wish it further.

Anon he will place the scene of the composition of the Epistle in North[?] Street Midhurst & then putting the wrong date sink under the table weeping.

Then with the most horrible curses on the heads of all drapers will run amuck around the room & only soothe his stormy soul by beating his head against the brick wall that luckily for humanity restrains & calms him & limits his violent actions.

Mr Frank before his fit came on told me to say that

Mr Frank & Mr George will glory in the hospitable reception of Mr Fred at George St. Godalming.

They are at present at Midhurst & will tramp to Godalming on Friday.

  *____*_____*_____*_____*____*

I am enjoying a short holiday before I begin business on Tuesday.

Give my love to father and
> believe me to be
>> Your very affecte
>> Brother
>>> H.G. Wells

N.B. (Also the good wishes of Frank to Dad.)

---

[1] Used here in the sense of a place or position

30. To Sarah Wells

Illinois, ALS

North Street
Midhurst   [Autumn 1883]

My dear Mother,

  The envelope is as acceptable as the sheet of paper is superfluous; in future, when wishing to hear from me, please send envelope as in the present case and a sheet of paper <u>with writing thereupon</u>.

The present glorious weather has induced me to make various lengthy walks, to the visible benefit of my health & injury to my complexion which walks have elevated the reputation of Midhurst and its neighbourhood for beauty greatly in my mind.

The commons are covered with a thousand shades of purple, blue & crimson. The sunshine lends a gentle richness to the plentiful fir plantations and wherever I go, the chalky old downs form a picturesque background.

Study progresses slowly for while this weather lasts I contemplate frequent half holidays nevertheless the progress though slow is done to make sure & hope that I succeed.

Last Sunday I dined, tea'd, went to church & supped with Mr. Byatt. He is extremely kind & we shall I think get on well together.

Remember me to all. Excusing this sudden termination as the evening bells are ringing.

                & believe me to be
                     Your affte Son
                       H.G. Wells

PS. A flower show is held here on Wednesday & I should like if possible to attend as I think Mr Byatt & most of the Midhurst people will go.

I also want a few sox as the ones that I brought from Southsea are almost falling to pieces.

Do not send on any account more than 2/6 <u>but if possible send postal orders as I cannot change stamps.</u>

31. To Sarah Wells

Illinois, ALS

North Street
Midhurst   [Autumn 1883]

My dear Mother,

        Your very kind letter arrived safe this morning.

I am very sorry that Frank is leaving Ballards just at present and I should like to see him if he would call on me while he is with you.

I do not think I should like to come to Up Park until I could say that I had commenced duty & was getting along well here.

It will please you to hear that usually the Grammar School has the curate down to instruct the candidates for confirmation every year.

So you see there is no excuse for me with which to evade that ceremonial any longer.
>Believe me dear Mother to be
>>Your very affte Son
>>>H.G. Wells

32. To Fred Wells

Illinois, ALS

181 Euston Road   Feby 1st, 84

My dear Brother,

I feel profoundly insulted by your silence. After my extreme generosity in bestowing on you a chop & subsequently allowing you to monopolise Kate [1] (in whom I am surrender all interest whatsoever), after losing money to you at nap[2] (1/2d) & in a thousand other ways earning your gratitude, allow me to maintain my indubitable right to respect from you and to state once more my impression that your neglect of correspondence is in the highest degree uncomplimentary to myself.
>Your aff Bwk[3]
>>H.G. Wells

---

[1] Who Kate was is unknown.
[2] Nap is a card game, which was often played at this time by military personnel.
[3] This mark is probably short for the nickname Buzzwhacker.

33. To Sarah Wells

Illinois, ALS

[London]   [17 July 1884]

My dear Mother,

>I have passed all my Science Exams.
>Human Physiology. 1st class Advanced (Queen's Prize).

Physiography,   "   "

Magnetism & Electricity "   "

Mathematics   2cd Class, 2cd stage.

I have not heard the results of the Art Exams yet.

This will make me a "<u>first class</u> certificated Science teacher" and If I have pased my Art Exams I believe that I shall also become a "certificated Art teacher".

Mr. Wilderspen is leaving us & Mr. Byatt proposes for me to take his place & to engage a special teacher for music. He will give me £40 per annum and a rise in about a years time. He will also let me earn what I can by teaching science classes which ought to bring me in something between £8 to £25 a year in addition to my salary.

As I shall draw salary for the next three months in a few days I shall be able to pay Mrs Walton's bill myself.

I have settled all my tailor's bill.

We break up on the 25th July (tomorrow week) Will there be any chance of a week at Up Park before I go to Bromley.

              HOORAY!

I am my dear Mother
    Your affectionate Goodfornaught
        H.G. Wells

                      Now an independent
                      Gentleman

Please excuse bad writing etc.
on account of good news.

34. To Sarah Wells

Illinois, ALS

47 High Street
Bromley   August 23 [1884]

My dear Mother,

    Mr. Byatt would probably prefer beginning the term work with a fresh master as changes in the midst of a session often produce confusion.

The entire cost of articles on list will be, I estimate, under £2.

I should like very much a short holiday at Up Park before I settle down here.

I have been contemplating trying to obtain employment for September if Mr. B. should not require me. I have already offered him my services.

Father seems to approve of the going up & down view. If more economical I shall endeavour to obtain a season ticket.[1]

I don't think there is anything more to say.
              & remain
                    Your very affte Son
                        H.G. Wells

---

[1] Wells was living at home with his father during the long vacation.

35. To Fred Wells

Illinois, ALS

47 Hai Stryt[1]
Bromli, Kent   September 25, 1884

Mai dyr Bryder,

    Yu wil notis on komensing the perysal ov this , an epipsal, and, on if ferst glans, asknyd apjrens about it; hwig iz oing tu de fakt ov its bying riten in akadens wid de rryles, wd reader in de alfabet, (fdr ier eir new ryter)of te niw spellig riform.

altho it me enkounter a konsiderabel dignty ov opostion from thoze pig hedid pypel thy sym to dilait in bloking the progres ov all impy=ryvment, yet ai ferli beliv that it wil bikom as usfal stail or speling bifor the end ov de senturi.

It is alredi ekstensivli used in skyls as an introdukton tu the riding of ordineri boks and it is a positiv fakt that a gaild me by toot tu ryed buks riten [....][2]

Wid best wishez
    Bileve my tu rimen
        Yurs veri sinsjrli
            H. G. Wels.

[1] In this letter Wells is indulging his sense of humour and his still rudimentary ideas about simplified spelling; he is also learning to use language in a variety of ways.

[2] This letter continues for three more pages, mainly dealing with the idea of simplified spelling. 'Punch' had carried several articles in this period making fun of simplified spelling, and this effort is Wells's response to that idea. The last two pages are concerned with the treatment of a head cold by applying plenty of rest.

36. To Fred Wells

Illinois, ALS

Atlas House
High Street
Bromley   [1885?][1]

My dear Fred,

You can see by the above that I am down here again with the Dad. And I take the opportunity thus afforded of writing to instruct you more fully concerning the nature of things in general at this noble establishment. I am particularly anxious to put the state of the case before you for reasons hereafter stated and I have already written a long letter to Mother showing the prospects of students in our school which I have requested her to forward to you. In that epistle you will find all that will interest you concerning myself and much doubtless also that will bore you; and in this therefore I want to give you a description of the Art School which is adjacent to ours with especially reference to the students who work in the studios of that establishment.

It is necessary, to be admitted to these studios free, to possess certain qualifications. These are as follows.

1. You must be a member of the industrial classes (which you are).

2. You must promise, that, after the training is over, you will become a science teacher and

3. you must display sufficient artistic talent to guarantee that the instruction will not be wasted upon you.

These conditions being complied with there is nothing to prevent you becoming a student here & securing the guinea a week towards your support as in the case of the Science teacher in the Science laboratories.

Supposing for instance that you, feeling that the prospects you have at present, are not of the most glorious kind, were inclined to endeavour to attain admission here. The task for one of your peculiar constitution would not be at all difficult. I have passed second grade free-hand and second grade model drawing and I can assure you that I have never done any work to prepare for either exam. [There] can be no doubt which of us has the most delicate appreciation of art. What I can pass second class second grade you undoubtedly could pass first class second grade with very little practice. Then there is geometrical drawing and Perspectives. For these you would have to purchases compasses, parallel rulers, ordinary ruler, and protractor. And you would have to work at them pretty closely but the leading principles once mastered, you would find little or no difficulty on your way to success in these branches of art. Neatness of workmanship, I may mention in passing, securing marks in the SR exams.

There are other sections of art you might also go in for but if you put in for the four I have mentioned alove you would get about 300 or 400 marks if you did pretty well at all. Now I may mention that several of our students got in our lab by coming up on two subjects only & some of them, had they got full marks for all they came up in, could not possibly have obtained more than 300.

I have gone in for these details because my dear brother, I have a suspicion that you are not altogether suited for the trade you are at present in, not that you are not a good draper, but that you would fill with better grace other positions in the world than those behind a counter. A training (obtainable in the manner I have shown) at our schools would qualify you as an art teacher anywhere. You might teach in one or two schools during the day and in the evening teach evening classes, under the Department & with half the work that you do now pull in from £100 or £300 a year. Of course you would have to scrape along rather close while in training but then the different prospects you would have would compensate for slight privations. You could if you got in next year, share my room & so effect a considerable economy in respect to lodging During the summer holidays you could of course always get a temporary crib, if you let yourself go cheap. //Keep & £15 say// and then when training was over you would be instead of an assistant an independent man, earning what many a manager in the drapery would like to get.

You can always set up for yourself and the capital required is nihil.

If you should think my letter at all worth considering on receipt of encouraging reply I will forward you the Art directory and a work on Perspective which will give you a better idea than my description of the advantages offered to those who like to work.

>I remain
>>My dear brother
>>>Your Affte brother
>>>>H.G. Wells

---

[1] This very tentative date is given because of the similarity of the handwriting with that of other letters from late 1884 and 1885. It is more 'juvenile' than that of his undergraduate days.

37. To Frank Wells

Illinois, ALS

Temple of Baal
The High Place   Kalendae Sextile
Bromley   [June 1885?]
                    (bats repaired & revetting carefully done)

Dear Geezer,[1]

>>Please write
>>Shall come down to Shrewsbury if you don't (Serious Honest Injun)
>>>So in a hurry.
>>>>Yours
>>>>>HGW

Geezer

>Pleasant is the Country in Summer
The butterflies are fluttering the balmy flowers around
and gnats in swarms & hornets in the woodland glades are found
Big Bumble Bees and wasps & things amid the heather hum
And we breathe an atmosphere of flies, now Summertime has come

>Lovely is leisure in the long Summer Days

Lo! The Sun is in the Zenith pouring down
On valley and on village field from house & town
    A flood of luminous blazing heat
On the fly surrounded kine in the meads. On the sheep
On the tourists (mightily booted) on the tramp asleep
    On picnic party & on children's treat
Through d[riv]ing clouds of dust on glaring roads
    Where is a vast procession toiling
  Bicyclists Tricyclists Excursionists
  Singing beer-ing howling tooting cheering
    yelling gal-ing smelling of much hair oiling
All slowly yet certainly boiling

The Glory of the Summer Night is to be Appreciated most when
    The fruit carts bound for London break monotonous midnight slumber
    The oaths of the drivers mingling
    With the sound of the harness jingling
    & the wheel & gravel thunder
    While the pale unspeakable glory of the Moon of the summer night
    Looks down on the fruit picking people engaged in a
        neighbourly fight
    The Song of the landrail
    Putting the nightingale
    To shame & to Flight
Wherefore let us all rejoice [2]

---

[1] This letter was probably written to his brother Frank. Letters to Frank tend to be written in a more jocular way than others.

[2] This account of some of the events of a draper's assistant's holiday was also recalled, although in a less derogatory light, in one of his uncollected pieces from the *Pall Mall Gazette*, 'The Holiday of a Draper's Assistant – Life in a Margin', (5 June 1894).

38. To Fred Wells

Illinois, AL

The Temple of Knowledge
Arts, Science, Philosophy, Religion
& Elementary Feliniculture (cat
has 3 kittens)
Euston Road
Smut City
England [Autumn 1885?] [1]

Frederick Joseph Wells

  Gloria in Excelsis mei Long years (3 months?) have rolled since I turned my noble self to write to your sublime majesty. Long and eventful time for lowly almost bestial thing that I was. Creature of hideous aspect. Plastered with South Kensington certificates. Evidence of honest cram - I have now become a holy - a respectable person entitled to wear a gown of some black stuff with pointed sleeves not reaching below my knees (if I enjoy being pelted by little boys) and to call myself an undergraduate of London University with the clear, the unavoidable prospect of becoming a graduate in October 1888 - a bachelor of Science - & the possibility (by licking the boots of the right professors) of becoming a scarlet clothed doctor before 1900. D.V. that is which being interpreted is - if the drains and draughts spare me & I hang not myself.
 I enclose a card[2] showing how we waste our time at the Schools. I am cultivating the brutality of speech, that used to drive Old Morley to caneings and the guvnor to awful convulsions of rage, at the therein indicated Debating Society - I find the fare that produces the most ecstatic enjoyment in the highly cultivated mind is the rankest & most uncalled for personal abuse or abuse of generally admired institutions witness my paper
  [remainder of letter missing]

---

[1] This letter is very tentatively placed here because of the handwriting and the nature of the way the topics are discussed. At this time students went through a course of study at the Normal School of Science, and then matriculated at the University of London to complete the undergraduate degree.
[2] The card is not present, but we can assume that it was a notice of a meeting of the Debating Society in which Wells was very active.

39. To Elizabeth Healey

Texas, AL   Easter, 1886

[*At the top of the page is a sketch of a person writing in a notebook while sitting on a stile. At the bottom of page 1 is a fanciful drawing of a skull with a crown, wearing the mask of tragedy. The first page is signed 'H.G.W. Easter, 1886'.[1] This poem was probably sent to Elizabeth Healey at a later date.*]

A Parable for Poets
(Inspired)

The grey sky glooms above me, the bare round-shouldered downs,
Like heavy yokels (which they <u>are</u>) my presence hail with frowns;
The village lies below me, the dirty ugly home
Of some two hundred mixtures of sorrow, spite and bone;
A ditch & hedge upon my left; the same upon my right.
A gloomy peewhit (squeaking); and nothing else in sight.
This is bad, but, in store, worse is: I am pledged to write some verses.

Can a mortal manufacture verse to suit the present age,
Philosophie-sentimental, sickly sweet or pompous sage;
While the east wind, dry, sarcastic, flings the dead leaves on the page.
Or in sudden bitter fierceness, blows his coattails round his ears
Fights him for his hat and paper, chaps his hands & makes the tears
Down his purple features dribble, as they have not done for years?
No. He cannot. And you never heard a poet person sing
Of the hopeful balmy springtime, who knew <u>anything</u> of Spring

Even as the worldly wise ones (knowing mankind) never can
Sing about the elevated nature of this Yahoo, Man.
Boast a mighty hate of shamming that itself is greater sham,
Hymn this rubble world of trouble, or in diverse manner, say
That the cooling globe is rolling onward to an age of day.

On they flood, O river, drift we in the moonlight,
With the oar blades slowly floating through the water
Or, returning lazily, babbling to the wavelets:
Silent mighty River, streaming to the ocean
On thy course attended by the fitful eddies

Murmuring and sobbing as they hurry onward
Underneath the beeches, from their deep black shadow
Comes the reedy sighing of the dreaming shore
Now a splash and ripple now a weird outcrying
Black against high heaven, stand the leafy [*illegible word*]
of tall ancient beeches:
And almost the river lies in kindred gloom;
Now and then the knotty trunks, like molten silver
Shine in the transient glances of the moon.
Glances, bright but fitful, through the gaps and shinings
Of the thin breeze-rippled cloud scum of the sky.

In our wake the bubbles, glorious for a moment
In the shining moonlight gleam & dance & vanish
Even as we mortals, frothings of dead matter,
Bubbles on a river, borrow light & shadow
Borrow joy and gladness, from the things around us.
Round the distant headland. ho! a light appearing
Like red Mars arising, lighting up its pathway
With a golden beam.
Voices, splashing, laughter; then a sudden stillness
Then with harp outringing solemn voices singing.

The roseate hues of early dawn,
The glories of the day,
The crimson of the sunset sky,
How soon they fade away.
A rosy hope lights early youth
Then follows, manhood's might,
The wisdom of declining years,
Another - Eternal night.
Time, like an everflowing stream,
Wears all our world away.
We die forgotten as a dream
Dies at the dawn of day.[1]

---

[1] Wells enclosed this poem, or a version of it, in a letter to Elizabeth Healey, 2 March 1930, dating it as having been written at Easter 1886. She selected the last eight lines, from her copy when she was preparing her proposed book on Wells based on his letters: the book did not appear however. The extracts from these letters are in Illinois, while the originals, or many of them, are in Texas. Healey sold the correspondence in the 1930s to raise money after her

husband developed a debilitating illness. Wells approved of the sale, and also began paying her a monthly pension. He also sent her an autographed set of his books for her to sell.

40. To A. T. Simmons [1]

Illinois, AL

The Elms
Minsterworth
Gloucester [2] [Summer 1886]

[At the head of this letter is a sketch of a hat stand.]

Dear Hats,

Your very comforting letter to hand. It has done some good. The Barometer rose one inch after I read it. Still my grief is terrible. The air is yet abnormally humid with my tears. Even now the glass is at 26, and people complain that the paper peels off the walls at a terrible rate.

The Severn Bore has not been seen or heard of for weeks.[3] Some suppose it was swept right out to sea when the first terrible torrent of tears poured over my cheeks on their eager course to the majestic repose of the <u>Englastic Review.</u> Some don't - All is doubt & despair & very damp indeed. The sexton kept baleing out the church all through the service last Sunday wid his hat.[4]

Scarcely had our parson given out his text, "The waters have come over my soul O Lord!" when the unanimous sneeze of the congregation blew him out of the pulpit.

The organ is no longer a musical instrument. It is a pump [*sketch of a person at the organ under an umbrella*] As for me, I am a wreck & a miserable sinner & the Lord ha' mercy on my sinful soul.

As for my chance of returning, Simmons, you are a Jesuitical sycophant. & even if it is possible to get another year at S. Kensington I don't think I shall come up.

I am so disgusted with the extreme poverty in which we have to live. If I can get over £90 I shant come There!

One matter I wish to consult you about.

How are recommendations

[remainder of letter missing]

[1] Simmons was a close friend and fellow student at Imperial College.
[2] The Wells family, or at least Wells and his mother, were spending a brief summer vacation at his Uncle Charles's farm in this place, which, according to Wells's letters, was incredibly dull.
[3] The Severn bore is a phenomenon in which the rising tide overcomes the river flow to the sea and reverses the direction of its current for a time at each high tide.
[4] Wells is sardonically describing a rain storm which had interrupted his holidays, which were very boring.

41. To A. T. Simmons

Illinois, ALS

The Elms
Minsterworth
Gloucester   [July–August 1886]

Cur of a Simmons,

  You cuss. I wrote to you on Thursday last asking you to forward a list of agent chappies for situations & here it is Monday & no noose which is a nuisance - You see tempus fugit & with tempus the engaging season, & with that all my prospect of getting a respectable berth.

Imagining that perhaps you are in London & the delay occurred in forwarding my note I have stuck immediate on this which I hope will fetch you in no time. Do please write by return Suspense intolerable.

If I don't hear from you before Thursday morning expect to read in paper of a respectable looking young man having run a muck down the nave of Gloucester Cathedral. Wirroo! Whoop!

[*A sketch of a person running amuck appears at the bottom of the page.*]

Do Write
    Your Wells

42. To A. T. Simmons

Illinois, ALS

Three Elms
Minsterworthy
N^r Gloucester   [Summer 1886]

The Advent of Learning in the West of England.
The domestic animals entertain a discourse on Indeterminate Equations of a degree higher than the first.

Dear Simmons (My Simmons)

      Book arrived safe. Many thanks.
This is a beautiful lonesome land.

    [A detailed 'Map of District' with sketches of animals and men drunk with cider]

This is a beautiful lonesome land. Consequently, vast opportunities for work. Spent the blessed Sabbath exploring for bacca. No blessed bacca to be got in the district. Consequently no bacca, no hindrance to work. Not a good looking [female] to be got here for love or money or any other purpose. No gallivanting about — More time for work.

*   *   *   *   *   *

A interval of some days is here indicated doorin which time I ave been hentrowdeuced to <u>the village school mistress</u>.

    [A sketch of a young woman's head labelled 'Plan of Schoolmistress', and another sketch of a young woman seated labelled 'Schoolmistress elevated'.]

Work all over. We are creatures of impulse. Hitherto my life has been a blank. Now it is a ——
  Goo night oflr. Ur go ome timornin Ur go ome timornin tidayli doshapear.[1]
    Yoursh,
      Wellsh

---

[1] This is either Wells's attempt at reproducing the local dialect, or, more likely, an indication that he had imbibed too much alcohol.

43. To A. T. Simmons

Illinois, ALS

Rus
Eternity   [Summer 1886]

Dear Simmons,

  Much meditation anent the scholarship has convinced me that
Jennings Estimable on account of his Wisdom & Knowledge & his Many Virtues, is yet, being an Official hardly a fit & proper person for the leadership of a Students debating society, & furthermore because he has been member for the space of one year only.[1]
  Burton for the last reason given [illegible words] Jennings & eke for considerations of a Personal nature already familiar to you is also unfitted for that exalted station.
  Taylor being altogether a vice sodden mass of vulgarity is to be noticed only on account of his self assertion & for rejection.
  Jones is ineligible because
    1. He is ignorant incapable & pedantic
    2. He is inelegant, vain & assertive
  & 3. He is subject to virtuous indignation (mote and beam)
  Simmons although the Slave of numberless vices is yet popular among our smokers. Has aquitted himself honourably as Speaker whereas Jennings has merely failed as Chairman [&] is except Taylor the Senior Member of the Society & enjoys My Approval - Moral, Plump
      Yours,
        Wells

[1] Each of these characterisations has a small sketch. Wells is suggesting who is going to be awarded a scholarship. All of these people are fellow students and friends of Wells and Simmons.

44. To Fred Wells

Illinois, AL

47 High Street
Bromley, Kent   August 31, 1886

Dear Fred,

    Accept my sincere thanks for razor - always laboured under a persuasion that that canary visaged footman Frederick had annexed it & had mourned it as forever lost.

Have resolved to return to Kensington for one more year. May as well learn a trade well; you know, if it is to be learned at all. Shall probably be pretty select as it is advanced geology and the number will probably be under ten.

No news from Frank. I fail to understand his position entirely. Do you know if he has any intention of chucking up the drapery or have you no inkling of his little game.

Very kind of you to display such a passionate desire to deserve to give Isabel such nice[?] gloves.

[Letter folded and damaged and this last sentence is therefore corrupt. Letter probably ends here, but it is difficult to be sure.]

45. To A. T. Simmons

Illinois, ALS

47 High St Bromley September 9th, 1886

Dear Simmons,

I am very sorry indeed that you are in the slightest degree offended by my Apparent Silence but in my sorrow I am consoled by the divine sense of Right doing and a knowledge of your calm impartiality. When you return to the way sacred to Robert of Chelsea you will discover an enormous quantity of correspondence which has Emanated from me and with willing tears confess that you misjudged me. I return to the Abnormal Science School in Geology, Pts II & III & with swelling heart hear of your contemplated onslaught on the gentle rabbit, the silent nervous snail and the meditative frog. Don't be too hard on them.

You will be made Secretary of the Debating Society on the strength of your umbrella, the majesty of your behaviour & the gloomy solemnity of your visage. A numerous band of conspirators have sworn it.

Have you heard from Burton & Smith recently? These very excellent persons contemplate doing a sort of Advanced Political Mission down in the Debating Society. I have volunteered my practical assistance. In fact, I believe remarks dropped (by a higher power) from my unworthy lips in the Pump Room Cheltenham into the ears of Smith like dust dropped into a solution supersaturate accelerated the definition of the potentialities of Smith's mind. This might end in Smith being an M.P. some day. Burton becoming the Isaiah of the XIX. & you one of H.M. Inspectors of Schools

Probably the best thing I could do in the cause of Social Improvement would be to take orders. It would irrevocably damage the Establishment.

I was at S. Kensington last Monday looking for venerated form. Having written about a week previously to the street of the Great Bob,[1] ordering you to write if you 'weren't' there, I consider you have broken an appointment and am duly affronted. Repent!
       Yours
        H.G. Wells

[A small drawing of a person labelled 'Gones' is at the bottom of the second page of this letter.]

---

[1] Another name for Robert of Chelsea, a church bell.

46. To the Average Man[1]

PLS

[South Kensington]   December. 1886

Respected Sir,

It was, in a more learned and less educated age than this present, the law that literary eruptions should be preceded by a sonorous dedication, by a moving appeal to some eminent person whereby his judgment might be distorted or overthrown, and the fiery flood of poetry, or scorinaceous shower of facts, or dense vaporous arguments, came upon him while disorganised and helpless.

This phenomenon of a dedication is imagined by many not to occur in the current epoch, save as an aborted, a complimentary, thing; but *this* is an error of some bigness. It is true the dedication is no longer, in many cases, a distinctly separable part, but it is equally true that it vigorously survives in the main portion of the Preface now always fixed to papyrean perpetrations. *Why* this modification has occurred is easily explained.

This Land has, unfortunately, become in spirit, democratic, whereas it *was* utterly aristocratic.

The appeal for favour has no longer to be to Eminences, but the Average Flat, and has undergone much adaptation. The eminent love open flattery, while with the vulgar an elevated confidence is more effectual. The dedication has become a prefatory dedication; no longer is it *"De Profundis,"*, but *"attendite, popule."* Nevertheless, the adamantine foundation, the fundamental, characteristic, dishonest object of the disarmament of justice, immutable remaineth. The Author no longer, with sheet and candle, bewails his frailties, but, like Cleopatra in the presence of Caesar, garbed in the thinnest veil of modesty conceivable, poses to suggest unprecedented gifts: yet the guilty consciousness is there still.

We merely mention these facts. We do not contemplate such an introduction to you, O Excellent Average Man; for we know full well you feel as superior to the vulgar herd as we do, and are confident of awakening a twang of sympathy in that Catholic Diapason, your mind, without much artifice. What we would here say is merely a dry indication of why this paper is published. The *personnel* of the Normal School of Science and Royal School of Mines is emphatically *recherché*. Every May the myriads of science students in the British Isles undergo gravimetric sorting. The noblest specimens reach this building.

Here, from north, south, east, and west, are gathered minds specially capable of acquiring, retaining and displaying systematic knowledge. Clearness of perception, imagination and order are alike *the* mental requirements of the scientist and the writer. We may, therefore, reasonably expect that our pages will be filled with right opinion well expressed.

If not, it seems to us that some such absurd explanation as these which follow will have to be accepted: -

That our fellow-students have no time for writing, which implies that they are committing to memory classified facts without opportunity for exercise in the re-sorting and displaying thereof; that, like athletes who, professing to train, merely eat, they are fraudulently cramming; or, that they are incapable of writing, which (as above hinted) condemns the whole magnificent examination fabric of the Science and Art department.

It is thus hard for us to imagine how anyone can deny that this periodical will contain great things.

Anticipating, therefore, your entire satisfaction, we would here record our sense of obligation to the compositor for his valuable aid in setting out our Magazine; to the boy who brought round the proofs for us to look at; to the compiler of "Nuttall's Dictionary", to whom we owe much, if not all, of our material; to the young lady (next door) who is practicing "Scales," and to whom is due much of the praise for the euphony of this introduction; and to the four fellow-students who, at a great sacrifice, *refrained* from offering us advice as to our duties. Less conventional and more sincere thanks must be expressed to those who have contributed matter to this issue. We hope that the number of contributors to No. 2 will be greatly increased, and shall be glad to receive help of *this* sort from all quarters.

I conceal from every eye beneath this calm, hopeful, even proud, exterior, the devastation of the furies, the fierce, ceaseless assault of fear, remorse, and despair. Like the Roman sentinel at Pompeii, or, better, like a responsible public official before an election,

> I remain,
>   O Average man,
>   Your faithful servant,
>   THE EDITOR.

---

[1] As Founding Editor of the *Science Schools Journal*, Wells began the first issue with a letter 'To the Average Man'. It appeared in vol. 1, no. 1, (December 1886), pp. 1–2.

47. To Mergrimes Peter Wells[1]

Illinois, ALS

[Bromley?] [29 June 1887]
from
Herr Busswhackier
Within the Gates

In Utter Darkness & Weeping Without
   Dated this 29th of June
   In the 16th year after the youth of Herr Busswhacker
   (or the 1887st year of the Common Era).

It pleaseth Herr Von Busswhacker
         To communicate in writing with Mergrimes Peter Wells to this purport.
                  (Seeing that the said Mergrimes Peter Wells hath ventured to express certain opinions of a devilish insubordinate & wrongheaded character contrary to the ideas of the said Lord High Absquatilator Herr Von Busswhacker concerning the Nigh Looming Vacation)

Herr Von Busswhacker ruler of the Universe hath decreed these 8 laws, as hereafter written.

Law 1.
   It shall be that Mergrimes Peter Wells do hath his holidays in September between Saturday the 3rd of September & Monday the 19th of September.
   Death shall be his portion if he have them not then.

2. & it shall be that Herr von Busswhacker do take his Imperial pleasures from Friday the 2cd of September to Sunday the 18th of September.

3. & be it decreed that the said Mergrimes Peter Wells do accompany the said Herr Von Busswhacker in his Vacational tours in Hampshire & Wilts in the capacity of valet.
   Horrible tortures awaiting his refusal.

4. And it is law immutable that the said Mergrimes do bear all expenses of the tour under penalty of a Painful Operation.

5. And it being his Lordships wish & desire
   - I   To see the New Forest
   - II   And to see Southampton
   - III   and to see Stonehenge
   - IV   and Salisbury Cathedral
   - V   and of Valentious camp
   - VI   and the camp of Clorius
   - VII and the cathedral of Worcester
   - VIII and his brother Frederick
   - IX   And other wild beasts & Lions

7. It hath pleased his Lordship to decree that the Line of March shall commence at Southampton whither the said Busswhacker & Mergrimes & other chattel hath been conveyed by boat & passing through the New Forest for 15 miles to Lymington where it seemeth good that Herr Von Buzzwhacker shall rest & he next day go on to Salisbury 27 miles & shall stay there all the next day Wednesday going on in the afternoon to Stonehenge with the Emperor of Salisbury (if possible) (16) returning in the evening & going on to Winchester the next day (22 miles) from whence Liss (20 miles) on Friday & UpPark Saturday (10 miles) being altogether a little over 100 miles.

6. And his Lordship hath decreed that Mergrimes shall buy a county map of South Hampshire & a part of Wilts & study the same.

7. & if the said Mergrimes disapproves of this plan he may communicate with H.G. Wells enclosing 7/6 on or before the second Saturday in July (after which no extra time is allowed as marking off for the sale commences immediately after; & the Saturday evenings after closing, are utilized for the said marking off) and the said H G W will run up provided with maps & arrange matters with him.

8. It may interest Mergrimes to know that the said HGW will come in a tight pair of togs patent cloth top boots.
                    a Tail COAT
and a most becoming hat, also a light tie
                    Believe me
                    Herr Busswhacker

[*Three small sketches of men, labelled 'Selevation', 'Nelevation' and 'Elevation' are at the foot of this last page of three.*[2]]

---

[1] This spoof letter, while addressed to someone by a name frequently given to Wells's cats, 'Mr. Peter J. Wells', is probably used here as a literary device for his brother Fred.

[2] This letter has many random spacings between words in the original. There has been no attempt to replicate them as they seem to have no special reason for their appearance. It seems unlikely that Wells and his brother took this trip, as he was teaching at Holt Academy when the dates came around. He did however take a similar trip while he was a draper's apprentice, and aspects of it appear in his popular writing in the 1890s.

48. To A. M. Davies

Illinois, ALS

The Holt Academy
Nr. Wrexham Denbigh   July 30, 1887

Dear Davies:[1]

By the grace of the great & good God, &, it must be added, reverentially but firmly, at considerable trouble & expense to myself, I have reached this locality without further accident than the loss of two books. Considering the small premium I pay in prayer for Divine insurance, I suppose I ought to feel grateful for the humble measures of protection. This is a desolate flat land. I expected the picturesque & behold.

      a view near Holt
A_1 - of course, myself
B - Strawberry pickers at work

S - a stranger.
C. The cetting sun
W. Wrexham.
H H[1] The visible (sensible) horizon.
P. P. P. P. P. P. strawberry plants.

or again: The Dee
average depth 3½ ft. shoaling

[another small sketch of a landscape with the river Dee]

Talking about the Dee. Can you tell me what you know about the London Library? Who ought I to write to? I and three other chappies here contemplate joining.
> Hullo! the chapel bell.
Farewell.   I go to meet my God.
> Yours
> Wells

---

[1] A. Morley Davies, a friend from his South Kensington college days. This relationship was as close as that with Simmons. Unfortunately it turned sour eventually.

49. To A. T. Simmons

Illinois, AL

Holt Academy
Nr. Wrexham
Denbigh   [end July 1887]

[A small sketch of the back of four students' heads appears at the top of the page, with a legend, 'Possible scientific adepts. At present in the raw state. Est-il possible?']

Dear Simmings,

I am hear.- Thanks to the great God who watches over us & protects & absolves us thereby from the moral responsibility of phoolish action. I am hier in this gloomy neighboorhood & I wish I was dead. The Dee is an ass of a river. It is inferior in beauty to the common concept of a Dutch canal: The people of Wales are not Welsh but Scotch; there is a gas factory in this rustic village & the girls in the Holt College for Ladies are to an extraordinary degree young - but with all the interior repulsiveness of features that is in fairer climes the destructive characteristic of extreme old age. The cricket field here is a muddy wilderness after rain and in the sunshine a lumpy sandbank. The boys are phoolish & undisciplined to an astonishing degree, & the chemistry cubbord is not worthy [of] the name containing mostly efflorescid salts in cracked bottles & many broken test tubes full of abominations left by the last Science master in c.'74. There is an utter absence of coherent system in the whole damned affair and I either take the management or go to the Devil.

My story is half written but prayer takes up such a time that I

[*letter breaks off in mid-page*]

50. To A. T. Simmons

Illinois, ALS

The Holt Academy
Near Wrexham   Tuesday, Aug 2nd 87

Dear Simmons,

      I hardly know how to answer your queries of the morning. Anent this Holt a letter is coming to you via Southampton which I trust will reach you in Finite Time. When we meet in the Abysmal, the Unfathomable, when we meet reunited in the bosom of the great All, I will mention a few curses therein contained if you <u>don't</u> get it - but then of course you will.

    I think you ought to do this. You ought to go on for Worthington,[1] if your hours are easy & matric' as possible speedily. If not you should communicate with agents at once before the good things are done for. In any case ascertain just as fully as you possibly can - even if it be by listening at key holes & cunningly opening letters addressed to other people - what the probabilities are of a demonstratorship being established. To ascertain this, it is required to know whether Worthington is influential in the proper quarter, whether he says he means to do anything & whether he is in the habit of sticking to his declared intention.

    Just at present the Boss is hunting round to find me and take me over to that there Ladies Colledge where I am to do the mathematics &
      [*sketch of two people embracing*]
Believe me, old chappy
        Yours very sincerely
           H.G. Wells

[1] A school teaching position was apparently available and Simmons was contemplating applying for the position.

51. To A. M. Davies

Illinois, ALS

The Holt Academy
Nr. Wrexham
                                      Wednesday
                                [early August 1887]

Dear Davies,

    I have just received your letter and with that alacrity to please my friends which is perhaps my most amiable though certainly not my greatest characteristic I write at once. Robbing therein my employer of time & work, & necessitating thereby the usage of graphite instead of that abysmal concentration called ink in the writing thereof.

You ask me for advice, my son, about that which I know little or nothing - nevertheless with that genial attention to requests that so endears me to all, I comply. Take my advice, sonnie, with a light heart. It cost me nothing. It will not affect you much. Here it is.

So far as my knowledge goes and so forth, generously stated is this.

Your intellect is of a high order & your reading has been extensive but I must tell you my conviction - for though it will [go] against your fine conceived notions in the matter - that you are defective on the aesthetic side, that your literary work is as bare of any native grace as is your style of dressing yourself. Consequently, in purely literary acheivement you will not excel. However you always make your meaning clear though sometimes not to the vulgar and there is no doubt that you possess all the capacity required for a monograph or suchlike essay where the succinct statement of fact to the initiated is the sole end in view. However, I do not think that you have a style that will take with the vulgar editor. I am afraid that you will meet mainly with disappointment if you trot round things in the general way.

I hope you are going back to South Kensington. I think - even at the cost of present poverty - you ought to push on there. The authorities approve of you. You are built for the work there & etc, & no one can do two things well at once & so on. I think this about completes the succinct account of things.

My boys - sweet candidates for cherubity - are beginning to get restless as I write. Even now I hear the whispering of the wings. Edward Rouse come here! Damn you - what the devil does this row mean. Go to Hell!
Write me fifty lines.

The trouble ceases. - Peace with the olive branch has entered. There is a silence. As before God. Tell me what you are going to do - the future & the present & believe me

yours in God
H.G. Wells

You know what I can do & what I can't do. If I can serve you in <u>any</u> way, ask & ye shall receive.

52. To A. M. Davies.

Illinois, ALS

Holt Academy
Nr Wrexham Denbigh				August 13th [1887]

Dear Davies,

First - Your imperious instructions. Burton is well and happy. He wrote a joint letter with Rowe (I think you knew Rowe the artist didn't you)[1] descriptive of vast doings on the Severn, portages, towages, etc. in which Burton enacted the role of Saint Christopher.[2] Since then I have not heard of him - sure indication of continued prosperity, for which I unfeignedly thank heaven.

I know nothing about the Nat. Hist. Museum business. Neither have I heard of other matters. You will not hear from the Dep. about your application until the end of Aug. or the beginning of Sep. so - ironical advice - cheer up.

The cry of the uncongenial environment comes also from Simmons. I also quiver. Here the folk are Presbyterian, Radical, and all that is altogether damnable, with an idiotic appeal to common repute, under the misnomer common sense.

However, I have a remedy. I have discovered a damoisel, beautiful, of extraordinary force of character, & higher culture. She is a minister's daughter. Quite by accident I sent you her first note. The letters are getting warmer now as per enclosed specimen. If it was not for the subtil but exquisite excitement of this connexion I should even now be stagnating toward death by [*word completely blacked out followed by what appears to be 'inattention'*] Return the enclosed it is an important link[?] in La plus nouvelle Heloise.[3]

Believe yours,
Slap in Christ & somewhat uncomfortable
H. G. Wells

---

[1] Burton was a schoolmate. Wells lived with him for a time in Stoke-on-Trent while recuperating from the football injury he sustained shortly after this letter; see letter 58. Rowe is Cosmo Rowe, the artist illustrator, with whom Wells lived in London later. Rowe drew some of the magazine illustrations for *War of the Worlds*.
[2] The patron saint of travellers
[3] J. J. Rousseau's famous treatise of finding young love and the process of discovery

53. To A. T. Simmons

Illinois, AL

Holt Academy
Near Wrexham
North Wales [mid-August 1887]

Dear old Chap,

I am sorry and glad that you have left that Portsmouth thing - glad first, because no man has any business in a place where he is not happy - if not in present time in expectation; and secondly very sincerely sorry that you have had this trouble in starting in the world after eremitism at South K. However, disregarding the loss of funds consequent on shifting & all that sort of thing, there is really very little harm done now except the loss of time - some month at most. Unless my estimates of the attitude of folks in general towards you are wrong, you have merely got to do this. To get in somewhere here where 'growth' is going on, and to behave as I have always known you to live, with scrupulous conscientiousness. The vast majority of men are scoundrels but many respect & all are anxious to deal with an Evidently honest man. It is one of those natural commodities whereof the demand exceeds the supply, and blessed is the man who hath such commodity. Tell me soon how you are managing & what you are doing. Why not try Keighley? It is still open, I suppose and the north is healthy & liberal. Keep up your pecker & believe on the Lord Jesus Christ.[1] & death & hell shall not prevail against you!

I am getting better here. The Boss is an ignorant fool, to be come over with astonishing facility. Moreover among these boors I have found a creature with a soul. She is a pretty girl, minister's daughter, teacheress in a high school. When we met we were enchanted. She has read Ruskin, Eliot, & an infinity of good novels. Now we meet surreptitously & spend whole hours, together by shady river banks, where I talk grotesque to her, and she very intelligently to me.

[*remainder of letter missing*]

---

[1] It perhaps ought to be stated that these phrases have no religious meaning for Wells and are simply a way of indicating how sophisticated he and his friends were.

54. To A. M. Davies

Illinois, ALS

[Holt Academy]   [mid-August 1887]

Dear Davies,

       I have been hunting for a letter from a damsel I have become friendly with here, for the past hour or so. Then, lo! I happened on yours. For God's sake return the other & believe me
                Yours,
                     In Christ
                     H.G. Wells
If I had sent that, well to some folks, I should be dead by now.[1]

---

[1] This is an emotional letter with large capital letters and scrawled handwriting. The sought after letter, unfortunately, no longer exists.

55. To A.M. Davies

Illinois, ALS

Holt Academy
Nr. Wrexham

Thursday August 23rd
or thereabouts. [1887]

Dear Davies,

    Incarnato Devilspit

Just you return that billet doux of mine by return, or - I swear by the God I don't believe in - I will drink thy gore clotted juice by the bucketful. I hope what vestiges of consideration you may have for me will prevent your provoking me to make myself sick in this disgustful way.

I suppose about now you are hearing of the providence of the high Gods of Kensington and I pray to him who sustaineth all, that you may hear now of those grim surprises they prepare for those that love them.

Just at present I am very happy but also foresee in the future, multitudinous evil to grow out of the pleasant summer. I am, of course, doing no work here. That - how quickly bad habits grow! - has already become an essential to my happiness. I am a lounger in the schoolroom, teaching without effort through the disciplinarian habit of mind fostered by former masters. I have a good deal of spare time - spent largely in the company of the before-mentioned Annie. I have a pound tin of Three Castles.[1] I have a French master who teaches me parler cochon & who is Atheist, Socialist, cuckold maker & all that is loveable in a comrade. I have a reputation for learning. Nobody capable of finding me out, a dozen fortunate minor accidents, and the capacity of forgetting the future.

Altogether I am to be envied, and in humbleness of heart & with smiling lips invoke a blessing on my less fortunate friends. There is a judgment behind though. Discipline will get out of joint & passion & work will begin. Annie's holidays will end in September & solitude will begin. The tin of tobacco will diminish to bottom dust. I shall sicken of my French Cochon, sacré nom de Dieu, Marchons! & the rest of it. Someone will ask me someday have I read A Kempis or Spenser: a dozen unfortunate accidents will obtain, dyspepsia set in & despair.

Just you write & tell us about yourself, my dear boy. Let me have a little shop, for which now I have reviving appetite. Above all return that letter beginning Dear Herbert - it is Dear Bertie now - as soon as possible.

    Believe me,
        Your loving brother in Christ,
            Wells

[1] A popular brand of pipe tobacco

56. To A. T. Simmons

Illinois, ALS

The Holt Academy
Nr. Wrexham   Saturday, Aug. 27th 1887

Dear Simmonds,[1]

I was dreadfully sorry to get your letter this morning. I wish I was capable of doing something that would actually & immediately make you cheer up from the mental abyss you have got into. From the sublime elevation of contentment, the only thing I can do is just to aim philosophical immutables at you & lacerate you & exasperate you out of inertia. Otherwise there seems to be no remedy for you in my power. Only a godly situation can do it.

Do not be a blasted idiot Simmonds and rush into a clerkship or English mastership or anything of that sort. That will ruin you for life unless God - an evil element - interferes.

Push for S K & classes for some thing of the sort of place from which they turn out fellows like Tate & co.

It is better that you should wash bottles where the conditions of things will render your elevation sure sooner or later, than to take a place where you will wear an unseparable sick hat & never have a chance of anything except marriage with the proprietors daughter, or widow, as the case may be.

Wherefore, my sonnie, shove for the big towns & the Institutions of Evening Classes. That is your sphere & the straight & narrow way to success for you.

Go to a science & art place at any sacrifice in preference to a private school where you will forget as well as fail to utilize all you have won more or less painfully at S.K.

The right place never drops on to the right man when he wants it.

There is always waste & delay in all human devices & transactions.

Rome was not built in a day.

Cheer up, lads, etc.

Sufficient unto the day, etc., etc., etc.

All this doubtless exceedingly true - but still nothing but definite arrangement actually pacifies the wretched uneasiness of mind that torments you.

I have suffered but the bitterness is now past. Still while I suffered there was no cure. Read, <u>do not smoke too much</u>, & get up a flirtation, a quarrel, & any other side issues you can devise to drain off the irritant spiritual matter.

The Meredith story is not yet ripe for telling.

Read novels. Blackmore, <u>Black</u>, Besant, May one of them be a new experience. Rousseau is a grotesque but somewhat sickly devil that may amuse you. Anything of Stephenson or Julian Sturgis is insufficient to while away dull care for a time.

Yours lovingly
Wells

---

[1] Some words in this letter are conjectural as it was written with a pencil on both sides of the paper, which was then folded. After more than one hundred years since it was written the text has become quite indistinct at the margins. Wells used a variety of spellings for Tommy Simmons's name as a sort of private joke.

57. To Sarah Wells.

Illinois, ALS

Holt Academy
Nr. Wrexham   [c. early September 1887]

Dear Mother,

I hope you will excuse the impatient letter I remember writing on Saturday. I quite forget what was in it but I have a very distinct recollection that I was in great pain & a nasty temper when I wrote it, so doubtless it was sufficiently bitter.

I am sitting up in an easy chair today and the haemorrhage has ceased so that I can now tell you what you are doubtless sufficiently anxious to know & that is what has been the matter.

I was playing football on Monday afternoon & got charged 'foul' (that is below the chest) by one of our bigger fellows.[1] The consequence was I was hurt badly in the loin, my kidney was crushed, my liver bruised & my intestines & muscles between the ribs & the pelvis mashed up more or less. Consequently I was in danger of departing this life by one or two different ways. The kidney might inflame, or the bowels, or I might have stoppage - a delightful method of dying of which you have doubtless heard tell before - or I might get weakened by the bleeding.

However by lying still & eating as much as I could under the circumstances, I have pulled through it all. On Thursday the Dr. said I was out of danger from inflammation, on Saturday my bowels acted. The bleeding has slackened off until it is just a few drops to colour the urine and I am still pretty strong.

However, I don't think I will be getting about much for some time yet. It has been a nasty time altogether & I hope you will forgive anything unpleasant I may have said when I had been fighting through it.

I shall want any stuff sent to me now that the worst is over but if you could spare me 10/- I should be obliged because I have spent most of my money in getting things I fancied.

   Love to father & Frank
    Believe me
     Your very affte Son,
      H.G. Wells

Tuesday -

I went to sleep in the afternoon yesterday so this was forgotten for the letter bag.

Your letter & kind enclosure came this morning. Many thanks. It is absurd to talk of Frank or you or anyone coming to see me. What earthly good would such an expedition be?

---

[1] Some accounts of this incident say Wells was refereeing the game, but the letter is clear evidence that he was actually playing when he was hurt.

58. To A. T. Simmons

Illinois, APCS

[Holt Academy,
Wrexham]   Tuesday - [Sep. 6th, 1887
                 from postmark]

Dear A.T.S.

  Please excuse prompt reply to your last. Had a smash at football yesterday week that prevented. Have had injured kidney & liver & suchlike hurts. Am now convalescing in a bedroom with 'nary' book to read. Beastly slow. Write me a long and amusing letter soon or I shall perish from inanition.

B[urton] has written twice. He has a job of some sort (investigation?) at Wedgewood The Potters. He is going to marry & whatnot. Have you heard? How is Bower. Where are Griffiths & Smith? I should like to hear of them if you know anything about them. Hope your little game is going on better now. <u>Do write a long letter</u> old chap & believe me,

Yours,

Wells

Where is Belcher? When does Hewitt go to Oxford? How did that competition for the museums end? Tell Hewitt I am hurt & ask him to drop me a line. Can you tell me if any of our chaps are planted about Bristol? [1]

---

[1] None of these other names are known today, but they are clearly fellow students at the Normal School of Science.

59. To A. M. Davies

Illinois, ALS

Up Park
Petersfield.
Monday   [Autumn 1887]

Dear Davies,

I never hear from you now so I conclude you are wallowing in Natural Science & its unscientific philosophy of progression, and forgetting all the vermin outside your scientific sphere. I <u>should</u> like to hear from you if you can spare a moment somewhen, about yourself, and about Clark & Jones, and the prevailing cliques just at present in the building. I am - see below - awefully hard up just now for amusement and even topics for meditation, so I hope you will see fit to spare - say half an hour - from the Advancement of Learning, for my sake -

I have had some painful experiences since I wrote you last. (I think, if I remember rightly my last letter was an exultant catalogue of sensual delights; bright weather, perfect health, pretty girl in foreground of a sunset by a pollard bordered stream, football, success & so forth.) Two days after I wrote you last

I got smashed at football - inside broken - and my circumstances suddenly changed to a barely furnished bedroom, agonizing pains, life destroying haemorrhage. I got up too soon from that - at the request of my excellent employer - and went to work while I ought to have been setting around, eating grapes & all that sort of thing, and the result was one of the [most] exhausting systematic collapses you ever heard of. At one time, I had - in metameric succession - in my body - acute bronchitis, howling raging dyspepsia, wounded kidney that the cold had got into, and at the caudal extremity - the piles. I had to come home to save my life & now I am living, artificially heated like an incubating chick, and fed on cod liver oil & fat. The kidney is quiet just at present, but there is a serious effusion round it that is going to play the very devil with me soon, and the lungs or rather the right lung - for the other - Thank God - is left - is going to congest and do for me on the first opportunity. I am a confirmed invalid for the rest of my days and I shan't be glad when it is all over.

I have a faint idea that God has sent all this to chasten me. If so he has certainly mistaken his man. I have learnt some wholesome lessons in human charity but I repudiate God more than ever. He's a beggar, he is.

My only chance now for a living is literature. I have done sundry things since I left Denbighshire but up to the present, I have had little success. I think the groove I shall drop into will be cheap novelette-eering - not with my entire approval though. I hanker after essays & criticism - vainly.

Write me a decent reply & I will feel grateful. Tell me anything distinctly new in biological thought. Are there any revelations in crystallography, atomic chemistry, or astronomy? What is this about Norman Lockyer?[1] So far as a newspaper paragraph is comprehensible, I gather that comets, nebulae & so forth are all meteorite clouds? Is that the notion & if so what the Devil impels that outrageous humbug to call it a new view? Has he got new proofs?

When you write tell me about Clark, Jones, Clarkson, Miss Healey, Ridewood, & Jennings. Remember me to these folks if you see or write any of them and mention incidentally that I have been smitten by Wasting Sickness and that my only excitement is the letter bag. Don't ask them to write, merely draw in words these pictures.

[*Two Wells sketches appear here: one to the left depicts Wells in a chair, 'Waiting for the daily mail bag', and in the second, he is slumped down in the chair, 'No letter! How the rest of the day passes'.*]

               Believe me to remain, A.M.D.
Yours
      Truly
            A Wreck,

Simmonds is at Southport Grammar School, and happy. Burton is at Wedgewood's in the Potteries, married, prosperous, happy and a political agitator. Bower is teaching science in Devonshire
Smith, E.H. still at home
Lewdes at Woolwich ? perfect & happy

---

[1] Lockyer was a well known astronomer who had just proposed a new theory of the genesis of comets and space dust of various kinds.

60. To A. M. Davies

Illinois, ALS

[Up Park] [Autumn 1887]

Consider this as an Epistle General & trot it around to all friends.

Dear Davies, and Ladies and Gentlemen,

    I am very busy just now so please excuse reports of progress. Enclosed are documents illustrating flourishing literary career. Don't return them for God's sake.[1] The small cheque relates to injuries sustained at Holt. I heard from Simmonds about their journal copy. Briscoe sent it in without any instructions to a Birmingham printer friend. So we may now reasonably conclude that the journal has gone to the Devil by this time.

Yours,
Wells

Beware of spurious imitations. The other creature who signs himself thus is properly E P Bath & Wells. I repudiate the connexion.

---

[1] Wells enclosed, and they remain with the letter, rejection slips from the *Family Herald*, 9 November 1887, for 'The Death of Miss Pickergill's Cat' and from *Household Words* 2 September 1887, for 'The Death of Miss Peggy Pickerskill's Cat'. The manuscript has not survived. Wells did get one acceptance from the *Family Herald*, but at the moment of writing [23 August 1996] it has not been located. The other manuscript mentioned is probably the next issue of the *Science Schools Journal*.

61. To A. T. Simmons

Illinois, ALS

Up Park
Petersfield   [Autumn 1887?]

Dear Tommie,

Stick out against a decent thing by all means. Why not advertise for private coaching if the time hangs heavy? - Southampton ought to be infested with jobs of that sort. I know of three men in your damned town who want practical work for Inter Sci - Bryt[?] & Holmes is two of 'em. I send you on the old thing again with all your suggestions carried out. If you approve - don't send it back. I have written to Fortnightly about it & will let you know if they will read it & you can send it on.[1]

Be a kind older brother & look at the spelling again - especially that French.

Kiddie

---

[1] This is probably the first piece for which Wells was paid. Frank Harris accepted it titled, 'Rediscovery of the Unique', *Fortnightly Review*, July 1891, pp. 106–11. Harris, (1856–1931) a well-known author and editor, later claimed to have been Wells's discoverer. He was fulsome about the young author in his autobiography, *My Life and Loves* (London, 4 vols, later 1 vol., 1922–7.) In this piece Wells expressed one of his fundamental tenets, that individuality within the group is illusory.

62. To A. T. Simmons

Illinois, ALS

Pay rental (rarely) Acres
Nye Woods
Rogate Hants   [end November 1887]

Dear Simmons,

I think I have unnecessarily alarmed you and myself. Dr. at Wrexham struck it a lot too gloomy. William Job Collins MD. MS B Sc etc tells me there is no consumption not a bit. Only acute bronchitis & congestion of the lungs & that if I stick in one room at a constant temperature I shall be as right as a trivet - which is the rightest thing on earth - before Christmas which has removed much anxiety on my part.

I came here Saturday. The journey took it out of me to an extent that surprised me. I didn't know I had so much in me.

Left Holt at 9:15 got home 8.10.

Pecker (thank goodness) well up. I rejoice over your classes. May perhaps see you Xmas?

Job in front of me now - to tell Cousin I have shifted & explain 'why' without alarming her.[1] Think I shall represent myself as ignominiously discharged.
Yours to an unlimited extent
Wells D G

'This is it.
It is rather slow but the Universe is getting thought out thoroughly.
The instrument round my neck is not a cravat. It is a thermometer to ensure a constant temperature.

---

[1] A reference to Isabel Wells with whom he was emotionally attached, and whom he would marry and divorce later.

63. To A. T. Simmons

Illinois, AL[1]

Ni. W^d.
Rogt.[2]   Sa'd^y [Autumn 1887]

Dr. S'ms.
      Hot wr makes me idl. Hard^{ly} energ^y to rite this 2 u. There r 2 wāz of com^g from Portsmth to R'g't.

Via Chicester & via Petersfld. Latter is prefbl.

Do this. Come up by 10.6 tr^n from Portsmth Town to Petersfld, where you must wate 35 min for tr^n to Rogate (11.20) No oth^r wa. Trains all rite in eve^n.

4 Gd's sake dont w^r a blk ct!

Wl mēt u at the st^n R'gte or mā b at P'fld.
        Thursd^y if fine
                if not sum oth^r dā.

[The remainder of this letter is a detailed sketch map showing all the areas where Wells was a familiar person.]

---

[1] This letter is in an envelope which, in the normal location for a stamp, has a sketch of a young woman with the words, 'This envelope not used owing to persuasions of the cousin to whom I trust you will be properly thankful'. It also has two sketches: one of a man in silhouette with a dog and a cat with the words, *'Immediate!'*. The other is a small sketch of a man, with the legend, 'This is *Him*'.

[2] This brief letter is partially written in a heavily abbreviated style. Wells is giving instructions for travelling to Up Park, and Nyewood, where he was staying briefly with his father and brother. The cousin, in fact, a first cousin, is Isabel Wells, with whom he was falling in love. Eventually they would marry.

64. To A. M. Davies

Illinois, ALS

Up Park
Peterfield
Hants.   Saturday, Dec. 3rd [1887]

Dear Davies,

If you expect this to be a rational letter you will be disappointed. I have been writling with pain all day - taking up books & chucking them about - rushing about trying to curse myself calm - doing brandies hot, capers [?], and unimaginable things. The idea of painting the human thorax with iodine[1] is jesuitical devilment - in order to stop a chap congesting you dip him into hell & so disincline him to die. Iodine is a deadly serpent to take to one's breast - so you mind. The first few days I painted myself, nothing happened. I was merely a pretty brown above the belt. Then the dose was increased, under a mistaken idea that I had been too moderate. Nothing happened, only the brown deepened. Then I got lavish. Now, — I have two square feet of burning itching irritation & half a dozen sore places maddening me as only sore places can. Yah! It reminds me of that jesuit head centre (Roffin?) in the Wandering Jew. Damn! Damn! Damn! <u>A few bars of the Marseilles</u>, Davies, there's not a soul here who has things to pitch about - not a solitary person to insult in the whole place. I musn't go out of this warm room, and I am in a sea of torment to which toothache is a babbling murmuring sunflecked troutsome rivulet. Oh if had Judd here! I mustn't even shout here, because certain people have feelings and weep if I do. Damn! Damn! Damn! Damn! Damn! Damn! God damn! God Damn! God!

After all though the iodine does me a world of good. My cough is better and a feeling of continally increased oppression has passed away. Still there are temporary feelings that must find vent.

I like the picture. Is it A.C.J. fretting about the futility of mountains? That is a new thing of mine. I am going to expose mountains when I get better. I cannot imagine how they have not been detected before. They are futile to the uttermost! Perhaps Jones has found it out. I charge mountains with being puerile, insidious, inappropriate, and inexpedient. Damn this iodine! You are right to say there is nothing new in Biology. Men like the current biologist never will get to anything new simply because they haven't yet come to understand the notions of the masters. What Bacon Newton and Darwin started building Woodwards will never complete. They will merely build their cottages and cultivate gardens on the top of the tower they ought - but can't - to lift upwards to heaven. Science is a tower of Babel to lift men up to heaven, up & out of the back of the God, i.e., the cruelty of nature. You can bring some old Ninevahs pottering round the abandoned building - with a microscope - and a finite ambition for the F.R.S. That's your current scientist. Yah! Curse Blast Damn!, This Iodine! I will write to Jones if you will let me have his address. What happens when Ridewood has found toe no. 6? Remember me to Richards and felicitate. Briscoe will smash the journal to a dead certainty. Why in god's name didn't you cook the meeting? I always did. May God leave iodine out when he makes another world! Damn! Damn its I'es. Hume, remember me to. Say I have been much altered by illness & have entirely given up swearing. Tell Wager, Richards, Reynolds, Hume, Clarkson & others (as per previous invoice) that I am too weak to write to them, or I would, but that I would so like to hear from them. The letter bag is my only excitement etc, etc. Tell Porter that if he has a photograph of himself I should especially treasure it. I wish you were capable of forgetting Smith's scandalous story about your Cantor Lectures. I had done it ages ago. Damn! everlastingly, irrevocably, Damn this iodine!

About yourself. You seem to be in a bad way, old chap. I guess from your letter you are debilitated, dyspepsiaized, or somehow collapsed as to the nervous system. Now let me warn you that this here sort of thing mustn't be let run. I was as sound as a Salvation Army drum, in the lungs before my smash but after that came weakness; and what at other times would have been a cough has just about done for me. You go off to a decent doctor at once, if my guess is right, and he will give you a prescription for a tonic, put you up to the right thing in exercise, and sound your chest, for a trifle. Be Warned in Time as Beecham of the pills hath it. If you don't go to the doctor you may go to the devil. I have been terribly lonesome myself before now, Davies, and I know just what you must feel in your solitary digs. If it will lighten in the faintest your load of lonesomeness to hear that I am not indifferent by any means to your welfare, let it be lightened. I know there are few chummable people for you at S[outh]. K[ensington]. The fellows feel personally injured by you, as a rule, because you have two, three, or more year's start of them. Damn! Ultra damn this Iodine! You are a smarting sore to the P.S. Have you tried chumming Jennings? He has a high opinion of you. He is a reserved beast though. He is either an oyster that is entirely shell or else he has a precious thick one. You can't get at him or at least I never could. I gave it up - the most disappointed whelk in creation - after two years. Still, you may find him cultivable. I recommend him to you as a most agreeable & improving companion and an impossible bosom friend. God blind - God cast into the bottomless slime, the devil who invented Tinct. Iod. May his eye's be everlastingly burnt therewith. It is awfully kind of you to offer me those books of yours, in return let me place my maimed self at your disposal. The books though, I don't think I shall need. Old Burton, most excellent of Christians, best of friends, & most visionary of Politicians, has sent me hosts thereof in large hampers. I believe all his store. Perhaps I shall be living at Burton's after Christmas, in which case your books may come in handy- when his are exhausted, so I shan't forget your offer.

I am sorry to hear about the London Library. Lewis's in Gower Street might perhaps be better to you than nothing - £1.1.0 pr. annum - Medical scientific only. Is there no public library in your parts? If you were artful you might shift Digs into a parish where is [*a long sentence completely blacked out*].

        Meanwhile
           Ever yours,
             H.G. Wells [*blacked out word*]

---

[1] This method of curing sore throat, bronchitis and similar maladies remained in use until the 1930s (as the editor can attest). Iodine has the property of intensifying its strength as the oxygen breaks down in the tincture which is prescribed.

65. To A. T. Simmons

Illinois, AL

The House of Captivity
Valley of the Shadows of Death [early December 1887][1]

Dear Simmons

Most Potent Grave and Reverend Signor

I have news for you of a piebald character. I am not worse than I was, but aware that I am much worse than that Earthly Evans at Wrexham told me. Collins, William Job of that ilk, MD, BSc, master of chiurgery, Senator etc. of the London University - Esq., brought down an array of instruments & went over my organism with me.[2] He thinks my kidney has a lovely effusion round it & promises something interesting in the tumour way, in about a years time. He holds out hopes of dyspepsia (chronic). He congratulates me on a thoroughly, disorganized right-lung and suggests darkly that if I want to stop all the bother I have only got to sit between a fire and an open window for a couple of hours & congestion of the lungs will manage it. He has borrowed a phial of piddle - my piddle - and taken it up to London. He explains that he has hopes of diabetes or even gravel for me. He would not insure my life unless he was me, myself for anything. He is sure I shall always be a chronic invalid. He wishes there were more like me. He wishes everyone played football. He wishes Good Morn. So much for Doctor Collins, William Job of that ilk, MD, BSc, MS SLU and his array of instruments.

I am to stay severely indoors for a year. I almost had the hole at your Gomorrah[3] but he says, to think of such a situation is contemplating suicide. I am to do nothing but sit around & [keep] warm. I must eat [*words missing due to deterioration of the paper*] [...] I die. [*a bit more of the letter is frayed and unreadable*] [...] non realistic fiction, & then I suppose I shall know by that time what has come to Lady Frankland's Companion [4] & be able to plan less discursively for the future.

I like the way you talk about yourself. So you never have fits of that unwholesome despondency now? I feel anxious about that because I know you as the best tempered & worst spirited chappie I ever encountered. 'Howsomever' that talk about marrying sounds unusually optimistic. Don't be rash. There is a girl being educated up to your level somewhere - wait. The following brief directions in choosing a wife may not be out of place here - (I am experienced. You can trust me.)

She may be religious but she must not be <u>too</u> religious - she must be <u>indifferent</u> - the slightest flaw here disqualifies - to all ceremonial whether religious or social. She must <u>unmistakeably</u> & greatly prefer you to anyone else in the world - especially must you make sure that she will prefer [you] to her children. She must be in perfect health & at least good looking. <u>She must be truthful</u> and She must understand cooking & household economy, baby linen, millinery and dressmaking. She must be jealous of your honour and have an education adequate to your position.

All these things infinitely important than pretty faces, charming ways, dainty dresses, talent, genius, or accomplishments - in a wife.

[*words frayed away*] Euston Road at Christmas.

[*at top of second sheet*]:

Letter from Wells to Simmongs!
Illness of Wells!
Thrilling Details!
A Pint of Piddle sent to London!
Examination by Council of Doctors!
Policy of Wells!
Novel finished!
Great Fire!
Wells on Wimmin!
Reported Return of the Piddle!

---

[1] Another hand has assigned a date of mid-November, but I do not think that is correct.

[2] A grateful Wells wrote a letter of endorsement for Collins's effort to be elected to the parliamentary seat of the University of London, see *University Correspondent* and a leaflet with the letter used as an electioneering device, 'Dr. Collins on the Educational Situation'.

[3] Wells was apparently contemplating a teaching position in the same location as Simmons.

[4] Another of the fictional pieces which Wells was attempting to sell to the *Family Herald*. Nothing more is known of it, although it may have been burned by Wells later.

66. To A. T. Simmons

Illinois, ALS

Up Park
Peterfield   Decr 13th 87

Dear Simmonds,

    I feel rather disappointed to hear that you are not coming until after Xmas but still I may perhaps have more to talk about then than now, so it is not altogether unmitigated sorrow. I hope you will have a gorgeous time of it with those brothers of yours. All our people will be here during the festive three days, to the envy of all the other servants & heart burning universal. I had a bad time about a week ago spitting gore-laden tissue secretly onto the fire to save my excellent mother from panic, collapse and privately preparing my mind for dissolution. But I am all right again now, comparatively, and working a bit at the writing. There is a grand plan on foot for a new great undertaking but I haven't the buoyant self confidence to finance such speculations now, so probably it will be like the seed sown on stony ground growing up & presently withering away.

You will let me know when you mean to come, because bloated aristocrats have to be studied, and sometimes the place is 'flushed' with valets & maids & such to a suffocating extreme.

Believe me Simmings
Yours ever
The Wells

67. To A. M. Davies

Illinois, ALS

Up Park
Petersfield   December 15th, 87

Dear Davies,

    I am glad that my letter gave you any satisfaction, & to hear that you are free from the inclusion of that vital rending Devil yclept dyspepsia. I had him in me while I was recovering from my internal smashup at football, but blessed be God, he was cast out by acrid fluids that even <u>he</u> couldn't endure. Cod liver oil is gorgeous stuff - too gorgeous sometimes making the gorge rise (latent capabilities of a pun here) unpleasantly. Iodine is doing me worlds of good & I am getting to regard a bleeding skin as a normal condition of my existence. Don't suicide rashly. It is curious to hear you doing the old fashioned speculation about the 'something we wot not of' after death. Are you really a spiritualist? I have just come on some fine reading that may please you in your present phase. Heine Prose Works (Selection) Camelot Classics. I think it will about delight you.

I will write to Jones when anything comes into my head to say to him, meanwhile please send in your next, brief message from me, "Hello, Jones", and enclose a slap on the back. Burton is at Newcastle Staffoodsheer. I blaguard him periodically about Ruskin but he clings to that blatant old mystic like a babe to his mother's teats. Stand old Fisher a bitter on my account if you see him, and ask him what he thinks of Home Rule, slap him on the back too if you get around that way & test him whether he smells of ale like he used, round the <u>other</u> way.

Hand my affectionate regards round to anyone you think needy & deserving thereof, & believe
Ever
Yours in the Lord.
Wells

N.B. On mature consideration, it occurs to me that the best way of getting you to read Heine will be to lend you the book which please expect in a subsequent post.

68. To A. M. Davies

Illinois, ALS

Up Park
Peterfield
Hants   Decr. 31st. 87

Dear Davies,

I am exceedingly glad to hear of your vigorous Atheism. It behoves us who deny, to make it as clear to the world as we can for the good of ourselves

& the world, that we think in this way. I am toiling now to attain the day when it will be possible for me to shake off the last vestiges of conventions; and I still hope to see it before I die.

I am very sorry to hear of your gloomy forebodings for next June; the more so that I am afraid there is justice in them. Jennings ought to be of use to you in the consideration of this matter. I know nothing about the things into which you want to get, only let me solemnly warn you not to try to teach [word obliterated] or in fact enter upon any employment that will lead to your forgetting the work you have done. Which piece of advice is almost as valuable as the old gentleman's "Never die before seventy - it shortens your years." Trust in the non diabolic theory of things, and don't bother about June till June comes.

Item - you might die before June & all the bother be wasted. Item - something might turn up. Why don't you have a shot at those scholarships that Hewitt bagged off? Jennings Hill (somewhere in Liverpool) and the various calendars will put you up to good things on that line.

For myself I am on the whole better. I danced three contra dances and waltzed a waltz on Monday; also did (not sang) a duet with my brother Frank, and was put to bed at half past four by the rest of our family; from which you may judge about my health. I am off to Burton about the middle of next month & shall stop a day or two in London on the way, with some relatives out Primrose Hill way. If the weather is sunny, I may look in at the old shop.

With best wishes for the New Year,
    Believe me
        Yours very faithfully
            H.G. Wells

69. To A. M. Davies

Illinois, ALS

[Up Park]   [early 1888?]

Dear Davies,

    Never Scoph at God. He is very ready to take offence, and even if you are not incontinently thunderbolted, he worms into you in a painful & incessant way that renders scophing a very unprophitable action. He has recently put in some consignments of hypochondria, as a reply to the jocular inquiry I have recently inserted in the Lord's Prayer as to whether he has no other judgement on hand, except purely fleshly afflictions. This renders me prone to neglect human intercourse in all its branches, & is my apology for arrears of correspondence - which fact please hand round. Chuck Ridewood's things about a little - from me. I have sworn a blood feud against Briscoe[1] for rejecting again M.S.S. of mine of an invigorating description. There is a novel in the Illustrated that ought to charm you by Black. Nothing turns up for me, and the workhouse & X roads grave yawn before me. I would sell myself soul & body for comfortable stabling & fodder and say - 5/- a week - but in my way, as in Balaam's is a God who is anxious not to be cursed - So asses tell me. The Lord bless you & keep you.

                    And believe me
                        Yours truly
                          H.G. W.

N.B. Don't scoph.

---

[1] Probably another student friend

70. To Elizabeth Healey[1]

Texas, ALS

Up Park
Petersfield, Hants   Feb. 20th, 1888

Dear Miss Healey

      Many thanks for your letter. It really came very opportunely and the flattery about anyone missing me from the debating club was distinctly beneficial. I have been experiencing lately what everybody has to experience who drops out of the marching column like I have done. There is a restiveness apparent even in those who still stay with me. "Why don't he die, or get well, or do something?" and the circle thins slowly but surely. Oh, altering the view of the case I have been shedding my friends ever since my failures distinctly set in. Some I got rid of because they were no use to a feeble person, sycophantic profit & loss sort of people, & some whom I did not want to loose, have taken the initiative, probably in a similar idea. Recently I have had a severe loss near home & here had to follow a very favourite delusion to the grave. Hence, energy & suicidall disregard of precautions, very acute and the great applicability of your letter as a tonic.

I am not going to leave England in the vulgar sense - about all you enquire - simply because I haven't the means to do it, but I expect to leave later on for a pleasant land where the warm is immortal & fuel at a discount, and I presume the higher development of matter proportionately exalted. I may drag a maimed existence in this accursed land of winds, wet ways, & old women, for three or four years or so. My mother is an old lady of over sixty, very garrulous about a sister of mine who died in 1864 [2] & certain great family events that mentally dwarfed her & her brother sisters cousins of the third & fourth degree, in 1825-30, but still she is sufficiently amiable, cognizant of current events, to render me anxious to survive her. That is my apology for not suiciding. I hope you will not consider it too unsatisfactory, & write & desire me to shed my blood as you used to do at S. K. words to be consistent.

By the bye - now I think of it - if you have any chance to have any friends in St Pancras who have votes in this free library business, and you come across them, just make them vote up and take all their friends to vote up too for the concern - I have a purely platonic affection for the parish of S. Pancras and if St. Pancras parish has a free library, I shall die happy.

Do you phonograph? I can phonograph, having acquired the art & a high rate of speed since I last wrote. I mention the matter because I think that perhaps it might enable you to treat me to a longer letter if you knew the art of the great Izak Pitman.[3]

What did Porter say? You speak of him with some severity. Did he revile his own sitters? Porter is a regular Scotchman for a joke. He builds it up brick by brick, & carefully expounds it, analyses it too, & suggests improvements. His archness even like the archness of a brick bridge is carefully gone over. Porter joking is like an elephant at the schottische.[4] Porter tries to tickle people with a beaver's weam - I mean a breavers beam.[5] Do tell me what he sed? Porter is always heavy, & with more body than spirit. Porter is a gorilla with a sapling, a lunatic with an overloaded gun, a rogue elephant, a blinded Polyphemus, an unbelievers dinner table (there is no grace about him) a great auk, a stork, a factory, & a dead wall. All that, & more is Porter.[6]

Come to Tea!

The needs of my nature & the flight of time demand that I should cease here.

Farewell

Write soon

& believe me yours very truly

H.G. Wells

[*A huddled figure is at the bottom of the page, captioned 'The Spirit of Consumption, After Blake'. Next to this cartoon is a man sitting before a fire, holding a book, and with very long spiky hair captioned 'No barber within ten (10) Miles' and 'This is me keeping off the spirit by means of phyres'.*]

---

[1] Elizabeth Healey, daughter of a professor at the Royal College, became close friends with Wells while they were students. The friendship continued until Wells's death. She played the roles of elder sister and confidante until he was well established in life. Later she becomes a recipient of many tokens of his friendship. She married a professor of mathematics at Bristol.
[2] This sister, Frances, died before Wells was born.
[3] Pitman was the classic method of taking shorthand of this period. Wells did not write any letters that I have seen in shorthand, but he might have used it to take notes at lectures. At this time the word phonograph had, as its primary meaning, 'to convert words into sounds', and specifically referred to the shorthand method taught by Pitman. Several of Wells's later works were published in shorthand versions and he wrote a squib or two for these methods of rapid writing later in his life.
[4] A form of dancing related to square and contra dances. It was widely practised in Scotland, along with reels.
[5] Wells's pun conceals his use of 'the weaver's beam', that is, the wooden roller or cylinder in the loom on which the warp is wound before weaving.
[6] Whom the unfortunate Porter might have been is not known.

71. To A. M. Davies

Illinois, ALS

Up Park
Petersfield, Hants   Feb. 22nd, '88

[*at top of page one, upside down 'Kick Ridewood in the shins for me.'*]

Dear Davies,

Your report to hand. Highly beneficial as I have been at the nadir point of dullness these two days. Was getting well & almost athletic last week - Walked 7 miles last Saturday. On Tuesday went out, got thawing snow in my boots. Today lungs positively <u>rustle</u> when I breathe. Air gurgles as it enters trachea. Cough up Swiss tinned milk in quantity. Expect to congest in a day or two. In which case, - farewell.

Congratulations on the gym. - Go on & get huge. - but keep away from sudden chills & wrap something over your mouth when fogs are on.

Bessemer[?] being a young fool naturally goes in for fair trade. He will do more harm to the cause he advocates than any Free Trader in the schools can. Wager on Shelley is like Clarkson expounding God Almighty. It is curious what queer beggars get drawn in by Shelley. E.H. Smith, Wm Burton, at one period. The Individualist Wager. Your honoured & esteemed self. There is probably <u>something</u> good about the beast. Don't tell Wager what I said about him but ask him to lend me his paper. - I won't hurt it only I always had a morbid taste for psychology. In order to beguile him to the loan I authorise you to state that I say anything you consider will flatter the said Wager. The Art Studentization of the D.S. was always a fad of Jennings's. It will make it effeminate & conservative or else blaguardize it.

I am very sorry about the age limitation to the Scholarship.

Thanks for the offer of Emerson's Essays. I have got Representative Men & English Traits and I don't like them. There is a lot of wilful insult in Emerson punning use of words, use of words with old etymological senses & far fetched figurative ones. He is hard to follow. At the same time I confess that [he] is richer by far than Heine for instance. - The meaning of almost all his sentences profound Only some of them I fancy will never be patent to me unless I run against Emerson after the Last Day. Somtimes I fancy his things are platitudes in barbaric ornament. - Country curates in turbans & sashes - Salvationists in this Ceylon outfit.

Thanks for the offer of books etc. I am tapping the curate here now & I am well set up. He gorges fiction. Any fugitive political leaflets -etc- forwarded might be acceptable & amusing.

        Believe me Davies
        Yours under Heaven
                H.G. Wells

72. To Elizabeth Healey

Texas, AL

<u>Uppark</u>
Petersfield, Hants.   Feb. 23, 88

Dear Miss Healey,

    I can never be sufficiently grateful for that letter. It was tremendous. The intimation that these epistolary seizures of yours are active and separated by periods of vague but considerable length was the only depressing thing about it. I am going to deal with topics seriatim.

About myself - I shall never join the Marching Column again. My youth went long ago - my life work will be to give as little trouble as possible in an uncongenial universe while I stay therein and not to leave too big a hole in anybody else's world when my creation terminates. -

I don't understand what you mean by contrasting "consistency" and truth on the authority of that dark and devious person, O.W. Holmes.[1] "Don't be consistent but be simply true." Such a sentence implies that truth is occasionally inconsistent, illogical, & self-contradictory; it subverts reason to partial impressions; & tends to urge us towards that altar where intellect & duty are sacrificed to emotion.

West Hampstead is not in St. Pancras. West Hampstead is N.W., new, respectable, conservative, articulate, detached or semi-detached, unsympathetic, and commercial. I hate West Hampstead and in fact the entire Hampstead genus, also S. Johns Wood, Regents Park and the whole of North London villadom - St. Pancras is old, dirty, immoral, drunken, radical Socialist, anarchist, inarticulate, crowded, sympathetic, starving, cheating, lurid, smoky and lovable; and yet there is a majesty also about St. Pancras that W. Hampstead has not - S. Pancras sins are deadly sins, its troubles are vital troubles; it hungers, and thirsts and longs. Hampstead's sins are social peccadillos, its troubles deal with matters such as making £150 look like £400, it dresses and performs and is satisfied.

I think perhaps I am wandering into the obscure regions of my private thoughts. Excuse me - your attempt to put West Hampstead into St. Pancras was very aggravating to me; don't do it again. I would rather you sent me drawings of Saints in Silk Hats.

On Porter I would have given - half a lung, say - to have heard Porter's idyll. I always thought Porter looked tallowy, but I never thought he was wicked, & had had the immortal flame lit. I should like to see the "companion of the fair sex" that beguiled him. I should guess she was a flirt & did it from habit.

On love and friendship. Your remarks about the comparative impunity of Porter amid susceptible beauty awaken reminisences.

In the course of an erratic career, I have been in the confidence of a very ill-looking curate. Some of his experiences were very touching.

[remainder of letter missing]

---

[1] An American poet and essayist best known for his *Autocrat at the Breakfast Table*, a collection of essays

73. To Elizabeth Healey

Texas, AL

Uppark
Petersfield, Hants Feb 28. 88

Dear Miss Healey,

I had no intention of dealing in sarcasm, no desire that my words should distraught [?], and deeply am I grieved if I have squashed you. When I avalanched, it was to squash a false notion of Providence and annihilate a mistaken geographical conception; but I fear I am like the elephant in my unpublished Fable.

<u>The Elephant and the Maiden</u> - said the Gangetic Maiden to the Elephant: "Lo I have been drinking the sacred water, and behold, a just-hatched crocodile hath entered into my mouth and hath been swallowed." Answered the Elephant: "Dear me! That's bad for your System. Permit me - I will squash it," and he did - and got no thanks -

Moral, Optional.

That phonographic inscription for anything that I can remember to the contrary may contain the clew of the Universe. I have forgotten what it was about & I am <u>utterly</u> unable to decipher my own phonography after four or five days have passed. I have an idea though that it reflected personally on a mutual friend so don't get any experts to it on any account whatever. I had rather explain what the eternal means by marking old mile stones with rain marks than explain what I meant, after aforesaid intervals of 4 or 5 days, by any shorthand I may have marked on paper.

Don't bother your mind about that letter of yours. It was delightful. I liked the length of it. - if it had been twice as long I should have liked it 4 times as much. - "directly to the square of the length." Moreover, two things were given for me to pitch stones at. Sometimes I fancy that that is the thing that gives me my profoundest pleasure. - To chuck things at things and break them. - I dreamt that I got to Heaven some time since & that I was made everlastingly happy by being allowed through a nightless infinity to smash the crystal sea to bits with lumps of jasper, sardonx, chalcedony & sapphire. This is my idiosycracy - This is my idiosnykracy - curious how some people spell! - my ruling passion - destruction. The ruling passion will be strong in death. I feel sure. Something of this sort: -

<u>Death Bed of the Infidel</u>
Chorus of Sorrowing Relatives

He has broken our hearts!
The Clergyman.
And his confirmation vows!
The Doctor
His breathing breaks. He departs!
To the land whereof there are no charts
& the law no leaving allows

[*a small portion of poem not present - torn paper*]

...eyes
... then this journey! Brandy neat!
[brought] a man back from the Judgement Seat.

The invalid, evidently with an effort, takes the offered brandy and without drinking drops the glass on the floor. It breaks musically. The invalid smiles & expires.

Clergman - the golden cord will hold no more.
The body is here and the soul is hence.
Chorus of relatives - (kneeling on the floor & searching eagerly).
Just as well with the glass on the floor.
It was one of our best & cost eighteen pence.

I have been going to Wm Burtons[1] ever since January, but the weather & one thing and another has stood between and turned [me] back even as Balaam was turned by the angel of the Lord. My doctor is the "person" who always sees the impediment. Do you follow? My room down there has been yawning all this time, & will, I fancy, until about the second week in March. If I can, I shall stop with some friends near Primrose Hill for a day or two on the way, & if it is possible, drop down to S. Kensington for an hour about lunch time if the sun shines.

I am glad you find my letters interesting. They bore most people insensibly[?]. I got this from my brother once.

Dear Herbert.

Your ltr to hand. From the gen'l tone I conclude you are happy, in an earthly sense, but there is no lack of happiness outside the fold of X- crucified. Do not mention Providence to me again in your let'rs please. I have marked certn passages in yr ltr with red ink & return it herewith. They are illegible. If of any import, please make a fair copy & they shd be attended to duly. Opportunity has two p's.

Yr. loving bro.
(In Christ)
Frederick Joseph Wells

I fancy F.J.W. would be a very hard enigma in a person even for you to tackle.

Here is another unappreciative letter from my eldest brother.

Dear old Man,
Write and tell us what that last letter means. G.V. well. and almost shot me yesterday. Curious old bird he is. - won't take out a license for his gun, is the latest new notion - Individual liberty! Tracts from Fred as usual. Love to Ma. Yours, Frank.

G.V. is his way of alluding to my noble sire. "Ma" is my respected mother. Another enigma.

[*remainder, if any, of letter missing*]

---

[1] William Burton, a former classmate of Wells, had obtained a position in Stoke-on-Trent. Wells spent some time at Burton's home later this spring in convalescence. The weather had been cold and wet and so he had delayed his trip.

74. To Elizabeth Healey

Texas, ALS

Uppark
Petersfield   March 2nd, 1888

Dear Miss Healey,

Many thanks for the latest instalment of cock-shies.[1] I detect your artifice. You put up nothing else about other people. You reserve your own ideas - except about Burton, the levèe, the doctor's second sight, & the wicked discontent you have with winter & the East Wind, all of them things giving no pleasurable smash when broken. To account for you & Burton not agreeing is difficult. To do so I must call attention to a Virtue of mine. This Virtue is Catholicity of Appreciation. All the first order of Poets - have it or had it (some of them are dead).

Here I make a digression. You sneer at my "death bed". You say my lines are lacking in metre. Miss Healey, metres are used for Gas, not for the outpourings of the human heart -. Again, you say my poem has no feet! Miss

Healey, (don't you feel the Vocative thrills?) The humming bird has no feet, the Cherubim around the Mater Dol^{sa} have no feet. The Ancients figured the Poetic Afflatus as a horse <u>winged</u> to signify the Poet was sparing of his feet!! But what <u>has</u> this to do with you and Burton - Nothing. You both - I am sorry for you but it is true - lack Catholicity of Appreciation. Burton hates Louis XV furniture, pure art, all sorts of womankind who are not distinctly indicated as good in the works of Charles Dickens, life without a leading idea, Conservatives, sin, as defined in the O.T., &, for some inscrutable reason, Tutton. (N.B., all this is confidential.) I hope you will not be offended by being classed with the "all sorts of womankind not", etc. Charles Dickens seems to have known only three women. Mrs Dickens, charming, but bordering on the idiotic, another young woman with force of character, whom he met with after his marriage, who is always feeling a lot & saying nothing as <u>Podsnap</u>, that Buddhistic Hindoo, used to say a cabbage did; and an old woman with "ways". That was his material. They keep on coming up like "tags" in a pantomime. So much for W.B. being unappreciative. You do not like people who are "earnest", you appreciate the abstract beautiful, & such things as LXV furniture adumbrates, you approve of, you dislike Radical persons (you are not aware of this but it is so). The O.T. is not your textbook of sociology and you have for some unscrutinable reason an aversion to Burtons Jonan pressure. - I, like a frog being amphibious in matters of opinion am appreciated by beings who are incapable of intercourse (v. my unpublished fable - the Frog, The Pike and the Stork).

I will speak to you unreservedly of Wager. For a young man to marry, who admires Shelley, indicates mental weakness; for a young man to marry who is not rich indicates considerable mental decay; & for a young man to marry Miss Watson is - to be mild with it - eccentric. I will confide my reasons. I am quiet but observant. I have watched her, carefully - for the sake of Simmonds - and I am convinced that <u>she is not human.</u> She is jointed all right but she is <u>perfectly inflexible</u> save at her joints and I feel assured that she is <u>constructed of some metallic substance probably aluminium</u> [two words blacked out] with the exception perhaps of her head. I can understand Wager loving her - he is one of those fragile beautiful poets with an ideal like a pitch plaster that fits anybody, but I cannot imagine his daring to suggest such a thing to her - she is so like a female policeman. Perhaps he was drunk when he came up to the scratch - [words blacked out] I cannot conceive of - I hope you won't object to the remark - Miss Watson being kissed. I am perfectly unable to imagine her doing anything but severely box the ears of anybody who attempted the faintest demonstrations of affection. I expect next to hear that Miss Pace has gone under the yoke. Do you remember them violets? I have long yearned to know who that Poor Chap was? Poor, poor, Chap! If Pallas[2] marries at all, she will marry her private secretary, just as old gentlemen sometimes marry their cooks to economize wages.

Porter has a huge cheek if that is what he means by the canon of beauty. 'Canon of beauty' is a medieval superstition but Porter loveth the ancients.

When I go to Burton's probably early in April I shall stop in London somewhere. Either with my relatives or at a den where the Landseer of this half century dwelleth in picturesque poverty near the areopagus of 'Midland Arches' where the Revolution of '89 is to begin.[3] It is a struggle between duty & pleasure. The advent will occur towards the end of the week. On Friday it will happen - I don't know which Friday I am sure. On that the day the downs will fade forever from my eyes - anything but tearful. Then I shall visit the brigand like establishment of my father & my eldest brother in a pine wood towards the wilds of Hindhead. Smoky whiskey will drown the sorrows of our parting, our eternal parting - because I don't think those two chaps will get let into heaven -, a rabbit will be sacrified to Hermes, a sacred pipe will be smoked, guns will be let off & perhaps a neighbour shot, and then I shall leave that hoary Pagan, old Silenus[4], my Father, and that changeling my brother to settle with the relatives of the Victim. Next I shall proceed to my billet in London. The sun will then set. On Saturday I shall come to South Kensington. The following will be probably advised of my approach, Davies, Bower, yourself. You will have mentioned the possibility of my being there to Jennings, who will exercise his own discretion about clearing out or staying. I shall be in the Bio. lab about Eleven. I shall then go to the Feeding Place about one. Go and smoke till 2. Do pictures if there are any new ones. The walk through the gardens to Praed St. - and that is the last chance anyone of the old set will ever get of setting eyes on me again till the day of judgement - because I am in consumption & shall surely die soon. The saddest parting of all will be with grimy old London - in which I had dreamt, until a few days ago, of working some schemes before I died.[5] I shall try & die in time for the June Journal - but this is getting melancholy -
    Please excuse my paper. Supply is low. & believe me
        Yours very sincerely,
          H.G. Wells

---

[1] Free throws at an object that cannot retaliate; derives from a game of chance. Wells is being ironic throughout this letter.
[2] A reference to Pallas Athena, an imperious goddess
[3] Wells is probably referring to Fitzroy Road, where many student friends lived. The Areopagus

was the name of the hill in ancient Athens where the oldest council of state sat and political debate took place. The Landseer comparison is probably to Cosmo Rowe, who acted as sort of super landlord in this student area. Edwin Henry Landseer (1802–73) was a noted artist who specialized in animal portraiture. Perhaps his best know work is 'Monarch of the Glen'and the bronze lions at the foot of Nelson's monument in Trafalgar Square. Wells's letters to Rowe are 89, 92, 93, 404 and one in volume 2.

[4] Silenus was a figure in Greek mythology, a demi-god, the son of Pan, who fostered and educated Dionysius. He was usually portrayed as drunk. Wells frequently referred to his father as Silenus because he was often in his cups.

[5] Wells is giving a mock serious description of what may be his last visit to his student haunts. There is an element of ironic self pity as he is well aware that his life expectancy may be cut short.

75. To Elizabeth Healey

Texas, ALS

Uppark
Petersfield [5? March 1888]

Dear Miss Healey,

<u>On the slating</u>? I apologize for calling your letter a collection of cockshies. It <u>was</u> not polite, & it reflected on persons discussed. I apologize for calling you "sin as defined in the Old Testament." I did not mean to. It was done in a linguistic convulsion when I was striving to say that a difference in ethical bases must involve an inevitable conflict of opinions. Why this hate of Burton? <u>Has</u> Burton ever set up as an "example of the Cardinal Virtues"? Have you anything against him? If you only knew Burton as I do you would understand that the only [*words missing*] I apologize for my venomous abuse of Miss Watson. My highest pleasure is vitriol throwing - now almost my only pleasure.

Do not get low spirited about your letter. The picture you draw of yourself in a sort of cavern of copybooks & rested[?] only by classes seeking oracles is very sad. I feel intensely flattered by the suggestion of being the ray that creeps in where there is no window - the unconventional ray. There is one objection that quite alters the picture, though, - In our correspondence you start all the topics. Permit me to suggest instead a cavern in the chalk (with flints) & the

Dying Saint Supernaturally attended & comforted.[1] My views about my heart are not a bit overdrawn. I am going down the hill like a toboggan. I did not say <u>near</u> Hindhead was the parental mud hut but <u>towards</u>. You perceive a distinction? I do not live with these two, because only by systematic poaching, garden stye[?], & hen roost raiding can they get food to themselves, and the house has only three rooms & there is a hole in the roof of one of them & one of the others is not boarded, and (N.B. I am inspired here) old Silenus, that once powerful and promising youth (only he married early & poor) My father, is usually cleaning his gun with paraffine, smoking tobacco that reeks of the everlasting bottomless pit, or sleeping loose on the victual strewn floor, while that misbegotten boy, my brother studies clocks & musical boxes at a bench near the window with a view to constructing a patent machine to kill rats and suchlike pests by a method combining the maximum of row & expense with the minimum of effect.

[*a sketch of the house labelled Nye Woods*]

I am glad to hear of Mr Cole's Coffee tavern. He is an excellent man, but too Christian to like me.

[*a line or words missing*]

The educated couple who start in that style ends in later generations in a progeny of ill fed, half educating weaklings. It is <u>not</u> selfish to marry for money or position. There are facts, and sentiment that talks against facts <u>must</u> go down. Thank heaven my ideal is unattainable, & I have a weak lung to keep me in the narrow way. Sentiment before there is comfort [is] provided the marrying persons. In many cases of course the husband <u>flukes</u> a position & it is all right, but in most, it means a miserable struggle to ward off inevitable collapse, a life of ha'penny economies, small pretenses, humiliations that fret all the admirable qualities on those of the husband, & weigh the wife double with the burthen of the work. I know all about these marriages because I am the victim of one.

[*Four lines heavily blacked out - it is just possible to see that they deal with his father and his drinking problem.*][2]

I must warn you that my app^{ce} as considerably changed since I was at that noble building in Exhibition Rd. Look for this.

[*A rather full figure swathed in clothes, hair etc. appears. Two marks, 'A' appear on the drawing, and the legend reads, 'a,a, is <u>not</u> corpus, but cotton wool, sundry shawls'.*]

I should like to hear all about the Art Schools Conversazione & anything else that you may have the patience to write to a rapidly decaying fellow creature. My cousin may be there.

>Believe me to remain
>Yours very sincerely
>H.G. Wells

P.S. If you happen to find yourself in the tremendous presence of Buchanan, will you remember me & ask him to send me a March Journal.

---

[1] Although this is an obscure passage, he is apparently urging Healey to establish herself as a sort of Delphic oracle.
[2] These blacked out lines come from a later censor, perhaps Wells himself, but unlikely.

76. To Elizabeth Healey

Illinois, ALS

Uppark
Petersfield, Hants.   March 10 [1888]

Dear Miss Healey,

Concerning Burton. I know most of the facts in the affair you mention against Burton. I did not know the matter had transpired. I do not consider it at all discreditable to Burton, save where the stupidity of his making himself specially amiable to a girl in Miss Wallace's (?) is that her name? position comes in. They both were intensely sentimental persons, phenomenally so, & interacting doubtless did some unconventional things. It wrongs Burton though very much to say he trifled with her feelings [*three words blacked out*]. My own conclusion in the matter was neither blame nor approval, but simply regret that they were not up to my standard of "matter-of-fact-ness" - and that she being more sentimental than he was most to be lamented.

The affair Burton generalized. I grant it "mean to trifle with the feelings of even a silly individual when one's faith is already promised to someone else", only the thing is constantly happening - has happened to my knowledge some dozens of times (not "to myself" please note) - almost invariably under the following circumstances. Ulysses finds his ideal in Pelenope.[1] They become engaged. Pelenope a divine thing. Ulysses goes away, to get a fortune say, or convert Trojans to proper views on social questions. Pelenope's letters at first glow, like her eyes used to do. Presently they decrease in length, and a certain someone becomes apparent, P having run out of her stock of endearing expressions, & [word blacked out] "suitors" becoming troublesome. Ulysses in distant parts finds the world stagnating. Calypso opportunely appears (or inopportunely.) Her conversation is interesting, her face very nice indeed to look at, and she is evidently interested in & anxious to please Ulysses. Ulysses behaves politely. Presently the Gods return Ulysses to Pelenope. Odyssey IV & V is the earliest instance of this trifling. It <u>is</u> mean, but that is man's distinctive quality according to some lovers of animals. It is hard to draw the line. Should a man who is [word blacked out] engaged deny himself all intercourse with the most amiable part of humanity, saving one unit, and should the Free Man - what ought he to do?

I am sorry you think my last letter vitriolic - I am naturally rough in my ways, but I assure you I wouldn't say anything to seriously lacerate your feelings for the world. I fancy you were in a considerably despondent state when you wrote. It is undoubtedly one of the beastliest things in life to have to drop into the treadmill of work & give up one by one all these nice aesthetic intellectual things that are the salt of life to non athletic people. I can sympathize with you thoroughly. At Holt I had to grind Euclid, among other things, into some wretched apologies for immortal souls at a Ladies College - not allowed to hit em or speak rough - only instrument of discipline, the tongue, suavely employed. "<u>Miss Taylor, the free handling of facts & the use of figurative expressions is less commendable in Geometric Exercises than in other branches of literature.</u>" "<u>Miss Meredith when you assume a proposition, proof is no longer necessary.</u>" "<u>I can wait young ladies, until your conversation is finished.</u>"

Sad fall truly from the Dyce & Foster[2] and a perennial combat with the great Judd. It happens to us all, though, if that is any consolation. Simmons has become just a worker, the ubiquitous B[urton] grinds like a slave, & has abandoned Ruskin almost, and at the end of it all there is nothing to show for either of them - so many lessons given, so many colours mixed & so much enamel perfected. I wish I could answer your questions and throw a pleasanter light on the monotony you complain of, for my own sake as well as yours.

Drawing near to death, that <u>WHY</u> ? presses heavier & heavier. "Cui bono?"[3] I doubt if "time will show".

I am glad you like Whitman. I have known him for 2 years nearly now, beginning with Leaves of Grass in the Cabinet of all Wisdom, the Dyce & Foster. I admire Whitman, but - is he a success? My ideal of success is entirely fruit[?]. You can only crop philosophy from Whitman, from Tennyson or Scott young men can gather real power, young women real grace of womanliness.

I really do approve of making wealth (not position) as an Essential to marriage. If I had the sticking power left in me I should try to start some persuasives against current sentiment. Some much belauded notions want utterly smashing. The "patient Grizel" is on notice.[4] the poetical weakling is another. - Something about Shelley makes me ill. That girl in Bleak House who marries a consumptive litigator is another abomination.[5] Petrarch[6] is fearful to my mind. Then there is the perfect gentlemam. The girl who won't marry because her lover dies or wanders, ought not to be made too much of. The religious sentiment is my special abomination - I have heard of young but emancipate men finding "The Saviour" had the first place in affections they had deluded themselves were entirely their own - and I feel for them. I am getting into dangerous waters - theology leads to first principles - and my first principle in the matter under discussion would I firmly believe horrify every other mortal I know.

        Believe me,
            Yours most sincerely,
               H. G. Wells

---

[1] Wells's spelling
[2] Building at South Kensington where the library was located in his student days, as well as classrooms in which he and Healey attended classes. Judd was a significant teacher of geology, and renowned for his extremely difficult examinations.
[3] 'Who benefits?' or 'Who is helped?'
[4] Usually known as Patient Griselda, the proverbiably meek woman
[5] Wells is referring to Ada Clare who marries the consumptive litigator Richard Carstone.
[6] The fourteenth century Italian poet whose love for Laura inspired a series of love poems. His passion is proverbial for its constancy and purity.

77. To Elizabeth Healey

Texas, ALS

Up Park
Petersfield, Hants
March 11, 1888

Dear Miss Healey,

    Many thanks for the number of the Journal. There is a clever fiction in it about myself getting better. I am glad that you are beginning to forgive

Burton even a little, you will esteem him some day. I do hope I didn't say disagreeable things in my last letter, if so, it was through that imperfection of utterance that is the blight of mortal intercourse and was the original incentive to the imagination of coalescent spiritual states perhaps - All mortal men have a savour of solitary confinement in their lives, the individual difference being a wall impenetrable by material method. The Buddhist nirvana is, in one of its many aspects a vague reaching towards the freedom of the imprisonment. I am afraid I am off at a tangent! Ware mysticism!

I don't think I have read Whitman about Lincoln. I'm glad you really enjoy Tennyson. Have you ever read Spenser? The glades, tangled underwoods, enchanted castles, & glistening streams of his land have a wonderful charm I find for me, and the moral intent is not repulsive by any means. Have you ever wandered in a genuine forest. Dean is not at all bad with its ancient oaks, but the enchanted castles to a properly imaginative person are satisfactorily represented by suffocating tree blasting, chemical factories, blazing iron furnaces, and blackhoused, black surrounded, black yawning, coal pits - it is wonderful how rapid the transition is between slaggy smoking swarming works, and quite perfect sylvan scenery, fit for Robin Hood or old Silenus even.

I do not approve of marrying objectionable people for money. I look forward to the sketch of the conversatazione with great anticipation. Yesterday, a sympathetic admirer, the lady of the lodge, sent me half a dozen of primroses which is better even than that poem - ? what was it? - "be still & wait", is all that remains in a too cribriform[1] memory - as anticipation of spring.

The Saturday when I shall weep over Kensington, in blasphemous reminder, is April 7th or thereabouts. (My Whittaker[2] is dated 76 & the computation of dates is therefore difficult to my enfeebled mind.)

Believe me to remain
> Yours very sincerely
> H. G. Wells

Perhaps I may try to get in a paper for the D.S[3]. on Friday the 6th.

---

[1] cribriform, meaning pierced with holes, sievelike
[2] The famous almanac, still printed today
[3] Debating Society

78. To Elizabeth Healey

Texas, ALS

Up Park
Petersfield, Hants   March 19, 88

Dear Miss Healey,

That correction of your report is very welcome to me for otherwise I should have had to give up all prospect of seeing the modern Babel again; the Brick Building where Men, if they only knew it, are reaching after God, & failing through confusion of nomenclature.

I shall not give a paper at the D.S.. That was said in an optimistic trance. I am about as fit to read a half hour's paper and live through the subsequent debate and afterwards go and breathe night air as I am to stroll about London with the dome of St. Paul's as a hat or catch tigers by hand in their native jungle. The doctor saw me last night. He seems to consider my inside original and interesting. He says that the internal arrangements that were mashed at football are by no means cured - "They are developing splendidly," says he with the most unmistakably genuine enthusiasm; "if you <u>only</u> live a couple of years" (tinge of despondency becomes apparent in his voice) "you could have a tumour as big as my head round that left kidney" "Will it hurt," I say with feigned indifference. "A <u>gon</u> izing," he answers unctuously - "Con - <u>vul</u> - sions. But there! Your lung will spoil that." I express my regretful sympathy. He bears up manfully. "There's a chance of a violent death <u>yet</u>", he says, "& Oh! <u>What</u> a <u>lovely</u> inquest!" "You are unsound throughout." - "I shouldn't be at all surprised, if you don't go bald soon."

P.S. I don't read German. I tried myself on the German article a few days ago & failed utterly.

I was very much interested in your account of the conversatzione and am especially glad to hear Miss Randell is studying the secrets of Aphrodite, & the Graces. I used to weep silently over her manifest disregard & frequent outrageous onslaught on their everlastings. It is an article in my creed that everyone ought either to dress beautifully or else be so slovenly and untidy as to be unique and picturesque - the latter alternative only for men and gipsies, of both sexes, I will add, on deliberation -

I do not believe in your kindly suggestion of sufficiency existing in a body. I know that, as I have always believed I am duller and with less of that self discipline, whose only hope [is] of dullness now or at any time of my perceptible existence. Can you give <u>one</u> of those numerous great men you airily allude to, who were "invalids or semi-invalids"? Blindness is not in the question, but physical impoverishment. I cannot recall one except Pope, & he would have collapsed & never written a line to live if his face had been on the grindstone of poverty.

There is a Sweny[?][1] exhibition somewhere on Bond St., where are some good pictures, I believe. I used to know the departed Sweny, through my cousin knowing a step daughter of his, & his story, which I will tell you somewhen, is a grim exposure of the so-called "extinct" Grub Street. [2]

Believe me now yours very truly

H.G. Wells

---

[1] Who Sweny was is not known.
[2] Persons described as working on Grub Street are hack writers. A street near Moorfields in London (now Milton Street) was the original source of the name.

79. To Elizabeth Healey

Illinois, Typed Transcription[1]

[London]   March 23, [1888]

Mrs Burton hates modern Radicalism. She and I sympathise most, of all parties in the world, with Wm. Morris and the Revolutionary circles in London, but he (Burton) shrinks from force. The 'Star' & Individualistic liberalism we would like to see scoured from the face of the Earth. The Commune which sank at Paris will rise next in London. That is the star we wait for. I am very sorry indeed that you are a Radical.

This is in the order of precedency -

Communists - Wm. Morris
Democratic Socialists - H.G. Wells -
Social Democrats - e.g. Champion
State (Imperial) Socialists (of the German type)
Moderate Conservatives - Raikes-Churchill types
Unionist Liberals, Goschen, e.g.
Liberals - John Morley -
Radicals - Bradlaugh type-

Tories - Primrose type -
Reactionaries (e.g. the Parnellites)
        (fair leaders)
Extreme Individualists - Auberon Herbert sort.

---

[1] Although Elizabeth Healey destroyed a few of Wells's letters to her, she made extracts of what she thought was important material. These extracts were typed out by her in the early 1930s and deposited with the remainder of his letters to her when he died. A few of the extracts are printed in this collection because of their value to our understanding of Wells's life and work. This extract deals with Wells's efforts to instruct her on political differences then noticeable in England.

80. To A. M. Davies

Illinois, ALS

Up Park
Peterfield
Hants   March 29 [1888]

Dear Davies,

      Just now I exhumed a rich brown fragment of paper with writing thereupon from the pit of breeches pocket. Imagining an archaeological[1] find of historical importance I set to work to decipher the electric flash symbols inscribed on the mellow matrix. "-ing" was perceptible also "-osity". but the other correlations failed to yield. One long flash (a long curving line) was at first rendered nuggets, but the true meaning was perceptible on inversion. <u>I saw at once</u> it was a letter to you. It had not been posted. Accept my sincere apologies for the omission, which doubtless has robbed you, to judge from the above, of a valuable theological bijou.

    I am coming to the Schools to have a look at your environment on Saturday April 7th (1888) so don't go & ride anywhere remote.

    Weather provocative of religious platitudes.
        Believe me, my son.
                Yours here & hereafter
                      H.G. Wells

---

[1] 'archaeological' has four question marks around it, one either side and one above and below the word.

81. To Elizabeth Healey

Texas, ALS

(Temporary) Center of
the Universe The 89th
of the 21st Year.

[29 March 1888][1]

Dear Miss Healey,

Many thanks for your kind & sympathetic letter. I am not a broken down invalid, I have merely had a revolution in my constitution - on the principle that a man who would revolutionize the World must first revolutionize himself - and I am now no longer an English person flourishing freely in the open air, but an exotic - It is sad to think I shall never grow in England again, but alas! too true. This last remark is jocquelar. I am rong in the lungs and shall go about henceforth like a bombshell with a proclivity to go off suddenly & unexpectedly - which is not a nice thing either for myself or my Envyrongment (this is the best spelling I can atcheve for environment) to think about. This passage is not humerous but pathetic.

I am sorry I cannot acceed to your rekwest about my litterery productshons - I am ashamed of them and desire only that my connection with them may seece on payment. Sharper than the cerpent's tooth is an unsatisfactory offspring, Miss Healey, and I trust that you will not mention my produkcions again. Clarque & Mrs Clarque I am glad to hier of. 'The great gentian work' is a longue firm fraud of some sort, I believe. I am glad Clarque is getting cleaner. Perhaps Mrs C washes his face for him or the atmosphere is less laden with dirt out there. The hermit of Davos rote to me sometime sintce. He is engaged in biler G which is n interesting sihence. You will be glad to heir that Smif E.H. is doing wel. I don't like your remarks about the world of lost things. I am not by any means a lost thing.

During my fflictions I have been much chastened. I am now to a large extent converted though I hope this will not diminish public interest as in the case of the 3 per cents after Goshen or Gochschen or Gosheschen - you know the man - had converted them - I have now written myself out and remain Simply a Shuck.

H.G. Wells

---

[1] This letter is postmarked Petersfield, where Up Park is located, April 1888.

82. To Elizabeth Healey

Texas, ALS; Illinois, Transcription

18 Victoria St
Basford
Stoke on Trent[1]

Monday
28 April 1888[2]

[A small drawing of a votive column with a burning sacrifice appears just above the salutation]

Dear Miss Healey,

Many thanks for your kind reply to that short jeremiad of mine. I am happy to say that this warmer weather has renewed my lease on percipient existence for a few weeks longer, and the blues have taken the wings of the morning & fled into the uttermost parts of the earth. To employ a metaphor that cannot possibly ever be worn greasy, the dying candle just now is in a state of flare before the final flicker cometh.[3]

You have probably heard me talk of a certain cousin of mine - in fact, now I think of it, you met her once at the Debating Society Conversatzioni - well, I am going to tell you sacred confidences about her. She has been engaged to me ever since I was an interesting & promising lad of eighteen. Living alone with her mother as she is and seeing very few people, I have reason to believe that I occupy a very considerable share in her thoughts, & when I die, there will be a very dreadful hiatus in the universe for her. Consequently I am anxious to see her surrounded by more friends than she has at present before the great renunciation occurs. To which end I shall esteem it one of those acts of friendship of the unreturnable sort if you would go & be pleasant to her & get fond of her & have her fond of you & so forth. I believe that you will like my cousin very much indeed & I [am] sure that she will - in fact - I know now that she has a very high opinion of you. Bless you my children, bless you. You will find her at home any evening after six[?] and on Sunday afternoons at a palatial second floor 12 Fitzroy Road Primrose Hill London N W within pleasant walking distance of the wildest parts of Hampstead Heath, Hornsey, Camden Town, Regent's Park, the Botanical Gardens, Marlebone Road, & many other places of interest & beauty too numerous to mention, & with convenient omnibus, railway & canal communications with all parts of the civilized universe.

I am glad you like Emerson.[4] I could make very little of Ruskin's[5] Queen of the Air when I ploughed at it, finding the Crown of Wild Olives vastly more congenial. Have you read Unto This Earth? It is a clear forceful exposition of the Socialist first principles that came to me simply like a heavensent revelation.

Sesame & Lilies finds great favour with that cousin of mine & is I think very nice myself. Emerson is rather too clever for me. He is like those gladiator fellows who used to fight with nets - always tripping you up & inextricably entangling you when you are thinking you are just getting at him. How he beguiles the innocent reader in that essay on Napoleon - blowing him & therewith all nineteenth century mankind, out into Colonial proportions, & then in the last paragraph with one diabolical little verbal pinprick collapsing the whole magnificent structure. It is magnificent but it is not essay writing.

I owe you a sincere apology about those mighty invalids you quoted to me. I contradicted you out of a cantankerous spirit. Darwin was an invalid & that I said about my father a gaudy lie. Also Carlyle a dyspeptic. Forgive the occasional crustiness of a dying man & believe me
          Yours very sincerely
          H. G. Wells

---

[1] Basford is not technically one of the five towns which make up Stoke-on-Trent, a county borough of Staffordshire. In fact Basford is more usually associated with Newcastle-under-Lyme. Stoke-on-Trent was not officially created until 1910 when a merger of Hanley, Burslem, Tunstall, Longton and Fenton was created. The usage of the general term to refer to the area of the Potteries, Arnold Bennett's 'Five Towns', is much older and it encompasses most of the Potteries district.

[2] Some of the extracts of this letter located in Illinois are dated 14 May 1888 but this is incorrect, as the date shown here appears on the letter itself. The sentence order varies slightly in the first paragraph of the transcript.

[3] Although it may seem that Wells is exaggerating his condition to Elizabeth Healey, he was very ill and did think that his days were numbered. His letters to Healey are much more open than to other correspondents. She was his confessor, his 'sister', his confidante at this time. It is this role which accounts for the continued closeness, not always as personal as here, throughout Wells's life. Other than business correspondence, more letters to Healey exist than to any other person, even though some were apparently destroyed.

[4] Ralph Waldo Emerson (1803–82) was a poet and essayist. His book *The Conduct of Life* (1860) was widely read. He was a close friend to Thomas Carlyle (1795–1881), author of *Sartor Resartus* (1833–4). Emerson was a leading figure in developing transcendental philosophy.

[5] John Ruskin (1819–1900) was a writer, art critic and a professor of art at Oxford. His works, *The Stones of Venice* (1851–3) and *Unto This Last* (1860) were important books for Wells. His recent illness had given him substantial time to widen his scope of reading, especially in matters not usually thought of as scientific. His letters to Healey in this period are a good indication of how his thoughts were evolving.

83. To Joseph Wells

Illinois, AL

18 Victoria Street
Basford
Stoke on Trent   Tuesday, April 29 [1888]

Dear Father,

   Remorse gnaweth at my vitals for my unfilial behaviour in not writing before to you, and I plead in palliation rather than with any hope of explaining away the blackness of my crime, that I have been seeking out interesting things to tell you about pots, and have heretofore been delayed by a cold & bad weather from going to Wedgewoods & collecting the same.[1] Considering the great reputation of the firm, I was rather surprised at the ramshackle state of their works, which are, with extensions & innumerable patchy alterations, the same that the immortal Josiah erected a century ago; they consist of big hive-shaped ovens and barn like but many storied buildings where the potters and the painters work standing towards each other at all angles, with queer narrow passages & archways penetrating them, with flimsy wooden staircases <u>outside</u> the buildings, and with innumerable windows opaque with dirt & crusted like bottles of ancestral wine with cobwebs & mouldy matter. There are grinding mills moreover which creak and groan as the mills within roar round and which are dim when you enter them with the dust of powdered felspar and chert, and these are served by men who are whiter by far than any other millers that I have seen.
   Through all this runs a canal and by the side of it are piles of blue and red & white clays & granite and red felspar waiting to be chewed up in the mills & spun around & moulded in the ramshackle buildings and elegantly ornamented and turned out, dishes & services, & ornaments & jars & utensils sacred to the Eloquent author of Lamentations and to the Service of Man.
   Burton[2] is concerned with the manufacture of the slip as the stuff which the pottery moulds is called, & and the mixing & invention of colours. The chief success up to the present has been a translucent coloured china, a thing hitherto deemed an impossibility. You know the beautiful effect of their white china — eggshell china as it is styled — well, by a very beautiful chemical contrivance Burton has managed to put into this white slip an excessively small quantity of colour - about a grain to a pint - and so, without rendering it opaque has produced a sea green, a jade, a rose pink, an ivory & a primrose

translucent china. They are making this now in some very beautiful forms - the sea green, for instance, is made in small plates & sugar basins & so forth, in shapes like sea shells & delicately lined with gold ornament to suggest the fronds & filaments of the sea weed & seamats. They are selling this stuff in the American market mainly obtaining such prices as one, two & three guineas for a small tea cup & saucer.

Burton has also turned out a new jasper (you know the Wedgewood jasper) of a rich greenish blue, a plum colour body, & a multitude of enamel colours, among the latter being a very exact imitation of that skyey blue that hitherto has been so characteristic of Japanese ware.

We are now seriously meditating a joint attempt to get a vermilion red, a colour as yet never known to have been produced in siliceous colours. To do so it will be necessary to go right outside of the known oxides which fix the basis of all colours in use, & try to obtain some salts which have hitherto existed only in theory. The brightest red hitherto has been

[remainder of letter missing]

---

[1] Although Wells's father was better known as a professional cricketer for Kent, his sports shop in Bromley also stocked china.

[2] Wells was recuperating in the Five Towns, with his student friend, Burton, who was doing research at Wedgewood's. Wells's interest in the silicas, as seen in his early fiction, may well stem from the experiments he conducted with Burton, and is hinted at in this letter.

84. To A. T. Simmons

Illinois, ALS

18 Victoria Street
Basford
Stoke on Trent   [c. May 1888]

Dear old Simmonds,

You must be calling me all the maggoty corpses on earth by this time for not answering that magnificent epistle of yours before. There is no excuse in particular forthcoming for the delay. You know I am a diseased poor devil with sluggish veins & clotted neurine & a muddy mind; I can only plead general unworthiness in excuse for my unworthy inaction. Never you fall ill, old chappie, while any decided hankering after life lasts in you. Inaction which is sublime while there is strength is the wretchedest thing in living when & in the outcome of weakness.

Bah! So much for myself and the plans you ask about, & the healthiness and happiness of the animal. I have reached such a pitch of uselessness that I know I am only cumbering the ground. Grrrr. Nice company I must be for dear old Burton! Eigh? I do hope you will do that matric next July. You will be a cipher if you don't. You are sure to pass if you go in for it.

Burton recommends you to keep your pecker up likewise cheer up & Hello. He also sends his love, wishes to be broadly remembered to you & hopes I will mention him to you in my letter. He is in hopes you are well & desires me to convey the best regards, wishes & kindest remembrances.

About them books if you will send me Gales address I will send it on to my mother who will send on to him the books he sent me.

   Art is long but life is short.
   Ars long vita Brevis.
Providence is usually on the side of the biggest battalion.
   Of Making of Books there is no end.
   Slow rises Worth by Poverty opprest.
    There is a Reaper whose name is death.
   Judsons Dyes are the best
      Yours,
       H.G.W.

85. To A. M. Davies

Illinois, ALS

18 Victoria Street
Basford
Stuck on Trent   [May-June 1888]

Dear Davies,

  I am a worm not to have written before to you, but I must plead bad times & lowness of spirit resulting thencefrom rendering possibilities of writing wholesome, <u>nil.</u> I have coughed up recently a lot more of gorey lung, so I am afraid the hungry maw will presently engulph the Prophet of the Undelivered

Spell, and the unwarned world hurry on to damnation. I hope you will let a chap know how things are with you. Ever since I used to pull your hair, curse God with you, & spoil your tools in the Elemgeollab, I have entertained the warmest & sincerest regard for you, A.M.D., and I shall be angry, & perhaps even murderous, if you don't write sometimes and let me know how you fare in your struggles against the Great Devil of Earthy Necessities. Burton feedeth me still with care & tenderness, and, were it not for a bubbling lung & an aching conscience, I think I should be fairly happy. 'But man was made for doing', my conscience tormenteth; and so - many sputters at authorship & much wrathful burnings of important efforts, & worrying after lame but not utterly important efforts that have hobbled off to editors, & gnawing of heart when they return, greasy & edgeworn. Some three shillings worth of sermon paper has curled up in pink spires to the God that made me a fool, but I persist (Burton victualling manfully). Some day I shall succeed, I really believe; but it is a weary game. After just a year of pegging away - Behold!

Item	1 short story	Sold	1 £
Item	1 Novel	35,000 words	Burnt 0. 0
Item	1 Novel Unfinished	25,000 ,,	0.0
Item	Much Comic Poetry	Lost	0/0
———	Some comic Prose Sent away Never Returned		
Item	Humorous Essay Globe, Did not return		
Item	Sundry Stories	Burnt	
Item	1 Story	Wandering	
Item	A Poem	Burnt	
			<u>etc. etc.</u>
Total Income (untaxed)			£ 1 - 0 -0

Are you going to tutor, or have you anything at S.K., or what are you going to do now the End of all Courses draws near.
     Give a chap a holler
     & Believe him.
      Yours in God
      H. G. Wells
Simmons prospers beamishly.
Burton doing really fine things at siliceous pigments.
All other chaps have dropped me.

86. To Elizabeth Healey

Texas, ALS

18 Victoria St.
Basford
Stoke-on-Trent [postmarked 2 May 1888]

Dear Miss Healey,

  Several times since I have been here I have begun letters to you but each time I have given up the attempt in disgust. I must most earnestly crave your pardon for my remissness. It is one of the most painful features of this form of human collapse, to feel continually power slipping away. Msy exertions to get here and the continued vile weather rendered this feature especially accentuated. I find walks that were even when I reached here, pleasant exercises, now become onerous exertions, and the effort required to sit down & write a letter becoming greater & greater every day. Which thing I hope is sufficient to get your indulgent pardon for my criminal silence.

 Burton is very much as he used to be, I find, doing really excellent work so far as I can tell in the investigation (on silicates & siliceous colourings) upon which he has been engaged. Mrs. Burton is quite beyond my powers of description - one of those rare people who are <u>not</u> to be classified smartly. They both take a care of me that makes me feel ashamed of my own unworthiness of the regard. Believe me to remain
     - in a sloppy sort of condition
      Yours very sincerely
       H.G. Wells

87. To Elizabeth Healey

Illinois, Typed Transcription, Extract [1888]

[...] There is a certain gamut of colours, complex all of them, visible to the unsophisticated world in April during a west wind, red-brown of tree-twigs, lichen stains of grey green and delicately blue green, greys of cloud shadow, and freshly broken pebbles, pallid blue of the sky, or richer blue <u>invariably broken by white</u>, distant violet-blues, and so forth, which I would recommend you, very earnestly to adhere to, it fortunately being possible to buy in these civilizing days, stuffs of soft texture and reasonable price in these shades.[1]

---

[1] There are some affinities in these word sketches of nature to a number of his later unsigned pieces in the *Pall Mall Gazette*, in this case, with 'Bleak March in Epping Forest', which appeared on 16 March 1894, and was later included in *Certain Personal Matters* (London: Lawrence and Bullen, 1897).

88. To Elizabeth Healey

Texas, ALS

18 Victoria St
Basford, Stuck on Trent   Jejewn 1888

Dear Miss Healey,

    Every day ever since my last, I have really been <u>hankering</u> to write to you, but somehow, lungs, or the will of the Lord in the form of disbarring accidents, have prevented. Now, however, an opportunity fortunately occurs, of which I avail myself with avidity.

There is really a fearful dearth of material from which to elaborate a letter to you, in this neighbourhood. There is absolutely nothing in the neighbourhood in which I can imagine you interested except myself, and it is written in the Book of the Polite Letter Writer that such a topick is forbid to a man as himself. However, taking the Polite Letter Writer by the shoulders & gently but firmly <u>moulding</u> him doorwards, his book following, - I am, Miss Healey, speaking generally better in spirits this day than I have been for some time - Certing saddening discoveries of mortal clayness having weighed much upon me since my journey from the tabernaculum of old Silenus & the move to this vale and hitherto prevented that lamblike gambolling of mind which is 1 of my most charming characteristics. The fact is, I had got sort of to believe that in that muddle of a cheap stamped tin universe gold might be found, & a little of yellow enamelled stuff I had grabbed in the belief disappointed me. I have righted now, I know now that the whole universe is a sham, a tin simulacrum of ideals, veneered deal pretending to mahogany. If I had not been an ass I should have understood that, when the cardboard religious structure I constructed in my kid - & calf hood caved in when I came to lean on it. Which it's raving I am, Miss Healey, & not to be minded. It's only my fun.

Miss Healey, this world is a lark of the omnimodus[1] - a screaming farce, the trifle before the Tragedy - of Death. Life is a game at bagatelle - the most serious things in it, eating & drinking & not getting your feet wet scarcely worth the trouble they take.

Write us a letter, & let us know how the gay world of Kensington gets on.
    & believe me
        Yours in the Lord
        H. G. Wells

---

[1] Existing in all modes of being, of all sorts

89. To Cosmo Rowe

Illinois, ALS

18 Victoria Street
Basford, Stoik   June or Junior [May 1888]

Dear Rowe,

I cannot conceive of any living thing having a less eventful existence than mine 4 the last 2 or 3 months unless it is that of the Paraclete before the creation (How <u>he</u> filled up <u>his</u> letters has not been revealed).

I cend you poetry & antiquities & my blessing. Burton (a character living here who professes to know you - a dissolute strange being) desires to be kindly remembered to you.
        Ewers (that is how they spell
            it here)
        H.G. (or J) Wells

[A drawing of a large sail boat is at the top of the paper. At the bottom is a man, Wells, with his lungs in view, and the caption, 'Right lung far from <u>right</u>. Left lung still left. H.G'.]

90. To Elizabeth Healey

Texas, ALS

18 Victoria St
Basford
[Stoke-on-Trent]   June 19 [1888]

Dear Miss Healey,

Many thanks for your nice letter whereof the only objectionable sentence was the one after the last. I was deeply moved to hear of the record of partings especially Wager's leaving away from his complementary soul. Excepting only myself I believe, Wager is the biggest fool I have knew of - his poetry certainly one of the gaudiest larks I have ever come across in the world of flaccid jokes. Emulation seizes on my soul even as I write! - & the rest of this letter - shall be in a light, but pleasing, poetical strain. (Please notice I burn with practical fire - I haven't the ghost of the faintest desire to mix with pen scratchings the twang of the lyre, and mingle this music in vain.) The weather is beauty, wind east, & I feel in a mood all my devilish self to reveal, & to scoff at the good and the true & the ideal [*several words blacked out*] like that thief chap who scoffed at the Lord.

Bother the poetry! It's too much trouble! But, don't you think there is a frightful lot of sentimental distortion of this important factor of human life called Love? The code of rules whereby two young people have to meet each other, go through all sorts of ceremonial and finally pass under the yoke, which exists in this effete state of humanity is one of the most ghastly difficulties that the ambitious writer of stories has to encounter. For myself, who am a doubter and contemner of almost all the amenities of social intercourse there is a simply frightful temptation to be glaringly improper in what I write - I am one of those beings who with the simplest and purest of lives, have the most shocking code of morals believable - but this is a personal detail & uninteresting, doubtless, to you. I am exceedingly glad Davies seems to be getting on to the S. Kensington establishment as a researchist - he is a chap who may someday do something about something scientific, sufficiently well to get somewhat distinguished in his own generation - but I am rather anxious about him as so much of his future depended on his continuance in London. I presume you will shortly enter upon a well earned holiday somewhere or other.

Then I shall expect - your excuse of excessive corrections & soul destroying bazaar duties no longer existing - voluminous letters giving exhaustive accounts of your physical state & your opinions on all matter of human life, interest & intercourse, without exception. Tell us about that bazaar. Was it a Church of England game? With the tooth exhibiting curate, baaing everywhere, and the parson's wife shrill & omnipresent, and the Sunday school doves clustering round the portly parson & the church old women very respectful & surreptitious & the middle class school master & his wife trying to catch the parson's eye & cutting the organist who is cutting the greengrocer who sings abysmal bass in the ?quire? (?choir) who is cutting the tinker whose wife cleans the church steps? Eigh, was it that? or was it a different game altogether in connexion with South Place Chapel - what is such a bazaar like? - without the parsonical element.

Stoke on Trent is not socially a gorgeous dream of happiness - lots of the people are decent brainless church goers of the black-coat-on-Sunday-or-burn-in-hell-for-ever type, lots of the rest are Evangelical beasts of the Card genus, the rest workpeople who may be summarised exhaustively as inveterate drunkards & free livers - so that, barring a few cosmopolitan china decorators and a transcendentalist Quaker or so of the Manchester school, there is very little enjoyable human intercourse available. Burton is doing very good work indeed for Wedgewoods, & bids for to become an authority in potting.

Write soon & tell me things in an Exhaustive way.
& believe me
Yours most sincerely,
H.G. Wells

The Chronic Argonauts is no joke. There is a sequel - It is the latest Delphic voice but the Tripod is not yet broken[1]

---

[1] At some stages of worship at the Delphi Oracle a tripod was offered with incense; after the ceremony, the tripod was apparently broken. The meaning and timing of this event is not well known. When it first appeared in the *Science Schools Journal*, *The Time Machine* was called *The Chronic Argonauts*. This letter marks Wells's return to fairly good health, and to reworking *The Time Machine* material for publication.

91. To Elizabeth Healey

Texas, ALS

12 Fitzroy Rd, N.W. August 5, 1888

[*A sketch of a Pan figure, playing pipes, with sheep (on wheels), tea, the sun, a bird and a tree, labelled 'Arcadia', is at the top of this page just before the salutation.*]

Dear Miss Healey,

Many thanks for your last descriptive letter, it brings with it an atmosphere of new mown hay in the dewy morning time cool with virginal breezes & trembling with the numerous twittering of young birds. At the same time the question arises, are somnolent cows in corn-fields, the only eutheria in your environment; I miss the melancholy criticisms of humanity around, which commonly give your letters such a plaintive charm. I have heard of the moorland home of Currer Bell,[1] a young woman whom I by no means admire, because being ugly she preached an incredible gospel of amiable ugliness.

Her and her sisters I regard as a most lamentable instance of that too common human failing of attempting to weave all one's characteristic failings into an ideal. Because I am rank and reedy, is that any reason why I should assert Jean Jacques to be the best specimen of <u>homo sapiens</u>; because I am prone to lapse into abuse, that I should accept Swift as entirely good, or because the recording angel scrawls insincere over my page, that I should shout and dance in the triumph of Benvenuto Cellini? But it is too much a feature of modern thought to echo the fox who thought the grapes were sour; we are anaemic, small chested, let us abuse carnality and exalt the Spirit. Our memories fail often, our wits slumber like gorged snakes, let us then revile clearness as superficial and insinuate profundity; we are poor, power and riches are vulgar. Before all things in a practical age, let the Ideal be something which we can without too serious exertion attain. Ideals in the Empyrean are like treasures laid up in heaven - medievalism - mad.

Tell me about the Sunday School treat. I should like to see you surrounded, wading, partially suffocated in a flood & atmosphere of children. I am fond of children - in Dickens & Victor Hugo & R.L. Stephenson. Elsewhere they are apt to be either dull witted or caricatures of flayed humanity after the Yahoo type.

My cousin sends best regards.
Believe me yours most sincerely,
H. G. Wells

[1] Currer Bell was the pen-name of Charlotte Brontë.

92. To Cosmo Rowe

Illinois, ALS

46 Fitzroy Rd. N.W. [late Summer 1888]

Dear old Ornament,

I am afraid to brave the elements on Saturday as my chest is still tender but I hope to see you soon. I am 7½ lbs heavier than I was three weeks ago & Lord knows when this Adiposity Boom will end. Tell Jennings the "Longman's Hope"[1] perished. I speculate "Whither?" Tell him I am "alone in London".
Faithfully yours,
H.G.Wells

[1] 'Longman's Hope' was an article in circulation, I believe. This letter has a drawing of a small Wells labelled: 'As I was', Wells larger, 'As I am,' and a huge Wells, 'As I shall be.' These weight gains are significant. He does not weigh much over 105 pounds (7½ stone), which is quite light, even for this time.

93. To Cosmo Rowe

Illinois, ALS

[Stoke-on-Trent] [late Summer 1888?]

Dear Rowe,[1]

On Saturday last a careful observer in the Euston-Road might have noticed an individual, wrapped up as if to avoid scrutiny, stealing carefully through the Metropolis on tip-toe and with numberless precautions to avoid recognition. [**or attract attention. Thus, his name was carefully concealed in his umbrella..**] [2]

This person was myself returning from Holt, the doctor having held out the most alarming prospects. **[in the event of my staying longer at that inclement situation..]** I had not time to call on you, so forgive me. Simmons is well and Burton happy. **[as a cricket]** Remember me kindly to mother and sister. How does the Birkbeck expedition prosper?

Write soon and believe me
        yours enjoying complete rest.[3]

                      H.G. Wells

---

[1] Rowe illustrated the book versions of *The War of the Worlds* (London: Heinemann, 1898), *Tales of Space and Time* (London: Harper, 1899) and the short story, 'The Sad Story of a Dramatic Critic.' Between 1884 and 1892 he maintained a large studio which he shared for a time with William Burton. When Burton started working in Stoke-on-Trent, Wells moved into his vacated quarters at 157 Euston Road. Wells had been living at 181 Euston Road, but had made a bit of money selling his work to Northcliffe's paper *Answers To Correspondents*. In Rowe's letter to the *St Pancras Chronicle*, 6 September 1946, where this letter was first located, he described these days of hope and youthful enthusiasm and this letter. Wells had just died when Rowe's letter appeared and the paper was pleased to publish it. Rowe told their readers 'H.G. has filled my life with many memories and I miss him very much. I get a dose of nostalgia if I go down Euston Road.'

[2] Bold type indicates words which appear only in the original holograph version of the letter.

[3] Another version of this letter to Rowe, heavily illustrated, is located in a collection of Wells's earliest poems, drawings and letters bound together and entitled, 'Mammonart'. One can only surmise that either Wells was particularly fond of the illustrations, or that they were added to a copied letter, for the two versions to exist. The drawings consist of Wells doing a visual exercise for a doctor; walking in a bent stance; in bed with an angel looking over him; and sitting by a fire, burning a parish magazine. The first notice of 'Mammonart' was in a 1947 antiquarian book catalogue from Bowes and Bowes, Cambridge; it apparently came from the archives of Cosmo Rowe. In 1947 'Mammonart' was on offer for £75 in this catalogue. The work is now in Illinois.

94. To Elizabeth Healey

Illinois, ALS

Nyewoods
Rogate
Sussex   Sept. 5 [1888]

Dear Miss Healey,

Just at present I am staying with that alcoholic savage, my father. He has won all my spare salary from me & gone to sleep on the broken down sofa. It is raining hard. This is the only piece of paper available. This cottage is our swampy recess, three miles from everywhere. Happy! Pardon my writing, but I <u>must</u> do something until the ancestral type wakes up & gets tea.

[*A small 'picshua' of Joseph Wells, lying on a couch, with two small figures looking at him. On a shelf on the wall is a bottle and a mug.*]

I do not approve of your disapproving of Wager. What business have people even to get engaged? The fact of it is, you display a very mistaken view of all that sort of thing in your remarks. You take it seriously. Neither Mr. Wager, Miss Watson, or engagements to many, are ever to be taken seriously. Mr. Wager is an ass, and he has that little learning which is a dangerous thing. He has read Shelley - he believes himself like him - He is insufficiently virile to be vicious, so he follows his great model along the Platonic plane. Until Mr. Wager sinks into his grave, he will be trying to get engaged to feeble minded female persons, & then publicly jilting them - perfunctory viciousness. Miss Watson, too, although I respect her to the extent of fear in her presence, still I am unable to take [her] seriously from the love point of view. I believe that familiarity might prove her a very nice fellow, but I am perfectly unable to consider of romance in stiff collars. And Romance <u>is</u> necessary to a love episode.

From experience & a priori, I object to engagements. They are a device of Mrs. Grundy,[1] or the devil. You know, I think, that I object to marriages as a general thing. The way in which two people after half a dozen weeks intercourse will bind themselves to burden & bore each other for the rest of their days, is perfectly disgusting to me. You can see for yourself that ninety nine per cent of marriages end in revolt or passive endurance and when two people will be loyal all through, the tie simply becomes a concession to circumadjacent Fetishism.

The class enterprise came to nothing after all. All the good places had made arrangements. Well — it will give me more time for my degree.

       He has woke!
          Believe me,
             Very sincerely yours,
                  H.G. Wells

I return to London on Monday.

---

[1] A narrow-minded person who is very critical of any breach of propriety (from a character in the play *Speed the Plough* by Thomas Morton, 1798).

95. To Elizabeth Healey

Texas, ALS

12 Fitzroy Rd, N.W.   Novr 21st, 1888

Dear Miss Healey,

      Your forgiveness is once more needed by your unworthy correspondent. I have not written before for the satisfying reason that I was incapable. For the last few days I have been most unaccountably wretched - not ill, but intensely miserable - an altogether unprecedented phenomenon. If I had retained the Bible as an authoritative companion to my dictionary, I should, I suppose, ascribe it to the burthen of original sin, and seek that Elder Brother who died to lighten our load. But under existing circumstances, it has been necessary to seek a cause, & that I am still seeking. The realisation of the disproportion of desire & possibility seem probable, but that I imagined was over long ago. Or it may be the quite purposeless way in which I am living from day to day. If the latter be correct, the disease is serious for I fail to see how epic unity can be consciously imported. I believe nothing strongly enough to let all other things group themselves around it, and it seems therefore not important that the disorder called ennui is my condition, a chaotic energy consequent on a failure of external excitement & increasingly liable to recur. In order to manufacture interest I am going to criticise a paper by Reynolds on Dec 14, & write one for Jan in the D.S., have written an abusive criticism for the forthcoming journal, & contemplate joining the Fabian Society, & otherwise involving myself. But all this is feeble & scarcely alleviates my dullness at all. It would be a kindness if you would irradiate my gloom next Saturday. My cousin will be home by three & we shall have tea at four. Do come.

                    Believing me
                            Sincerely yours,
                                              H.G. Wells

[*An illustration of a thin stooped figure, with hands in pockets is at the bottom of the page.*]

96. To Elizabeth Healey

Texas, ALS

The Watchtower
12 Fitzroy Road
Mount Primrose [1888?][1]

Dear Miss Healey,

  Walt Whitmaniacal, inchoate, dishillant, demiurgic, cataclysmal birth of a new philosophy (supreme democratic Cockney, etc.) hitherto has in the cosmic whirl, gatherings & scatterings hither & thither, engaged my time entirely et je ne was pas able ecrire eine litterae. The persons stading-on-a-relation-to-the-poet-of-democracy not dissimilar to John the Baptist named Whitman has been the displaced atom around which my universe has crystallized. I, even ego, je, Ich, H.G. Wells, am resolved to sing, perform, figure, express, voice, whistle, symbolize, howl, schriek, project, the democracy of London Cockney - cosmic, Anglo-German-Yiddish-Italian ice cream - French laundress- Lascar crossing sweeper - Swedish sailor & Russian refugee, polyglot people of the New Old World, distillation, decantation, compaction, scum of the universe, London centred, - Chant with steam-whistle Democratic siren accompaniment the deeper & the truer, the hitherto voiceless, the future-foomige, ewigest, of all humanity, superseding aristocracy overcoming, taking the shine out of.
  Come O barrowger, cauliflowerifem costermonger! O 'Array, chantant "Deux belissima ocula noir "! O mealy faced clerks! beer-puffed publicans! cornet compelling housepainters out of work! mousy mothers! dirty children! Cerulean butchers! Corduroyclad & odoriferous, porters & bricklayers! Grant getting, superstitiously slapping board-school teachers! Salvationis miles avec monstrissimum os & drum! Soapless foreigner hirsutus! Come! dis je Come! just as you are into my poem. My chant of the new age, my chaotic, unique, colossal Londoniad, Democraticiad, psalm of the common life. Thus am I thinking & working now, in throes of Phoenix climatrix.[2]
  My cousin sends her love & wants to know when we shall see you again over here.
    Believe me
     With best wishes
      Most sincerely
       The Poet of the New Democracy.

[1] It is difficult to date this letter, Wells and his student friends lived at both 12 and 46 Fitzroy Road in this period, moving from flat to flat as their finances improved, or space was available, such as when Burton moved to Stoke.

[2] This wonderful gallimaufry of words, and veritable salmagundi of sounds occurred because Wells had discovered Walt Whitman's *Leaves of Grass*. His cousin is Isabel, who was close to Healey.

97. To Fred Wells

Illinois, ANS

12. Fitzroy Rd. NW [late 1888]

Dear Fred,

    Very many thanks for the pretty box of biscuits which are now being munched by us in solemn convocation of dessert. When shall we expect you for the Pantomime? If you can get away early, Saturday would be much the best day because then you could spend the greater part of Sunday with us. If you have to come up on Saturday, it might be convenient if you were pressed for time not to come over here till after the play. I could meet you at Waterloo, take you in to Jennings' den on Chancery Lane & have some tea, go into Drury Lane (which is close by) & then come on here. Do you know that Irving is going to produce "Macbeth" at the Lyceum for the new year & that promises to create a tremendous sensation? There are performances of the pantomime at 3:30 that you might see if you could perhaps get up early enough & wanted to do so. Give my love to Frank & Mother & the G.V.
        & with best wishes for the New Year,
        Believe me
        Yr very affte br
                Bertie

[*small sketch map of area*]

98. To Elizabeth Healey

Texas, ALS

[London] [perhaps 1888 or 1889[1]]

Dear Miss Healey,

How is Providence dealing with you? With me that eccentricity goes on in his usual interesting way, no chariots on the one hand & no thunderbolts on the other. He sent a toothache which I pretended not to notice - I believe that is about all he can do - & then he got friendly & accepted an article. Nothing decisive you observe. I have been cycling for a week, Guildford, New Bognor, Arundel, Pulborough, Reigate and I must admit that the weather was really very good & no tampering with the brakes & so forth on hills. Either he has been sending good books & is trying to reform or he is saving up for some crushing effort. Perhaps he is writing a version of my book with a quill from the wing of the Angel of Death with cholera in the cistern.

Let him.

He is a poor creature, this God, and I pity him from the bottom of my heart. I bear him no ill will. Leave me alone, O Lord, is my prayer & I will do the same by you. You have things in a mess, but I am not a God, I cannot help you. I can give you advice if you like. But God you are not much of a man, leave me alone at any rate. Else I will canvass against you. I will make your position unbearable. I will jeer and make a mock of you.

So I pray bullying God.

Yours ever,

H.G.W. [*a little stick figure*]

N. B. This is jocular. I am not insane. With best wishes.

---

[1] There is some guesswork about this letter. The prayer also exists in typescript, undated, and in the second half of another letter in holograph. The first version is in Illinois and the second in Texas. I believe this is the way they should fit together. A few of the Texas items are only partially available, and they are fitted together by deduction from times, topics, placement in the files and handwriting. Although Sarah Wells had a strong but unquestioning Christian faith, the other members of the family apparently had no faith. Wells rejected her beliefs early in his life and this prayer, along with several short poems which do not appear in this collection, are clear indications that he was shedding her religious influence rather steadily. Oddly enough he continued to use expressions with religious connotations, such as 'for God's sake', for the remainder of his life. He also had a religious epiphany of a sort during the First World War, which produced a book he later repudiated, *God, The Invisible King* (London: Cassell, 1917). The best place to explore this aspect of his thinking is in *First and Last Things* (1908), revised at three

different times later in his life. The last version, *The Conquest of Time* (1942) was written to replace *First and Last Things* (London: Watts & Co., 1942) and it is influenced by Einstein.

99. To A. T. Simmons

Illinois, ALS

[Up Park] [1 January 1889]

[This letter has several sketches. One is of four rather horrified people at a table with the caption, 'The way they take a <u>novel remark</u> at Up Park'. On an enclosed page there is a sketch of a 'chemist' in a pharmacy. A broken retort with a black liquid spilling out is marked 1888. The chemist is warming a dish, marked 1889, with his hands. A large mortar and pestle are nearby. The caption to this drawing reads, 'Time, The Great Healer. May he be mixing you a good dose for the New Year'. On the second page is a drear dark figure, staring into a fire, writing his correspondence. It is marked, 'This expresses all there is to tell you'.]

Dear Tommy

Things are very dull here. I am dull - deadly dull. I am getting better & go for walks & eat well & get up Correspondence lessons but O God how dull I am! Oh God how dull! They are all dead - purely automatic. Look at the devils [*small sketch of a black hand*] Each of 'em have fifteen remarks to say over & they get through the lot each mealtime. "The days draw out nicely." "The frost continues." "The poor souls without coals must suffer!" & so on. They are <u>damned</u> <u>phonographs</u> <u>bloody old talking</u> <u>Dolls.</u>

Let me know all about your things & for Gods sake write soon to your friend, the

      Meek Pietist
      <u>H.G.W.</u>

100. To A. T. Simmons

Illinois, AL

12 Fitzroy Rd NW   Feb 4th 89

Dear Simmons,

Many thanks for the letter and your kindly self sacrifice in sounding the ambiguous William [Burton]. I have written him a letter suggesting a sort of compact of separation & silence. If things get talked over & talked over between that wife & him in the way they evidently have been since I parted from them in all apparent lovingkindness, God knows how great my sins will be in a year hence. Quite sufficient at any rate to rob me of every friend who gets into Mrs. Burton's sitting room. You even are evidently shaken, & in quotation, "A friend should bear a friend's infirmities[?]" is visible between the lines of your most kind letter. So far as I can recollect, my sins were such as these. I was ill in a way that made me low spirited & dull witted & the amount of heavy sentiment in the atmosphere sometimes bored me beyond concealment into irony or argument. Then the continual dropping of

[*The letter deteriorates, or changes character here, and the second page is a series of cartoons which carry the message. 'Burton! WhaddyoutakeMrWellsfor? Mrs. Burton secundus?'*]
[*a cartoon of a man in armchair startled by a voice, then a man tiptoeing with a wand of some sort*]

Of all the <u>Bloody</u> insults.
[*a sketch of two persons rolling on the floor*][1]
[*This is all that remains of this letter*]

---

[1] There may be more sketches which belong to this letter.

101. To A. T. Simmons

Illinois, ALS

12 Fitzroy Rd, NW.   Febr 8. 89

Dear Tommie,

Don't be absurd. Them was ony my gaimes when I talked about your seeming to be cooling, & ony my defective elingquence in seeming to be cool. Between us, old chappie, there is scarely any need of elaborate assurances & pledges to ensure our continued friendship & sympathetic comprehension. The thing is not of man's devising or agreeing but of nature's persuasion, an elective affinity, a mutual fitness & necessity.

Wherefore, o Simmonds rejoice or weep as it beseemeth thee, for thy interaction with me is as inevitable as $H_2SO_4 + 4 H2O$ yea even to the cracking of the vessel! Neither attempt to find things too clearly crystallized in words for the phenomenon of crystallization is too often the follower of evaporation or cooling. Comprenez esker vu? By these fruits ye shall know them. Consider your back slapped, your hair ruffled & your hand fervently gripped.

I wrote the Great Burton saying that I had received a fatherly letter from you expressing a question as to my estrangement. I further dilated on the points:

(1) that I was unprincipled mainly in theory & that of us two he was the more disingenuous in action & that he was most unprincipled in his inner self.

(2) that my social backslidings (specified to some detail) were entirely due to the mistaken estimate of his unconventional sincerity which I had formed on his own declarations. Especially that any remark hurting & hitting him were due to the contacts of the social & moral habits & his commercial position (swapping men - making 2 men do the work of 3 etc.)

And that remarks hurting Mrs. B. were especially in salutary direction of pointing out that Longfellow's sentiment led to gush & uselessness, by the use of parable & destructive criticism. Doubtless I was acrid. I was the skeptic in the household of Faith - the Faith that their lives were a lot better than those of other people. I do not think I ever expected to lose you or any part of you by my difference with Burton, & I believe too that Rowe is more akin to me than to them. Believe me
        Old Ornament,
            The Unchanging

102. To Elizabeth Healey

Texas, ALS

[Address unknown]   [May 1889]

Dear Miss Healey,

>We regard May 17th[1] as the brightest spot in our Common Future.
>and remain
>>Complacent & Expectant
>>I.M. & H.G. Wells

[*various drawings of people and animals on the lower half of the page - with a title - 'Cases of Sympathy'*]

---

[1] This was the date of their formal engagement.

103. To Fred Wells

Texas, ALS

46 Fitzroy Rd., NW1   May 28th, 89

Please note the change of address

Dear old Man,

A letter presupposes a great & imminent occasion, which, briefly, is as follows. We, the girl & I, have tickets for a certain 'aughty art sworry held yearly in the South Kensington Museum. But an evil thing impedes the ravishing delight - we should otherwise feel rushing through our hearts. Your brother has no "war paint", no black & shapely evenin' dress. He turns in this extremity to your fraternal resources, to save him from the anguish of a terrible disappointment, & not only him, but the young woman whom it is his exalted function to "take around" & "trot about". The soiree is about the 3rd or 4th of June. You have therefore just time to look spry & send off them there things & earn the gratitude of perhaps the most promising young man you have ever known.

You will see that we have married.[1] We are still in the same road but now close to Primrose Hill & Regent's Park Rd. instead of to Chalk Farm & the democratic Camden Town. The apartments we are in are much more convenient in every way than those above the hymn playing she-parson, as we hope you will soon testify for yourself. There is a corner for a bicycle at any time, & always the possibility of storing away a slender and flexible young man like yourself. So that you have only to send on a postcard to lett us to slay the fatted calf, broach the wine casks, & to get in, during this season, ice & a quart of scent for the bathroom.

I continue to dodge death in miraculous ways. Pending that I am working for my Intermediate University (Junior Tripos) in Science, & writing fitfully at various schemes for stories, though I have been at it for two years or more, now, there is yet all to learn in the art of fiction. But, failing death, I mean to learn it, & that learnt, to write & print, & printing, to succeed & sell. Resolution & persistence are the keys of Earth & heaven, & I set the bound at forty within which there will be praise or reward.

Things continue well at Kilburn. My hours of duty are reduced this term, & I get a fortnight off for the exam, clear without trouble for a substitute. The results of that exam, by the bye, come out in August. We get a vacation of seven weeks, beginning early in August, & running well into Sept. Some part of that time I hope perhaps will coincide with yours, & if so we might get up to some larks together. During Isabel's fortnight we have some idea of all three of us going into the country together - perhaps if we could get apartments in some farmhouse or the like, in Surrey or Sussex. Midhurst would be a jolly place to visit but then it stinks with people who know me. We have also thought of Cotswold. The idea is a combination of weald forest & heathery common. We don't want the sea with the bathers & boatmen & minstrel abominations. What sort of country is it round Redhill, Dorking, Godstone[?] & about there? Any knowledge you can offer about Sussex or Surrey will oblige.

Awaiting those clothes.

Your venerable Brother
Bertie

---

[1] Not literally

104. To Fred Wells

Illinois, ALS

46 Fitzroy Rd. NW.   May 30th, 89

Dear Fred,

They art come. The family happiness is again complete. Dissipated wine card found in one pocket, significant programme in another crowded with names of victims, cross against two of these, in another, menu of the hotel Continental (Feb. 3rd, 89) - Query how did it get there? I am afraid, my brother, your moral reformation is incomplete.

Thing happens June 6th, after which I will as speedily as possible send off in return. Are you going to see the Academy or the New Gallery this year? Do you still take an interest in botany or insects?

Yours in faith,
H.G. Wells

105. To H. E. Hedley [1]

Sothebys, AL

46 Fitzroy Road, N.W.   3 June 1889

Are you or are you not going to the Art Schools Swarry or Sworry? because if you are & if you have no serious luggage, you have got to come & go with me who have much & need the aid of a friend... My burthen is worse than that which Christian left the City of Destruction, first, those two ladies whom you already esteem & admire & who (this - in strict confidence) consider you the takest-about young man they have ever met; secondly, a lady who requisitioned me in an imperious manner to escort her, her maiden aunt & cousiness, thirdly certain friends of my cousin who may or may not bring a he-attendant - they are three in number, young, witty & beautiful - & who therefore may be considered as the sixth, seventh, & eighth, of my responsibilities. Now I am weakly, shy, & devoid of entertaining converse, & unless I am relieved from this octadicity (N.B. scientific joke) I shall die...

[1] In December, 1969, Sotheby's auctioned three of Wells autograph letters signed, and one envelope, addressed to H. E. Hedley. One of the letters began 'Dear Old Hedley', and another ended with 'Yewers in the Lord'. On the envelope Wells drew a sketch of a man holding his nose, about to drink poison, labelled 'Hedley F.R.S/Physics', and in a note says, 'Excuse the Mr. but I have forgotten your soon-to-be famous initials'. There are a dozen sketches in these letters, including one labelled, 'a dark & lonesome soul amidst the hum of Manchester's social life'. In addition there is a sequence of a dozen small sketches, labelled, 'A study in congenial souls'. Hedley became Principal of the School of Science, Kidderminster, and wrote many school science textbooks, several in conjunction with R. A. Gregory, later Sir Richard Gregory. Wells also spells the the name as Hedleigh, but the correct spelling is Hedley. The whereabouts of these letters today is not known (Sotheby's *Catalogue*, 9 December 1969, p. 143).

106. To Fred Wells

Illinois, ALS

46 Fitzroy Rd NW　　　　　　　　　　　　　　　　　　　　June 18th, 89

Dear Fred,

　　　　I would have liked to come to that great show in the Windsor Great Park, but unfortunately I am fast in the University quicksands, being sucked down swiftly to the Intermediate Science, and struggling without hope, but as honour demands, with all energy, to avert the inevitable failure. I am fit for no festivities till the thing is over. I should make you anxious & dispirited by my weird conversation. My mind runs on kinetic energy, equations to chords of contact, binomial theorem, Mendeleff's theory, macrosporangia, & fields of magnetic force. I should chalk chemical equations on the pig pens, & try to dissect the prize bull. I should think of vegetable morphology among the taters & seek for square & cube roots among the wurzels. Not yet, my brother, not yet until this terror be overpast.

I am going to make Isabel pack up them clothes and send them on as soon as possible.

Remember me kindly to any Williams cousins extant. I still cherish the most cousinly feelings though their faces & ways have well nigh vanished into the unfathomable forgotten.

　　　　　　　　　Love from all.
　　　　　Affte Brother,
　　　　　　HGWells

107. To Fred Wells

Illinois, ALS

46 Fitzroy Rd, NW   [early July 1889?]

Dear Fred,

By this post those evening things of yours are forwarded. I am sorry for the delay in sending them, but hitherto my state of cram has prevented my attending to such matters. I have had a week of examinations now & most of the Pass work is over, except some practical stuff in Zoology & Chemistry, but the whole thing will not be concluded till the 31st, as I am trying Honours in Zoology. I have been, so far as I can judge my own work, pretty fortunate in the subjects that I have sat for, up to the present. My holidays from Milne's School[1] begin on the 1st of August & run into September (16th). How do you propose to spend your holidays? I believe we shall go down to Leith Hill, all three of us for a fortnight or three weeks, but other than that I have no plans. If we get some blazing weather I may run down to Nye Woods,[2] but it will want gorgeous weather indeed, to make that place bearable for long. I shall want some idleness after all this fug at the University, too. Suggestions will be welcome.

        Yours fraternally,
        The Buzzwhacker

[*A sketch of four persons writing an examination while a gowned figure invigilating appears at the bottom of the page.*]

---

[1] Henley House School in Kilburn where he had been teaching since January. A. A. Milne, son of the proprietor, was one of Wells's students, and it was here he met Alfred Harmsworth, later Lord Northcliffe, who was a former student of the school.

[2] The name of the house and village in Sussex where Wells's father and brother were living. His mother was still at Up Park.

THE LETTERS: 1880-1903

108. To Fred Wells

Illinois, ALS

46 Fitzroy Rd, N.W. August 7th, 89

Dear Fred, [*small sketch of Wells*]

All the fug of that exam is over. Your brother has been measured for a holiday suit (see above)[1] has purchased a pink sport 2/11 shirt, a straw hat, & is now about to seek fastnesses of Whitstable in company with Aunt Mary & Isabel. Address, therefore, <u>until the 24th</u>
>Black Cottage
>Swalecliffe
>Whitstable, Kent.

The results of that exam was second place in Honours Zoology for your brother.
>Write to me some day, & believe me
>>With best wishes,
>>Your Affte Brer.
>>H.G. Wells

*<u>P.S. Did you get your dress suit all right?</u>
N.B. Shall we get a glimpse of you at these holidays? Look out for University lists in papers.

---

[1] The reference is to the sketch in which Wells is modelling the new suit.

109. To Fred Wells

Illinois, ANS

46 Fitzroy Rd. N.W. [August 1889?]

Dear Fred,

Just a little book, which I hope will please you, and my very best wishes for a long & prosperous life. I am sorry it comes late but I have been

away from all decent bookshops until now. Better late than never. Keep your head clear & your body active, believe on your brother, & happiness to yours.
Fraternally yours,
The Busswhacker

110. To Sarah Wells

Illinois, ALS

46 Fitzroy Street
Regents Park, N.W. <u>August 7th 89</u>

[At the top of the page is a small figure, dressed in cap and gown, administering a spanking with a besom to a person lying on his lap. It has a caption, 'Labore est Honori'.]

Dear Mammie:

It is all over, your son are past that exam, & have got the second place, Honours in Zoology in addition to that pass. There is one more exam and then your son will be a Batchelor of Science of the Imperial University of the British People. Your son is at present packing up his one other shirt & his best hat & collar to go to Whitstable with Aunt & Isabel. He will be there until Aug 24th. & soon after that he hopes to run down to Nye Woods for a week or two before the toils of the Christmas term begin. His address until the 24th will be,
   Black Cottage, Swalecliffe, nr Whitstable, Kent.

[Just over three lines have been blacked out, by a later censor. Some of the words are barely decipherable, and the sentences may refer to Joseph Wells's drinking problem.]

Have you heard from Fred lately? What is the date of his birthday? Give my Kind remembrances about promiscuously & with love from all of us.
   Believe me, your most affte son,
         Bertie

Look out for University list in paper.

If you want to tell people about that - it is a very good thing indeed - say
>Second in Honours in the Intermediate Examination in Science.

At Cambridge they call the Intermediate "Junior Tripos" or simply "Tripos".

I have one more exam for a degree.

The degree I shall have is
>Batchelor of Science
>written thus; B.Sc. (London)

It is equal to an Oxford or Cambridge M.A.

111. To Elizabeth Healey

Texas, ALS

46 Fitzroy Rd. N.W.　　　　　　　　　　　　　　August or thereabouts '79[1]

Dear Miss Healey,

　　　The humble apprehensionion grows stronger each day that your unworthy correspondent has met with his deserts, that henceforth - The thought is really a dreadful one, he writes in fear & trembling, praying so far as he is capable that it is the pressure of exams, the fog, the rain, the frost, anything but <u>that</u>, which causes your silence. Write only to say that the merciful hypothesis is right, and

>[*six gambolling stick figures at the bottom of the page*]

>Otherwise

>[*five mourning figures at a crossroad near a marker*]

Cousin Isabel too wants to hear of you, the more so as on the 18th there is Student's Soiree and she would go to meet you, but will hear of no other attraction.
　　<u>Ars longa vita brevis</u> as Plato says: do write.
>　　Believing me,
>　　　　Faithfully yours,
>　　　　　　H.G. Wells

---
[1] Clearly a joke for '89

112. To A. T. Simmons

Illinois, ALS

46 Fitzroy Rd. N.W.   September 18th '89

Dear old Beamish,

I am quite pained to hear of your respectable self suffering from blue devils & loneliness by the shores of the Drieed-up the sea.[1] Look not upon the bacco while it is red, or even golden; shun it; it is company indeed, but company like the mermaid that will drag you down into the unspeakable blue & destroy you. How much do you weigh now? Turn neither to the right or to the left but remember always you are a pilgrim after ponderosity, a seeker of sebaciousness, a feeler after fat, an anxious awaitever of adiposity, and above all things, cheer up! The B. Sc. awaits you & you will sink profoundly in my opinion if you do not wipe off a first in Physics & Chemistry. (This statement subject to the interposition of Providence of course) On second thought, perhaps I will not cut you <u>dead</u> if you get a second Honours in Chemistry. But you <u>must</u> try both - It will be absurd if you don't. You don't risk your degree, going in for honours, remember - vide Regulations. Start going over the d——d old Syllabus now in an ample way, making notes, & not bothering about remembering details just yet. That is what I am doing now. My selection of subjects will disgust you. Mental & Moral, Zoology, & Geology - & I am resolute - It won't last beyond Xmas though - to bag honours in all three. They are my three best subjects & the competition is really not heavy. I find I have done most of the psychology & a good deal of the Logic required for the pass, already in a discursive way, so that I am ever so much stronger than I dreamt I was in the M & M, before I looked the subject up. The stuff, you know, comes on again for the Teachers' Diploma of L. Univ. & also for the Fellowship of the C. Preceptors,[2] which is really not a bad thing to get. Besides - this is confidential - there is so much humbug in M & M Science that I believe it will be particularly easy for me with my special gifts in that direction, to collar the D. Sc. A thesis on the Influence of Evolutionary Hypothesis in Religious Thought, or the teachings of Dalai Lama, is decidedly inexpensive compared with one on a new theory of Crystal Structure or the physical condition of super heated liquids - one is so many days in the B. Museum & so much ink & paper; the other means a laboratory & material in gaudy profusion.

When you write during the next year don't forget to mention the exam each time - I want sadly keeping up to the work. I find it stimulating to speculate who out of Tate, Hewitt, Simmonds, P.L. Grey, & little Georgie will collar most Distinction. Arise O Simmings & be strong! Buckle on thine armour!

I mourn old Burton as one dead, Swallowed up by a wife and a situation among lowly souls. The corpse or sarcophagus Burton came to London with his proprietor a few weeks ago. They trotted to all the sights, Tower of London, Windsor Castle, Happy Hampton, & so forth. They did the heavy swells in some hotel & dropped in on the unfortunate Sirrie Rowe twice during their visit, for ceremonial calls of about an hours duration. She had been looking forward to their visit all the summer & hardly felt that she had seen enough of them. The fact of it is, that fool hasn't an introspective grain of independent soul in him. He follows the inspiration of his nearest influence, & all he deserves is his life sentence with that obese country girl, who naturally feels antagonism in anything more refined than herself. They are both getting very fat, & affecr the style of important people in the potteries. Oh God! Almighty God! & this was the Burton who longed for things spiritual, who hungered, I verily believe, after righteousness! Simmons, my son, we male brutes [*half a dozen blacked out words*] are utterly lost if we attempt to be a weaker wessels prophet.- Our only safety is in charming someone whom we can imagine at all events, to be something infinitely better than ourselves, & constituting ourselves the reverential guardians of the shrine. Get a girl who has to be lived up to, is the counsel of yours in God.

The Hoary Sage,
H.G. Wells

---

[1] Where this is located is not known.

[2] The College of Preceptors set standard examinations and certified teachers.

113. To A. T. Simmons

Illinois, ALS

46 Fitroy Rd, N.W.   Sep. 24th, 89

Dear old Image,

It is easy to infer from the last lengthy epistle that you find a weight of spare time on your hands. It is an ill wind that blows noone good, & so I get the benefit in readable letters. So also, it would seem, has the fallen Burton.

And he wrote you a very affectionate letter in reply, but subsequently neglected the correspondence. More or less connected with that is the tone of the second sheet of yours to me. You are resorting to that heresy about the duplicate nature of the beast man. You yearn for <u>moral</u> not <u>mental</u> development [&] want to be a <u>sincere</u> man rather than a <u>clever</u> one, feel that even a comfortable post & duties faithfully discharged without the element of exalted sentiment means to a large extent a life wasted & so forth.

My dear old chappie, man isn't a double barrelled gun, so that you can let out with one half of him & not the other! If you depreciate (a) the intellectual, & (b) worldly activity, you pave the way for (a) well meaning & quite mischeivous actions or (b) sentimental & unconscious selfishness. In other words, perfect sincerity without wisdom or toil is as foolish a thing as salvation by faith. There is no doubt as to the sincerity of a cabbage, it is as perfect as its freedom from sin. Knowledge, the power of matured resolution, a store of energy; these make men glorious souls if you will read your prophetic Carlyle aright. That sputter of '<u>sincerity</u>' '<u>a fixed faith</u>' '<u>honest sincere men - not clever</u>' is not our prophets teaching. It is a kind of Burtonian - little Bethel - gloss on his writings. It means fluctuating round a formula, & saying you are immovable, it means prevarication & convenient conventionality, posing[?] as truthfulness, selfish isolation pretending to be moral exclusiveness, foolish following of hastily assumed "principles." You can not be truly sincere by resolution & self government. Sincerity is essentially internal harmony. I thank God, Simmonds, if you find yourself not as many men are, a half hearted compromise of godliness, self deception & deliberate humbug. Sincerity is a gift. - All the rest depends on your wisdom & energy, whether your sincerity be a barren stick or no. Become efficient, become powerful to the limit of your possibilities, & then do your best to shape the world in your hands to the form your heart desires.

There are two deadly sins. Vanity & meanness - shun these more than adultery, murder or parricide. Make your brain & body a cunning instrument in the hand of your will, and dissociate your mind from sympathy with the weapon. Disabuse yourself of the illusion of identity, associate yourself with the great humanity of making, teaching, conquering the dead world. Be an enthusiast devoid of sentiment, a dumb prophet like Moses, a materialist in earnest. This is the true gospel of

       Faithfully your friend
       H.G. Wells

(N.B.) You will probably jeer but I am going in for the Excellent distinction of
    L.C.P.

Licentiate of the College of Preceptors this Xmas. It is a little sought thing involving very sound exams in English Subjects, Theory & Practice of Teaching (i.e., Mental & Moral), Mathematics (up to Analytical Conics) & Nat. Sci. The two latter well up to the Int. B. Sci. it appears to me.

114. To Sarah Wells

Illinois, ALS

46 Fitzroy Road, N.W   Oct. 14th 89.

Dear Mother,

I hope you will excuse my not replying at once to your letter. I think it was mean of me to let the time slip by, but really I have been very busy with different odd jobs in my spare time, doing some maps for Mr. Milne, cramming for an exam at Xmas, & so on, and one is not always in the mood to sit down & write a letter worth reading. Poor little Mummie! I hope before many more of your birthdays go by, we may see you in a cozy little home of your own & shabby, scandal loving Up Park left to congenial souls. What a tawdry mess of dull-brained, spiteful, useless people it is, to be sure, that we four louts have left you among, to have all your fine feelings wounded everlastingly! Sometimes, dearest Mother, I think of you so dolefully and remorsefully that I have to fall to abusing the governor to keep my spirits up. Well, well, there is a little vial of wrath for his portly indolence a filling, that will be administered if he isn't careful. I wish I could write you a letter fuller of comfort than this. For want of a better subject I have to fall to talking about myself. I prosper now like a green bay tree. I have been weighed and had my muscle prowess tested again & I find I am a pound heavier & my grip of the hand twenty two pounds more than it was when I had it measured in June. That means a great deal to me, for it is the assurance that I am entirely free from any thing of the "<u>wasting</u>" description, of which I was not <u>quite</u> sure before. And my position as a teacher is improving steadily. Dear Mother, I wish I could tell you how much I am anxious to help you on in your many trying experiences. I often think how I have hurt you by hastiness & of the many brutal things I have done to you, cross letters written & feelings disregarded. Really, I am very sorry for these, I grieve over cross letters I have too often written you perhaps more than you think. Sometimes it seems to me that I may have lost some of your affection by these things, & by what you may have thought unsympathetic coldness — you know I never was given to demonstrations of affection. Do let me now assure you of my respect & tenderness for your dear devoted life, & do not forget it if any time you are in trouble. I know now, far better than I did in the old days, how the sense of one being to whom our sorrow is sorrow helps us against the heavy trivialities that sometimes almost bear us down. So that I want you to read this subscription to my letter not as a usual formality but as a truth, really believe me.

                Your most loving son
                      Bertie
Isabel & Aunt Mary send their love.

115. To A. T. Simmons

Illinois, ALS

46 Fitzroy Rd, N.W.   Octr. 17th, 89

Dear old ATS,

      Concerning Ridges,[1] who writes to me evidently under the impression that at any cost he <u>must</u> be jocular with me, what shall I do? Things are thus; I can use Jennings's[2] rooms at any time - the poor old chap has gone off on a sea voyage, do you know, & I have been spending evenings with him lately & getting even intimate & affectionate with him before he started - but I am rather engaged for Xmas. I am going in for L.C.P. and that will take all my Xmas holidays up to Jan. 5th, but I think I am quite free at Easter & our school will not probably keep in vacation at Xmas until the 14th or 15th. Perhaps it would be best to do it by the week. The best thing I could do is leave it all to your friendly mediation, I know you will do better for me than myself. You know Ridges, what he <u>can</u> pay & what he cannot, you know me, & all about it. What do you say to taking him every morning from 10 to 1 for five days for a guinea? I would do that if he is a deserving case, & your friend really. I could do the special types with him in that way in 20 lessons or less leaving him the Lab for the afternoon to work out the demonstrations more fully by himself. If he is a chap who is really hard up & trying I would do him for much less, for I have a keen sympathy for the struggling man. On the other hand if he is raking in about £50 or £60 res., he ought to pay more. I leave myself unreservedly in your hands, only remember I cannot spend more than 3 hours a day in my holiday times; that is the important point.

Do you know how I flourish? when I wrote before I don't think I had been over to that anthropometrics place again. I weigh 114¼ as against 113½ last June. grip *78* as against 66, & blow 202 as against 208 - an insignificant difference, this latter, for the chap says a cold will produce a fall of as much as 30; & I had a cold.

The B.Sc. will be on the shelf till after Xmas. I am swotting just now, at Todhunter's Analytics & Algebra - punctually[?] I have got into pole & polar & have dabbled in Quanternious[?] - moreover the Mental & Moral goes on well. & I have done a lot of Gogerfree & History & Eng.Lang. & Lit, which things are required for the L.C.P. But geology & zoology are forgotten things.

How goes it with you? That foreign class you go to I hope breaks in on the monotony of your days. Wire 'em! Remember Grey & the glory of Honours.

        & believe me
          Always
A foolish, vain, & erratic being,
    but most sincerely yours,
        H.G. Wells

Ridges addresses me as T.D. Wells,
                      46 Fitzroy Rd.
                           S.W.

Will you damn him for me?

---

[1] Apparently a college friend, who was seeking special tuition, but who is unknown today.
[2] Jennings was another college friend.

116. To A. M. Davies

Illinois, ALS

12 Fitzroy Rd.   [late 1889?]

Dear Davies,

If you can drop in tonight we shall be pleased to see you. Rowe will be here, & we shall probably organize a rubber of the sublime game.[1]
Yours reverentially,
H.G. Wells

[A series of small 'picshuas' adorns the bottom of the single page letter. It is labelled 'theory of the degradation of an Octingzoon'. A tree stump turns into a human, by taking its hands from his pocket. The caption reads, 'Takes his hands out of his pockets & Eureka'. Beneath the sketches is written, 'In support of which theory witness the vestiges of the coelenterate mouth of the top of head of the human infant'.]

---

[1] Probably whist

117. To A. T. Simmons

Illinois, ALS

46 Fitzroy Rd NW   [late October 1889]

Dear Simmonds,

Make any bargain you like with whatshisname. The terms you name would be quite satisfactory - he, I suppose, fetching along instruments & buying the beasts. Only remember there is to be only one week at Xmas beginning <u>after the 4th</u> on account of the L.C.P.

I am very sorry to say Jennings is so ill as to have to leave Kensington & take a voyage to Australia. I am getting up an address & it will come along to you in due course for your subscription & shilling. It will greatly strengthen his position at the Birkbeck, now in some peril.

Things jog on. I grind at various subjects, mainly just now, at Mathematics

& Mental & Moral. Logic is more reasonable than I expected. I am getting quite interested with the Higher Algebra & Trigonometry & really think of substituting that for Geology. I have dipped into calculus & put off anything but the formidable thing I expected. The Augustan Age, the great Literary Period, seems over.

Yours, a pompous failure
H.G. Wells

118. To Elizabeth Healey

Texas, ALS

46 Fitzroy Rd, N.W. Sunday, Novr 16, '89

Dear Miss Healey,

Vile east winds, creaking wheezing lungs (I can hear the things work & gurgle like the pumps of a sinking ship), the drying up of my brain, an incubus of puerile facts, accumulated for a useless examination; this much & more also is my excuse for not writing before. How can one turn out any kind of letter; even the savage kind, with one's own littleness & death as dominant facts in one's mind? But now I have been nursed back into a kind of phosphorescent brightness of soul again, iodine, paregoric, & strychnine have made me (on paper) a man again, and I write.

I have verged closely on your world during the interval though. You said in your last letter that you were going to the Photographic Society Exhibition, & we, having some tickets, went there with a hope of seeing you. My cousin declares that she saw you once by a fitful flash of limelight,[1] during that outbreak of photographic meteors, but you must have fled before the display was over. Last Sunday I went to South Place to sign a certain declaration addressed to Jennings, & found myself at last, hot but happy, listening to four energetic persons with fiddles, & seated some two seats from your respected father.[2] But he was rapt in the music & escaped my respectful salutation. And today, he, being short-sighted, almost trod upon me as I stood in the refreshment room at S. Kensington. In the refreshment room, too, I met Lanchester, you remember him? a conspicuously dirty person, even for S. Kensington, & formally attached to Hewitt.[3]

My mind is exercised at present in drafting a thesis on Froebel[4] for the L.C.

P. I find it difficult however to refrain from sneering at that eminent person & more so, at his biography /ess? or ix?/ & feminine devotees; most so at our none too respectable profession. But really the cant of Educationalism[5] is so very thin, that there is little choice for a topic. And Froebel did at least invent "bricks," even if the Baroness von Mareuholz Bulow <u>does</u> claim that he taught little children through nature (with a big N) to know God & based his everyday work on German metaphysics.

Jennings went for New Zealand on the 14th.

Apologizing, on behalf of the weather, for a dull & disappointing letter, & enclosing Isabel's love.

> Believe me,
> Very faithfully yours,
> H.G. Wells

---

[1] Here, I believe, he is referring to the flashes of primitive cameras. However, the phrase was also used in theatres to indicate a greenish spotlight, and the usage, and the meaning of being centre stage persists.

[2] Healey's father was a professor at Imperial College.

[3] Lanchester and Hewitt are unknown.

[4] Friedrich Froebel (1782–1852) was a German educationist. He was influenced by Johann Pestalozzi (1746–1827) a Swiss educationist. Froebel followed the teaching of Rousseau, urging 'natural' techniques with children. He wrote *How Gertrude Teaches Her Children*, a book on Pestalozzi which was the subject of a Wells essay. Froebel carried these ideas into 'instructive play' for children and created the first kindergarten in 1836.

[5] Wells's 'sneer' at the vapid nature of much educational theory

119. To A. T. Simmons

Illinois, ALS

46 Fitzroy Rd, N.W.   Decr. 4th, 89.

Dear old Beamish,

I am sorry for my silence, but really, thank God, there is so little to write about, the world goes so mildly - it is like riding a cow - that you have lost nothing & I have gained a postage stamp and otherwise there is no harm done at all. The postage stamp came in useful too. I asked for a rise & got £10, negociated for less time, & gave notice, went to the agents, interviewed a man or so, wrote a letter or two, got sick at the prospect of having to leave London, & was reconciled, & we are going on for another year & mean to be so happy, me & the little eminent educator at Kilburn. Work goes on moderately for the B.Sc. I am working four subjects because I cannot decide between mathematics and geology, but belikes it will be the latter because of the factor of time. Beyond myself I know of no interesting thing to speak of. The L.C.P. seems a fairly safe thing for Xmas. I am as ready for it as for any exam I ever sat for. Davies is going in for Matric. & we have worked each other up in Dates, Etymologies, & geographical niceties to an extraordinary pitch; & I feel as much at home on the focus of a parabola as if I had been born there. Well, I have written enough to show that I love thee still, & life is short. Tell me whether we may see anything of you about Xmas & accept my blessing.

Believing me always,
yours,
A shrivelled ambition
That bust frag.
Wells.

120. To Elizabeth Healey

Texas, ALS

46 Fitzroy Rd., N.W. January 24, 1890

Dear Miss Healey,

There was cutting injustice in that of yours; you promised a monograph on Birmingham, you know you did! You went down to Birmingham "to see men and things" (a phrase not my own & which I consider slightly wanting in gallantry). You were amused, you reveled (?) ll (?) — old friends were forgotten, solemn & solemnly anticipated promises were discarded, the envelope of jeer never came, but, instead, this crowning wrong. So that as I write now a manly sorrow weighs me down - you will notice it more particularly in the drooping of the "g's" - and I might for all the mirth that is in me be that eminent young scientist, Fowler.[1] But why dwell on the horrible picture of my grief? With an affectation of carelessness I pass to indifferent things.

Do you, I would really like you to confide fully, believe you have a soul? is it immortal? state briefly how you came by it and your general ideas as to its nature & destiny; are you it, or is it an amplification of you? and so on.

Psychological research having failed to put up any adequate ghosts, I am trying to mark down an immortal soul but there is a prejudice on the parts of the people I hitherto have asked on the matter - they seem to suspect ridicule.

Or are you only a vortex of material atoms (I have sometimes suspected you of being a vortex of material atoms) or simply a recipient immaterial in a dependent organic relation? Any information you can afford will be greatly appreciated.

In the last few months I have noticed

Davies has just been in for an hour or so & I really cannot say for certain what it is I have noticed; I think however that it was that the Universe is being rapidly de-psyched for me. You know that the Poor Indian sees souls in trees and hears them in the Wind - Then as Man advances toward my level Souls cease in inanimate and finally in much animate things. Finally the whole Universe becomes a comical, but somewhat wearisome, puppet show, the motive strings visible enough but the upper part of the strings in some inexplicable manner shrouded.[2]

[*a drawing of a person sitting, labelled Death, with three marionettes next to Death*]

Please excuse frivolling. Really no <u>serious</u> topics to hand.
Faithfully yours
H.G. Wells

---

[1] Fowler is unknown.
[2] Virtually a complete draft of this letter also exists in Illinois, but it is minus the drawing.

121. To A. T. Simmons

Illinois, ALS

46 Fitzroy Rd, NW   Jany 25th, 90

Dear Simmiviges,

Sterility - not of affection but ideas. Barren as Sarah, as Arabia Petra, as Fisher's pate; yea even unto the desolation of a scientific monograph has my unproductiveness come. Would it interest you to hear of Olenus, Polypterus, or "my boys"? Nay! I know there is a limit, even to the patient attention of you, O Simmingues, my aramanthine[1] friend.

You <u>know</u> Ridges - why should I write of him? He <u>paid</u> before the lessons began. One thing occurs though! I am to go to Cambridge, <u>fare paid</u>, to interview Briggs[2] the autocrat of the U.- Corres. Class about doing some work for him in Biology. I do not think that it means opulence however and check all sanguine thoughts. Let us be meek!

No news has yet come to me of the L.C.P. - nor of anything or anybody. I am dry, Saharaesque, Atacamaitic, <u>Praeter ea Nihil</u> (Butter's spelling Bk). I revel now in a free Saturday & sometimes spasmodically work, but mostly I sleep. I have recently been sleeping about a good deal lately on sofas & chairs. I have been recently been inhaling camphor for catarrh. Do you prefer Brompton Specific to Kay's Comp^d Essence, Linseed? I rarely think. When I do it is on the human soul. Have you one about you? Talking of these things reminds me that I am to ask you to forward your photograph to G.W. Gregory, F.Z.S. F.G.S. Natl Hist M^m, Cromwell Rd, S.W. for transmission to Jennings. I have also promised to ask Hadleigh but think it would be nice if you did that for me. Also anybody else you can put up. Album is to be sent to him with sufficient mugs for a school treat, a normal school treat that is.

You wrote something in one of your letters about your persuasion as to a Rector Mundi & similar matters. Am all in the dark myself, & should like something conclusive.

Isabel sends a hearty slap on the back.

Faithfully yours,
Height 5' 7½",
Complexion fair, age
circa 24, name unknown.

[*a small sketch at the bottom of the second page depicting Wells in bed, with the title, '<u>Good Night</u>'*]

---

[1] Wells may mean adamantine. In any case the word indicates that Simmons is a steadfast friend.

[2] William Briggs was principal of the University Correspondence College in Cambridge. Wells was about to be made a member of staff.

122. To A. T. Simmons

Illinois, AL

Le Rue Fitzroie
Inte Primrose Rd. [1890]

Dear old Simmongs,

Life is hollow, death a rest after much unnecessary wearinness, the organic is a freak of the inorganic, & it can never be known. The thought of these things makes me sad, though I try to bear up & smile.

[little smiling head with tears]

Do not go to Chelsea. We want you here.
    Oh damn it! don't go to Chelsea.
A.T. Simmongs, if you go to Chelsea I —
    But what am I,
        Dust!
Again I am sad.
    Well, I will write again when I am not sad lest my sadness cleave unto thee.
    "Tralala!" I cry, my voice choking
    with tears.
        <u>Tralala</u>

[a very small figure at the extreme bottom left of the page]

123. To A. T. Simmons

Illinois, ALS

46 Fitzroy Rd. N.W. Feb 9th 90

Dear old Simmonds.

Among all the pleasant things that have been dropping in lately the pleasantest of all was your letter of congratulations. I <u>do</u> like being slapped on the back by my friends. It is just you & one or two others that made the great hard-up break bearable and now there are some inklings of success. It is the thought of sharing the glee of it with you that makes it really worth having & persevering after.

Gregory has asked me to get your photo & Hadley's[1] (I have lost his present address) for the album to go to Jennings. G.W. Gregory F.Z.S., F.G.S. British Museum of Nat. History. Cromwell Rd. S.W. is the man collecting the stuff for the album. Isabel is going to do my mug for you, soon - they are rather busy now -hence the delay. [2]

Do you know Holland[3] has the Berkeleinn[?] fellowship at Owens? Davies likewise gets a lift to 30/- Jennings is reported better. Clarke's in London but I have not seen him.

Reverting to the familiar & congenial theme, did I tell you that I am running the F.Z.S.?[4] On Monday I started the demonstrations at Booksellers Row. - Altogether about 35 students at the three classes - mostly assistant masters, some of considerable antiquity. Everything seemed to go all right. Fernando neglected them a bit at the end so that they are excessively grateful for any pains taken with them.

Plenty of work to do altogether - feel quite an active useful person. My boy gets top place Euclid at Coll. Preceptors Exam. Pace too high though - life a bubble - smash at any moment.

    Always yours,
     The good rather than great

Wells

P.S. Did I tell you saw Hewitt at Cambridge, big pipe - very jovial splendid chemical lab. Sent his love.

---

[1] Gregory and Hadley were fellow students and were creating a photographic album to be sent to their friend Jennings who had migrated to Australia.

[2] Isabel Wells was employed as a colour tinter by professional photographers.

[3] Holland was apparently another school friend. Owens College later became the University of Manchester.

[4] These are examinations prepared and administered by the Fellows of the Royal Zoological Society.

124. To Elizabeth Healey

Texas, ALS

46 Fitzroy Rd, N.W. Feb. 9th, 90

Dear Miss Healey,

Excuse the pause. I have been suffering keenly. With all due respect I cannot but think that Providence has been sky-larking in an undignified manner. I write with the weighty anticipation of some great calamity upon me. The good fortune that has come on lately cannot last - it cannot last. I know Providence too well.

The Correspondence College (vide large advertisements) started it. The highly certificated & honoured person who did their biology has gone to the Cape - a glittering apotheosis to Professorship. The college casting about for a worthy successor chose me. - poor leetle me! They even speak of paying me something for accepting this honour, so great is the generosity. The sudden accession to great wealth makes me giddy - I go about doing foolish things. A few days ago, for instance, I paid a person a bill.

Just after that Holland,[1] also gone now to the Gods, offered me some classes, nice healthy classes of his, all taught & ready & nothing to do but take the grant, but that I had to decline - practically the first & only time in my life when I ever declined a good thing.

And then the College of Preceptors' eggs hatched out, the plunder amounting to £20. I go sick & damp & cold all over when I think of the responsibility of this possession - whether it should go to found a new hospital or endow a teaching University for London or buy a new hat (which I want badly) is more than I can decide.

I am an L.C.P. I pray daily that I may be worthy of this great honour, ;and that I may bring no stain upon the noble college of which I am a university member. I know that heretofore there has been a certain levity, a low & most unbecoming levity in my words & acts. Perhaps the L.C.P. (under Providence) may send as ballast to the dangerous lightness of my disposition. For this especially, I pray.

> And praying,
> Remain
> always very faithfully yours
> H.G. Wells

[1] Holland, of whom nothing more is known, was an instructor at the Correspondence College when Wells became a member of the staff.

125. To Sarah Wells

Illinois, ALS

46 Fitzroy Rd NW Febr 25th, 90

Dearest Mother,

    Those snowdrops are still living, that you sent last week. It was so kind of you to think of us & send them to cheer up our room. I have also had Sunday newspapers from you & a Bromley one from Aunt Hannah from which it appears you have a most energetic & examinable son. I suppose the great Horace sent you that Midhurst one & composed its classic periods.

    You will like to hear that very probably I shall be elected a fellow of the Zoological Society (F.Z.S.) next March and also perhaps, a member of the College of Preceptors. There is just one more period of steady study - up to the Degree, Final, or Greats next October & then I hope to begin the great and momentous business of casting about for some abiding & remunerative resting place.

        With love from all,
           Believe me Dear Mother
             Your most affectionate Son
                Bertie

126. To A. T. Simmons

Illinois, ALS

46 Fitzroy Rd N.W. March 8 '90

Dear old Simmons,

    I am exceedingly glad to hear you are in for honours in three new[?] subjects. I have been raving about these damned dates myself for weeks, &

have decided to chuck Milne at Midsummer, but then Briggs has promised a minimum of 20 hours work per week (i.e. £2) before the exam &, with success, £165 a year after it. So that I don't feel now very much doubt about what to do in my own case but I am certainly in doubt about yours. You see at Southport you are, in your line, the boss man & have the monopoly in the district. In London the competition is heavy. You will have all the job of making yourself known & respected over again if you shift. Still, London is the place of unsuspected possibilities, and you <u>must</u> take honours for the degree - Even board school teachers can pass.

Then again in offering you my advice I suspect it, I am of a sanguine disposition & what I desire I can always manage to see advisable & possible & I <u>should</u> like to have you in London old chap immensely. With this warning I give the following council. Chuck Southport & commence enquiry for classes or a school in London <u>at once</u>. Don't be particular about pay if the work is light & good. A year on £80 would be well spent if you got a first in Physics. But I would not leave the crib question till December because most of the really nice things go in July & September, & at all events advertise at once & send to the agents.

The following chaps are in for the degree Watson, Grey, Rager, Hewitt, Hume, Hadleigh, Tate - a devil of a show altogether - Gregory, my rival taking all my subjects.

By the bye - A. M. Davies took 10th in Honours this time & is trying for the Zoology schol. I wish him luck & rather fancy he will get it.

With best wishes from Isabel.

Very faithfully yours,
H.G. Wells

127. To A. T. Simmons[1]

Illinois, ALS   Spring, 1890

<u>STOCK EXCHANGE INTELLIGENCE</u>
<u>GREAT BOOM IN WELLS</u>

We have to announce a surprising run upon the H.G. Wells limited ordinary and Debenture A in consequence of the
Entirely Unexpected Improvement
in the prospects of that concern. It began with the spontaneous gift of one half

holiday placed at the disposal of the Enterprise by J.V. Milne over & above the covenanted quantity. This was the first pattering of the approaching fall. The next thing was a
    Mysterious Communication
from a person of the name of Briggs requesting the honour of an interview at Cambridge & offering the company
    His Fare
there & back. In the meanwhile Holland offered to hand over two excellent classes in going order at Highbury, he having won a Berkeleian scholarship at Owens, and vague rumours came from the College of Preceptors of circumstances favourable to the company. It was on Saturday last that
    The Storm Burst.
Briggs turned out to be the University Correspondence College with examining work, vice Fernando who has passed to higher things. This week it has taken the shape of over £2 and promises to run to more. Then came, on Wednesday, the College of Preceptors results.
    Honours - Eighty Per Cent
on 15 papers out of twenty - establishing my pedagogic position & <u>all</u> the prizes I had dared to hope for, £20, in all, vide Educational Times. Compliments from Secretary, Enthusiasm in school, the town
    Painted Red
on this auspicious occasion. The only shadow in the prospect is the necessary resignation of those
    Highbury Classes
in view of the time required by the U.C.C.
  Rejoice with me O my Friend!
  Believe me
    Always most faithfully yours,
      H.G. Wells

---

[1] This letter may have been circulated to others as well as Simmons.

128. To Elizabeth Healey

Texas, ALS

46 Fitzroy Rd. N.W.   March 22nd, 90

Dear Miss Healey,

The grim demands of duty forbid it. On Thursday, the Thursday of that dazzling assembly, it is my bitter fate to slash the ruddy carrot & guide the gleaming razor over the shrinking paraffine - I have a class in Botany. While you thread the mazes of the crowd & exchange criticisms on startling strangers with all thy friends, I shall be moistening my sombre blackboard with bitter tears & explaining phellogism in a choking voice to my unsympathetic class. And my cousin did so want to go too.
But the warp of life is tears.
    Sadly & so lonely yours
    H.G. Wells

129. To Sarah Wells

Illinois, ALS

46 Fitzroy Rd N.W.
Vide Whittakers 275   Saturday [April 1890]

Dearest Mother,

Just a line to say "alls well" and to thank you for the flowers. Since I last wrote I have received the accompanying notice, which gives me the run of the Zoological gardens, museum & library & the imposing addition of F.Z.S. to my name.[1] I have also been elected a member of the College of Preceptors. These are not great things but they give my position in London and the teaching profession a much greater stability than it had before.

I shall not leave London at Easter, but early in May, if it is convenient to you. I should like to run down for a couple of nights & see the wild flowers. In the long vacation I shall be reading hard for the B.Sc. degree Exam^n. With love from all.
    Your very affte Son,
    Bertie

[1] Wells is referring to his formal election as a Fellow of the Zoological Society. The certificate (below) is in the Wells collection at the University of Illinois.

Zoological Society of London,

3, HANOVER SQUARE, LONDON, W.

March 20th 1890

Sir,

I beg leave to inform you that at a General Meeting of the Society, held this day, you were elected a Fellow of the ZOOLOGICAL SOCIETY OF LONDON.

I have the honour to be,

Your obedient Servant,

PHILIP LUTLEY SCLATER,

Secretary.

130. To Elizabeth Healey

Texas, ALS

46 Fitzroy Rd, N. W.
Regents Park April 20th, 1890

Dear Miss Healey,

I am a miserable, overworked, underfed, mean-spirited, indolent hack of a human. This at once explains my silence & enforces its pardon from your generous heart. I am a trite & vacant repetition of the foolish endless monotony of mortal generation - can you therefore condemn my letter?

Just now I am having a few holidays & getting through them somewhat sombrely. Human desires are manifold & endless, human possibilities small, we dare not do the thing we would, there are impassable bars to our being so that we smoulder all our days.

Why toil on in this vale of tears?
>Faithfully yours,
>>H.G. Wells

[A drawing of a penitent angel appears on the page opposite.]

131. To A. M. Davies

Illinois, ALS

46 Fitzroy Rd, NW   May 10th, 90

Dear Davies,

> Would it trouble you to drop in (on business of pressing import) Sunday.
>> Believe me
>>> A copepod (disguised)

[Under his name are five drawings showing people walking along first in rain and then sheathing their umbrellas.]

132. To Elizabeth Healey

Texas, ALS

46 Rue de Phrenzie du Roi   [late Spring 1890?]

Dear Miss Healey,

> Life is a weary alternation of work, mealtimes, & sleep beginning in darkness & ending in death. At present my pilgrimage is singularly deficient in any variation in the above triserial succession.
>> Awaiting better times.
>>> I am
>>>> Very faithfully yours,
>>>>> H.G. Wells

133. To the Editor, *Educational Times*[1]

PLS

[London]   [late May 1890]

Sir,

While admiring the hopefulness of the numerous registration schemes that have lately been advanced, there are two points upon which I feel tempted in the absence of any more authoritative voices to offer some remarks. The first of these, which was incidentally mentioned in Cheltenham, is the want of restriction on the employment of totally incompetent assistants. It was pointed out in that debate that an unqualified assistant would no longer be able to recover salary. Without wishing to question the great convenience and practical efficiency of this provision, based indubitably on a keen appreciation of the business relations of private schoolmasters, it may yet be asked if some further guarantee could not be required - as, for instance, making continuation on the register dependent on the maintenance of the proper staff. Otherwise, there is an apparent unfairness in inflicting a serious risk on the unqualified assistant, and none on the master who may decoy him from board, counter, or plough, by the promise of munificent pay.

The unconditional admission to the register of all unqualified persons now engaged in misleading the young of the middle classes, seems to be a condition common in all the schemes proposed. The idea is too strongly established to encourage opposition now. It is interesting, however, to point out that registration will be accepted as a satisfactory guarantee of a teacher's capacity in a very considerable section of the public. Many a dubious prospectus, at present, mainly dependent for its attractiveness upon a poetically treated view of Hevingly House, Mr. John Kidd's exotic diploma and the airy indication of visiting and foreign masters and a resident cow, will be endorsed by that solid-looking guarantee, "Registered Teacher". That will be the immediate and most actual fruit of the register.

To make qualifications within a definite time one - and not the only - condition of permanent registration, is not only perfectly reasonable, but would probably give many masters an enviable intellectual stimulus for which they would, I am sure, be ultimately very grateful indeed.

                                          Obediently yours,
                                          H.G. Wells

[1] This letter marks the first of Wells's formal statements on pedagogy. It appeared in the journal on 1 June 1890, p. 264; Wells was editor at the time.

134. To A. T. Simmons

Illinois, ALS

Fitzroy Rd NW   June 1st [1890]

Dear Old Image,

  I am dreadfully grieved to think of that postcard that came here with white lips & slender teeth & asked me why I had not written. I did write - a beautiful letter - but believe me the thing has gone astray. And I am ill, Simmons, old chap, worked out, in fact, dead, and it is hard to think ill & write harsh post cards to a dead person, one who creeps about in dread every moment lest some undertaker claim him as his lawful prey & pop him away & bury him. Moreover I was really going to write you again just before I died. But that bother of my dying upset me, I am no more ready to be buried than a little boy is to go to bed at seven o clock, & that together with Milne's work & Briggs his work & the Degree exam, make my mind such a painful litter - you can't fancy it. People are beginning to fancy though that there is a little wrong somewhere, I can see it from the way they look at me, and last Saturday I got quite mixed about the abdominal appendages of the skull of the sporophere conceptacle of Vancheria cuniculus & all my students seem to have stopped taking notes & some of them stay away - quite a lot of them in fact & for my own part I fail to see why they should all bring their sticks & umbrellas with them into the laboratory & it _was_ dishonest, say what you like, to collar my scalpels & razors. Why _do_ people object to being painted with osmic acid - it is dear enough I should think for the most fastidious taste? 12/- for quite a small bottleful!
  Oh Simmons Simmons! I did not mean to write anything but a pleasant sober letter to you, but my own little troubles will creep in somehow. We shall both be so glad to see you when you come to London & I mean to ur worry you sometimes to take me for walks & rest my poor little overcrowded brain a bit. I have got so much work & worry & such a damnable cold in my head.
  Read this out loud

The apples were gone excepting two rotten
They hunted around; Master Tommy had gotten
    The auntie (a grieving)
    Because he'd been thieving
Obtained a small birch twig & leathered his [*last word blacked out*]
    Believe me
        Faithfully yours
        H.G. Wells
Not genuine without the signature.

135. To A. T. Simmons

Illinois, ALS

46 Fitzroy Rd. N.W.   June 4th, 90

Dear old Tommie,

    I am so sorry - so dreadfully sorry to have made you anxious about my mental health & prospects. It is really not quite so bad as it looked in my letter, it was Sunday & I had a bad cold, two things that always incline me to larking & I believe I wrote a letter after my supper beer in red ink & codded a little, only just a very little, about my poor little brain. It is not true that I have an illusion that I am a corpse any more than that I am a little teapot. - there is really not a grain of truth in the insinuation. Neither did I talk about - what was it? - the spherophyte of the Rabbit; and they have not hidden the razors, and they come regularly, & I paint no man's face with with osmic acid - why should I? No Simmons it was supper beer & rolling did it, & I am as sorry as ever I can be to have made you so sorry for me, believe me.
    Really I am not overworking <u>very</u> much. I am bowling occasionally at the Eton & Middlesex & draw crowds. They gather all around behind me - for safety. Really, Simmons, this is not lunacy (it strikes me the last sentence is a bit overcoloured & may make you anxious). What I mean to convey is that I play cricket sometimes, & I get other exercise as well. One has to be so very careful using hyperbole with elderly (but nervous) people.
    You won't mind my being a little amused, will you Daddie? But really to

write such an extreme unction kind of letter to a young fellow of my exuberant width & weight (8 stone 5 lbs sir!) - but then the red letter! I must be careful.
Benediction to best of friends,
Faithfully yours,
H.G. Wells

136. To Fred Wells

Illinois, ALS

College of Preceptors
Bloomsbury Square, W.C.   July 5th, 1890[1]

Dear old Fred,

Just a line to mention the fact that you have a brother in London to whom your memory is a precious possession and wild flowers very acceptable. Dog daisies, dandelions, violets, in fact anything in that way, the meanest flower that blows - a LARGE BOX.

I hope you keep healthy and happy. I am overworked of course, but my appetite is still unimpaired and while that lasts, I will keep happy.
"Our jokes are little but our hearts are great."
Tennyson
Believe me,
Very respectfully yours,
Bertie

[on opposite page, with a drawing]:

What is this? Why do the people in the tram car shrink from his presence? Why, in this hot weather sit in a heap together? Can it be — Satan? Or the Hangman? Or the Whitechapel Murder (er)? NO — it is none of these things. It is simply a young biological demonstrator who has been dissecting with a large class that particular form of life known as the Dog Fish (scylla canicula). HE STINKS.

---

[1] Also appears in *ExA*, ch. 6 §7. The flowers were for botany teaching at Henley House School.

137. To Fred Wells

Illinois, ANS

46 Fitzroy Rd, NW   Aug 16th [1890]

Dear Fred,   [*a caricature of a man walking*]

Isabel went to Blandford this morning. Plenty of room if you care to come. Do as you like, of course. I will test your mind vigorously if you care to come.
   Yours,
     The Buzzwhacker

Love to <u>Ma</u>

138. To A. T. Simmons

Illinois, ALS

46 Fitzroy Rd. N.W.

The Abysm   [perhaps August 1890]

Dear Tommie,

I think you do the wise thing. It ought to be a comfortable step, I think, & that young man Hayden[1] is the joint author of the well reviewed Latin composition book, Briggs pub. Why not go in for Paedogick seriously. I believe it will be the most paying line for you - science in teaching & all that Wolverhampton [?] is a place that will double your salary with science teaching.
  I am in hell. Why, I don't know. ? indigestion. Have never had anything like it before.
I am rotting about with scraps of work.
Have you seen J of Ed? W.S. article therein & a "par" from a distinguished pen. Problem,which is it? He has taken another little paper, but says nothing of pay. The first review in Ed. Times on Seeley's book is me. What do you think of it? Nothing else. Globe has rejected an essay which I send you with a

vague idea of your having better luck? Anti-Jacobins or the Saturday Review or shall I rewrite it?[2]

I am really & undeniably in Hell.

      Yours (damned)
      H.G. Wells

---

[1] Hayden was an instructor in the Correspondence College.
[2] None of these reviews and articles have been traceable as at the time of writing (28 September 1996).

139. To Fred Wells

Illinois, ALS

46 Fitzroy Rd.
N.W.   [December 1890?]

Dear Fred.

 We have been thinking of sending Mater a Xmas present of some gloves and we thought you might know her size. If so will you let us have it.

Will the death of Mrs Saunders[1] alter your Christmas plans at all? The mater wrote & said there would be no festivities & that she thought it would be dreadfully dull for you - as no doubt it will be. You know that we should only be too glad to see you here. I have some idea of getting a room in the road for you & Frank for the Xmas days so that I should be glad to hear some from you about it.

You will be pleased to hear that I have taken

* I left this blank but although I have waited for days & send to the University every day the lists are not up yet. So I send now without it.

    With best wishes
     Trusting to hear from you soon & to see you at Xmas.
Believe me your very affectionate Brother,
        The Busswhacker

---

[1] Mrs Saunders is not known.

140. To Fred Wells

Illinois, ALS

Up Park [1888][1]

F.J. Wells is seen misbehaving himself & interrupting the dance. The dismay of his mother is apparent in the doorway. Mr. J. W——s has just had his favourite corn trodden on by one of the outside curiosities.

Dear Fred,

Just a few lines to let you know that I am still upholding the glorious name of Wells in these parts, and that I continue to remain
      Your veru affectiionate Brother
      Bertie

P.S. You must not think that I have forgotten you because I have not written, but just now we have so little in common in our pursuits that it is rather difficult to produce an interesting letter. You will doubtless be glad to hear that my prospects have improved a good deal since I saw you. At that time, I think I told you, I was painting diagrams & mounting specimens for Jennings my old chum in the zoological school. That has kept me going up to now but next

January I begin as a non resident assistant at a "highly respected" school at Kilburn. I get £60 a year, partial board (dinner & tea 5 days in the week) and certain Examination results. This is not very good, but there are the advantages of living at home in comfort, and of having plenty of spare time, to set against the relatively low pay. The latter consideration especially, since it will enable me to finish my degree of B.Sc. by next September twelvemonth & so command a salary of a hundred and fifty or two hundred. Isabel & myself are bringing the art of living on very little, very happily to a high state of perfection. Since you were here we have set ourselves seriously to making our room look bright & cosy , & I should really like you to see how jolly we are. When the roads are fit - and if the cold weather lasts that will be soon - you must come up & see us. Do you get a Saturday half holiday? We are just a little bit cranped for room by living in apartments, but still if you do not mind a shake-up in the drawing room, we shall always be pleased to accommodate you for a night. Do you get Monday (Christmas Eve) & are you coming through London to Up Park? If you want to put us in your plans for the Holidays do by all means. It is improbable that we shall have anyone to see us this Xmas except Rowe & his sister or Miss O'Leary, who are all three artistic jolly sorts of people, and so we could have our Xmas festivities on Sunday or Monday (Monday of course is the jolliest day) if there were a chance of seeing you on that day.
    With love from Aunt Mary, Isabel, & myself.
          believe me, dear Fred
              I am your very affectionate brother
                Bertie

Of course, if you intend dropping in on us you will let us know.

---

[1] There have been various attempts to date this letter. December 1888, 1889, and 1891 have all been suggested, and the possible reference to marriage to Isabel suggests Christmas 1891, but the references to his new position at Kilburn have now convinced me (at proof stage, too late to reposition it unfortunately) that the letter should be placed just before letter 97.

141. To Fred Wells

Illinois, ALS

46 Fitzroy Rd, NW   Tuesday [1889-90]

Dear Fred,

If it is fine on Sunday come by all means with your model mannered man but don't come if this atrocious weather continues until Sunday week. But if it is fine London is very pleasant now.

I was in bed last Saturday & Sunday with influenza & am all to pieces but hope to be all right with warmer weather now.
>Awaiting you
>Your very affte Br.
>Busswhacker

142 To Elizabeth Healey

Texas, ALS

[Address unknown]   [1890?]

[A sketch of Wells adorns the top of this letter.]

Dear Miss Healey,

We were at that museum Shindig & looked out for you. I thought I saw somebody in a dark red dress who might have been your sister - but I was not sure & her attention was occupied.

Miss Hall[1] is an owl. I always keep straps & things like that & material, like thought, is free.

If you want to do dogfish & need help I can come & superintend or you can come to my afternoon entertainments at any time you like. (They are on Mondays, Wednesdays & Fridays from 2 to 4) and dissect any type you feel worried about but then I should have to keep the class going as well as you, & it would be done "surreptitious".² I am always at your service for any material you want - or information for Intro Biology.

                Faithfully yours,
                H.G. Wells

---

[1] Who Miss Hall was and what this sentence means are unknown.
[2] Wells was offering demonstrations in dissection for the Briggs Tutorial College, located in Red Lion Square.

143. To A. T. Simmons

Illinois, ALS

University Correspondence College
Cambridge
46 Fitzroy Rd NW[Holograph]   [December 1890 or January 1891]

Dear old Tommy,

    Isabel went today & saw the lists again. She says that Hewitt is first in Chemistry (scholp.) and that there are no other names she knows on the list. The Physics examiners have driven a hellish plough this time.[1] Watson is top & there are two other first classes (Possibly Schott & ? ? Porter) <u>There are no seconds</u> & Hadley is first of the thirds & John T, bottom. When the Examiners chuck human beings about like this, there could be little mercy for your explosion on the practical morning or for any inadvertency. Hadley who only took Physics is the most unfortunate of any of our Normal School going up to the present - he & Woodhouse are the only ones not in first class honours of our gallant seven, & altogether there are only twenty first classes. "He hath exalted the humble & meek & numerous first class passes hath he sent Empty away." Trust in God, Tommy, & try to come to London. We had a leetle party on Saturday & lo! a voice came forth & spake saying " Would that Mr. Simmongs was here!" Whereat we wept.
                Believe me to be
                  Moving Godward.
                  H.G.W.

---

[1] The examiners had been especially strict in their awarding of marks.

144. To A. T. Simmons

Illinois, ALS

[Address unknown] [late 1890 - early 1891]

Dear Tommy,

You are reported to be loafing about Southampton. thus

[*a sketch of a lounger*]

So, I send you something to do.

Do read it through, there's a good chap. - Correct all the spelling - Mark any parts in pencil you don't like - jerk in any suggestions - hunt up the address of the Universal Review & what they say to contributors - Write any advice you can give - and in fact, sparkle up & do the correct thing by it <u>if you think there is anything in it</u>. - Then let me have it back & I will recopy it & send it on its wanderings. I wrote & offered a paper to Longmans & they consented to read one, & have it now. I pray night & morning I may never see that paper any more till I get a proof of it.[1] But it is <u>Too</u> much to hope.

Yours,
The Boojum[2]

---

[1] The paper is lost.
[2] Probably a reference to the final verse of Lewis Carrol's *Hunting of the Snark* (London: Macmillan, 1876), 'In the midst of the word he was trying to say, / In the midst of his laughter and glee, / He had softly and suddenly vanished away – / For the Snark *was* a Boojum, you see.'

145. To the Editor, *Educational Times*[1]

PLS

[London] [late December 1890]

Sir,

Every teacher who is interested in the welfare of his profession will be grateful to Mr. Quick for his polemical treatment of Herbert Spencer's <u>Education</u>. The student who is contemplating the servile assimilation of that work must almost inevitably be set thinking, even against his will. With this in view, it may possibly be simply the expression of Mr. Quick's own intentions that he is too severe upon his author, and, through him as a representative, on science.

In the first phase, there is an initial doubt, of which Mr. Spencer is not allowed the benefit, regarding the meaning of "education". Throughout he seems to use that word in the popular acceptance of "schooling" and this opinion is certified by the absence of any specialised and technical definition. This deficiency Mr. Quick counts as a blameworthy omission, and supplies by "a judicious supervision of the development of an organism", which is a continuously overexcessive simplification of the meaning in the vulgar tongue. These amplified meanings are a prominent feature of recent discussions. Mr. Ruskin inverts our "ideas" of "riches"; Mr. Buchanen[?] explains that most people called Christians are not, and most who are not are; while "we are all Socialist nowadays", is almost proverbial. In this case, education is stretched to cover the purchase of feeding bottles, and patent egg incubators are brought within the purview of pedagogies.

When we recognize the different standpoints taken by author and critic in this matter and remember that <u>Education</u> was written less for schoolmasters than for a public which identifies the word with "book-learning", the objection to the order of Mr. Spencer's topics loses much of its force.

Mr. Quick, with perfect justice, objects himself to an unjustifiable amplification of the term religion and science, whereby matter of fact is made to invade and blot out matters of faith. But, while it is not desired to defend the passage criticized, an immediate confusion of the two on the assertion that granted science and religion are true, science followed faithfully will lead through wider and wider causes to that incomprehensible Cause, unthinkable dualism, that wide realism, which science can never enter, of "world realities" <u>outside phenomena</u>, cannot possibly be defused by the realism of hallucination, as far as I can see; and Mr. Spencer's statement that art and religion are amenable to scientific analysis no more destroys their distinctness and value than does the discovery of hydrogen and oxygen the integrity and necessity of the ocean.

It is, however, certain that science can be made extremely interesting and comprehensible to the young, while the results of direct school teaching in religion and art are, at least, extremely dubious. This latter does very probably involve a loss of spontaneity, a precocious piety, sentiment, or amateurness, learnt by heart. It is this kind of instruction above all against which Mr. Quick's charge of giving the child what is good for the man should be directed. The gist of Mr. Quirk's argument in this matter, is, however, to make the existence of the essentially adult religious and aesthetic interests a reason for grudging science a fundamental share of the child's school course.

Throughout, the tone of Mr. Quick toward science is one which the meanest pretender to purely scientific teaching may very justly resent. He speaks of "all the sciences" as one might speak of such incoherent and heterogeneous things as the Latin classics, and complaining that Mr. Spencer wants them all taught, proceeds to speak of specialization and of the varying states of life to which men are called. Here again, while Mr. Spencer speaks of the educational groundwork of sound judgement and universally necessary knowledge, Mr. Quick points to adult needs, and he entirely ignores the intrinsic unity of science. The great doctrine of energy binds together the phenomena of physics, chemistry and biology into an inseparable whole. The teaching of physics, for instance, without unified mathematics and chemistry can only by a corruption be styled science teaching but Mr. Quick appears to be under the impression that one may take a science and teach it exactly as three or four discontinuous literary fragments are sometimes taught to a boy as literature.

Equally objection may be taken to Mr. Quick's opposition to "practical skill". Scientific knowledge, as the term is used in Education, is a more intimate knowledge of things and deeper appreciation of their inter-relationships. Whenever possible, as at the Universities, the method of instruction is by dealing with the things themselves - the knowledge is the knowledge of eye and ear and finger-tip. At the South Kensington Royal College of Sciences, the students spend four hours or more experimenting, surveying, dissecting, or analyzing, to every one spent in the lecture themselves.

Even the widest laws of science are not theories, but continuously verified facts. The student of science is, above all, the systematic student of tangible things, - the eminently practical person. The distinction between theory and practice is notoriously a provisonal one in favour of those unfortunates who are obliged to extract their knowledge laboriously from woodcuts and letterpress - fact at second hand. Yet Mr. Quick in the face of modern science teaching, misinterprets all that Mr. Spencer says of science in relation to man's callings, and charges him with "attributing success to a knowledge of theory in cases where it depends far more on practical skill". The science Mr. Quick contemplates evidently smells strongly of the midnight oil, while Herbert Spencer's is the science of spectroscope and scalpel, balance and slide-rule, the museum, the workshop and the open air. Few, I think, will disagree with Mr. Quick's unmistakable aversion to the speculative, hearsay science he has in view, but there are many who will fail to find in his remarks the quietus to the claims made by the science teacher for a generous increase of his share of the school time.

    I remain, Sir, obediently yours,
    H.G. Wells.

[1] This is a letter to the editor of *The Educational Times*, 1 January 1891, pp. 30–1, in which Wells comments on a recent essay by R. H. Quick on Herbert Spencer, which had appeared on 1 December 1890, pp. 523–6. Throughout the period from 1890 to 1895 Wells and others debated the possible future curricula, especially in the University of London which was in the process of being founded. The piece to which he is responding here was entitled 'On Herbert Spencer's Education', which originated as a talk given at the College of Preceptors meeting on 28 November 1890, at which Wells was present. Wells was, of course, the editor of the magazine, so the letter is a fiction to that extent.

146. To A. T. Simmons

Illinois, ANS

[Address unknown]   [February 1891]

Dear Tommy,

    I send you a draft of the paper we spoke of to show you I had not forgotten it - but I do not think it will do. It is too colloquial and too devoid of epigram. I will try another draft. I also send my paper on Retrogression with a letter to an editor & I would be glad if you would send it, if approved of, (with an envelope for return), to Cornhill or ? The Illlustrated ? or to any scientific magazine you think more suitable. It has been to Longmans. ?Unionist Review? ?Strand Magazine - I have not seen it. I shall burn the damned thing if it comes back again so you had better address it for return to yourself at Southampton - let me never hear of it again until it succeeds. Is the reference to the Fortnightly indiscriminate [*a few words missing because paper frayed*] I like your papers. You preach the true gospel. Have the Godly raged against you & the good imagined a vain [*illegible word*]. Keep me posted up in the controversy.

  W. Burton is giving public lecturess on pottery in the Burslem town hall with a mayor-person as chairman, Rowe tells me.

    Vita brevis.

I wrote to Fortnightly to say I could wait for printing[?] & said I had an idea for a paper on "The Universe Rigid", but I did not want to hurry matters but to accumulate ideas. Told him I might write about Easter. He says he will be pleased to read it whenever I find it opportune to send it - but I shall not forward it I think until the first one is published even if I write it by then. I shall introduce the universal diagram I think & other matters of current conversation.

                  Yours in God
                    H.G. Wells

147. To the Editor, *Cornhill Magazine*

Edinburgh, ALS

46 Fitzroy Rd. N.W.　　　　　　　　　　　　　　　　　　　　Thursday 4/2/91

Dear Sir,

I have written a short paper on "Zoological Retrogression" (a little under 3000 words) which is I think readable & amusing.[1] I have therefore avoided any moral though the human application of the scientific fact is kept in view. It is suggested that man is utterly degenerate & that there is considerable hope of his extinction by some coming Beast in the future, but the suggestion is made in a grave & decorous manner & by the way. The staples of the feast are seasquirts & mudfish. If you will do me the honour to read my paper I think you will find it likely to suit a cultivated taste. As I am quite unknown as a writer I may perhaps plead that I am young & have only just finished my university work with double honours (a first class in zoology) at the London B.Sc.

　　　　　　　　　　　　　Faithfully yours,
　　　　　　　　　　　　　H.G. Wells

---

[1] This paper, although rejected by the *Cornhill*, had a wide circulation. It first appeared in *The Living Age*, vol. 191 (10 October 1891), pp. 363–7; then in *Gentleman's Magazine*, vol. 271 (December, 1891), pp. 246–53, and, in an abbreviated form, under the title, 'Degeneration and Evolution,' in *Scientific American*, vol. 65 (10 October 1891), p. 228.

148. To the Editor, *Educational Times*[1]

PLS

[London]　　　　　　　　　　　　　　　　　　　　　　　　[end February 1891]

Sir, - Mr. Quick's reply to the somewhat disconnected remarks I made upon his paper, narrows our differences down to three matters, and contains a very definite statement of his position regarding them. As they are things of fairly wide interest, I will venture, with your permission, to continue this discussion, the more readily since I have found more to dissent from in Mr. Quick's reply than in his previously expressed opinion.

The first and least of the differences raised was the question of a definition.

I do not think I gave any ground for the charge of suggesting that Mr. Spencer would have us read "book learning" for "education"; I said "schooling", which is a very much wider thing. Still, if Mr. Quick prefers his own rendering and makes a point of adhering to it rigidly, there need be no objection if he will only tolerate a narrower use on the part of other people. But he read *Education* in the light of his own definition, and that is not following the indisputable maxim that "people who want to get at the truth cannot be too careful to understand one another". Under the circumstances, it is simply my duty to press him gently, but firmly, to take that egg incubator, in addition to the feeding bottle and the perambulator he has accepted, as a pedagogic property.

The next point at issue is of much greater importance. I am glad to hear that Mr. Quick does not consider the difference of theory and practice the difference of fact at second-hand and fact at first-hand, and that he intends by "the study of theory" (and, I presume, "science"), the study of "generalizations", because it brings us into agreement at the starting-point, at any rate. But the word "generalization", like most other of those treacherous tools we have to use to get at one another's thoughts, may convey several meanings. I can best illustrate my idea by an instance. One may see in Mr. Galton's Anthropometric Laboratory certain multiple photographs of students and others, obtained by superimposing individual portraits in such a way that a vague, foggy, collective face resulted; such a face would be an instance of a *blurred* generalization. In the same laboratory, on the same persons, certain definite facts of proportion and average of immediate value to the railway director, detective, doctor, artist, hatter, and ready-made tailor, had been ascertained, and were of the nature of *exact* generalization - they fitted all the cases. Now, if physical science, like the science of education, is yet in a stage of blurred generalization, I will admit all that Mr. Quick said against theory or science in relation to practice, but I hold that the generalizations of physical science are exact and immediately applicable. An enormous mass of human duties and actions are application of scientific generalizations, as Mr. Quick points out, and to me it is certainly not so obvious as it is to Mr. Quick that the more that a man knows about these the less skilfully can he employ them.

Of course, if Mr. Quick chose to assert that the laws of physical science *are* blurred generalizations, his position so far would be as good as mine, if it were not that he has already written, "we cannot value too highly the laws of science," and so, I take it, subscribed to their truthfulness. Either a scientific law is to be compared to a picture or photograph - a something *like* the phenomena represented, but getting away from them - or it is like the mirror of a laryngoscope that brings one nearer to the source of outer symptoms. The alternative is not to be decided in half-an-hour's thinking or by discussion;

the answer must arise from habits of thought - from the educational influence of a lifetime. There are authorities who find the maximum of truth, beauty and mental value in the Greek classics and who regard science as the fermenting soil from which spring such matters as Eiffel Towers, äerial advertisements and heterodoxy. To such minds the suggestion that art and literature are things of the market-place, and that science is the veil of the temple, appears absurd.[2] Curiously enough we owe it to Mr. Quick that the attention given to Froebel by educationalists has been largely increased, and Froebel before all things was the prophet of teaching, through perceptions of phenomena, and by implication and in fact, by direct statements, of the religiousness of science.

H.G. Wells

---

[1] Letter 146 was responded to by Quick courteously, but not completely dissociating himself from Wells, on 1 February 1891, p. 69, in 'The Limits of Science'. Wells then offered a final comment in the issue of 1 March 1891, pp. 154–5, entitled 'The Value of Science'.

[2] In these letters to the press Wells very clearly lays out his view of the sciences and the modern needs of education. Versions of these ideas recur throughout his writing. In a sense he is using them as a way of working out his own educational philosophy.

149. William Briggs to H. G. Wells

Illinois, TLS

University Correspondence College
Burlington House
Cambridge   15 June 1891

Dear Mr. Wells,

I am pushing on the negotiations with regard to your successor as briskly as possible and will then let you know definitely with regard to the correspondence work, but I need scarcely wait for that. I shall be only too pleased to accept the offer which you made, perhaps I may be able to improve it but cannot say definitely until I have arranged terms with your oral successor.

I trust that you will recover your health completely and unless the new man turns out to be your alter ego, I shall only be too happy to ask him to send in his resignation and take you back again as I have been more than satisfied with your work.

As you will be staying on as correspondence tutor I trust that I shall be able to accept your book and in fact the thing remains as you originally put it, namely that you will let me have the first refusal at £45.

The time you propose taking with the Matric. Botany lessons is quite satisfactory.
                    Yours faithfully,
                         W. Briggs[1]

---

[1] There appear to be no letters remaining from Wells to William Briggs, the proprietor of the Correspondence College where Wells taught briefly, and where he corrected papers at the time of his serious illness. Several survive from Briggs to Wells and merit inclusion because of their content.

150. To A. T. Simmons

Illinois, ALS

46 Fitzroy Rd N.W.
God Knows the date -
see envelope   [June 1891]

Dear Tommie,

       Just as though it was as sad as all that! I really did not mean to make you as funereal as your letter shows you.

Just see the enclosed letters. I declined Milne's of course, but is it not good, all the same?

I am going to do 12 hrs a week 44 weeks a year, for £60 for Briggs.

Did I tell you the editor of F[1] is going to use <u>Rediscovery</u> next month & has written me to come & see him about <u>Universe Rigid</u> (which has been printed) next Monday?

It is not so bad - it always was half expected.[2] Cheer up, & if there is an excursion <u>come</u> up & see me.
                    Yours a la Pope, Coleridge etc.
                         <u>THE</u> H.G. Wells
Please return Brigg's letter - and the other.

---

[1] *The Fortnightly Review* (Frank Harris) had just accepted his article, 'The Rediscovery of the Unique', vol. 56, (n.s. 50 in the new numbering system) (July 1891), pp. 106–11. This was his first breakthrough. For the other article mentioned see letter 155.

[2] Wells is referring to the fact that he had had a bad relapse, with some internal bleeding. It was

a serious blow to his life's hopes, as it seemed as though he had reached the top of the pile with his teaching and with his writing. The previous letter from Briggs is an acknowledgement that Wells has had his relapse and they were scaling back his work for the Correspondence College.

151. To Joseph Wells[1]

Illinois, ALS

46, Fitzroy Road, N.W. Monday, 15/6/91

Dear G.V.

I have sent you your glasses - they were done long ago but I could not forward them on account of my illness - they were forgotten in fact.

I had influenza about three weeks ago, and congestion of the right lung on the top of it. I have had to resign my classwork with Briggs, and so I am - now that I am a little stronger again - hunting around for work to do at home.

I wrote to Mother four or five days ago but she has not answered my letter.

It is no good going into the details of the disaster. It is a smash. Still [it] is not so impossible now as it would be if I did not have a degree. My thing is to come out in the next <u>Fortnightly</u>[2] and if they send me copies I will send one to you. The editor has written for me to call on him, about a second paper they have taken and perhaps there is something in that.

                Faithfully your son,
                    BERTIE

I have had to pay a substitute for all my classes.
Marriage postponed - for ever?

---

[1] Also appears in *ExA*, ch. 6 §7.
[2] 'Rediscovery of the Unique' (July, 1891), pp. 246–53. Frank Harris rejected the second article, 'The Universe Rigid', which is no longer extant, on the grounds that it was not comprehensible. According to recently discovered letters, printed in this volume, Wells withdrew the piece voluntarily, see letter 155.

152. To A. T. Simmons

Illinois, ALS

University Tutorial College
London, W.C.   July 6th, 1891

Dear old Tommie.

  How one can trespass on the kindness of an old friend! I am writing of damnation. Why have I not written? Because I am ill? Nay. Because I am in the shadows? Nay. Because I have forgotten you for awhile? Nay - that were impossible. The sun has been shining - The world has smiled green & therefore happy - little birds on the tree have twittered welcome to me, little flowers turned their faces to me & they hyptonized me with their glowing eyes. I have been under an hypnotic illusion - That I was Pan - the great Pan ([*illegible word*]) - <u>one</u> with the brown earth, the blue ever changing sky - the rich grass & the distant hillsides. How the devil can a landscape write a letter?

  You will infer from the address at the head of this letter that I am probably at Up Park - this view is correct. I have been thereabouts for 3 weeks but I go up on Thursday or Friday or Saturday to do a last week's work before the Exam. I thank God I am not as other Pulmonaries; I weigh 8 stone 8 lbs and against 8.4 a fortnight ago. & [?] 8 when you saw me. I cough not neither do I ache. For which, & for other mercies, let me thank GOD (& Collins)

        Your servant,
        H.G. W.

Howes has been trying to get me a special job at Oxford (museum) but E.R. Lankester says he is in treaty with another man, but promises to keep my name in mind. Have you seen any notices, good or bad of it.

[Also at the top of the page, where this post script is located, are the words, 'Cum mouton petite an dem top'. A rough translation, 'small sheep are grazing,' appears beside his description of the hillsides.]

153. To Elizabeth Healey

Texas, ALS

46 Fitzroy Rd, N.W. August 1st, 1891.

[sketch of Wells with 'a gigantic indolence' sitting on him at the top of paper]

Dear Miss Healey,

I grieve at your positive orders for a letter because as you see I am overwhelmed by a gigantic indolence. When I am not, when they pull him off & shake me & de-flatten me, then there will be much to do. There is my shattered future to contemplate.

[a sketch of a man looking at four building stones]

- it is to be reconstructed. I am really working very hard in this season of the dog days to open up a retreat before the dogs come.[1] I [am] willing to <u>think</u> numerous letters to you but I cannot write them because I really have no time. But you have plenty & with the inspiration of a new county & fresh people I expect something much more than small sheets of note paper writ large. It is more blessed to give than to receive.

& believe me,
Always very faithfully yours,
H.G. Wells

---

[1] Dog days are a period in August when Sirius, the dog star, is very noticeable in the sky. It is thought to be a period of warm, pleasant, gentle airs; a time for indolence and vacations.

154. To the Editor, *Educational Times*[1]

PLS

[London] [mid-August 1891]

Sir, - May I call your attention, and that of your readers, to a matter a little off the main line of school work - to the troubles of some of the science masters who prepare pupils for the College of Preceptors examinations? It has been repeated so often, that any one repeating it again must needs apologize in doing so, that examinations, for good or evil, are the preponderating influence in the determination of what shall and what shall not be actually taught in schools. Doubtless the fancies and prejudices of parents have their effect upon the prospectus and time-table; but the working schoolmaster knows full well that the edict of the examiners is universally considered as the final verdict upon his work, and, far more than anything, is the maker or destroyer of his prosperity. In thousands of schools, therefore, examinations guide the teaching, and the responsibility for the character of that teaching devolves upon examiners, who indirectly direct it. Undoubtedly, for instance, the want of insistence upon oral tests and retranslation into English, in the language teaching of the immediate past, has done much to confine such work to the easier exercise of simple translation, with a cram, when the examination approaches, of the accidence; and there are thousands, as a consequence, in the position of the writer, who can read French easily without being able to speak or understand a spoken word of it. In this matter the College has recently set an example in the foundation of an, at present, optional test of conversational ability. The College has also recently lightened the yoke of obligatory subjects, and these indications of a liberal spirit are an encouragement to those who imagine that room for improvement exists in other directions, and notably in the department of science.

The great objection made by many adverse critics of the claims of the science teacher is that much of what goes under the name of science is merely "information", and that of what Mr. Herbert Spencer himself would call the "unorganizable" kind. Now an unfortunate difference of opinion exists as to how far scientific facts are organizable, how far they can be built together into one coherent and independent structure. Those who have specialized along the scientific line assert a wonderful unity in diversity exists in their field, and belittle the harmonies and and allusions of literary study; and it certainly appears to the writer that the opinion of scientists in this question is of slightly greater value than that of literary men, for there are few scientific men so illiterate as not to be familiar with the beauties of some literary masterpieces, while there are many men on the classical side who know little or nothing of science. But leaving this wider question, I think that all teachers will be agreed that a subject that is so taught as to be merely an information accumulation, without any mental exercise except that of the memory, is of very little value, and should be mended or ended as part of the school curriculum.

Now, if we ask whether Natural History, and especially the branches of Zoology, Botany, and Geology, as the examination papers of the College of Preceptors determine and exhibit it taught, is anything more than an accumulation of information, I am afraid that our answer must be NO. And, in order to justify this statement, an examination paper in Zoology, set this last midsummer, may be called as a witness, and itself examined. The first Zoology paper has been selected, but the others have much the same character, and as the writer considers, faults.

VERTEBRATA
Elementary Section

1. Give a classification of the *Mammalia*, and indicate the differences of structure whereby the divisions you enumerate are distinguished.
2. Describe, and show by diagram., the circulation of blood in a Mammal and in a Fish respectively.
3. What are the *Rodentia* ? Why are they so called? Mention some that live in Britain.
4. Make a list of the chief kinds of lizards (*Laecertilia*), and state where they are to be found in a state of nature, and anything in particular that you know about them.
5. Give the proper names to the different kinds of Fish that are brought to market, and state whereabouts in the British seas and rivers they are severally caught.

ADVANCED SECTION

1. Classify the *Monkeys*, and point out in what aspects the *Chimpanzee*, *Ourang*, and *Gorilla* respectively present the nearest approach to human structure.
2. Enumerate *either* (i.) the freshwater crustacea of the British Isles; *or* (ii.) the Birds frequenting the rivers, marshes and coasts of these islands; and point out in either case the localities abounding with the species or kinds you mention.
3. In what respects do Birds differ in their organization from Mammals? What are the chief Orders and Families of Birds?
4. Give an account of the *Ophides. What are they?* What are their structural characteristics? What are the habits of different kinds, and where are they met with?
5. On the Outline Map of the World mark the areas where different kinds of crocodiles, of Bears, and of Sirenia and Cetacea are respectively known to exist.

Where praise is due it should be given, and the second question in the Elementary Section is certainly a good one; it demands a knowledge, and something more of a verbal knowledge, of wide and important facts; but here our praise must end. There are two fundamental objections to this paper: in the first place, over an immensely wide subject, containing endless departments complete in themselves and capable of independent study, there is apparently no choice of questions; and in the next place, it is a paper that directly encourages "cramming". If anyone had tabulated the classes, orders, families and genera of vertebrata, and given that and some thirty or forty definitions to a class of boys to learn by heart, and had drilled them a little with an atlas of blank maps, questions 1 and 2 (imperfectly), 3, 4 in the elementary, and 1 (in part) 2 (?) 3, 4, and 5 of the Advanced would have been done, and they might even have got a "special" or so; while the success of pupils familiar with the museum and zoological garden, and to whom the interdependence of structure and mode of life, and the bearing of systemic position and habit upon structure had really been rendered clear, would have been, to say the least, doubtful. It is difficult to imagine any explanation of the inclusion of "freshwater crustacea" in a vertebrate paper, that is not a little uncomplimentary to the examiner. Finally, attention may be called to the vagueness of Question 4 in the elementary -"*anything* ... you know!" and to the disproportionate difficulty of 5 in that section and 1 in the next. It seems to me that for a teacher to be very successful upon papers such as this, a gallop through a zoological miscellany, coupled with a cram such as I suggested above, would be the only possible course. Now this is the character of the College of Preceptors Natural History at present. Need it remain so?

There is one thing that can easily be done, and that is to give a wide choice of questions; at present, the country schoolmaster who has tried to show an animating and unifying soul in hedgerow, river bank, and moor, and the London teacher who has availed himself of his vast resources in museum and zoological collection, are equally "out of it."[2] The suppression of "classify", "enumerate", and "refer to their orders" from the papers will alone suppress the process of unintelligent list cramming. But there are wider possibilities in Zoology yet, and more sweeping changes to be suggested.

Almost alone among examining bodies the College of Preceptors ignores the "type" system of teaching biological science. The first great exponent of this method was Professor Huxley, and it is now the one recognized by the Cambridge and London Universities and at the Royal College of Science. Instead of a scramble over endless unmeaning names, ending in a vague, inaccurate, and often misleading knowledge, a few types are dissected, the dissections drawn, and comparisons instituted and homologies traced between them. This is really an intellectual and a manual training combined, it interests almost all boys and fascinates some, and it leaves a permanent effect in after life. The dissecting instruments need not cost 5s per head, and among the most instructive types are the rat, the sparrow, the frog, any fish, the cockroach, crayfish, worm and amoeba. But, the College of Preceptors, instead of promoting this kind of work, raises an obstacle in its examination papers. I do not by any means wish to suggest that the "type" system is the only one, but simply to point out that at present an indubitably excellent way of going to work is entirely disregarded, and thereby discouraged.

In view of all these things, it seems not unreasonable to ask that the College should reclassify its Natural History subjects, and offer some kind of syllabus for the guidance of teachers. No one could be more willing to confess incapacity than the writer, but with a view to provoking those who are abler to action, he ventures to suggest his own ideas - not, be it understood, as a standard, but as an irritant. Five papers are suggested, each carrying one hundred marks, and of which - to prevent schoolmasters giving disproportionate time to Natural History - no candidate should take more than two.

They are :-

(1) Vegetable physiology, as illustrated by such a type as the bean plant, and the compared structures of such types as the pine, the fern, the moss, and any common fungus and alga. (A science properly speaking.)

(2) General morphology of the flowering plant, and the study of the common British natural orders. (A training in observation and drawing for rather younger boys.)

(3) Comparative Anatomy of the animal types mentioned above.

(4) Descriptive Zoology, with especial reference to the relations of form and habit; classification and distribution. (For younger pupils.)

(5) Physical Geography and Geology, with a number of questions (of which only one must be done) in the stratigraphy of different selected districts defined by a syllabus. Questions on the names and horizons of fossils should not occur. Paleontology, requiring, as it does, for its proper comprehension, a sound and adanced knowledge of Zoology, and being largely a memory subject, can hardly come into the scheme of a well-planned school, where the mind is developed and the memory dulled with better things.

Trusting sincerely that my remarks may lead to some dissension, and eventually be of benefit, I remain, Sir, very obediently yours,

H.G. Wells

---

[1] At this period of his life Wells was mainly interested in teaching, and science teaching in particular. Writing to the editor of *The Educational Times*, he commented on these matters in his letter, headed 'School Zoology' which was printed in the issue of 1 September 1891, pp. 400–1.

Wells proposed, in this long letter, a complete reworking of the curriculum. Within the same year he wrote two textbooks to attempt to achieve this end. What is also interesting here is that he is offering a very early preview of what C. P. Snow after the Second World War would call the 'Two Cultures'.

[2] Wells had had practical experience in teaching school zoology in both the situations he describes. This letter is a penetrating criticism from within. The College of Preceptors, of which Wells was by this time an elected member, certified teachers and set standard school examinations.

155. To the Editor, *Fortnightly Review*

Texas, ALS[1]

46 Fitzroy Rd. NW   Sept. 5th, 91

Dear Sir,

    Some days ago I left a copy of '<u>The Chronic Argonauts</u>', a story you had very kindly promised to read, at Henrietta Street. I need scarcely say that whatever advice you can give me, for its disposal, will confer a great favour upon me. That other matter of an eviscerated paper called the <u>Universe Rigid</u>[2] I shall be only too grateful if you will forget; the idea I was trying to express has now been put in a far more effective way than I could ever have done by Professor Lodge at the British Assn.
               Believe me,
                    Very Sincerely yours,
                    H. G. Wells

---

[1] This letter exists in copy form at Illinois as well.
[2] The 'Universe Rigid' is the essay, or has the same title, as the one that is variously described as having being set in print, being rejected as 'incomprehensible' and in this letter, as having been withdrawn by Wells. This little mystery will remain as no trace of the paper remains.

156. To the Editor, *Cornhill Magazine*

Edinburgh, ALS

46 Fitzroy Rd N.W.   Sept. 13th '91.

Stamped Envelope Enclosed

Dear Sir,

    With this is a paper "On the Mental Condition of the Specialist" which I imagine might be of interest to the readers of the Cornhill Magazine.

    As I have only recently taken my degree & commenced to write, & am probably unknown to you I may mention that I have contributed to the Fortnightly (July), the Gentleman's Magazine (September), The Journal of Education (Aug & Sept) & other educational papers.

            I am Sir
                Very faithfully yours
                H.G. Wells

As the paper is Zoological I may say that I took first class honours in Zoology at the London B. Sc. & wrote on Zoological Retrogression in the Gentleman's Magazine.

157. To Elizabeth Healey

Texas, AL

[Address unknown]   [perhaps Sep 19 [?] 91
                                                       from blurred postmark]

[*a figure struggling up a very steep hill, 'onward and upward'*]

Dear Miss Healey,

    Any news is welcome. I have nothing to write about i.e., myself. I removed to 28 Fulham Road[1] in Putney, S.W. on Saturday next. What is our crime? Why are we not visited - called upon? Why do our buns harden their hearts & our tea stagnate? I proposed these questions, Miss Healey, with plaintive severity. What have we done?

[remainder of letter missing]

---

[1] A mistake for Haldon Road

158. To A. M. Davies

Illinois, ALS

28 Haldon Road
Wandsworth, SW   Tuesday [Autumn 1891]

[A sketch of two persons engrossed in a book adorns the top of the writing paper.]

Dear A.M.D.,

Many thanks for your charming present.[1]
It is fine stuff, that last part, is it not? Can you come over & see us on Saturday about 6 & have some tea. - There will be a Miss Hunter & a Miss Hodgkiss here - I don't know whether you know them? If you can come don't trouble to write.

                Yrs.
                    H.G.

---

[1] An attractive well bound copy of the novel *Peter Ibbetson* by George Du Maurier

159. To A. M. Davies

Illinois, APCS

[Address unknown]   2 October 1891[1]
[by postmark]

Dear Davies,

Have hunted about Edgware Rd & Praed St but disappointed to find nothing cheap. Rooms up this way range about 5/- & 6/- if you like to try on Sat. aft. (If so, call) i.e., With fare for a week to Praed St, 7/6 to 9/.
                     Yours in the Lord
                      H.G. W.

---

[1] This post card could be 2 October 1889, as the date is very smudged. Accompanying the card are five visiting cards from various establishments which rented rooms. They are those of Mrs. William F. Spittle (no address); Mrs. Ivison, 61 Devenport Road, Shepherd's Bush; Mr. Y. Parkes, 48, Star Street, Norfolk Square, Paddington whose card carries the hand written advice, '8/6 with full attendance, Rather shabby place'; Mrs. Coxhead, 19 Portsea Place, Connaught Square, W., also with a handwritten note, '10 with full attendance. Very nice room & landlady'; and E. Shreves, 34a Gloucester Place, Portman Square Apartments.

160. To Elizabeth Healey[?][1]

Texas ALS

Moving on September 2   October 29th, 1891

[No salutation]

     Sorry to hear you belong to the society.[2] Now you are too ethical as it is. I think these societies where people cluster in a heap in order to be good & do good & spread a good influence are a mistake. I intend shortly to start a rescue movement for these perfect[?] & Good People. To [illegible word] up & mislead em, to teach them a lesson to get the people to swear, to dress badly, to make fusses & do ugly things, to be vulgar.

Malevolence in all these things is the only way to persuade 'em to come down & be kind to other people.
                  Obediently yours,
                  H.G. Wells

---

[1] This letter is indecipherable in places, so the reading is problematical.
[2] The context suggests the Ethical Society.

161. To A. M. Davies

Illinois, ALS

28 Haldon Road
West Hill, SW
Oct. 30th 91

Dear [*an ink blotch*] Davies [1]

We were sorry not to see you Tuesday - took it for granted that you would come from your letter. This is the foulest pen [*another ink blotch*] I ever handled, by the bye, & I work in a mood bordering on phrensy. Never criticize stuff <u>after it is printed</u> except to praise or because your enemy wrote it. You ask in your letter when I am to be married - I am not going to be married.

Come over and see our new home. & me & my wife (to whom I was married October 29th). [2]

    & believe me
        Your new afft friend
            H.G. Wells

---

[1] Another word is completely blotted out before Davies.
[2] The day before this letter was written.

162. To A. T. Simmons

Illinois, ALS

28 Haldon Rd
West Hill, SW
November 13, '91

Station East Putney
Telegrams Southfields, Wandsworth

[*The paper has a tiny gryphon sketched at the top as though it were a crest.*]

Dear Tommie[1]

Your blessing has rendered my happiness complete. Write to Martin J. Cole for amphioxus - to Davies, who is at the schools to ask Ritzel or whatever his name is to send rabbit skeleton - & if you want a D.F. skel^{n2} you must macerate and prepare it yourself - but only the head & limbs need be done. H.G. Wells on the Elementary Comparative Anatomy & Development of the Vertebrata is just being finished. Howes has seen scheme illustrations & parts written up & promises to revise proofs - he likes it & thinks it will sell 'like wildfire'. The cheapest micro going is W.B. Cleves at £3. 7/ 6. - a cheap good weapon with an excellent 1/6' objective (& 1/2 in. of course). I am sweating to finish book for press. I am fired by the furies of necessity & toil all my hours. Looking forward to a Beamish presence in the household at Xmas. I remain, Yrs in God

H. G. Wells

---

[1] This letter is written in Wells's tiniest and most precise script. He was in the process of preparing the *Textbook of Zoology* for the printer. Howes, the demonstrator at Imperial College mentioned later, wrote an introduction to the work. This is one of the very first letters written by Wells from the first house he lived in with Isabel. They had been married for just two weeks. He needed money to cover the cost of moving, and to provide for his parents. Simmons had apparently begun some teaching responsibilities in the field of scientific demonstrations. At this time, individual students did not do dissection; the methods were demonstrated by another person.
[2] A dog fish skeleton

163. To Frank Wells

Illinois, ALS

[Address unknown] [mid-December 1891]

Dear old Boy -

You <u>must</u> come up this Xmas. The missis says so. Do come & cavort around. Come up on Monday or Tuesday next. I shan't get any peace till you do come.

Yrs,
HGW

It will strengthen the Mater's position if we stand off from Up Park this Xmas.

164. To the Editor, *Educational Times*[1]

PLS

[London]   [c. end February 1892]

Sir, Some few months ago I called attention to certain weakness of some of the Science papers set at the Pupils' Examinations. May I again trespass upon your space to discuss the same subject further. My original letter, I regret to say, led to no reply in your columns, but I remain, nevertheless, persuaded of the necessity for some ventilation of the matter. To attain this end I shall now lay down certain propositions, and I propose, unless they are previously sufficiently disposed of, to embody them in resolutions to be put before the next General Meeting of the College.

It is simply stating the unanimous agreement of all educational writers to say that book-science is, perhaps, as useless and objectionable a department of school work as it is possible to imagine. I believe I am outside the realm of controversy altogether, when I express the opinion that the mere rote learning of a text-book, however well written, cannot be science at all. That is, indeed, simply a paraphrase of your conclusion in your January issue. The College of Preceptors, which has always exercised, as modern teachers must gratefully admit, a directive, as well as a representative function in middle-class teaching, should, I take it, do nothing to recognize such teaching, and all that is within its power to reform or destroy it.

I attempted, in my previous letter, by instancing questions actually set, to demonstrate that, so far from doing this, the College is really encouraging the objectionable method, and, I may now add, it is discouraging those who walk in the right way, by setting no stamp of approbation upon better taught pupils through the medium of practical examinations. I am afraid that my criticisms may have appeared to the reader - if there was a reader - as levelled mainly at the College Natural History examiners, but, excepting that they appear to be steadily set against the doctrine that in such subjects as theirs, without a syllabus or recognized order of teaching, a choice of questions is advisable, I fail, on further consideration, to see what they can do to produce any change without the prior action of the Council of the College. All that an examiner, under the present conditions, can do, in the way of thoroughly examining, is done in, for instance, the "Sound, Light, and Heat" papers of Mr. Loewy, and the next steps necessary to improve the present conditions of science teaching in middle-class schools appear to be (a) the establishment of a directive syllabus, and (b) the institution of practical examinations.

With regard to (a) it may be pointed out that at present the teacher and examiner are entirely in ignorance of each other's ideas and methods. It is only by a careful examination of the College chemistry papers, for instance, that the fact comes to light that the chemistry in question is almost entirely the chemistry of the non-metallic elements, excluding the carbon compounds, that experimental demonstrations of the orthodox type are advisable, and that analytical work by boys will be thrown away. And there is no guarantee that a new examiner may not recast the subject to his liking, put all the stress upon replacement and quantivalence, for instance, and practically insist upon analytical work. Such a state of affairs as this renders teachers of small knowledge no assistance, and leaves teachers of higher capacity in considerable anxiety as to their final section of success.

With regard to (b) there is no doubt that a dexterous teacher, may, by clear examination and plentiful note-book drilling, prepare quick boys to pass any *written* examination without practical work; while, on the other hand, many boys may have a great deal of really useful knowledge, and may even be sound thinkers without the gift of luminous exposition. But it is late in the day to plead for the absolute necessity for practical work in science teaching, and for what goes with it, and indeed often precedes and stimulates it, practical examination. Four or five years ago I anticipated with easy confidence the immediate advent of practical tests in the College examination scheme, and it is largely as a reminder that I am now making these proposals.

H.G. Wells

---

[1] Wells waited a few months after his previous contribution to the debate over the curricula at the University of London, but he returned to the issue with this letter, entitled 'The College of Preceptors Science Examinations', which appeared on 1 March 1892, p. 140.

165. To Elizabeth Healey

Illinois, ALS

28 Haldon Road
Wandsworth, S.W.   May 2cd 1892

Dear Miss Healey

Your letter was a boon. I was very glad indeed to hear you are jolly & interested. I really see no hardship in your having a good deal of your own undiluted society. I think if you saw more of yourself you might get a better opinion of yourself than you have at present. Cultivate the relationship & let it ripen into friendship. But eighteen hours to travel 572 kilometers (I always thought these were things like gallons) is almost too much even for your company. What a blessing you had no entertaining person with you who undertook to 'make conversation'. For my own part when I am weary or in pain or ginned I detest the solace of companionship. The companion blocks out the responsible Deity behind & the finite gets sworn at instead of the vile infinite beyond. Travelling alone among a strange people is a great opportunity for spiritual growth. You are dissociated from the petty familiar. Clearly in the bother of tickets, the trouble of luggage, the weariness of waiting, is the parable of human feebleness in contest with the next & Unknown & yet lawabiding manifest.

Since writing to you last my opinion of Saint Paul has altered very considerably. I have a kind of idea that Saint Paul must have studied my writings & have attempted in a vague misleading way to anticipate their publication. I am casting about to find someone who has a Bible & who is willing to sell it, & when I can procure a copy I intend studying this person's lucubrations in detail.

I believe that a tract upon the True Annals of Christianity - based on Professor Green would be of the greatest service to the Broad Church party of this country. Christianity without Theology, without Morality, without any concept of Duty or any influence whatever upon Life - a refined Christianity desirable mainly as a substitute for the repulsive label of Atheist is the article I propose to deal in.

Howes by the bye is backing me for the Marshall scholarship & I have sent in the necessary form for a teachership in training. If I get the one & do not get the other, I shall be in a nice little mess. If you happen to know the Science & Art Department at all I shall be glad if you will speak to him on my behalf.

I and the Head of the Household have become tricycle riders of the most prominent type. We smashed up one machine, sold the pieces & bought another. With this we have.

(a.) Frightened a pair of horses belonging to some aristocrat & scared the aristocrat. He swore by means of his coachman at us.

(b.) Ran into a tramp (democrat) who swore for himself & several others.

(c.) had several delightful journeys with occasional interludes of sorrow as when we got a tyre loose & had to hunt a blacksmith about Wimbledon in the afternoon. They had been watering the streets at Wimbledon & the roads were muddy. Likewise it was the afternoon & the quantity of afternoon -walk, young ladies & young men with chaperones, was frightful. Fancy yourself dusty above and muddy below, your hair getting loose, a heavy machine to push up an incline of 45°, the fatigue of twenty five miles just ridden upon you. Heaven bless you from such. In your final reports, for heaven's sake do not say too much about these idiotic things slight & long, insane explanations of sane proceedings.

    & believe me,
     Very faithfully yours,
      H.G. Wells

Why sign your name, Elizabeth?

166. To Fred Wells

Illinois, ALS

West Field Cottage
Crawley   May 15th [1892?][1]

Dear Fred,

  Just a line to say we got here all right yesterday. We left West Hill at 10. Stopped half an hour at Cheam & rather longer at Reigate & reached here at a quarter past four. - 30 miles. Our machine is a good strong Marlborough Club (double & band brake?) & runs along very decently. Of course as this is a first ride of any importance, we are a little stiff to-day but I hope weather permitting we shall run all right tomorrow. I have just joined C.T.C. I see DuCross[?] is chief counsel for Berks and Heelow for Wokingham. I suppose that is your DuCross & Heelow? Hope to see you next Sunday all right. Come up in morning[?]. You might perhaps let me know your route & when you expect to get to us so that we might perhaps run out & meet you.
     Yours always
      H.G.

---

[1] This letter, written in a cramped hand, fills the bottom portion of a large piece of paper which has a half page sketch of Wells and Isabel on a tricycle of the period. As the letter is to Fred, and mentions Wokingham where he worked, I assign it the date 1892.

167. To Sarah Wells[1]

Illinois, AL

[London]　　　　　　　　　　　　　　　　　　　Wednesday evening
　　　　　　　　　　　　　　　　　　　　　　　[21 September 1892]

Dear Mother,

You observe a doubtless familiar figure above, keeping his 26th birthday. In the background are bookshelves recently erected by your eldest, who came up here Thursday and has been doing things like that ever since. He has laid hands upon all the available reading in the house and seems to be going at it six books at a time. Isabel is at work doing some [knitting].

[The last three lines appear on the verso of the document where there is also an illustration of Fred, sitting near the hearth reading, surrounded by books. Isabel is also sketched, knitting. Remainder of letter is missing.]

---

[1] Also appears in *ExA*, ch. 6 §7.

168. To the Editor, *Educational Times*[1]

PLS

[London] [late November 1892]

Sir, The paper by Professor Laurie which appeared in the November issue of <u>The Educational Times</u>, is one which arouses a considerable amount of dissent in my mind. I was, unfortunately, unable to attend the meeting at which it was read, and, even had I been there, I should not have greatly cared to venture a criticism upon it on the spur of the moment. Under these circumstances, I shall feel myself greatly indebted to you for your courtesy if you will permit me now to question his conclusions. I am strengthened in this request by the fact that Professor Laurie's paper is not merely a criticism of opinion, but a proposal - pretty plainly made - to remove Herbert Spencer's work altogether from the reach of young teachers.

We are told that Herbert Spencer's teaching is not Christianity. This itself is a very serious consideration to many, but to me it does not seem to be a very serious matter, so long as his premises are good and his arguments sound. If his testimony is true, though his profession may be agnostic or atheistic, he must, as far as he goes, harmonize with Christianity, if Christianity is also true. His limited wisdom will be better altogether, I hold, than the foolishness of the orthodox. If his testimony concerning education is false, it falls by its own defect. In either case the direct reference to Christianity, in a nation where the profession of Christianity is as good as all the virtues, lacks as much in fairness as it gains dialectically. To speak of Christ and Spencer as teachers diametrically opposed begs the whole question. It does not follow that a man who does not call himself Christian is Antichrist, or that he who saith, "Lord, Lord," is a soldier in the hosts of heaven.

And now, coming to the real arguments of Professor Laurie's paper, it appears to me that the case he has made out against Herbert Spencer rests chiefly upon the - to me - strange meanings he attaches to "proximate end" and "natural". Only allow that Herbert Spencer intended by some strange aberration, the same things, in these words, that Professor Laurie conceives, and the whole of the vigorous chastisement of the paper is nothing more than Herbert Spencer deserves - yes, even to the holding of the comparison of his teaching to "Roman thought" an insult to the latter.

[For] "Proximate end" Professor Laurie reads "end" simply. The word "proximate," however, has a certain qualifying effect. The end a soldier may be fighting for may be the liberty of his country, but the proximate end of his fighting may be simply to get a bayonet under another man's midriff. "Proximate" means, in fact, the more immediate, the nearest of a series. It is hard, however, to avoid drifting to the conclusion - and harder still to accept it - that Professor Laurie regards [it] as a clipped form of "approximate". He writes: "The attainment of a proximate end in the *sense of an approximation to an ideal end!*" Is this a misconception or a misrepresentation; or can Professor Laurie explain the thing away?

Unless the proximate end of education is simply a respectable livlihood for respectable people - a lowly thought that does not seem to have occurred to Herbert Spencer - is it not the preparation of a child for the "business of life"? Professor Laurie has not told us his own idea of the true proximate end, and it would be interesting to see wherein it differed from that of Herbert Spencer.

That Herbert Spencer has no place, in his philosophy, for high ideals, is altogether new to me. The chief impression the "Data of Ethics" left upon my mind, was the profound conviction of the reasonableness of self-sacrifice, and the folly and unnaturalness of individual selfishness. This man, Herbert Spencer, himself, has been undeniably sowing truth with a single heart - which, I take it, is the intellectual part of the service of God, and to speak of him as the prophet of "beer and skittles", simply because he has not yet reached the same spiritual level as Professor Laurie, is distinctly hard. Professor Laurie, from his higher standpoint, has, as it were, hurled the crucifix at Herbert Spencer's head. I do not propose, in a discussion such as this, to follow this example and to deal too frankly with sacred things, but I cannot resist calling attention to the consistency of the passage: "According to Spencer, Christ on the cross, and all the crucified and self-sacrificed martyrs, were enjoying the greatest sum of pleasure possible for them.... According to Spencer, it was foolish of Christ and the others; they were mistaken. They were blind to their environment." Either this is self-contradictory, or it contradicts Professor Laurie's statement elsewhere that Herbert Spencer regards pleasure as the only sane human end.

After this it is not surprising to find that "natural" means, to Professor Laurie, "physical", and that the mutual affection of parent and child is unnatural. We are told: Poor "Spencer gets so muddled over his natural reactions that he begins, towards the end of this chapter, to see that he is somehow wrong, and says that the disapprobation of the parent and teacher is itself 'a natural reaction'." I have carefully gone over the chapter, and I do not see, myself, that Spencer is "muddled", and, even if he is, it would have more become Professor Laurie, as an exponent of the higher morality of the Christian, to have used a gentler and more charitable word.

These are my chief objections to Professor Laurie's paper. If it were not for these, I should be inclined to regard it as one of the most valuable, as it is certainly one of the most important, of recent contributions to educational science. Even as it is, I have read it with the greatest interest and benefit. But, these objections, unless they are disposed of, completely destroy Professor Laurie's case for the addition of Herbert Spencer's "Education" to the *Index Expurgatorius*. - I am, Sir, very faithfully yours.

H.G. Wells

---

[1] Wells continued in his role of defending Herbert Spencer's ideas on education in this letter, which was given the title, 'Professor Laurie on Herbert Spencer', 1 December 1892, pp. 516–17.

169. To Fred Wells[1]

Illinois, ALS

[Haldon Road, London] [January 1893]

Dear Fred,

Of course mother can come here and live with us.[2] She will not be happy, however, if Nyewoods is not kept on. If I keep her will you contribute 3/- a week or 12/- a month to that concern. I propose to leave things entirely in Frank's hands there and to pay all money to him. If you will do this I will see to all the rest myself. Let me hear. Very busy - excuse more.

Buss.

You stick where you are, my boy, and don't let this little affair upset you.

Write and tell mother to come straight here, bag and baggage, and assure her it will be all right with the G.V.

---

[1] Also appears in *ExA*, ch. 6 §7.
[2] Sarah Wells had been dismissed from her position as housekeeper at Up Park. Joseph Wells, her husband, and her second son, Frank, were living in Nyewood in fairly precarious circumstances, as their only income was from Frank's work mending watches. Fred had been happy in his draper's job at Wokingham but he had just learned that a possible position in the firm was not to be his as it was now reserved for a son of the owner. Wells was forced into the position of 'head of the family' by these circumstances. Sarah remained with Wells and Isabel at Haldon Road until late April when she went to Nyewoods with Joseph and Frank. Fred, by then free of the Wokingham imbroglio, moved into the Wells's spare room, while investigating a number of opportunities, one of which was a possible family drapery and watch shop. Fred eventually found a position in South Africa as a draper.

170. To the Editor, *Educational Times*[1]

PLS

[London] [late January 1893]

Sir, The admission made by Professor Laurie that his address was a popular one, the purpose of which was to rouse, and in which platform language was used, for emphasis and effect, may sufficiently explain much to which I presumed to raise objections in your December issue. Perfect charity, I understand him, was set aside by rhetorical necessity, in the use of the word "muddled", and I would plead, therefore, a similar excuse for my missile of "unchristian". I must apologize, unreservedly, to Professor Laurie, if it appeared that any charge of conscious misrepresentation was made or hinted at by me - and I am afraid that my letter may have been read in that sense; but, at the same time, I still believe that Professor Laurie *has* - quite unintentionally - misrepresented the view he criticized.

Dropping, if I may, the controversial style, I would state this: that Professor Laurie misrepresents Herbert Spencer by using (1.) "proximate", and (ii.) "natural" in a different sense. The difference, with regard to proximate, is best illustrated (with the help of the printer) thus: -

$$\begin{array}{c} b\ c\ d\ e \\ A\ B\ C\ D\ E \\ e \end{array}$$

In this arrangement, A, B, C, D, E, represent successive steps, or acts, beginning at A and ending at E; and e and e are points near E. A person aiming at E as his final end, has B, on the way thereunto, as his proximate end, as the word is used by Herbert Spencer. But Professor Laurie reads proximate end, as a final aimed at, near to, but not quite the same as, E; if E represented the ideal end, e and e would be "practical or proximate ends", as I interpret Professor Laurie. Herbert Spencer speaks of "gradual approximations to an ideal", meaning the successive stages on the thorny path, B, C, D, E to E, the ethical ideal. Professor Laurie suggests the idea that Mr. Spencer recommends an easier route, b, c, d, to a spurious substitute for E at e. I would ask Professor Laurie if this is not the case.

Then, Mr. Spencer uses "natural" in such a wide sense that psychology might be spoken of as one of the natural sciences, according to his use, while Professor Laurie's meaning is such that he would omit psychology from a list of these; and to Mr. Spencer, "pleasure" is that quality of association determining impulse in its direction, while the meaning given the word by Professor Laurie in this discussion is the end of sensual desire.

It would be gross presumption for me to pretend to decide in these differences. What my first letter was intended to point out was that, through their misdirection, Professor Laurie had failed to join issue with Spencer at all on his most important points, but had wandered after and belaboured an approximated Herbert Spencer with a muddled mind.

I admit the absurdity that has arisen by my writing as though I were defending Mr. Spencer. At the same time, Professor Laurie's praise of Mr. Spencer, and his admission of the value of his work, is a very welcome postscript to his lecture. It is well known that Mr. Spencer engages in no controversy, and this being the case, the discussion by an outsider of Professor Laurie's criticisms is less an impertinence than it would be otherwise be. The question whether Mr. Spencer be an agnostic or no is beyond the range of my knowledge or curiosity, and it scarcely affects the essentials of this matter.

I am, Sir., etc.,
H.G. Wells

---

[1] Professor Laurie responded to Wells's comments on Herbert Spencer's philosophy by accepting some points, but he also claimed that Wells had exaggerated in order to arouse the interest of a popular audience in the real meaning of the subject. Wells responded good-naturedly to this accusation in his letter, 'Professor Laurie on Herbert Spencer', in the issue of 1 February 1893, p. 78.

171. To Elizabeth Healey

Illinois, Typed Transcription, Extract

28 Haldon Road Monday, Spring 1893

[...] I had almost sent in P.P.C. cards on Thursday morning, but it occurred to me in time that they were out of fashion.——Really I have had a very bad attack this time, and there is no more teaching for me for ever - However I am not dead yet and I think I may promise with safety to write further when I am better. But I thought I would let you know now because I am still lying on my back and almost the only pleasure I have is reading letters of condolence. Write a good one to

yours ever
H.G.W.

172. To A. T. Simmons

Illinois, APCS

[Address unknown]　　　　　　　　　　　　　　　　　　[Spring 1893?]

Dear Tommy,

　　　I caught a little cold on Xmas eve - began to spit a streaky sputum about Boxing Day & now I am in haemorrhage. Have chucked oral classes in favour of Andrews & on the advice of Doctor Collins - shall probably go to Hastings for a month. He reports no tuberculosis & thinks my prospects of a long life are very much greater now than three years ago - says I have distinctly gained ground & that this attack if repulsed may prove the last effort of the enemy. Otherwise I should not have considered it worth while to throw up work. Still it is very annoying you will admit. I keep on <u>Correspondence</u> of course. How are things going with you. Write me a long letter old boy & forgive the postcard. No envelope visible & too depressed to hunt 'em.
　　　　　　　　Yours
　　　　　　　　　　　　The Pietist

173. To Amy Catherine Robbins[1]

Illinois, ALS

[Haldon Road, London]　　　　　　　　　　　　　　[c. 22 May 1893]

My Dear Miss Robbins,[2]

　　　When we made our small jokes on Wednesday afternoon anent the possible courses a shy man desperate at the imminence of a party might adopt, we did not realize that the Great Arch Humorist also meant to have his joke in the matter. For my part, I was so disgusted, when I woke in the dismal time before dawn on Thursday morning, to find myself the butt of <u>His</u> witticism, that I almost left this earthly joking ground in a huff. However by midday on Thursday, what with ice and opium pills, and this soothing bitterness and that, my wife and the doctor calmed the internal eruption of the joker outjoked, and since that I have been lying on my back, moody but recovering. I <u>must</u> say this for chest diseases; they leave one remarkably cheerful, they do not hurt at all and they clear the mind like strong tea. My poor wife has had all the pain of this affair, bodily and mentally, fatigue and fear. For my share I shall take all the sympathy and credit.

It was very kind of you to call this morning but my wife would like to have seen you. Next week - if I do not go to pieces again - I expect I shall be coming downstairs, and a visitor who would talk to me and take little in return, would be a charity. Will you thank Miss Roberts[3] for the letter of condolence which - quite contrary, as she must be aware, to all etiquette, following your bad example - she wrote to my wife.

I guess class teaching is over for me for good, and that whether I like it or not, I must write for a living now.
              With best wishes,
              Yours very faithfully,
              H.G. Wells

---

[1] Also appears in *ExA*, ch. 6 §7.
[2] This is the first letter (there may have been a few notes prior to this) to Amy Catherine Robbins, who would fairly soon become his second wife. She was affectionately known as 'Jane' by Wells.
[3] Adeline Roberts later become a well-known London physician. She and Amy were students in the laboratory where Wells was teaching. The three of them had begun the practice of taking tea together, after the laboratory exercises, at least once a week. There is some slight indication that the two women were initially vying for Wells's attention. For a later letter to Roberts see volume 4.

174. To Amy Catherine Robbins[1]

Illinois, AL   May 26th, 1893
                                                                                                    Thursday

OFFICIAL BULLETIN

Mr. Wells tasted meat for the first time since Wednesday the 17th (18th?) yesterday, he also turned over on his side and sat up with assistance - cheerful. No recurrence of symptoms of haemorrhage, no fever. Slept well. To day stronger. Has eaten an egg, some boiled mutton, and other trifles. Pulse quiet, no fever or inflammation. No blood or clot expectorated now for eighty-five hours. Much stronger, able to sit up and turn about without help. <u>Getting a little troublesome.</u> Insists on writing letters in ink to everybody he knows -

quilt spoilt and two sheets ditto - also in preference to tinkling little bell, upsets table when he wishes to call attendance - also wants books to read and if those procured are not to his taste throws them at nurse - also plays Freddie at draughts and insists upon winning. Hopes are entertained that he may get up by Saturday. No definite plans. Possibly a month at Ventnor, and then if practicable remove from London.

It is particularly requested that in all letters of condolence it shall <u>not</u> be remarked that it may be for the best after all.[2]

---

[1] Also appears in *ExA*, ch. 6 §7.

[2] A classic example of Wells's writing, both in tone and information. This bulletin was apparently sent to those who enquired or wrote to him and Isabel. They were not on the telephone at that time.

175. To Amy Catherine Robbins[1]

Illinois, ALS

28, Haldon Road
Wandsworth, S.W.   May 26th. 93.

[This letter has a sketch of a rather unshaven Wells, with his knees up, lying in his bed.]

My Dear Miss Robbins.

Your unworthy teacher of biology is still - poor fellow - keeping recumbent, though he knows his ceiling pretty well by this time, but no doubt he is a-healing and by Saturday he will be, he hopes, put out in the front parlour in the afternoon. But he will be an ill thing to see, lank and unshaven and with the cares of this world growing up to choke him as he sprouts out of his bed. However that is your affair, only you must not make it a matter of mockery.

During my various illnesses I have derived much innocent amusement from letters of condolence but your Vice-Principal Briggs thing capped it with a brief note written by Miss Thomas and signed,

John Briggs[2]
S.T.

After that I can believe the story of the typewritten love letter signed by a pardonable slip of the pen, Holroyd, Barker and Smith.

Remember me kindly to Miss Roberts and Miss Taylor, especially Miss Roberts. Tell the girl not to trifle with Bronchitis, whatever other giddiness she may be guilty of. And believe me

>Yours very faithfully,
>H.G. Wells.

P.S. I think he will not be fit to see you before Sunday but I will write you before then.

>Yours faithfully,
>I.M.W [3]

---

[1] Also appears in *ExA*, ch. 6 §7.

[2] The reason Wells knew this letter was a joke was that Briggs's name was William, not John.

[3] One of the few early instances of Isabel's calligraphy; later there was quite a full correspondence between her and Wells and her and 'Jane'. By writing this postscript she was attempting to salvage her marriage, as she said later, because she had come to realize that Amy Catherine's interest in the sick teacher was beyond general student politeness.

176. To Elizabeth Healey

Texas, ALS

6 New Cottages
Meads
Eastbourne[1] [June 1893]

[*a sketch of a man, with spade, shovel, and rolled up trousers, in the sea*]

I am trying to rejuvenesce by throwing myself perhaps with artificial zeal, into the innocent pursuits of seaside childhood. I mend but slowly. Yesterday we came near to a relapse and to day to my disgusted imagination there is nothing but a long perspective of relapses to the inevitable end. Your Briggs[2] garden party letter did me good. Before it came I found a consolation for my illness in the thought of that party but if you, escorted by the exhuberant Lowson & the fancy Dibb was there, I am sorry we could not come. Do you not think on the whole that Briggs & his brigands are a painful exposition of the failure of the examination system? Did you meet Barlow, Hayes, Shipham or Gladstone. They ought to wear their certificates about with them for they constitute their

only claims to human sufferance. Have you heard how Ewan is? He has been very ill indeed. With fondest love from Mrs. Wells & best wishes, Believe me
Yours very truly,
H.G. Wells

---

[1] Wells and Isabel spent much of July in Eastbourne as he attempted to regain his health.
[2] Her letter describes a garden party for the Correspondence School staff which Wells would normally have attended. Healey's letter to Wells is in the Illinois archive.

177. To A. M. Davies

Illinois, ALS

28 Haldon Road
West Hill
Wandsworth, SW   Aug. 4th, '93

Dear A.M.D.

      The house hunt is finished. Sutton on chalk, pretty house, pretty view Alas! more rent than this. Some alterations but we can go in, in about three weeks time if that suits you. About the house I propose to pay you £5 as rent for the time since quarter day and you will pay the landlord. Mrs. Wells very busy now but she will make out list of fittings & prices as soon as possible.[1]

If you would like my bookshelves you can have them for 30/-. I shall be glad if we may leave tricycle house & send for it when we want it.

It is a blessed thing to have a home again.
Yrs ever,
H.G. Wells

I believe Isabel wants to trade a bed & one or two other things but I think she had better negociate with your sister or you.

[*The opposite page has a drawing of the new house, 4 Cumnor Place, Surrey.*]

---

[1] It is clear from this that Davies is relieving the Wellses of their lease and some of the furnishings.

178. To Fred Wells[1]

Illinois, ALS [Summer 1893]

[Three sketches illustrate the letter. The first, at the top of the page, shows four figures walking, linked together with a rope, marked as Mr. F. J. Wells, Mrs. F. J. Wells no. 1a, Mrs. F. J. Wells no. 2, and Mrs. F. J. Wells, no. 3., with the words 'more to follow'.]

[A second sketch shows Wells, dressed in cap and gown, invigilating a group of scholars.]

[At the bottom of the sheet is a cat, sitting disconsolately, with the caption, 'O for the touch of a vanished hand & the sound of a voice that is still'. To the right, Wells, his mother, his Aunt Mary and her daughter, Isabel, with two cats, bow, as they take their exit.]

My Dear Freddie,

I have nothing to tell you except to keep your courage up & work hard & bear in mind that there are plenty of sympathetic friends over here anxious to hear about you whenever you can write.[2] Things are going very evenly with us. We have not found a home yet but we have hardly hunted for it. I have been & am very busy. I have almost written my share of Gregory & Wells' Honours Physiography which I arranged for a day or two before you sailed & a lot of small coaching jobs have dropped in for me, and next week (which will be about the time of your landing at Cape Town) I shall be sitting in glory above my room full of candidates.

 Izzums sends her love to you. Mummie is writing to you herewith.
   With love from us all, & best wishes
    Your very affte brother
     Bussums[3]

---

[1] Also appears in *ExA*, ch. 6 §7.
[2] Fred Wells had recently migrated to South Africa in an attempt to find work, and establish a business.
[3] Wells's family nicknames were all variants of Buzz, Buzzwuzz, Buzzwhacker, and here, apparently used with Isabel, is Izzums. The origins of the names are unknown, but his brothers used the name as long as Wells lived. A more sedate family name was Bertie, which was also widely used.

179. To Fred Wells

Illinois, AL, Extract

[28 Haldon Road[mid-August 1893]
West Hill
Wandsworth, SW]

[Dear Fred,][1]

[...] wish you could see it.

[*a sketch of the new house*]

This style of thing. There are plentiful elm trees behind & we are within reach of Banstead Downs, very fine breezy hill country. Your kitten went off with Miss Creigh before we left Haldon Rd & Thomas is with us & says he prefers the new home. I am getting quite portly down here & Aunt Mary is herself again. I am still taking it easy - doing a few articles & science notes. I am barely paying expenses but that really does not matter until I get a bit better. I am not fretting about it. I have been asked to write articles - which is much [better] than making them on spec. for <u>Knowledge, The Ed. Times, Science & Art & The Correspondent</u> and indeed I might be doing a lot more than I am. I am doing the "Science Notes" in the <u>Journal of Education</u> & <u>Knowledge</u> if ever you see these papers.

Isabel is very well & has been very busy with the floors, the blinds & all that kind of thing.

Have you found a job out there for me yet?

The postman has just arrived as....

[*remainder of letter missing*]

---

[1] The first and last pages of this letter are missing.

180. To Amy Catherine Robbins[1]

Illinois, ALS

6, New Cottages
Meads Road
Eastbourne   Tuesday [Summer 1893]

My dear Miss Robbins,

Your humble servant has been at this gay place now for eight long days. He has been led out daily to an extremely stony beach and there spread out in the sun for three, four or five hours as it might be, and he has there inhaled sea air into such lung as Providence has spared him, sea air mingled with the taint of such crabs as have gone recently from here to that bourne from which no traveller returns. His evenings have passed in the marking of examination papers and correspondence tuiting, and his nights in uneasy meditations on Death and the Future Life, and Hope and Indeterminate Equations. Moreover I have sorrowed greatly over Miss Roberts. When I was near the lowest point of my illness she sent me a wicked book by some evangelist - a word I have long used as a curse - about how that Huxley will not look his (the evangelist's) substitutes for arguments in the face, how that geology supports the Book of Genesis (which is a lie) how that the Gospel of St. Mark was written before A.D. 38 (which is idiotic) and all those dismal things. Egged on by this wicked book I wrote two letters to Miss Roberts blaspheming her gods, saying I knew God was a gentleman and could not possibly have any connexion with her evangelist and the like painful things. I am sorry now because I certainly was uncivil, but this particular form of Religion arouses all the latent 'Arry in my composition. But I know Miss Roberts will never approve of me any more.

This Providence has seen fit to increase the tale of my wife's troubles by sending her mother very ill. Of the two she is much worse than I am now, and I am still in a hectic unstable condition. A more serious man than myself would be horribly miserable at his inability to play his part of man in all these troubles. Everything is pressing on my wife's shoulders now, and I dare not exert myself to help for fear I shall give her a greater trouble still.

I sincerely hope you are working hard for your examination. I shall take anything but a first class pass very much to heart, so that I hope you will out of consideration for a poor suffering soul who must not be depressed by any means, do your best. I am looking forward to visiting Red Lion Square next week and seeing you again and conversing diversely with you.

Very faithfully yours,
H.G. Wells

Concerning literature to which you would have directed me, I have done nothing. One dismal article full of jocularities like the rattling of peas in a bladder has seen the light in the <u>Globe.</u> Moreover I tried a short story for <u>Black and White</u>, which impressed me when I had done it as being unaccountably feminine and acid - much what a masculine old maid would write. What <u>Black and White</u> thinks of it I do not know. I think my mind stagnates. It is blocked up with a lot of things. I shall come and talk to you a long time I think and deliver myself.[2]

---

[1] Also appears in *ExA*, ch. 6 §7.

[2] The *Globe* piece was 'Animals at Play', 29 September 1893, p. 7. Another piece appeared in this magazine the following week, 'The Noises of Animals', and three others by the end of the year. He did not appear in *Black and White* until the summer of 1894, after James Pinker became its editor. This letter to his student, who was soon to be his wife, indicates some development in their relationship.

181. To A. M. Davies

Illinois, ALS

[London] [August 1893]

Dear A.M.D.

I rejoice to hear it. I am very sorry I was out this afternoon but I am at your service tomorrow or Thursday night. Wednesday Gregory[1] is coming over on business. Whatever I can do to facilitate your coming in I will. We will do all we can to store away your stuff. Respecting one or two little details, oil cloth in the hall, blinds, & so on I can sell you them at 3/4 cost if I can ascertain what that was, and you approve of them. There are some curtain rods and so forth you might like too. However of that when I see you.

I am <u>looking</u> as well as usual again now - rather better if anything, but this time Davies I know the vanity of these things. I am going to take no more risks. It is hardly needed now.

Yours ever,
H.G.

---

[1] His college friend and co-author Richard A. Gregory. They wrote *Honours Physiography* (London, 1893).

182. To Amy Catherine Robbins

Illinois, ALS

4, Cumnor Place
Sutton   [probably late August perhaps
                                          early September 1893]

Dear Miss Robbins,

I am in the tail end of the stream of congratulations, but I am happy to say I was the first person not in the confidence of the University to see that you were in the first division. And our Adeline has passed in Biology, she and her riotous school of boys, or at least Wells and Johns. Miss Saunders is in the second class, and one Miss Knight - you will remember a romantic young thing with expressive dark eyes, is, I am very sorry to see, missing.

Everyone will be in superlatives about this success of yours but as a matter of fact it is a mere beginning and not at all beyond my expectation. I should have been secretly disappointed if anything else had happened. You must not touch degree grinding for two or three years yet, though it is time for you to select your subjects. You must take an honours degree - that is a mere debt you owe your disinterested teachers.

This choice of degree subjects is a very serious one, and one you ought to make now. For mental greatness - such as mine - you must attack the biological group. I sincerely regard mathematics as on a lower level intellectually than biology. On the other hand you have done enough in mathematics to show you can get to brilliant things in that direction, while your biology is a brief growth of one year. However we must talk over this when you return. It will of course affect your attack upon South Kensington very considerably. I am glad your visit is to last another week. Putney for the last three days has been a melancholy oven. However I hope you will return before we leave here, because I would very much like to deal with the matter of the future at a greater length than is possible in a letter.

My wife sends her sincerest congratulations on your success. How did Painter get on? They have let me sign an article in the Pall Mall Gazette, by the bye, and signed articles in dailies is a distinct advance for a poor wretch like me.[1]

                Very faithfully yours,
                H.G.Wells

---

[1] Wells may have thought they were to give him a by-line, but none has been located at this time. He did receive an occasional by-line in the *Pall Mall Budget* for his stories of 'scientific romance'.

183. To the Editor, *Educational Times*[1]

PLS

[London]   [late August 1893]

Sir, With the possible exception of the minister of religion, no kind of man has been, and is, so exhaustively criticised as the schoolmaster. Individually and collectively he is worked over, no detail neglected, from his collars to his conduct of his immortal soul. The informal council of the parent, the pupil, and the disinterested relation is always in session, and to these has been added the educational writer. Beside the schoolmaster the general practitioner in a village is a free man. Even over the boundary of his professional duties he is pursued, and his behaviour in society and his vacation employments, are the matter of well-nigh classical criticisms. He carries too much of the tone pedagogic into his lay conversation - that is an old complaint, and now there is added that he gathers himself together in his vacation in conferences, guild meetings, and the like, preferring his own kind to common humanity. Moreover, someone has discovered that he marries, with singular frequency, within his class. Doctors do not marry lady practitioners, nor the clergy sisters of mercy; masculine artists would sooner marry their models than their proper feminine equivalents - but statistics show that those who profess education mate within their calling more than any other kind of people. This is made a reproach to us. It is stated - and nothing could be more evidently false - that schoolmasters and mistresses are inflated by their schoolroom authority until none but teachers are good enough for them, that other adult humanity is to them merely so many fugitives, across an age limit, from salutary discipline, and the like.

But the truth of all this is, it is not the schoolmaster who has, in disdain, cut himself off from common men, but the general public which has, to a perceptible extent, put us in a class apart. It is the perpetual sense of criticism, and the absurd conceptions formed by the public of what a schoolmaster should be, that give so many of us an air of being consciously not as other men. The public *will* have its schoolmaster Sabbatical in garb, loving them best when they seem to be clad, morally and physically, in ready-made mourning; its ideal teacher may not sing nor play nor dance. If he smokes at all, he smokes after bedtime up the chimney, and that mild tobacco. And their conception of our range of conversation is peculiar. We are supposed to delight especially in etymology, the verification of quotations, and nice questions of pronunciation; and talk in which we join is commonly politely wrenched around to these our topics. Moreover, it is expected of us that we should speak with language of unnatural polish, and our spelling and our handwriting must be devoid of the grace of variety.

As for wit, a witty schoolmaster is to the public eye clearly an immoral one, though a special kind of joking, as gay as the distant firing of great guns, is allowed him. These are some of the many conventions that are forced upon us. We must observe them, because no teacher can educate if he is not trusted with pupils, and so it is not of choice but necessity that many of us wear at least the exterior aspect of prigs. With the parent, that is, the public, the teacher is always on his guard, lest it be discovered that he is, after all, but a mortal man, and "the imagination of his heart only evil continually" - just as the parent's is. Of course where the parent is [in] education this isolation is at its least; the happy few in the upper ranks of the profession can almost afford to be taken for common men, and it is mainly upon the teachers of the lower middle working classes, that this burthen falls, of being set apart in a deliberately "superior" call from ordinary humanity. Thus it happens that we are very much alone, and we must seek our fellow teachers in order to unbosom ouselves and let the bow of behaviour unbend. Teachers gather with teachers, and marry teachers, for no love of the teacher, but of humanity. Among ourselves we can set aside the armour of solemnity the public has made us wear, and taste the dear delight of human intercourse without pretence. That is the true and honourable reason of that isolation of which the critic unreasonably complains, and, indeed, no vain sense of superiority such as he suggests.

I am, Sir, etc.,

H.G. Wells

[1] Although Wells continued to think and write about the issues of pedagogy, both the curriculum, and the goals to be striven for, by the time this letter was printed, on 1 September 1893, as 'Scholastic Isolation', he was also writing seriously for magazines like the *Pall Mall Gazette* on many other matters.

184. To A. M. Davies

Illinois, ALS

4, Cumnor Place
Sutton, Surrey [c. September 1893]

Dear A.M.D.,

      Will you please do whatever you can for Cycle house. e.g.
-sell it (any price)
- have it taken to pieces & packed up & sent here (in which case I will pay expenses, of course.)
-give it in charge of the police
-Paint it red, take it up on Wimbledon Common & leave it.
- Set fire to it
-Give it a plain hint to quit.
Ask Lees to move it.
- Buy a dog to live in it. - it would do beautifully for a dog.
When are you both coming to see us?
              Affectionately
              HGW
I have written twice to Wood imploring him to buy it.

THE LETTERS: 1880-1903

185. To A. T. Simmons

Illinois, ALS

4 Cumnor Place
Sutton, Surrey   Sept. 7th, [1893]

My dear old Tommie,

     I have not written before on account of manifold matters, but for Gawds saik don't think I am going the way Burton went. I have been moving & I am trying certain little experiments upon the world, & the like excuses. It is hard that I should have to write things to you. Can you come up to do a day or so's Jawing on your way to Tellenhall. We are all straight here & have a bedroom for you if you will come. Madam is just as anxious as I to see.
     Do come. There's a duck.
          & believe me
            Ever yours,
              H.G.W.

[A sketch of Wells, with the words, 'Getting quite plump again' adorns the opposite page. In fact, the sketch shows a person with a pronounced embonpoint.]

186. To Amy Catherine Robbins

Illinois, ALS

4 Cumnor Place
Sutton   Tuesday [late 1893?]

My dear Miss Robbins,[1]

     I am rapidly developing into the galosh wearing, comforter adjusting, sky watching creature Mrs Robbins would have me become. A certain homeopathic dose of bronchitis has gotten a footing upon me - It puts me in sympathy with all the old women. - & I crave your pardon but I do not think I ought to come to London tomorrow. It is really nothing serious, but now my life is not worth insuring, it has become exceedingly precious to me out of sheer perversity. There is some credit in being alive a year after you ought not & I do not propose to give Providence a loophole. The account of the bronchitis is to be settled in four days according to the best authority, so I hope to come with Isabel on Saturday. It is really a judgment on me for breaking the Sabbath, for I had to go to Kensington in the damp on some press work.

Let me know what Briggs says to the picture & what has become of lessons ii iii iv ?

But really this lung of mine is the greatest affliction ever human being had. - but Mrs Robbins & her Visitor. Chance just tickles you under the rib, & you become feverish, ill tempered, all the nice easy feeling that makes work delightful vanishes. I am resolved I will have very little more of this annoyance. I will breathe with gills. Perhaps it would be easier to go abroad after all. I have a horrible vision of the rest of my life, flying from England, outward bound, with a red bogie in the form of a right lung behind me, then precipitate flight back to England again pursued by a blue devil in the shape of dullness & lonliness.[2]

I think I shall write a big book on the genius of a Cheerful Man. It is only a light, buoyant person who <u>can</u> know anything of sorrow. Your depressed people collapse like concertinas under their first grief - it lasts a lifetime. But your versatile person goes down a different abyss daily, he tastes here & sips there & becomes a perfect encyclopaedia of woes.

I could go on - I think with this letter for the rest of the day. I revel in myself, especially when I am not well. But possibly you do not share my tastes.

The point is, I am not coming to London tomorrow.
>With best wishes to Mrs. Robbins
>>Believe me
>>>Very faithfully yours
>>>>H.G. Wells

---

[1] Although this is not a love letter, it is rather warm to be sent to a student in one's laboratory class.

[2] Wells is attempting to deal with the problems of his life in this extended metaphor. His various illnesses created tensions, but so did the fact that he was beginning to fall in love with Catherine while still attached to Isabel.

187. To A. M. Davies

Illinois, ALS

4, Cumnor Place
Sutton, Surrey   Thursday [late in 1893]

[*a sketch of two persons bowing to something, perhaps the invitation, in front of them*]

Dear Arthur Morley,[1]

On behalf of Madam & myself, I beg to accept your invitation for Sunday next <u>provided that it be as fine as today.</u>
Yours ever,
HGW

We will arrive somewhere in the forenoon perhaps about eleven, because I am not allowed out after dark.

---

[1] 'Arthur Morley' were Davies's Christian names.

188. William Briggs to H. G. Wells[1]

Illinois, ALS

University Correspondence College
Burlington House
Cambridge   7th November 1893

Dear Mr. Wells,

I am in receipt of yours of Monday. Would it not be well to alter the Biology Tests, Short Course, from the commencement. If the men get into a grumbling vein by finding what they are having is what they had before, dissatisfaction may remain throughout the course.

With regard to the biology illustrations, I should be glad if you would arrange with Miss Robbins, even to the matter of fee, £5 seems to be both a large and a small sum, large absolutely for such work, and for work which has been done before, but small when it is regarded as a specialist's work.

I am rather hoping that she will do the work mainly as a work of love, and I shall be pleased to thank her in the preface.[2]   [!!!-HGW]

I will send on to you any suggestions which come in for the Vigilance Prize. Copies for review went to "Knowledge" and "The Practical Teacher". When the new edition comes out, I will see that it goes to "Natural Science" "The Lancet", and "The Medical Magazine" etc.

W. Briggs

[A second sheet in holograph says]:

Please put Miss Robbins to do illustrations as soon as possible. Copies may be next month.

---

[1] Some correspondence from Wells from 1893 has disappeared. Wells himself may have destroyed some of it after requesting its return (at the time of *In the Days of the Comet*, and later as he prepared his *Autobiography*). For this reason, I have chosen to print a few letters to him from others which describe important events.

[2] Wells drew the diagrams for the 1st edition of the *Textbook of Biology* (London: W. B. Clive, 1893). Some reviewers found the illustrations cramped and not well done. Amy Catherine Robbins did the illustrations for the 2nd edition (*On Vertebrates and Plants*), and received £5 for the work. In his introduction to the 2nd edition, Wells gives Robbins credit for redrawing all the illustrations, and close inspection indicates that this probably is the case.

189. To Fred Wells[1]

Illinois, ALS

4, Cumnor Place
Sutton   [November 1893?]

My dear Freddie,

I suppose if I write to you now, this letter will reach you about Christmas time, and I daresay you will like to have our good wishes in season, even if we have to send them off unseasonably early to reach you. But over here already we are beginning to think of Christmas, there is a hard frost today and the roads are all hard, and last Sunday there was the first fall of snow. All the bookstalls are bright with the Christmas numbers of the magazines, and the London shops are getting brilliant with cards and presents. My two books[2] have been published now, and I have been writing articles for all kinds of publications since you left. The stories I wrote do not seem to be a great success but I have found a good market for chatty articles, and I am doing more and more of these. I had a cheque of £14 13s from the Pall Mall Gazette the day before yesterday for *one month's* contributions. Not bad, is it? But that may be a lucky month. However I am not drawing on my small savings, thank goodness, and I am keeping indoors, and I think pulling round steadily. How are things going with you? I hope everything glides along, and that you are striking root in South Africa. Do you ever play draughts or chess? If so I hope you are improving, for your play with me was simply abominable.

Isabel and Mummie and the Cat are well, and we find ourselves very comfortable in our new home. We are only about twenty minutes walk from the downs, and we can go by Banstead and Epsom to Dorking over them all the way. We have had a lot of Sutton people call upon us, so that we already feel much more at home than we did in Putney, where the London custom of ignoring your neighbour is in fashion.

I have not been to see either Father or Mother since you left us but I daresay I shall run down there some of these days. I judge they are all right. Neither have I seen Frank now for some months.

I think now I am almost at the end of my news. It is not a very eventful record, but as someone has written, we are happiest when we have least history. Things have been going easily with us, and so I hope they may continue.

With very many wishes for a happy Christmas and a prosperous New Year.
   Believe me my dear Freddie
    Your very affectionate brother
     The Busswhacker.

Isabel and Auntie send their love.

---

[1] Also appears in *ExA*, ch. 6 §7.
[2] *Honours Physiography* (London: Joseph Hughes, 1893) and *Textbook of Biology* (London: Clive, 1893)

190. To Sarah Wells[1]

Illinois, ALS

4, Cumnor Place
Sutton   Dec. 15th, 1893

My Dear Mother,
 I had hoped to run down to Rogate for a day or so before Xmas to settle my accounts with father and to wish you all a pleasant time, but I am afraid it will

scarcely be possible now, so I am sending a little cheque (payable to father) to pay for what he has done for me and the balance I hope *you* will dispense in making things festive on the great anniversary. As Frank has possibly told you I am still contriving to make both ends meet by writing articles. There are two more when the previous ones are returned. Did the G.V. notice that To-Day[2] had a note and a sketch about my million year man?

I and Isabel are going off this afternoon to stop with Mrs. Robbins at Putney until Monday - you will remember Miss Robbins who came to tea one Sunday - and we are going to a concert tonight with them. My cold and so on it is needless to say are better, or I should not be doing this.

We are looking forward to Frank's visit directly after Christmas.

With love from all.
Believe me dear Mother
Your affectionate Son
Bertie.

It is not all jam this book writing. Part II of my Biology has been slashed up most cruelly by this week's Nature in a review.[3]

---

[1] Also appears in *ExA*, ch. 6 §7.
[2] This piece is virtually identical to the 'The Man of the Year Million: A Scientific Forecast', which, with an illustration, appeared in the *Pall Mall Budget*, 16 November 1893, and without the illustration in *Pall Mall Gazette*, 6 November 1893.
[3] The review was more concerned about the illustrations than the text. The 2nd edition, with drawings by Amy Catherine Robbins, followed within the year.

191. To A. M. Davies

Illinois, AL

4, Cumnor Place
Sutton, Surrey   Dec. 21st [1893]

My dear A.M.D.,

I have been a letter in your debt since before the concert. I can only plead I am a miserable poor sinner unfit to live, and that I have had a great deal to think about lately to the utter disorganization of these social duties. Isabel wants to know whether you will have a slow print or a platinum type of her,[1] & whether you think we are going to pay all your expenses every time you get so elevated as to go kicking holes in your ceilings, & when you will be back again from the place vile enough to shelter W. N. P. Did you read the creature's review of my book in Nature? If I was not sure of my greatness it might have hurt me, but as it is I am only sorry for the creature's relations and the children - if any - who will bear his shame. My dear

[*remainder of letter missing*]

---

[1] These are methods of printing portrait photographs used at the time. Isabel was a colour tinter for a photographer.

192. To A.M. Davies

Illinois, ALS

4, Cumnor Place
Sutton, Surrey   27. xii. 93.

My dear Davies,

    I am really very glad to taste the tone of happiness in your letter. I do sincerely hope that it is an anticipation that will be realised. You know me, I hope well enough, to know that I do wish you well with all my heart. You are not a man to show feeling - you err on the other side - but I am assured that beneath your rather punctilious honourableness there is enough tenderness & sentiment to make & keep any woman happy.

    It will always be a matter of self-congratulation to me to know that you made me one of the first recipients of your secret & that you proposed to introduce your Miss Greville to me in the tone you have done. But I am very much afraid that I shall never be able to enter at all into your married life. I have been in very great trouble all the past year - all the greater because it has been my own private affair. My own marriage has been a very great mistake. I love my wife very tenderly but not as a husband should love his wife, and - as quickly as possible - we are going to separate this new year. This is putting a very great confidence in your hands. Our determination has been our absolute secret until now. I shall get this house off my hands, & we shall return to different parts of London before the end of January. We are parting not in anger, but in sorrow, because our tempers, interests, desires are altogether different. In the end I suppose the thing will be talked about and I want you to understand clearly, & when the time comes to say, that my wife has been noble loving & faithful to me as very few wives can be.

It is I that am doing this, & I am doing it because I love another woman with all my being, & it seems a hideous thing to me to continue this comfortable life of legal adultery simply because I cannot have the woman I love.

I do not know whether I shall run counter to your principles, but there is always a subtle discredit attaches to a man who disregards the matrimonial recipe. In sexual matters my good name will be smirched. The popular mind makes no distinction between sentimental and sensual aberrations. You have, if not for your own sake, for Miss Greville's, & your sisters, to think of what the world will say as our separation leaks out.

I trust implicitly to your power of keeping silence.

And remain, as ever,

Your sincere friend,

H.G. Wells

The worst of the separation will fall on my wife. Even at the cost of a little trouble, your sisters should keep up the acquaintance & do a little to make her feel less lonely. I trust to their goodness for that.

193. Richard A. Gregory to H.G. Wells[1]

Illinois, ALS

5 North Court
Westminster, S.W. 1   November 9, 1934

[...] the most charming thing to me in the Autobiography is the continued affection which you express for the old friends of the R.C.S. - Simmons, Jennings, Burton, Miss Healey, E.H. Smith, A.M. Davies, myself and others. Tommy has gone, but I am sure all the others will be as proud as I am to be among the figures on your life's stage.

It is curious how closely in many respects my own early mental developments followed yours. Before I came to South Kensington I had read Henry George's Progress and Poverty, and tried to get satisfaction out of Paley's Evidences but failed. I wonder now why I had not come across Darwin's Descent of Man, but you seem also to have missed this work before you came to London. Like you, I tried all sorts of chapels and churches, including the Halls of Science of the secularists and the Salvation Army, and although I was never confirmed, I have been "converted", whatever backslider I afterwards became. Like you also, I am glad to have been able to keep my mother and father while they were alive; and even when you lent the historic tenner I was allowing them £3 a month.

When you had decided to leave Isabel, you asked me to come to Cumnor Place to see you, & you told me on a stroll toward Banstead what you intended to do. I remember very well seeing your trunk in the front room ready for you to take with you on the following morning. I called once at Mornington Place when you little expected me, for Jane was there, & when you let me know of this in a few words, I quickly retired. For several reasons, it was a memorable Sunday to me when I came up to Mornington Crescent to be the witness at your wedding. Dozens of other incidents come into my mind as I read the work, and I am happy to recollect all of them, & cherish the hope that we may still remain together for some years yet.

   Always Affectionately Yours,
   R. A. Gregory

---

[1] The following extract is in response to the publication of Wells's *Autobiography*. It is included here as it gives a picture of the end of Wells's first marriage to Isabel, and the beginning of his second to Amy Catherine which seems a worthwhile contribution at this point. A portion of this letter also appears in W. H. G. Armytage, *Sir Richard Arman Gregory* (London, 1957).

194. To A. M. Davies

Illinois, ALS

7 Mornington Place, NW   [c. January 1894]

My dear Davies,

  Thanks very much for your opinion & your letter. With regard to enquirers, please do not volunteer any information. Say, to anyone that asks, I have removed from Sutton & that you have reason to believe there is some domestic trouble, but what it is you are not in a position to say. I think the Roses might, under proper promises of secrecy, be told so much as you know - if they ask you, that is.

    Yours ever,
    H.G. Wells
(I propose to tackle Miss Healey myself.)

195. To A. T. Simmons

Illinois, ALS

7 Mornington Place
N. W. [c. January 1894]

Dear Tommie,

    Thanks for your long letters. It is going all right with this animal but I am really frightfully busy. Cash is an urgent necessity of course & if only I could get about 32 hours in a day it would be very well indeed with me. My short stories are going at last. - Truth & St. James'. I have hope of making the best of my P.M.G. papers into a book. It makes my heart ache to see the educational papers so dull without me, & to be unable to get anything done for them. What a gorgeous book The Cloister & The Hearth.[1] (6d bookstalls) Don't miss it. It will just suit you. Mrs. H.G. Wells liked the story about a perpetual motion machine in the Tellenhall. Mag. Did you write it?
        Yrs,
           (In all Godly things)
           H.G.

Hawley Institute shop vacant £250. This weeks Nature Hewitt has gone to People's Palace for Chemistry.

---

[1] Charles Reade (1814–84), the English novelist is best known for *The Cloister and the Hearth*, which was published in 1861.

196. To Sarah Wells[1]

Illinois, ALS

7 Mornington Place, N.W.   Feb. 8th, 1894

My dear Mother,

    Do not be anxious about me. This trouble of ours is unavoidable, but I really do not care to go into details. Isabel and I have separated and she is at Hampstead and I am here. The separation is almost entirely my fault. I am with very nice people here and very busy. Yesterday I went over a microscope factory for an article for the Pall Mall Gazette similar to the one I sent a proof of to the G.V.[2] Did I tell you that they had made me one of their reviewers? I keep very well, no cough in the morning or any of those troubles. I hope Frank will run up soon to see me and reassure you. Let me know when he is coming as sometimes I am away all day. Love to the G.V. I will see to that Zoology soon. Ask him to send a letter card to Ellerington saying that no more B.Sc. Zoology will be sent for four weeks to give him an opportunity of getting the work up to date.

> Your loving son,
> Bertie

Will Father send me one copy each of the scheme for Zoology and for Biology and of the last lesson and test he has of each of those courses please?

---

[1] Also appears in *ExA*, ch. 6 §7.
[2] His two microscope articles 'The Very Art of Microtomy: The Subtle Beauty of Next to Nothing', *Pall Mall Gazette*, 24 January 1894, and 'In A Holborn Factory : Some More Microscopic Objects', *Pall Mall Gazette*, 5 March 1894, have never been collected, although they are quite stylish pieces. The latter part of the letter is puzzling, unless Wells's father is correcting correspondence school lessons.

197. To A. M. Davies

Illinois, ALS

7 Mornington Place, NW [1894]

My dear Davies,

I was very glad indeed to get such a long & familiar letter from you. I have thought of writing once or twice, but I was a little doubtful of your attitude & besides I have really been very busy indeed. I am very glad of the change in your views regarding our excellent Herbert Spencer - a noble & wondrous thinker but lacking humour, the trick of looking at things with two eyes, the stereoscopic quality that makes a view real. The way you put it 'individualism in ethics, socialism in economy' expresses I think my own position as well as yours. Come along on Thursday. Let me know by post card at what hour you are due. We usually have tea at 5:30 or 6.

My career has been uneventful, without either evil crisis or triumph. P.M.G. keeps loyal. By the bye, there was a good figure of Martin J. Cole in the <u>Budget</u> last Thursday week & last Thursday one of a creation of mine, a certain taxidermist (this last number has five things of mine, by the bye - you might do worse than get it) I have also responded to an invitation by the <u>National Observer</u> and that old corpse of the Chronic Argo is being cut up into articles, one last Saturday (Time Travelling) one next number & possibly others to follow. It is quite recast. You might let me know what you think of it in the new garb.

I object to Bernard Shaw rather. He is such a giddy creature.[1]

Yours ever,
H.G.W.

Short Stories are going after all. One in Truth & another in St. James's

---

[1] George Bernard Shaw (1856–1950), playwright, critic and friend of Wells. Their letters have been edited by J. Percy Smith (Toronto, 1995).

198. To the Editor, *Pall Mall Gazette*[1]

PLS

[London]   [c. 9 March 1894]

This letter speaks for itself. It is as tasty as their tombs. I had not Messrs. Daniels or any other stonemasons in particular in mind when I wrote the article, but if they like to wear the cap, I see no reason why I should exert myself to prevent it. Their circular[2] certainly gives them a strong claim, but I should be sorry to rob any other "monumental" mason by assigning my strictures unreservedly to them. I fail to see any reason why they should regard themselves as *par excellence* the bad stonemasons, though some of their patterns - 29, 42, 45, 94, and 103, for instance - are certainly most unseasonably funny, and the majority of them are very ungainly. As a nervous man, not in the best of health, I have some reason to anticipate, as a consequence of their gruesome joke, a nightmare of their monuments out of their catalogue fighting to sit upon my chest; but their uncharitable hope that it will finish me is, I trust and believe, a mistaken one. Rather, I should imagine it a new inducement for me to cling to life and escape them.

> The Correspondent in Question.

---

[1] Wells had written a story about stonecutters, 'The Mode in Monuments', *Pall Mall Gazette*, 6 March 1894, p. 3. This letter is a sarcastic response to a strong protest by Hy. Daniel & Co., which was published entitled 'forty-four years experience of the monumental trade'. Wells's response is signed, 'By the Correspondent in Question', and appeared in the edition of 10 March 1894.

[2] Which they had sent to the paper.

199. To the Editor, *Pall Mall Gazette*[1]

PLS

[London]   April 11, 1894.

Sir, I am delighted to find Mr. John Williams has been good enough to notice my little paper, though the impassioned tone he adopts, his angry italics, and the way he throws about such encomiums as "fool" and "washer-up of greasy plates" suggests that he has scarcely taken my efforts to show the reasonableness of his views in the right spirit. Really I did not "strike a blow at the flat earth" - I have too much respect for my knuckles; I struck a blow at the unreasonable prejudice people entertain to the proposition of the University Zetetic Society. I stated that this is only one fact that Mr. John Williams cannot get over; only one little fact- and I gave him, very generously, all the rest of the arguments against the flat earth. I showed that his opponents have tried to draw him to a false issue, and the question of water curvature has nothing to do with the shape of the solid earth. That concerns the theory of gravitation - an altogether different matter. But the point is that Mr. John Williams cannot explain the apparent rotation of the stars around *two* points in the heavens, round a south as well as a north pole. He may write a letter all in italics and pepper it with notes of exclamation and write "fool" in every line, but he will not touch that difficulty. Mr. Alfred Russell Wallace and the doubtful Christianity of this nation have nothing whatever to do with this discussion. If Mr. Williams replies I venture to prophesy he will dance round this one proof that the earth cannot be flat in a very amusing manner.

His argument from the Manchester Ship Canal is lovely. "If the world be a globe, how is it that one end of that Canal is not 217 yards lower than the other?" Simply because "higher" or "lower" means, respectively greater or lesser distance from the earth's centre, and the datum line is part of a terrestial circumference. I anticipate one of two delightful things: either a dignified silence on the part of Mr. Williams - he might instruct his solicitors to say he declines the discussion - or he will, in his inimitable style, dispose of this difficulty about the south pole of the heavens. But anyhow I think we may feel assured that Mr. John Williams is going to be entertaining. I am, Sir, yours, etc.

The Writer of the Article

---

[1] Wells had written an article, published in the *Pall Mall Gazette*, 2 April 1894, entitled, 'The Flat Earth Again', which dealt with the idea that the earth was flat. It produced a sarcastic letter from John Williams, and a prolix letter from 'R.Z', in response, the latter complete with a diagram, which was published on 13 April 1894 (p. 11). This is Wells's response to Williams, who was President of the University Zetetic Society.

200. To Elizabeth Healey

Texas, ALS

12 Mornington Rd, N.W.   June 11th, 94

My Dear Miss Healey,

Can I rely upon your discreet silence under the terrible & altogether mysterious shock I am about to inflict upon you? Explanations are among the things that come with the fall. In Paradise there were & in Heaven, there will be, none. The fact of it is I have done something rather dreadful - at least from the current feminine point of view - and I think I have no right to correspond with you while you are unaware of this. I will not give you the details - they are only fit for a Daily newspaper. But jesting apart, as you know I jest most when I feel most - things are grave. Isabel & I are living apart - she is at 52 Broadhurst Gardens N.W. - and she will divorce me.[1] It will be a kind thing on your part to us both if you do not try to learn any further particulars & if you will keep this matter a secret. Believe me that it is no small matter to terminate a correspondence that has flickered now for - how long is it? Seven years? But I am afraid it must be done. You really cannot go on professing the acquaintance of a person who has given his wife full grounds for divorce proceedings without running the risk of a certain amount of explanation if the particulars should transpire[?].

    I remain therefore
        Very sincerely (but henceforth quite silently)
            Your friend,
                H.G. Wells

---

[1] At that time in England, the only possible grounds for divorce (except for a very few Catholics who could obtain annulments) was proven adultery. A very good novel on this subject by A. P. Herbert, who later became a friend of Wells, is *Holy Deadlock* in which the plot revolves around the phony adultery games which sprang up in certain hotels. Herbert sponsored and saw through a private member's bill which introduced other grounds for legal divorce. This is one of the very few times in which a private member's bill was actually enacted. The novel, a best seller, was instrumental in achieving this result.

201. To A. M. Davies

Illinois, ALS

Tusculum Villa
Eardley Road
Sevenoaks   [Summer 1894]

My dear Davies,

    Thanks for your letter. I infer from your adhesion to Briggs that the Inspectorship did not come off. The correspondence has been given to a Miss Abbott. Simmons has taken B.Sc. Geology. Do you care to take on B.Sc. Zoology?[1] If so I will hand it over. I surely hope you will be happy when you are married. Your Miss Greville, I hear, is a friend of Miss Healey's. You are a true friend to warn me of my literary falling off. The bother is I have got to live & during my epoch of excellence not an editor would look at my stuff. This decadent style seems to have caught the fancy of Marriott-Watson, Henley[2] & one or two others, & I must needs disregard your warnings a bit - I am afraid - until I am in a less dependent position.

    Believe me,
        Yours ever,
             H.G.

[1] These references are to the Correspondence College teaching which Wells had been doing. This letter marks his commitment to full-time writing for his living.
[2] Marriott-Watson and Henley were important editors. Marriott-Watson introduced Wells to the *Pall Mall Gazette* and found a home for his short fiction in the *Pall Mall Budget*, while Henley serialized what would become *The Time Machine* in the *National Observer*.

202. To Elizabeth Healey

Texas, ALS

University of London
Burlington Gardens, W.   July 16, 1894

Dear Miss Healey,

    I am shifting my address, for three months at least if not permanently to Tusculum Villa, Eardley Road, Sevenoaks. London got a bit too much for me some weeks ago, & I am up here to fulfill an engagement I had rashly incurred at this Exam & to pack up for a permanent retreat. Since I last wrote to you about my literary vices, I have fallen still deeper into the mire, going from humorsome articles to short stories - I have hatched out half a score of single sitting stories for the P.M. Budget and I have some Strange Stories under way for Truth.[1] There is talk of a book, and where it will end, I don't know.
                      Believe me
                      Very faithfully yours,
                          H.G. Wells

A kind of informal connection with the P. M. G. has sprung up and I have been cherishing it for all I am worth.[2]

[1] A large number of Wells's short science-fiction stories appeared in the *Pall Mall Budget* under the general title, 'Single-Sitting Stories' prior to their collection in book form. *Truth* also published at least two stories, 'A Bardlet's Romance', 8 March 1894, and 'How Gabriel Became Thompson', 26 July 1894, pp. 208–11.
[2] Another letter which exists in holograph form as well as a typed transcript. The typed transcript contains this line, as well as the material above, but the line does not appear in the written version. It may well be part of still another letter, or another page, which no longer exists.

THE LETTERS: 1880-1903

203. To Joseph Wells[1]

PLS

Tusculum Villa
Sevenoaks, Kent   August 10th 94

My dear Father,

  I had intended to come along this week but more delays have arisen and so I suppose I had better fill up the gap with a letter. I thought Frank who came up to see me a few weeks ago would have explained affairs to you. The matter is extremely simple. Last January I ran away with a young lady student of mine to London. It's not a bit of good dilating on that matter because the mischief is done and what remains now is to get affairs straight again. Isabel left the house at Sutton and went to Hampstead where she is now living (at my expense) and she has now got through about half the necessary divorce proceedings against me. I expect to be divorced early next year and then I shall marry Miss Robbins.

The house at Sutton the landlord took off my hands upon my paying the rent up to June. Since then I have been in apartments with Miss Robbins (passing as my wife) but now Mrs. Robbins has joined us. She owns a house at Putney and has let that now on a twenty one years lease at a rent of £90. We think of taking a house down here - as we are not very comfortable in apartments - and settling down. My wife will take her degree of B.Sc. (of which one examination still remains) and go on with me with literary work.

About my work. The P.M.G. is still my bread and cheese. I do from six to ten columns a month and get two guineas a column. I have been doing work for Briggs that brings in about £60 a year but it takes too much time and I am resigning that. I am also dropping the Journal of Education which comes to about £12 a year and takes nearly a day a month. I do Educational Times work from 2 to 5 or more cols. a month at half a guinea col. and in addition drop articles at Black and White and the National Observer, when I get the time free. Then there are short stories which are difficult to plant at present, but I expect this series in P.M. Budget will get my name up. They are paid at a slightly higher rate than articles but are much more profitable in the end because they can be republished as a book. Besides that I have been writing a longer thing on spec. and have been treating through an agent to get some of my P.M.G. articles published as a book.

I think that is a pretty complete statement of my affairs. Naturally things are a little tight with me at present as the divorce business is heavy but after that bill is settled I see no reason why things should not get easier with all of us. I shall have to pay Isabel £100 a year or more, but my income by hook or by crook can always be brought up to £350 and it may be more in future. Mrs. Robbins is going to raise the ready money for our furniture by a small mortgage on her house and the interest on that with the ground rent will come to £30 out of her £90. Still I don't expect to be pinched and I have no doubt that I shall be able to do my filial duty by mother and yourself all right.

My health hasn't given me any trouble, save for one cold and a bit of overwork this year.

Give my love to mother and believe me,
Yours ever,
Bertie

Of course I want you to hand this to mother to read as well. Mother will remember Miss Robbins - she came to tea one Sunday afternoon.

---

[1] Letter appears in *ExA*, ch. 6 §7. I have never seen the original.

204. To Elizabeth Healey

Texas, ALS

12 Mornington Rd, N.W.   Sep 1894

[*a small sketch of a woman's head*]

Dear Miss Healey,

Thanks for your inquiries about the Great Man. His Chronic Argonauts are with a fact hound (& author of a slang dictionary) named Henley. His other works await the grace of publishers readers against their ignominious return & the <u>Pall Mall Gazette</u> is getting tired of him.

Of common people - Davies has stopped writing to me but I'm going to look him up herewith & I don't seem to have seen anyone else of our mutual acquaintance for ages. Concerning Miss Calvert - <u>Why</u> Physics?

Reverting to graver topics, we abandoned Sevenoaks about three weeks ago & I have been intending to write to you since with great persistence. Do you know how things are going with the <u>Educational Review</u>. Oh! - your loyal admirer Simmons (or Simmonds) was here yesterday. He is still at Tellenhall

& save for certain baldness shows little of the waste of years. It is a remarkable thing that he is unmarried. He stands, a bare & desolate summit, above all such petty accidents of this earthly life. By the bye, A. E. Taylor is a sub-inspector at a £150.

Sic transit gloria mundi Baccalaureii nascitur non fit.

Yours ever,
H.G. Wells

205. To the Editor, *Royal College of Science Magazine*[1]

PLS

[London] [September 1894]

Dear Sir:

Why the Associateship and why the Gown? A mere F.S.Sc. expedient! Why not the Associateship and the Cocked Hat? The College of Preceptors authorises those who have its diploma to wear not only gowns, but hoods and bands of purple; but for all that, A.C.P. is not more reputable than A.R.C.S. We want something more distinctive. To catch the public, why not authorise the Union to placard London with some leave-taking bill as -

THE VALUE OF THE A.R.C.S.
Worth a Guinea a Week!

or-

HAVE YOU TRIED AN A.R.C.S ?
Warranted Free From Any Ingredient But the Purest Science!

or again -

EMPLOY AN A.R.C.S. AS SCIENCE MASTER
AND
INSURE YOUR LIFE FOR £1000!

But meanwhile, all unknown to you, Sir, they are going to turn the R.C.S. into a constituent college of the great University of London that is to be, and then everyone shall [get] his B.Sc. without any heart-burning.

Speaking seriously, the scholastic value of the A.R.C.S. is so small because it conveys not the slightest guarantee that the holder has any qualification, as a teacher, except knowledge. He may be absolutely ignorant of method, of the simplest requirements of the discipline, or of the aims and ideals in general, as distinguished from scientific, education. He may even be ignorant of his own ignorance. I have no doubt that many a passed teacher in training, or A.R.C.S., could tell a story of failure due to this cause. The addition of a gown - a difficult thing to wear well - will merely be an added encumbrance. Until the serious study of method is added to the R.C.S. course this pedagogic insufficiency will remain a serious obstacle for the new-fledged A.R.C.S. Possibly the Union might consider this. Something might be done if a R.C.S. Teachers' Club could be formed for the purpose of studying educational science, and the preparations, delivery, and criticism of lessons. If the idea commends itself to any students or to any members of the staff, I should be very glad if I could take a share in the organisations and earlier meetings at least of such a club.

H. G. Wells

---

[1] At this period in his life, Wells still considered himself a professional teacher of science. Much of his writing at this time dealt with pedagogy, curricula and professional standards. He took part in a controversy over whether a distinctive gown should be worn by students at the Royal College. This letter appeared in the *Royal College of Science Magazine*, vol. 7, part 1, no. 57 (October 1894), p. 17. The controversy ran from June 1894 to March 1895. Wells edited the first three or four issues of the magazine. Several correspondents, as well as the current editor, welcomed Wells's suggestion of a Teachers' Club in the issues of November 1894 and January 1895.

206. To John Lane

Hofstra, ALS

12 Mornington Rd., N.W.   Sep 10th [1894]

Dear Mr. Lane,

Thanks very much for yours. I'm very glad you can use some of my stuff & shall be happy to talk matters over whenever it is convenient to you. I would like to give whatever is selected a careful revision before it went into a book. - Some of it is a trifle raw, & almost all was written under the spur & sent in to the P.M.G. at once.[1]

Yours very sincerely
H.G. Wells

[1] This letter and letter 208 concern Wells's third book, the first that was not a textbook. The collection of pieces from the *Pall Mall Gazette* was entitled *Select Conversations with an Uncle, Now Extinct and Two Other Reminiscences* (London: John Lane, 1895). Three conversations were not reprinted, but two of them can be found today in Patrick Parrinder and David C. Smith, eds, *Select Conversations ...* (London: Wells Society, 1993). The other two pieces have been reprinted by John Hammond in his edition of the uncollected short fiction, *The Man with a Nose* (London: Athlone Press, 1984). The uncle in the pieces is made up of character traits shown by Wells's father and his brothers. Lane was famous for the small sums he paid for books, and he was not in a hurry to accommodate Wells here, as is obvious from the second letter. The book was dedicated to Richard A. Gregory, although his initials were incorrectly given as R.A.C. for R.A.G.

207. To the Editor, *Nature*

PLS

[London] [Mid October 1894]

Mr. Crump (vide p. 56) though adopting a critical form and tone, really endorses the grounds of my suggestion that the Science and Art department should dissever itself by an age limit from school science. He is inclined to be especially severe upon the defects of the government examinations because they are controlled by scientific men, and to excuse the proper school examining boards because they have - according to Mr. Crump - attempted to examine without any qualification to do so. But I fail to see why eminent scientific men should be expected to be experts in elementary science teaching, any more than distinguished *littérateurs* , in the art of teaching to read, and it seems to me - in spite of Mr. Crump's "absolute" denial - that examining boards, neither professedly literary nor scientific but professedly educational, are more to blame in following and abetting the department's premium upon textbook cramming. The fact remains that the London Matriculate ignores practical teaching of any kind, and that the "practical chemistry" of the Locals and College of Preceptors is essentially the same test-tube analysis as the South Kensington examination. Anyone who knows the London matriculation examination - witness Miss Heath's concluding remark - will appreciate the quiet humour of Mr. Crump's allusion to it "as awakening and developing the powers of observation and reasoning".

H. G. Wells[1]

[1] Wells had written a short piece for *Nature*, 25 July 1894, pp. 300–1, which had stirred up

considerable interest, as he had claimed that although science needed popularisation, most scientists were too abstruse and abstract to do that very well. W. B. Crump responded to the piece as did a Miss Heath on 22 November 1894. O. Henrici also responded on the same page urging that mathematics be included in the pupil curriculum no matter who taught the subject. Wells's letter appears in *Nature*, 29 November 1894, p. 106. He had just given a talk before the College of Preceptors, 'Science Teaching: An Ideal and Some Realities', which was part of this long discussion in various venues. See the *Educational Times*, 1 January 1895, pp. 23–9, for the piece on science teaching; the talk was delivered on 12 December 1894.

208. To John Lane

Hofstra, ALS

12 Mornington Rd., N.W.   Nov 14/94

Dear Mr. Lane.

Will you be able to do anything with that stuff of mine? I have one or two other things - if you care to go through the lot and make a book of any of it.

Yours very faithfully,
H.G. Wells

209. To Elizabeth Healey

Texas, ALS

12 Mornington Rd N.W,   Nov. 14/94

Dear Miss Healey,

Ars longa - vita brevis, which being interpreted means I have been letting unconscionable time slip by without writing to you. But the advent of 4 Gilehurt reports from the Saturday Review have set me hunting for your conclusions re co-education - which were unfavourable, I believe? I don't know where my copy of your report has hidden itself. Let me know if they weren't as

I've alluded to "it". All four books are bad, about as bad as they can be, except Miss Burstall's.[1]

Things go very evenly with me. I do my two or three articles a week & that with a little reviewing meets my responsibilities but my books hang up the publishers & no article as yet has created an epoch. So far my greatest success has been a review of an American book that seems to have drawn one Kelley[2] from America (with a revolver?) to scare the harmless publishers of the <u>Educational Times</u> with ominous requests for Mr. Wells. (his head on a charger) but nothing came of it - I only heard of it after my life was safe. With the best of wishes,

Yours ever,
H.G.
as ever

Have you heard from Isabel? I'll be glad to hear all I can of her. She does not say much in her letters.

---

[1] Wells misspelt Miss Binstall's name. Wells reviewed four books for the *Saturday Review*, 1 December 1894, pp. 576-7 (Supplement) under the title 'Girls' Schools in America'. The books were A. Zimmern, *Methods of Education in the United States*, S. A. Binstall, *The Education of Girls in the United States*, A. B. Bramell and H. M. Hughes, *Training of Teachers in the United States* and M. H. Page, *Graded Schools in the United States*.

[2] No response to Wells's review appeared in *The Educational Times*. What is even more problematical is that there are seven articles by Wells in this time period, so we do not even know which article had excited Kelley's attention.

210. To Sarah Wells[1]

Illinois, ALS

12, Mornington Road, N.W.   5/12/94

My dear little Mother,

I'm anticipating Christmas and sending you a little present (I wish it could be larger). I'm keeping very well this Christmas and at about the same level of prosperity. I don't do so much for the <u>P.M.G.</u> but I do stuff for the <u>Saturday</u> which is rather better pay and I have some hope of the <u>New Review</u>.

This day week I am giving my lecture at the Coll. of Preceptors. There's nothing settled about any of my books yet but I think there will be two if not three in March.

Let me hear all about you. Have you heard from Fred?

Yours very affectionately
Bertie

[*The next page is a sketch, with Wells toiling away at his desk (with a quill pen). There are three inserts in the sketch: one of a man walking, another of Wells sitting at his desk, looking at a clock, and a third of a female figure in a mob cap, entitled 'Fat little Mother'. The text below reads: 'Little Bertie writing away for dear life to get little things for all his little people sends his love to Little Clock Man and Little Daddy and Little Mother'.*]

---

[1] Also appears in *ExA*, ch. 6 §7.

211. To Elizabeth Healey

Texas, ALS

12, Mornington Road, N.W.   22/12/94

Dear Miss Healey,

Just a line to wish you a Happy Christmas. You may be interested to know that our ancient Chronic Argonauts of the Science Schools Journal has at last become a complete story and will appear as a serial in the <u>New Review</u> for January. There was a puff preliminary in the P.M.G. last night (Friday). I'm praying it may go. It's my trump card and if it does not come off very much I shall know my place for the rest of my career. Still we live in hope.

Believe me,
Yours ever,
H.G. Wells

[*a sketch of a bewildered man looking at a mirror*]

212. To Elizabeth Healey

Illinois, ALS

12, Mornington Road, N.W.   25/12/94

My dear Miss Healey.

    I'm very much obliged to you for your letter. Is there anything I can do to help Isabel?[1] I don't know how she is situated even. I want Miss Davies to live with her. I know they're very fond of each other.

I hope you'll go to see her if you possibly can and I'd be very glad to know about her. She writes to me but it's scarcely to [be] expected she would tell me very much.

It's a dismal tragedy & it's <u>entirely my doing.</u> Don't blame anyone else. I can't stop the hum of Death. So far as I can see all that is possible for me is to go with my own work & keep her at least from urgent material necessity and give her the possibility of change & new interests. But beyond that the less I come into her life the better. She wants friends, sympathy and interests.

The Roses are people she might like - I don't know. But I can not go about finding friends and interests for her, can I? They must come at least from natural accidents.

Believe me,
Yours ever
H.G. Wells

I hope you'll get some rest this Christmas. Looking over it, this seems to be an egotistical letter.

---

[1] Although Isabel's life story is not well known from 1895 to 1900, Wells was able to hear of her activities through Healey who remained close to Isabel. Wells paid alimony to her, but this letter is referring primarily to loneliness. Some of the text of this letter is problematical.

213. To J. M. Dent

George Locke, ALS

12, Mornington Road, N.W. 2/1/95

Dear Sir,

I am greatly flattered by your letter. At present however I am scarcely free to avail myself of your kind offer to consider some of my work. The <u>Time Machine</u> is on offer to Heinemann & I have reason to think he will take it. Aepyornis Island is disposed of in a collection of stories to Methuen's & I have promised to let Mr. Watt - the literary agent - have the disposal of a story I am now writing. It is a trifle gruesome, will be about the length you name, & is, I think, absolutely novel, but I understand he has already some kind of informal arrangement about it. I had another in hand but I don't like it & have put it on one side.[1]

Although I have nothing in hand at present I should very much like to have a place in such a series as you suggest & in a month or so I will try to get something sketched. Will you mind my offering it to you through Mr. Watt? He has done most of my business so far.

Yours very faithfully,
H.G. Wells

---

[1] Wells had shown himself to be a promising author with his work in *Pall Mall Gazette* and *Saturday Review*, so some competition had begun. Heinemann did take *The Time Machine*, the 'gruesome' book is *Dr. Moreau* and the short story collection, *The Stolen Bacillus and Other Incidents* was published by Methuen. Wells was not going to let Dent go however, as the next paragraph indicates.

214. To the Editor, *Nature*

PLS

[London] [early January 1895]

May I call attention to Prof. Lodge's method of "silencing" me in your issue of January 10.[1] It bears very closely upon this very question of the effect of psychical research upon the investigator's reasoning. He quotes the preface of Mr.

Podmore's book to show that that gentleman is not a "bigoted upholder of the certainty of telepathy," and the casual reader would scarcely guess that, in truth, I never asserted that he was. I complained of the very air of open-mindedness in that preface to which Prof. Lodge's quotation witnesses, and showed by an instance, that in the body of the book question-begging occurred which was all the more dangerous on account of the liberal tone of the opening portion. I made no objection to the individual prosecution of psychical research - only to its public recognition before it has produced more definite results than it has done so far. So much for the "silencing." It shows either that Prof. Lodge had not read my review, or that he has misunderstood it; and in either case it enforces my contention that these investigators are over-hasty. The phrase "irresponsible detractor" points in the same direction.

H. G. Wells

[1] On 6 December 1894 Wells had reviewed F. Podmore's book, *Apparitions and Thought Transference* in *Nature*. There were two responses to the review, on 27 December1894, and 10 January 1895, by Sir Oliver Lodge, which Wells answers here in the issue of 17 January. Karl Pearson also commented in this same issue. Wells and Lodge would clash again. Oliver Lodge (1851–1940) was a physicist, then teaching at the University of Liverpool and was a pioneer in the study of radio-telegraphy. He later became the first principal at the University of Birmingham. Karl Pearson (1857–1936) was a distinguished mathematician increasingly concerned with eugenics. He is regarded as a father of modern statistics.

215. To the Editor, *Royal College of Science Magazine*

PLS

[London] [January 1895]

Dear Sir,

The amount of reply to my remarks upon the great gown proposal is a little oppressive. Mr. Grime is very kind and flattering, and I can only say that I endorse his suggestions and shall be very glad to do anything to forward his proposals. The other letters demand fuller answers. "A.R.S.M." objects to my statement that A.R.C.S. is of low scholastic value, because it implies no knowledge of method, on the ground that B.Sc., which is equally without such implication, is preferred. But the preference for B.Sc. is, I think, due to the fact that a certain literary qualification is involved. I am under the impression that the market value of a pass B.Sc. with a gown and without teaching experience, is no higher than that of an A.R.C.S. who has matriculated. With regard to his second point, the method and discipline required in a boys' school are essentially different from those employed at your College, as I pointed out in Nature (September 27th). Mr. Nathan's proposal to institute a diploma of F.R.C.S. seems to me to be premature while the value of the A.R.C.S. seems to be established in the popular estimation. He is wrong, moreover, in supposing that the College of Preceptors diplomas are given only to those who have been engaged in teaching; the A.C.P. is awarded, upon examination, to those who have merely attended twenty-four lectures in psychology and method. "W.H.W." has the will for sarcasm. So far as the material points of my letter go, he is entirely in accord with me; but he is evidently upset at my want of respect for his gown aspirations. So he begins very severely with "second-rate comic journal", "deplorable want of originality", and "anxiety to be funny" and presently behold him, half-way down the column, unable to restrain his real appreciation any longer, with my cocked hat clapped on his head, and his own miserable little addition of a coloured feather, chuckling up the Exhibition Road, and clearly persuaded the whole is his own original joke! That, Sir, is a feather in my cap. I say it without anxiety, and I thank "W.H.W." for his most delightful - because unintentional - compliment. I am also glad to find I have contributed to his education, and that he now perceives in what manner the demand for a gown is related to teaching qualifications. Then he goes on to say other things, meant unkindly, no doubt: dark insinuations about "cramming institutions (now so popular)", and "books, written especially for the examination", but if he will reread his letter, he will find that in his abortive research for something to sting me with, he has altogether forgotten to intimate what are "the real points at issue" which I have missed. I fancy he is trying to support the view that the A.R.C.S. should have a gown, not because it would be of the slightest use to him, but because (*a.*) the London B.Sc. has one, and (*b.*) it need not be worn; yet these are scarcely convincing pleas. "W.H.W." should study some little crambook in logic. However, I freely forgive him his bad logic, and absurd animus for the sake of his adhesion to my views.[1]

H.G. Wells

---

[1] The controversy over whether an academic gown should be worn by holders of the degree continued. This letter appeared in the *Royal College of Science Magazine*, vol. 7, part 4, no. 60 (January 1895), pp. 115–16. Others continued to comment on this issue in this number and elsewhere. Wells was also repelling an attack on his and Gregory's book, *Honours Physiography*, which had appeared in 1893 and, although he specifically described it as not being a cram book, that is essentially what it was.

216. To John Lane

Hofstra, ALS

[12, Mornington Rd., N.W.]   Feb 2, -95[1]

Dear Mr. Lane,

I've had the ill luck to miss you twice, so I am writing about the book we have under consideration. The points to consider are how to make a book out of the miscellaneous collection in hand. The things I have written fall into four classes

1. Altogether I have now written about fifteen or sixteen essays in which scientific theories are treated in an imaginative manner. I've had five in the Saturday, since Harris took it, one in the Fortnightly, and the rest are from the Gentleman's, The P.M.G. & The Globe. I've been wondering if such a book would sell. The only thing of the kind you have in your bundles of my stuff, is the Man of the Year Million.

2. Then there are numerous articles of which you have a bundle & of which I have as many more at home here.

3. Dialogues

4. Short stories & sketches.

Perhaps if you would return my bundles I could overhaul them & rearrange them. The more I think of the suggestion I made you of a kind of humorous book the less I like it - at least as a beginning. A collection of scientific papers such as I have suggested would appeal to the same class of people as the "Time Machine" story I have running in the New Review. I'd be glad if we could get to something definite about this stuff soon.[2]

               Believe me,
                 Very faithfully yours,
                   H.G.Wells

---

[1] There is another date in Wells's hand, 20/1/95, which suggests that this letter was held back before it was posted. Also, at the top of the page in another hand, perhaps Catherine's, are the words, 'Breakfast, [*illegible word*], 10 o/c.?'

[2] This letter is important in a number of ways, as it shows the young writer on the verge of success but in the hands of someone who worked at a different pace. Wells was able to sell some of his scientific stories in *The Stolen Bacillus and Other Incidents* (London: Methuen, 1895), but only a few of the others appeared in his lifetime, mainly in *Certain Personal Matters: A Collection of Material, Mainly Autobiographical* (London: Lawrence and Bullen, 1897). The pieces in *The Plattner Story, and Others* (London: Methuen, 1897) were mostly written after this letter. Some of the scientific articles have been republished in recent years by Robert Philmus and David Y. Hughes, eds, *Early Writings in Science and Science Fiction by H. G. Wells* (Berkeley: University of California Press, 1975).

217. To Joseph and Sarah Wells[1]

Illinois, ALS

12 Mornington Road, N.W.   5/2/95

My dear Father and Mother,

Thanks very much for your letters in the last few days. It's very kind of the Father to say £40 a year will do to go on with. However, I think I can manage £60, though just now is a tight time. Take £10 of the £15 to go on with and put £5 by for next quarter, say, as an experiment. You know the method is to put the cheque I send into the savings bank - which will take cheques now - and draw on whatever you want as you want it. Later on I hope to do better things for you if I can only get hold of a little money. It's a dream of mine to get you into rather a better house, either by buying one or leasing it but that can't happen this year and may never happen. Whatever success I have, you are responsible for the beginnings of it. However hard up you were when I was a youngster you let me have paper and pencils, books from the Institute and so forth and if I haven't my mother to thank for my imagination and my father for skill, where did I get these qualities?
   Believe me my dear Parents
                              Your very affectionate son
                                                      Bertie

---

[1] Also appears in *ExA*, ch. 6 §7.

218. To Elizabeth Healey

Texas, ALS

12, Mornington Road, N.W.   26/2/95

My dear Miss Healey,

   How are you going on? I've been expecting to hear from you. For my own part I have prospered until just now. Walter Low, one of the finest & most lovable of men is dangerously ill & I am afraid dying. He's been my intimate friend for a year & a half. We have hunted our exams together & done a thousand things in company. You may have met him perhaps at Cambridge - he [is] one of Briggs' tutors. I would willingly give God all the rest of the N.C.C. staff to redeem him. When one thinks of all the surplus population & remember that this man has a wife & three little girls of a hundred interests & possibilities, his death seems the most ghastly travesty of all the good I had thought of the world, even in its sadder phases. However, it is no good howling.[1]

I shall look to you to quote my books to me so soon as they appear. "There's Select Conversations with An Uncle (now Extinct.)" a book of cheerful rambling which Lane has in press, The Time Machine, which will follow this in June, & The Stolen Bacillus in September. Don't miss these treats.

& believe me
Yours very faithfully
H.G. Wells

---

[1] Wells is not exaggerating. Low was his best friend at that time and it was his first loss of a close friend or relative. They had met at Briggs's and immediately became close companions. Low had great promise, but all he left was one book in Briggs's series of cram books. He worked for part of the eighteen months with Wells on *The Educational Times*. Wells provided some funds for Low's wife and family. One daughter, Ivy, became a novelist, but she is better known as the wife of Maxim Litvinoff, later Foreign Minister, as well as USSR Ambassador to Britain.

219. To A. T. Simmons

Illinois, ALS

12, Mornington Rd, NW   [Spring 1895]

[*A sketch of a studious man, labelled 'A.T. S.' is at the top of the first page.*]

My Dear Tommy,

I don't know whether or not I owe you a letter. Anyhow here goes. I'm in a gorgeous state of cockiness just now, as Dent & Co. have agreed to buy a book - a new one - of which they have only seen the first sixty or seventy pages. It's brand new - not the Beast People idea - but a thing about a Vicar & an Angel, grotesque and humorous. The Island of Doctor Moreau is on offer with Methuens & an American firm, & from what Henley says of it it's going to go. I've just been seeing about a little house in Woking & I shall go there I hope in the course of a month & put in some good work. Heinemann hestitating to put the <u>Time Traveller</u> on the bookstalls at 1/6 - & go for a big sale, or make it a 6/- book. In the first case he will have it out by Whitsuntide. <u>The Referee</u> gave it two columns of notice last Sunday. I feel just like we used to do before our exam list came out, & most of my leisure goes in calculating 15% of this or that. I expect I shall be out of my misery by June.

You see Tutton[?] as a senior Inspector I suppose? I haven't seen or heard anything of Mills, but I expect he'll have a damned hard time. Gregory had an article on helium in last months <u>Fortnightly</u>, I see. A.V.J. is back in Hampstead & fat enough for two of us. He says he is earning nothing, & seems rather more opulent than ever. I've heard of nobody else lately - except Rowe, whose just the same as ever & cursing Burton for some new wrongs. Don't forget to vote for Napier & with God's blessing upon you.

      Believe me
       Yours ever,
        H.G.W.

They've put me on to novels with the <u>Saturday</u> & I've chucked the <u>PMG</u> drama.

220. To the Editor, *Royal College of Science Magazine*

PLS

[London]   [February 1895]

Dear Sir,

Why I should go on writing letters to you is a perennial source of wonder to myself. I gain nothing by it - yet this is a mercenary world - and palpably - for where is the Teachers' Club? - I am doing no good. Moreover, I lay myself open to learn that such exasperating persons as W.H.W. exist. It is a matter of sentiment, I suppose; the memory of those happy days when I was always receiving blue forms, underlined red, for smoking through some demonstrator's keyhole, whistling on your magnificent staircase, absenting myself without leave, and coming late, failing those absurd examinations that give you such heart-searching times in your first year, and living crescendo on Wednesday afternoon to pianissimo on the subsequent Tuesday. And the memory gets mellower as we get further away from the real thing. However, much as I am interested in your affairs - it should charm you to think that I am the only old student not on the staff who cares a rap about you - I tire of this attempt to convert your College to the necessity of studying pedagogics. Your students run into side issues and your staff maintains an attitude of gentlemanly aloofness, so I give it up forthwith. But, at any rate, I've warned you. As I once heard an "educational reformer" say to a private schoolmaster, "You wait until Acland comes to you."

Mr. Nathan's suggestion that the study of method might begin when the Associate has secured his position as a teacher seems made in forgetfulness of the fact that the discussion really grew out of the difficulty the A.R.C.S. sometimes finds in securing that position. And I must insist that until the market value of the A.R.C.S. is assured, it would be unwise to confuse the public with an F.R.C.S. I don't see any objection to "premature" because it is divisible into three syllables. As for W.H.W., what am I to do with him? He's on my hands, so to speak. I began it by larking about with his funny little gown proposal. I suppose it was wrong of me. By way of reply he wrote a letter neither witty nor funny, but simply ill-tempered. To that I replied with admirable kindliness, as you must admit, showed his want of logic, and forgave him. Now here he is again with the same ungracious phrasing, the same huffy offence. "Pretend to criticise", indeed! I simply knocked his childish proposal of a Gown into a Cocked Hat - and there it remains, beyond salvage. I give him up, too -

Yours etc.
H.G. Wells[1]

---

[1] The editors responded with a brief statement of regret, couched in irony, and the affair ended. Wells's letter and their response appeared in the March 1895 issue of the *Royal College of Science Magazine*, vol. 7, part 6, no. 62, pp. 165–6.

221. To A. T. Simmons

Illinois, ALS

12, Mornington Road N.W.   [c. March 1895]

Don't be such a miserable hound, Tommy – your troubles all of them are mere vexatious straws - or stomach. Go to.

I'm just up from a bed of sickness - a kind of cheap influenza or something. Moreau is still unfinished. After you left I began the beggar again from the very first page & set him up quite different & much better. Since then I've hacked him about a good deal. He's far from shipshape yet. About the middle of Feby I discovered I was likely to become bankrupt so I've had a spurt at occ articles again. Made Grant Allen howl in the Saturday over his blessed old Woman Who Did - my first novel review.

Love from both of us & do try and rise above these informal little frettings & pickings.

Yours ever,
H.G.

222. To the Editor, *Pall Mall Gazette*

PLS

[London]   March 18, 1895

Dear Sir, - May I have an inch or so of space to reassure the readers of my delightful little article on "Argon",[1] who may have been set a-doubting by the letters of "Your Science Correspondent" and "Accuracy"? The article was written merely to bring out in a readable way the pretty point about the specific heats which your science correspondent missed, or mentioned mysteriously - I forget which - in his notes and I doubt if one of your readers would for a moment confound his style with me. The slip by which I wrote "Reynolds" for "Ramsay" was an unfortunate one, which I regret without any indecent shame - for all of us make such mistakes at times, and, I am inclined to think, the best of us most frequently. You see, I propose no tu quoque.[2] And "Accuracy" is right about chlorine being denser than argon; frankly I forgot chlorine - I'm not a chemical specialist. Only don't let the moral be missed. Here were striking facts going almost unnoticed by the general public because they were presented in exuberantly accurate, highly technical, very unreadable reports and notes; a benevolent writer, pitying what he conceives to be the dumbness of the chemical person, kindly interposes and explains; and forthwith comes this fierce correction on two or three quite unessential points. And these scientific people have heaps of other delightfully interesting things, which they will probably resent the common writer handling until he has studied the whole hierarchy of research and read all through the "Pogg Ann" and such like attractive records. A specialist in constantly changing results of any branch of science can generally point out some inaccuracy in a paper upon his subject by a man of broader culture. And the man of broader culture can in return appeal to a certain grave dulness that ensues from a weight of facts. I conceive it is choice for the general reader, between occasional inaccuracies and permanent boredom, and for the scientific investigator between being sketchily treated or ignored. It was, perhaps, an excess of sketchiness to confuse Professors Ramsay and Reynolds. I don't wish to extenuate my faults.

Yours, etc.,
The Writer of the Article

---

[1] One of the more interesting scientific events of the mid-1890s was the isolation and discovery of a new element, argon. Wells wrote at least two articles on the element, but he made some slight errors in his description of its characteristics. This letter, published in the issue of 18 March 1895, p. 4, 'The Strangeness of Argon', corrects these mistakes.

[2] Essentially a retort to a critic, 'You, too' as in 'You, too, have made errors' or 'You're another'.

223. To Elizabeth Healey

Texas, ALS

Lynton
Maybury Road
Woking   [Spring 1895]

Dear Miss Healey,

Thanks for the cutting. I'm having rather a good time just now with the notices. - but some of this sweetness will certainly beget sourness soon. The Weekly Times & Echo, the Referee, the Review of Reviews, & several other papers have men cover the column - so has the Realm. Le Gallienne in the Star remarks that a thousand years in my sight are but as yesterday & compares me cheerfully to the talented author of the Bible. But really it is very generous of these men. I don't intend to go on shouting in this way. Don't lend that copy of yours too widely mind - the public has got to buy the thing. "Select Conversations" is out. It's a limited edition & I'm doubtful if I shall let Lane run over the 500. It's been well praised in two or three papers, but it seems to me pseudo-scientific, so innocence[?] is the line for me to take just now.

Yours very faithfully,
H.G. Wells

224. To T. H. Huxley

Imperial College, ALS

Lynton
Maybury Road
Woking

May, 1895

Dear Sir:

I am sending you a little book that I fancy may be of interest to you. The central idea - of degeneration following security - was the outcome of a certain amount of biological study. I daresay your position subjects you to a good many such displays of the range of authors but I have this much excuse, I was one of your pupils at the Royal College of Science and finally: the book is a very little one.

I am Dr Sir
Very Faithfully yours
H.G. Wells

Professor Huxley[1]

---

[1] Thomas Henry Huxley (1825–95), biologist and the leading British exponent of Darwin's theory of evolution. This note accompanied a presentation copy of *The Time Machine*; it is located in the *Huxley Papers – General*, vol. 28, pp. 233–4 in the library of the Imperial College of Science. Huxley did not respond; he died shortly afterwards.

225. To J. M. Dent

George Locke, ALS[1]

12. Mornington Road, N.W.   May 1st, 1895

Dear Sir,

    I am receipt of your letter of yesterday's date. With regard to the book <u>Some Trivial Incidents</u> [2] I should be quite willing to let its publication stay over until Xmas, & in that case we could postpone settling the terms of the agreement at present, though I may say that I prefer to have a royalty on each copy. I should however explain that, of the the three books of mine which are about to be issued, one is a book of dialogues - to be published in a limited 500 edition by Mr. Lane, the second to appear will be the <u>Time Machine</u> now appearing in the <u>New Review</u>, while the third is the only one likely to clash with the book in your hands — being a collection of short stories of adventure differing entirely in style & method from those you have. [3]

With regard to the fantastic romance - which I have in hand for you, about 10,000 is already written & the rest planned, so that I could probably let you have the complete story by the end of this month.[4] If you would care to see the portion already done I should be pleased to send it to you. I should be quite willing to leave the American publication also in your hands, on the terms of a royalty of 10%. In the event of your proposing to postpone the publication of this also, I should like to avail myself of the interval to give it a serial appearance. I think however that in form & style it would be well adapted for the "Iris" series.

        Believe me
        Very faithfully yours
                H.G. Wells

---

[1] This letter also exists in a holograph draft at Illinois.
[2] This is the collection put together from his journalistic 'middles' (short filler pieces used in magazines) we know as *Certain Personal Matters* which was not published by Dent however. They were probably content with *The Wheels of Chance* which has remained available on the Dent list until very recently.
[3] The Lane volume was *Select Conversations with an Uncle* which, because it was published in an identical edition in America, was not really a limited edition, although it was part of Lane's Mayfair Series. The book was reprinted and made available again in 1931 in an identical edition. In recent years, other 'Uncle' stories have been discovered and an edition of 'Just *Uncle*' pieces, has been published by the H. G. Wells Society, edited by Patrick Parrinder and myself.

Since then I have located still another 'Uncle' story, 'The Advancement of Humanity: A Serious Discussion', *Pall Mall Gazette* 11 June 1894, p. 3.
[4] This book is *The Wonderful Visit* which, in fact, came out before *The Wheels of Chance*.

226. To William Heinemann

Illinois, ALS

12 Mornington Road NW   May 14/95

Dear Mr. Heinemann,

   I have been expecting to hear from you about the <u>Time Traveller</u>. I'm afraid people will be forgetting <u>The Review of Reviews</u> and <u>Referee</u> notices if the book is not fired off at them soon. I'm quite prepared to place myself in your hands with regard to price, get up &c, only if the price is to be 1/6 or lower I think I ought to have say 20% after the first 5000. But I don't want to haggle about details of that sort - the important thing to me is to get the book published. There's one point I have been thinking over & that is, that an initial publication at a low price involves some risk of the book being scantily reviewed. We appeal I think to a public which reads reviews. Don't you think an immediate publication at a minimual price of 4/- say with the ordinary discount followed by a cheap paper covered issue for the Christmas bookstall time wd be possible.

 By the bye has the book appeared in America? I have hopes for it over there.

 Pardon my troubling you, but naturally I am in considerable suspense.
Yours faithfully,
H.G. Wells

The following publications wd I think look at the book with friendly interest.

 The <u>Saturday Review</u> (the editor was praising the thing to me the other day).

<u>The National Observer</u>
<u>Nature</u>
<u>The Observatory</u>
<u>The Journal of Education</u>
<u>The University Correspondent</u>

The Educational Review
The New Budget
The P.M.G. & St. James's Gazette

I've had numerous signed articles in all of these things & fancy that a certain proportion of their readers wd. go for the book. I have indeed a kind of small public of my own in this constituency.

P.S. The extensive changes I have made in the early part of the book should prevent <u>Mudie's</u> binding up the <u>New Review.</u> If they did, we could make a fuss in all the newspapers & advertise the thing.[1]

---

[1] This remarkable letter provides a look at Wells, the new and anxious author, along with Wells, the careful vendor of his contributions. He did in fact have articles in all the journals he mentioned. The letter, seen in draft in the Rare Books Room at the University of Illinois, has some marks (possibly in crayon) across the fourth page, but they seem to have been added later. This is an important holograph letter about his first significant novel.

227. To Grant Richards[1]

ALS

Lynton,
Maybury Road   June 15 [1895]
Woking

Dear Sir,

I have no story in hand of the length you specify, but I will get one done before July 7th. Seven guineas would I think be a fair price - what do you think? - two guineas a thousand.

      Yrs very faithfully
      H. G. Wells

---

[1] The next two letters were originally published in Grant Richards's *Author Hunting by an Old Sportsman*, vol. 2 of his *Memories* (New York: Coward-McCann, 1934). They concern Wells's short story, 'The Argonauts of the Air', which appeared in *Phil May's Winter Annual* (Christmas 1895).

228. To Grant Richards

ALS

[Lynton,
Maybury Road
Woking] July 7th, 1895

Dear Sir,

I've just discovered to-day is the 7th - I hope you'll give me this one day's grace.

I'm sorry I've not had time to have this story typewritten, but I think it is all right.

Don't be too dispirited when you read it if the story does not seem to jump in the earlier two thousand words of it. I've made that go quietly in order to enhance the wobbling flight and smash of the flying apparatus at the end of it.

With apologies for sending you the rough MS.
    Believe me
    Very faithfully yrs
    H. G. Wells

229. To Elizabeth Healey

Texas, ALS

12, Mornington Road, N.W. [Summer 1895]

My dear Miss Healey,

  Have you also dropped me? What is fame - the admiration of the Referee, the applause of the Review of Reviews, if it is tempered by the neglect of all respectable people? I become an outcast. Davies drops me, Jennings writes me to see him when his wife is out. I feel a tainted wretch in the presence of the ridiculous[?] Briggs. The Educational Times selects anybody but me to edit it. I feel that I am kindly treated when some pretentious nobody calls upon me with an air of infinite patronage & behaves like a district visitor in the house of a fallen woman. Consequently I am driven to consort with publishers & sinners. Of course it will all make copy - seen in the retrospect - but the humour of it is bleak enough now. But it's rough on my wife who has no interest in publishers nor taste for sinners. All of which, as you will no doubt observe, simply shows that I didn't ought to have done it. In a week or so we shall be in a home at Woking - Lynton, Maybury Road, Woking is the address.

Yours ever,
H.G. Wells[1]

---

[1] Wells always wrote in this jocular manner to Healey when he was under stress. This letter is one of the finest letters to indicate an author's mood, while the reviews are being written and before they are read.

230. To William Heinemann

Illinois, ALS

Lynton
Maybury Road
Woking   [August 1895]

Dear Mr. Heinemann,

You asked me to name terms for the <u>Island of Doctor Moreau</u>. The following wd. I think be fine.

<u>A.</u> If published at 6/- 15% on the first 2000, then 20% up to 7000, then 25% onward.

(<u>B.</u>) If at 3/6 or any lower price 15% up to 6000. 20% up to 16000 & 25% onward.

With regard to the American rights I think they had best go to you if you take the English & Colonial, at 10%. The American edition might go into Canada.

In either case a cheque on account of royalties of £100 to be paid on the completion of this agreement.

The book not to be published before November 15th 1895 or later than April 15th 1896.

The agreement on these terms would not be terminated. I am clearly entitled to that.

Yours faithfully
H.G. Wells

231. To A. T. Simmons

Illinois, ALS

Lynton
Maybury Road,
Woking [c. 1895]

My dear Tommy,

I will do all I can for you. Do you care about prices? Because I daresay I could plant you on to such a paper as <u>The Realm</u> if ever I sh<u>d</u> chance upon Earl Hodgson, very easily, but he pays - Good God! - infinitesimally.

I'm writing towards midnight & with a splitting headache. - the results of an <u>E</u>cker[1] of 24 miles to Liss on my bicycle. - white fog all the way, ruts like iron, flints now on the roads. Many an easier journey has been counted a saint for righteousness.

God bless & keep you,
Yours ever,
H.G.

Latest quotations on the per thou market Seven guineas English serial rights, two American Short story of six thousand words in Pearson's Monthly. Work it out.

Abused wife sends greetings.

---

[1] Wells probably means excursion, although he may mean reconnaissance.

232. To Sidney Low[1]

Illinois, Typed Transcription

Woking Oct. 26th. '95

Dear Mr. Low,

I must thank you for your very kind letter, and for the admirable review you gave me. It's not very often that one learns anything from a press notice, but certainly I owe you my thanks for very genuine and helpful criticisms. I should have rewritten the book.[2] I set out merely to jest, and the deeper applications are by the way.

Yours very faithfully,
H.G.Wells

---

[1] This letter and others written to Sidney Low, the brother of Walter Low (see letter 218), appeared originally in Major Desmond Chapman-Houston, *The Lost Historian: A Memoir of Mr. Sidney Low* (London: John Murray, 1936). I also read these letters in transcription in Illinois, before I was alerted to the original by my very good friend, John Green, of the H. G. Wells Society.

[2] Wells is referring to his published work, *The Wonderful Visit*, see letter 239.

233. To Grant Allen

Yale and Illinois, ALS, Typed Transcription

Lynton
Woking [late Summer 1895?]

Dear Mr. Allen,

Your very kind acknowledgement of my book is more than I expected. I'm glad indeed that you like the work of it. But there is one little matter which I feel bound to mention to you in view of your good opinion. You allude to possible reviews. I think before you say anything in the book's favour that you should know that I wrote the review of The Woman Who Did in the Saturday. So far as essentials go I hold by that review now, & any apology I could make for the Bank-Holiday flavour of its style, the window smashing midnight-concertina-playing tone of it, wd I am afraid be a little belated now. But I sent the book to you, not in your aspect of prominent critic & with any designs upon your criticism, but simply because I wanted you to read it. I have as sincere an envy for the almost instinctive way in which you get your effects in your short stories & for your scientific essays, as I have — shall I say dislike? for your vein of sexual sentiment. It's an unpleasant explanation this, but I have brought it on myself by my action in sending you a copy of my book. That was really not an appeal to you as a public appreciator. Apart from the difference in temperament that comes out when I read your fiction, I flatter myself that I have a certain affinity with you. I believe that this field of scientific romance with a philosophical element which I am trying to cultivate, belongs properly to you. Hence the book I sent. And you go writing 'Keynotes' that I cannot admire, goading me into ill-mannered & even unfair reviews, when there is this fantastic wonderland unexplored.[1]

I cannot imagine that you will do anything but dislike me after this incident, but I trust that at any rate you will give me credit for not aiming at your public support.

Yours very faithfuly,
H. G. Wells

---

[1] Allen responded that he had known Wells wrote the review and that no damage was done to their association, see letter 221. A printed exchange had already occurred, but Wells's name was not published. Wells's review appeared in the *Saturday Review*, 9 March 1895, pp. 319–20 and it was answered by Allen on 15 March 1895, p. 351.

234. To Fred Wells

Illinois, ANS

12 Mornington Road, NW [end of 1895 - beginning of 1896?]

Dear little Freddie,

Thanks very much for your very brotherly letter. I can scarcely detail all that has happened to me yet, but do not think of me in any way as collapsed or ruined. I am in apartments here & am writing now for The National Observer, Black & White, the PMG & Truth & doing very well indeed. I will write you a long letter soon but just now I am working very hard indeed, & feel scarcely in the vein for epistles. So I send this card just to fill up the time. But don't worry. I weigh 9 stone 3 lbs, earnt £40 last month & am altogether very cheerful.

Yours ever,
H.G.W.

235. To Sarah Wells

Illinois, ALS

12, Mornington Road, N.W. [late in 1895]

Dear little Mother,

Thank you for your letter. I daresay Freddy is having a good time & will come back with dozens of diamonds sewn into his coat linings, in a year or so more. My address for the next week or fortnight will be the The Glen, Sidmouth, Devon. I shall send you a P.M. Budget in a few days - the last you will ever see - for the proprietor who is an American millionaire & who owned it to please his wife, has lost her, & hasn't the heart to see it going on any longer. I'm off tonight to the Haymarket Theatre & then no more work for a bit! Give my love to Dah dah & Frank. I've had the papers all right & am much obliged to him. And many thanks to Frank for the clock from us both. Don't be indignant at the American's indignation. I had knocked his book into splinters, & as he had no answer he naturally fell to abusing me. Several of the Chicago papers quoted my review against Parker who is being denounced as a 'hum bug', pretty roundly & no wonder the poor soul 'cussed' when an independent stranger in England rose to witness against him.

I'm enclosing the review which you three little people may like to read.
      With love all round
       Yours ever
        Bertie

236. To Sarah Wells

Illinois, ALS

12, Mornington Road, N.W. [1895]

My dear little Mother,

Many thanks. Tell me when you are coming along. Before you go back I want you to go with me to a theatre. I can get you some nice reserved seats at a play you are sure to like & I'll call for you & take you. High Life

Below Stairs is on now if you would like to see that & there is a delightful play, A Pair of Spectacles at the Garrick Theatre.[1]

There's no harm done yet by your little trip & if you go back soon there probably won't be. Forgive me if I worried you.

& believe me Dear Mother
>Your very affectionate son
>Bertie

---

[1] Wells reviewed plays for the *Pall Mall Gazette* from January to April 1895. He reviewed 'A Pair of Spectacles'. 'High Life Below Stairs' would have appealed to a person who had spent more than half her life 'below stairs'. It is quite possible that this was the first play Sarah Wells ever attended.

237. To Sarah Wells[1]

Illinois, ALS

12, Mornington Rd. N.W. Sunday, October 13th [1895]

My dear Mother,

Just a line to tell you that I am back with my old landlady here for three weeks (getting married). We've been up about a week. My last book seems a hit - everyone has heard of it - and all kinds of people seem disposed to make much of me.[1] I've told nobody scarcely that we were coming up and already I'm invited out to-night and every night next week except Monday and Friday. I've had letters too from four publishing firms asking for the offer of my next book but I shall, I think, stick to my first connection. It's rather pleasant to find oneself something in the world after all the years of trying and disappointment.

What is Fred's address in Johannesburg? I'm rather anxious to know. I sent a copy of "The Wonderful Visit" to him just before I had your letter, addressed to Messrs Garlick. I'd like to know all about him. There's no doubt that country is rising at an immense pace. I know one of the bank managers and might be able to help Fred through him. He was my colleague at Milne's school. He's a Scotchman and bound to die rich, a long headed friendly man who might - if he chose - put Fred up to a lot of good tips. His name is Johnston. I'm getting his address from Milne.

Love to the Dad and Frank.

Your very affectionate son,
Bertie

---

[1] Also appears in *ExA*, ch. 6 §7.
[2] *The Time Machine* was published by Heinemann in May 1895.

238. To Grant Richards[1]

ALS

Lynton
Maybury Road
Woking						Nov. 6/95

My Dear Sir:

It's awfully good of you to go writing up a reputation for me, and I will gladly do what you ask of me. I was born at a place called Bromley, in Kent, a suburb of the damnedest, in 1866, educated at a beautiful[2] little private school there until I was thirteen, apprenticed on trial to all sorts of trades, attracted the attention of a man named Byatt, headmaster of Midhurst Grammar School, by the energy with which I mopped up Latin - I went to him for Latin for a necessary examination while apprenticed (on approval, of course!) to a chemist there, became a sort of teaching scholar to him, got a scholarship at the Royal College of Science, S. Kensington (1884), worked there three years, started a students' journal, read abundantly in the Dyce and Foster Library, failed my last year's examinations (Geology), wandered in the wilderness of private school teaching, had a lung haemorrhage, got a London degree B.Sc. (1889) with first and second class honours, private coaching, <u>Globe</u> turnovers, article in the <u>Fortnightly,</u> edited an obscure educational newspaper, had haemorrhage for the second time (1893), chucked coaching and went for journalism. <u>P.M.G.</u> took up my work, then Henley (<u>N. Obs.</u>), Hind (<u>P.M. Budget</u>), set me on to short stories. Found <u>Saturday Review</u> when Harris bought the paper. <u>Review of Reviews</u> first paper to make a fuss over <u>Time Machine</u> - for which I shall never cease to be grateful. <u>Referee</u>, next. Brings us up to date.

Books published -
Textbook of Biology. A cram book - and pure

                    hackwork (illustrated grotesquely bad - facts imagined.)
Time Machine
Wonderful Visit
Stolen Bacillus
          Forthcoming -
The Island of Dr. Moreau Jan. 1896

   I am dropping all journalism now, and barring a few short stories to keep the wolf from the door am concentrating upon two long stories - one of these is a cycling romance (I am a cyclist), the other a big scientific story remotely resembling <u>The Time Machine</u>. I am trying to secure a serial publication of these in 1896 - if ever I get them finished.
   But this is enough of facts. Use any you fancy and believe me
   Always yours very sincerely,
                    H.G. Wells

---

[1] This letter appeared in Grant Richards, *Memoirs of a Misspent Youth, 1872–1896*, (London: Heinemann, 1932) with an introduction by Max Beerbohm, on pp. 327–8. Richards reviewed *The Island of Doctor Moreau* very favourably in the *Academy* and this letter is in response to a letter offering to promote Wells and his work.

[2] When this appeared in the *Memoirs*, beautiful was changed to beastly. However, that may simply be rapid reading as Wells's hand is cramped in the original.

239. To the Editor, *Blackwood's Magazine*

Edinburgh, ALS

Lynton
Maybury Road
Woking   Nov. 29/95

          [*at top left corner, '30/11/95 Wrote to Decline'*]

Dear Sir,

          I have almost completed a story of 50,000 words. It describes the sensations & adventures of a draper's assistant during a ten days holiday tour upon a bicycle. He becomes involved with an elopement, & finds himself (through no fault of his own) with a lady (in rational dress) & a bicycle upon his hands. He is pursued by the lady's friends. The story is built to divide conveniently into pieces of about 5000 words each. I shall be glad to hear if you have any opening for this story. A fairly novel sentimental interest runs through the whole, & the generous allowance of bicycle should, I think, appeal to a certain section of the public. Of my published work it is most like 'The Wonderful Visit'. It has no "scientific" element.

Yours very truly
H.G. Wells

240. To the Editor, *Saturday Review*

PLS

[London]   10 December 1895

Sir, It is impossible for one who is so deeply indebted to the present London University[1] as I am to pass by the misleading article in your last issue, "The Duke and the Crammers", without a protest. The question is a special one, and overmuch left to those immediately interested. The Duke of Devonshire has shown in this business an unexpected breadth of sympathy. Like Sir John Lubbock, he has evidently studied the matter broadly and carefully, and the advocates of one of the most tawdry of all the cheap and nasty reform movements that Liberalism has produced in its decay, may count upon one more honest and enlightened opponent to their persistent enterprise. The illinformed reader would imagine from the tone of your article that the new scheme proposed some splendid addition to the teaching facilities of London, and that a dishonest crew of "crammers" obstructed this for their own ends. As a matter of fact, no new teaching body, no new buildings, no new professors, are to be provided. I challenge your contributor to state any definite enlargement that would certainly ensue if this Gresham[2] scheme operated. The point at issue is not enlargement, but contraction - a monopoly of teaching. The essence of this precious "reform" movement, apart from the demand for an easier medical degree, is to exclude the non-collegiate students, to force such non-collegiate students as have the means into the empty classrooms of those whom your contributor calls the "ablest men in the educational world", the energetic movers in the matter, and to prevent all together the poor selfeducated man from obtaining the worldly advantage, the honourable hallmark, of a London degree. To do that your representative of these "ablest men" sticks at nothing, not even at the assertion that a majority of the country graduates are favourable to the scheme, not even at the self-contradiction of invoking heaven and earth to deprive Convocation of the rights of voting a plan which asserts Convocation has already approved.

Then this attack upon the University by Correspondence. What does it really mean? The ill-informed teacher will imagine, on the one hand, some seedy rogue "cramming" - what a magic word that is! - his gaping, attenuous customers, and on the other the wise, grave professor, like a father in the bosom of his family, giving individual attention to his select following, saying that apt memorable thing and that, cherishing, developing. But the facts! I claim to know two typical establishments passing well: one a University by Correspondence, a cramming shop, the other a great scientific school- the Royal College of Science to be explicit, college elect of the wonderful University that is to be, if the public conscience permit it. Take the mathematical instruction. In the former you actually have teaching such brilliant and original investigators as Mr. Bryan, a Smith's prizeman, one of the youngest of the Fellows of the Royal Society, and Mr. Barlow, as scholarly if less original a mathemetician. In the latter the bulk of the actual teaching is in the hands of (comparatively) unknown men. In the latter establishment, too, the professors, as your contributor knows as well as I do, being preoccupied by the keen competition in research, lecture a minimum of lectures, talk a text-book that is, and never come into personal contact with their students at all. During my three years of instruction, save for a rare "Good-morning", I never spoke to any professors at South Kensington - Professors Huxley, Guthrie, and Judd - except in the case of the latter. And most of my conversations with Professor Judd were devoted to points of discipline. This is the usual experience of South Kensington students, and it is probably the general rule in college teaching; you cannot expect celebrated men to spend their lives teaching the rudiments. The personal teaching in the college is almost entirely in the hands of men not a whit above the crammers and in many cases the College instructors eke out their incomes by "cramming" of an evening. In the University by Correspondence you have teaching, now, a former demonstrator of the Royal College of Science, and another of its outlaw teachers has recently gone into "genuine" teaching in a university college. Again, a Royal College professor was formerly a Correspondence tutor. You have one and the same man, here a heaven-sent teacher, and there a scoundrel crammer. And as at the University by Correspondence, I can assure that, save for the intervention of the postman, they teach geology by correspondence at the Royal College of Science; assistant teachers at a guinea a week give out instruction papers, and the students work accordingly. The stress is sustained by frequent and stringent examinations. There is not a pin to choose between the two methods. I have, too, the note-books of the Cambridge Morphological Laboratory, in which the same "cut-and-dried" method is carried far beyond the University-by-Correspondence system as it is known to me. And when as Doreck Scholar I inspected and reported on the school of Professor Sylvanus Thompson in Finsbury, a couple of years ago, I found the same mechanical cramming, by instruction papers and class examination, in full operation in that institution. Yet he is one of the leading "ablest men" in this movement. Where more than two or three students are gathered together there are necessarily instruction papers and delegated teaching in the midst of them. And the proposition that private teachers are necessarily dishonest teachers and endowed professionals the reverse, is certainly not the axiom your contributor would have your readers suppose.

But apart from the natural indignation excited by the pot calling the kettle black, I have little interest in defending the University by Correspondence. All teachers in big classes must necessarily mark against originality, and Mtr. Blank's class in matriculation Latin and Professor Judd's class in elementary geology are mechanical for much the same reasons. The point upon which I am more concerned is the closing of the worldly advantages of the degree, the withdrawal of the encouragement to self-help it offers to the outside man, the cobbler's 'prentice who reads of an evening, the literary bricklayer, the ambitious shopman and their class. That is a type of energetic man the country cannot afford to stifle down in the interests of the reputedly able and certainly very assertive professors of London. It is, to mention haphazard the names that come first to hand, the class of Dalton, Joule, Miller, and William Smith, the founders of modern chemistry, modern physics and geology, of Shakespeare, Burns, and Blake, and a host of lesser but still honourable citizens. Scholarship is an admirable thing in its way, but the greater need of science and literature alike is energy and originality. After all, the finest scholar in the world is but a parasite on originality. And London University, with its hard examinations to all-comers, has been for many years now an open, a stimulatingly difficult, but a possible and encouraging way from down below there, to a position as teacher, as journalist, or what not, to a breathing space wherein a young man of this type may find his possibilities. So long as *his* way keep open, open beyond any risk of tampering, the "reformers" may, for all I care, tinker as they like with the rest of the University structure, organize boards of fellows and high professors, reconstruct the charter to give one another honorary degrees, put an easy medical degree upon the market, and enrich this great Metropolis with a University worthy of its County Council. Other graduates [are] perhaps more squeamish, but, whatever else they oppose, the exclusion of the rank outsider is the vital objection in their opposition.—

Yours, etc.,

H.G. Wells

---

[1] Wells was passionately attached to the University which had afforded him such wonderful education. A move to modify the University of London curriculum standards, therefore, drew the comments in this letter, published 14 December 1895, pp. 803–4, under the title 'The Threatened University'. The editors of the magazine opposed his views in a note printed after the article.

[2] Possibly a reference to an economic 'law' coined by Walter Gresham to the effect that bad money drives good money out of circulation. The 'law' was in wide circulation at the time because of some nations moving to silver rather than gold to back their paper medium. One of the proposed plans for London University was also drafted by a person named Gresham. Wells may be making a double pun.

241. To the Editor, *Saturday Review*

PLS

[London] [c. 1 January 1896]

Sir, - Professor Thompson repeats the statement already made by you in an editorial footnote, flatly contradicting my assertion that the exclusion of the private student from the degree examinations is the root idea of the present London University "reform" movement. If this movement is not to exclude the private student, what *is* [it] to do? I challenged your contributor to state any positive addition the reformers would make to the teaching facilities of London, and that challenge is, of course, open to Professor Thompson. The reform is to annihilate the "crammers". I learn from your article, and how it is proposed to close the way to the pupils of the guerrilla teachers, while leaving it open to the untaught private student, I cannot conceive. Professor Thompson writes gaily of the proposed scheme of reform making "elaborate provision for including" these private students. The elaborate provision consists of creating a special board for their benefit, a Board largely under the control of the London professors, to whom the "crammers" and those stubborn originals who prefer self-education are absolutely antagonistic, and endowing this board with practically unlimited powers of regulating the ex-collegiate pupil's course of study. The fact that the Gresham scheme, excluding the ex-collegiate students, and the Cowper Commissioners' scheme, including them, have been supported in their turn by practically the same body of advocates shows how much good faith there is in the proposal. We who oppose these schemes, therefore, simply decline to believe in that "elaborate provison", and as our only security for the better definition of these vague promises of consideration, we insist upon the right of Convocation to veto any scheme unsatisfactory upon this point. But however else the "reformers" change, they are absolutely determined that the veto must not be exercised. How can we trust them? There is nothing to prevent the ex-collegiate student being "included", much as a bear includes a casual antagonist. So far from convicting me of a "good downright thumping - misuse of language" - as Professor Thompson puts it in his animated way - I think his letter will, in the judgment of every thoughtful and impartial reader, simply illustrate the levity with which the interests of the ex-collegiate students are treated by him and his fellow-movers in the matter.

My statement that the Finsbury College is, educationally, on a level with any "cramming" establishment he deals with in a similar fashion. It is, he says, "pure fiction" that the teaching is by mechanical instruction-papers under stress of frequent and stringent examinations. "Examinations are held as seldom as possible", he says; and adds, in his airy way, "once only in each term". Yet surely it is possible to be less frequent than that - the "crammers" pupil is examined once a year or so. On the score of "stringency" he does not add, as well he might, what percentage of the students entering his college successfully complete their courses. Do sixty per cent survive? Of instruction-papers he almost seems to say "there is none". There were. The instruction-papers in his college, unless they have been destroyed since my inspection, are simply printed demonstrations, and can only be intended to economise [on] personal teaching. If the use of them was not necessarily cramming, then I submitted that correspondence teaching was not necessarily cramming. That was my position, and Professor Thompson's denials do not touch it.[1]

Yours, etc.,

H.G. Wells

---

[1] Wells continued his general discussion of what forms the 'new' University of London and its curriculum should take. This letter was in response to one of the faculty at Finsbury College, Sylvanus Thompson, and forms an interesting note to English higher education in that period. It appeared in the issue of 4 January 1896 on p. 17, under the heading 'The London University Question'. The editor continued to argue against Wells in his comments.

242. To J. M. Dent[1]

AL [early 1896]

[Dear Mr. Dent,]

Herewith is the M.S. of my story, "The Wheels of Chance,".... It will begin serial in To Day in April & will be free [for] book publication in September. Colles is trying to secure American serial rights publication. Jerome has set aside his normal six-months stipulation ...

---

[1] A holograph letter, two pages, about 150 words was offered for sale in 1993 by Ferret Fantasy, catalogue Q99B. This letter is closely related to others which follow, dealing with editors, publishers, and agents as he became better known. Maurice Colles (d. 1926) was his American agent at the time.

Jerome K. Jerome (1859–1927) was a writer, editor and humourist. He became co-editor of *The Idler* in 1892, and founded *To-Day* where Wells's serial was appearing. He edited a volume, *The Humours of Cycling* (London, 1899) to which Wells contributed a short piece, 'To A Perfect Gentleman on Wheels'. Jerome is best known today for his novel *Three Men in a Boat* (London: Dent, 1889).

243. To An unknown correspondent

Boston, ALS

Lynton, Maybury Road
Woking
Jan 2nd /96
[recipient date stamp Jan 13 1896]

Dear Sir,

I have just completed a story of 60,000 words which will appear here serially in Mr. Jerome's Today. It is a purely humorous work & describes the sensations & adventures of a drapers assistant during a ten days holiday tour upon a bicycle. At the outset he rides rather badly & experiences the usual fatigues of the beginner. He becomes involved with an elopement & finds himself (through no fault of his own) with a young lady (in rational dress) & a bicycle upon his hands. He is pursued by the lady's friends. The young lady is a highly educated girl of advanced views which she has derived mainly from books & the humour & a touch of pathos at last arises out of the contrast between her & the uncomplicated, half educated, commonplace, sentimental & well meaning shopman. The details of bicycle riding, carefully done from experience, & the passing glimpses of characteristic scenery of the south of England, should, I think, appeal to a certain section of the public.

Of my published works the story is most like "The Wonderful Visit". It has no 'scientific element' & it is entirely free from "horrors". It is longer & more carefully constructed, & far more carefully written than anything I have done hitherto. I shall be glad to hear if you are disposed to offer for the American rights of such a book. I am prepared to accept the following terms, for a one & a half dollar book — 10% up to 1000 & then 15% with a cheque on account of royalties of £20. The story will begin to appear in Today in April & will run out in August. I have made no arrangement for American serial rights, & unless I do, the book will have to be published in America in April or May.[1] As my time is so limited, I shall be glad if you will send for the book only if there is a fair prospect of your publishing it. I could post the typewritten copy at once on receipt of a cablegram.

I am, dear sir,
Yours very faithfully
H. G. Wells [2]
[in another hand, 'See letter book, Jany 16, 1896']

---

[1] Macmillan published the book in the States. There was no American serial publication and, in the event, the *Today* serial ran from May to the end of September.

[2] It is interesting to compare this precis of his novel with letter 239 offering it to *Blackwood's Magazine*. This letter, using many of the same exact phrases, is, nevertheless, a much more sophisticated document. Wells is still acting as his own agent in great part.

244. To an unknown correspondent

Illinois, ALS

[London] Jan 13/96

Dear Sir,

Since I wrote you I have concluded an agreement which fills me up with short stories until October next. I'm giving most of my time now to a long story. If you cared to give six guineas a thousand for English & American serial rights - of a 3000 word story, I might be able to get it in. Otherwise I'm afraid I'm not free to do you anything until October.

Yours very truly
H.G. Wells

245. To Fred Wells[1]

Illinois, ALS

Lynton, Maybury Rd.
Woking, Surrey   Friday, Jan. 24th, 1896.

My dear little brother at the Seat of War,

How goes it with you? For a day or two in the new year, while Jameson[2] was astonishing the world, I was seriously anxious about your safety, and I should have cabled to know if all was well, had not the wires been choked with graver matter. I suppose we shall soon have a lengthy and vivid account of the whole business from you. Here things have been of the liveliest, war rumours, all the Music Halls busy with songs insulting the German Emperor, fleets being manned, and nobody free to attend to the works of a poor struggling author from Lands End to John o' Groats. Consequently a book I was to have published hasn't been published, and won't be until next March. You see how far reaching your Uitlander bothers are?

I'm going on very well altogether. I made between five and six hundred last year, and expect to make more rather than less, this year. I've married and ended all those troubles, and I've just taken a pretty little house at Liss with seven decent rooms and a garden and things all comfortable for the old folks. They are moving in next week. Frank is to expand his watchmaking business and altogether I think things are on the move toward comfort. I was down there about Christmas time and all three seemed very well and jolly. Frank's business seems picking up. The new home is one of a dozen or so decent little houses, and within comfortable reach of a church.

I'm riding a bicycle now and went a few weeks ago to a place called Odiham which may perhaps awaken old memories.

Since I wrote the above I've received your letter. I'm glad to find you're all right. As you say, the Invasion was a Capitalistic enterprise, though Jameson himself is a gallant man enough. But the Transvaal has no business to intrigue with Germany for all that. Do you see any papers now? There's usually something about me in the <u>Review of Reviews.</u>

Go and see Johnston if you possibly can. He's a first rate man you'll find. Some of these days I must come and see you out there. I hope you're getting on all right with the Dutch language and your business. What are the chances of opening for yourself out there? I should think that if you could pick up Dutch and master the habits and requirements, you'd have a better chance than you had in this crowded country. Don't dream of any speculation in gold mines or that kind of thing. Stick tight to your savings. If you want to invest trust old Johnston. He's a first rate, square headed, thoroughly honest man. What do you think of your move out of England? It wasn't so bad for you altogether - was it?

However time slips by. I've got to write a story before next week for a new monthly magazine, so I mustn't write any more now to you.

    With kindest regards
      Your very affectionate Brother
      The Busswhacker

---

[1] Also appears in *ExA*, ch. 6 §7.
[2] Sir Leander Starr Jameson (1853–1917) was a British colonial administrator in South Africa. In 1895 he conducted an attack on Boer settlements in the Transvaal from his base in Rhodesia. The raid was unauthorized and led to more trouble with the Boer settlers and eventually to the Boer War.

246. To an unknown correspondent

Texas, ALS

[London]   Jan . 25. /96.

Dear Sir,

  I have a short story by me in the rough which would run to about 2,500 words, & I think I can finish this for you. Is the 1st positively the latest date you can give me for delivery? I have some other work on hand which is pressing.

        Yours very faithfully,
        H. G. Wells

247. To Morris Colles

Indiana, ALS

Lyton
Maybury Road Woking   Jan 26/96

Dear Mr. Colles,

When sending you the synopsis of the <u>War of the Worlds</u>, I do not think I mentioned that I do not wish it to be offered to the <u>New Review</u> or the <u>Graphic</u>.
Believe me,
Yours very faithfully,
H.G. Wells

248. To Morris Colles

George Locke, ALS

Lynton,
Maybury Road Woking   [received 25 March 1896]

Dear Mr Colles,

The final instalments of the <u>War of the Worlds</u> are now in the hands of my typewriter,[1] as soon as they reach me you shall have them.
Yours very faithfully,
H.G. Wells

---

[1] A now obsolete word used as a generic term for typists, stenographers and other office workers until the first decade of the twentieth century.

THE LETTERS: 1880-1903

249. To Morris Colles

George Locke, ACCS

Lynton,
Maybury Road,
Woking   12-4-96

Dear Mr. Colles,

    Thanks for your letter. I'll certainly let you know if there's any attempt to bag the <u>W of the W's</u> behind your back on the part of the people you name.
                  Yours ever,
                  H.G. Wells

I've just refused the <u>Graphic</u> a short story at 4 gns a thousand. They rejected the "Wheels of Chance" & I want to make them feel I'm disinclined to do any more with them. So don't take the W of the W round that way yet, whatever you do. In three months' time they'll be ripe for it.

250. To Elizabeth Healey

Illinois, Typed Transcription, Extract

[London]   [late Spring 1896]

[Dear Miss Healey][1]

[...] I hope you've read The Island of Doctor Moreau, and I do hope that you don't think [it] merely a festival of 'orrors. You may perhaps have seen that the good Jerome has joined the select band of my believers, and that I've got a serial in To Day illustrated with incredible violence and vulgarity - Also between ourselves I'm doing the dearest little serial for Pearson's new magazine, in which I completely wreck and destroy Woking - killing my neighbours in painful and eccentric ways - then proceed via Kingston and Richmond to London, which I sack, selecting South Kensington for feats of peculiar atrocity[2] ...

---

[1] Extracts are all that remain of some of Wells's letters to Elizabeth Healey, who destroyed them around 1903. The remaining bits were willed to the Wells estate and now are part of the Illinois collection.
[2] Wells is referring here to his 1896 novels, *The Island of Doctor Moreau*, *The Wheels of Chance* (in *To-Day*), and *The War of the Worlds* about to appear in serial in *Pearson's Magazine*.

251. To Cyril A. Pearson[1]

ALS

[Address unknown]　　　　　　　　　　　　　　　　　　[Spring, 1896?]

Dear Sir,

　　I've seen your first number of the new series & it seems to me first rate. I'm immensely flattered by your invitation to contribute. At present I have nine stories in hand for various people & thinking over an offer for five more. I doubt if I can do any more for a few months. What do you offer?
　　　　　　　　　Yours very truely,
　　　　　　　　　H. G. Wells

---

[1] I do not know the provenance of this letter. I am using a xerox copy which has no location on it, and I infer the name of the recipient from internal evidence. *Pearson's Magazine* was just beginning in the Spring of 1896, and Wells published two stories in it in August. C. A. Pearson (1866–1921) was a newspaper proprietor who later founded the *Daily Express*. The two stories, 'In the Abyss', *Pearson's Magazine*, August 1896, 'The Rajah's Treasure', August 1896, are problematical in themselves, in one case not being republished in England until after Wells's death. Their only contemporary publication is in *The New York Times* on successive weeks in July and August 1896.

252. To Joseph Conrad[1]

ALS

Lynton
Maybury Road, Woking　　　　　　　　　　　　　　[late May, 1896]

Dear Sir,

　　I am very glad indeed that my review of your book was to your liking. Though I really don't see why you should think gratitude necessary when a reviewer gives you your deserts.
　　Since you don't make the slightest concessions to the reading young woman who makes or mars the fortunes of authors, it is the manifest duty of a reviewer

to differentiate between you and the kinds of people we thrust into the "fictions" at the end, the Maples and Shoolbreds of literature.

Where the irony of an author thanking an anonymous reviewer comes in, is in the fact that the latter is almost invariably an unknown man and quite incapable of the workmanship the traditions of journalism require him to discuss in such an authoritative manner. I, for instance, could no more write your "Outcast" than I could fly. But, unlike the huge majority of reviewers, I do happen to have written an (unsuccessful) book or so and to have learnt something from my failures of the method of the art.

If I have instead put my finger on a weak point in your armour of technique, so that you may be able to strengthen it against your next reviewer, I shall have done the best a reviewer can do. You have everything for the making of a splendid novelist except dexterity, and that is attainable by drill.

Looking forward to reading your next book - I do not know whether I shall still be a reviewer then - believe me
> Your sincere admirer,
> H.G. Wells

---

[1] This letter was saved very fortuitously. When G. Jean Aubry began his *Life and Letters of Conrad*, he was given a packet by the family in which some twenty letters from literary colleagues were found. These were made into little booklets for each author and then into a box, 220 copies in total, which were sent out to members of 'The First Editions Club' in London, under the title *Twenty Letters to Joseph Conrad*. Other letter writers in this group were Stephen Crane (2), Edward Garnett (4), Rudyard Kipling (1), George Gissing (2), John Galsworthy (1), Arnold Bennett (1), James Gibons Hunecker (1), E. V. Lucas (2), Constance Garnett (1), Henry James (3), and Wells himself (2). In his introduction to these last two letters, Aubry quoted extensively from Wells's review of *An Outcast of the Islands* which was the occasion for this letter. The second of the two is located in volume 2 of this edition.

253. Joseph Conrad to H. G. Wells[1]

Illinois, AL, Extract

[Capri, Italy?] May 25, 1896

[...] If I prized the review before I knew who wrote it - it became still more precious now when the name of my kind appreciator is known. Strangely enough - almost five months ago when turning over the last page of "The Wonderful Visit', " in the full impression of the extraordinary charm and suggestive realism of this book I remember reflecting - with contemptible bitterness - that a mind that [could] conceive and execute such work was absolutely beyond my reach. That, to a man who could think and write so anything I could do - or attempt to do - would probably never seem worth a second glance.

This is a shameful confession but you know how difficult it is for a common mortal to kick himself free of his own clamourous careers. [...][2] Your books take hold of one with a grasp that can be felt. I am held by the charm of their expression and of their meaning. I surrender to their suggestion. I am delighted by the clearness of atmosphere, by the sharp definition even of things implied - and I am convinced by the logic of your imagination so unbounded and so brilliant. I see all this - but this last I am probably unable to see.

Pardon uncouth outburst of naive enthusiasm. I am, alas, forty and enthusiasms are precious to me and to be proud of. [...]

---

[1] Wells reviewed Joseph Conrad's novel, *An Outcast of the Islands* in *Saturday Review*, 16 May 1896. The review was anonymous, but Wells wrote to Conrad soon afterward to reveal his authorship. Wells to Conrad, undated, late May 1896, in G. Aubry, ed., *Twenty Letters to Joseph Conrad* (London, 1926), see letter 252. Conrad wrote back to thank Wells on May 18, and followed with this longer letter. Because so little of the Wells side of this correspondence survives, only letter 252 and another in volume 2, I have chosen to provide a few examples from the Conrad side.

[2] Conrad goes on to say that he knows *The Time Machine*, *Wonderful Visit*, *Stolen Bacillus* and *Doctor Moreau* were on their way 'to my island' (Capri, where the Conrads were staying).

254. To Grant Allen

Illinois, ALS

Worcester Park
Surrey   [date unknown]

[This letter is decorated with two sketches, one of a house built on London clay in dry weather, the second is the same house after a rain. The first house is upright, while the second is leaning.]

My dear friend Allen,

Thanks for your letter and for your suggestion of a trip. A sprained wrist however keeps me off wheels & besides the house is full of workmen - who require a MAN about, so I understand. I'm very sorry to hear the third novel [*illegible word*][1]. Publishers are I think (saving plumbers, painters & decorators, builders, & the asses who live by selling obviously unsuitable chimney cowls) the most stupid human beings. There is no publisher in London (now Lane has gained money & lost enterprise) with the intelligence & originality to set fashions. Fashions in book productions are the result of office mistakes or the physical violence of authors. You started an uphill fight not quite perfectly perhaps but with admirable vitality & now in the stress & nadir of your fight the camp followers bolt with the ammunition.

Our warmest regards to Mrs. Grant Allen & yourself.

Yours very faithfully,
H.G. Wells

---

[1] This is probably a reference to the third (and unpublished) novel in Allen's trilogy. Wells reviewed the first two, see letter 265.

255. To John Lane

Hofstra, ACCS

Lynton
Maybury Road
Woking   [May-June 1896]

Dear Mr. Lane,

I shall come & sit on your doorstep for that account of mine if you don't mind.[1] And, incidentally, here is a masterpiece of mine running serially in To-Day - a humorous novel containing allusions to 'my uncle'. Also you have an advertisement of the Mayfair Series in the same paper - which omits my 'Select Conversations'. But clearly if this book has not sold so far it will sell now to some of the To-Day readers. Several have written Jerome gushingly about the serial. - I should think a timely advertisement would go far to clear the edition.

Yours ever,
H.G. Wells

---

[1] John Lane, one of Wells's earlier publishers, was a notoriously slow payer, and this letter may reflect that failing.

256. To Fred Wells[1]

Illinois, ALS

Brosley [July 1897]

[*This a fairly heavily illustrated letter. At the top left is a caricature of his father, fresh from croquet. A few lines down, opposite, is a smaller sketch of his mother. There is also a small cartoon of Wells, and further down the page a line of ships (Royal Navy) from the Jubilee review at Spithead which he had witnessed. The letter, which has no salutation, is to his brother Fred in South Africa.*]

This does not represent a Dutchman but an elderly gentleman of distinguished manners who has recently been staying at Heatherlea, Worcester Park, Surrey. He plays chess with considerable skill, draughts and whist - croquet he learned rapidly - and he answers to the names of "Gov'ner" "Dad" or the "Old Man" with equal facility. When returning to Liss he took away all the tobacco and a box of Brosley clay pipes. In the place of him a short lady of pleasing demeanour is shortly expected (as per accompanying illustration). She will probably be here on the birthday of her middle and favourite son, whom she speaks of variously as "Freddy" "Fezzy" "Fizzums" and "Master Freddie". Needless to say his health will be drunk on that anniversary both at Liss and Heatherlea with the warmest feelings. This person (illustration) it is scarcely necessary to explain is your long lost brother Buss. You will observe that he has with growing years and prosperity developed - a projection which he keeps in bounds only by the most strenuous bicycle riding. He rejoices to say that things go very well with him, books selling cheerfully and so forth, in spite of the Jubilee.[2] And speaking of the Jubilee he saw nothing of it whatever, except that he went to see the ironclads - hundreds of 'em lying all along Spithead and the Solent for miles and miles and miles. - He went round the show twice in a steamboat accompanied by [*finger pointing*] that chap! And while he was going round, the King of Siam in his yacht came out of Portsmouth Harbour and every blessed ironclad let off a gun (illustration). This is a sort of Birthday card really. I've heard from mother once or twice that things were going very well with you and I was very glad to get your own letter. May your good luck keep on for you deserve it richly. Many happy returns of the day and a light heart to you, old boy!

From Buss.

---

[1] Also appears in *ExA*, ch. 6 §7.
[2] The Diamond Jubilee was the sixtieth anniversary of Queen Victoria's accession to the throne. Although this letter is dated 'July 1896' in *ExA*, and was positioned in this volume on that basis, it seems to have actually been written in 1897.

257. To Grant Allen

Yale, ALS

Heatherlea
Worcester Park
Surrey   Aug. 25th [1896]

My dear Grant Allen,

I hope sincerely that you have not been inconvenienced by getting no reply to your invitation to us - but the enclosed letter will partly explain the matter. I lost your letter, as I did all letters in the heat of the 'move', & sent my reply to Jennings hoping it would reach you; I couldn't remember any more of your address.
Kindest regards from us both to Mrs. Allen.
> Believe me,
> > Yours ever,
> > > H.G.W.

258. To A. M. Davies

Illinois, ALS

Lynton
Maybury Road
Woking   [1896]

My dear A.M.D.,

You shall be met duly. 'Tis terrible to think that the Star paragraph is a distortion of information supplied by myself.[1] (Tell it not in Gath - or elsewhere) in reply to a polite letter. I am trying vainly to recall the slightest justification for the Devil's statement. All I can think of is the possibility of confusion between Huxley & Henley whom I also mentioned in my reply. However it can't hurt Huxley much & nobody will remember a paragraph in the Star in three days time. Large number of new works is magnificent.

I seem fated to association with Huxley. The Bookman demanded my portrait & so forth & went & printed it face to face with his - a kind of 'disgust & impudence' grouping. Looking forward to a pleasant time.

Yours ever,
H.G.

[A small sketch of two people/dogs appears at the bottom of the last page of this letter.]

---

[1] I have not yet seen the *Star* story. Nevertheless Wells did not keep copies of his correspondence at this stage, except occasionally in draft, and he may well not remember what he said in answer to the journalist's request. The letter we have was saved by an autograph collector, not a Wellsian.

259. To J. M. Dent[1]

Illinois, ALS

Answering Sep. 11. 96

[Address unknown]   Sept. 12, [1896]

Dear Mr. Dent,

I'm obliged by your frank letter. But to be equally frank, I don't intend to bind myself to any publisher upon his mere promise to publish my books. My transactions with Heinemann have been a lesson to me. I let him have three scientific romances on that understanding, The Time Machine, The I of Dr. M. & the next scientific romance I write. Then he disappointed by funking the "Island" pitifully because the Chronicle slated it.

At the same time I recognize the justice of your remarks. Vigorous pushing of one book does sell the next. What I think might serve as a fair arrangement would be something of this sort: - If you sell, say 7000, of the W. of C. @ 6/- within a year then you shall have the refusal of the British rights of the next book at a certain spec. price. That might be more perennial.

Following are fixtures.

        Sep 1896. Wheels of Chance
        Spring 1897 Short Stories, 2cd vol.
        by Methuen.

Sep 1897 nothing - or a sensational
story (written and with Mr. Pinker)
of 20000 words to keep in the reviewing
Spring 1898 A scientific romance by
Heinemann (his third) which is to be
serialized - Pearson's Mag. or the
Cosmopolitan of America in April, 1897.
No further arrangements.

A sentimental humorous story in hand. Title (in confidence) is Love & Mr. Lewisham. Expect 80,000. Doing nothing else till Xmas. L & Mr L has to serial here or in Am. Impossible for Sep 1897 - earliest expected to be Sept 1898 wd certainly suit your [plans]

H.G.W.

---

[1] This letter and the following ones in draft, (260, 263, 265) were letters negotiating with J. M. Dent. It seems clear that Dent knew that large profits were likely to be had from Wells, but it is equally clear that Wells realised that he was a potential gold mine. Although Pinker's name appears, and he was handling some of Wells's output, Wells himself was his own agent. These letters were all to be reworked and typed by Catherine Wells who, as can be seen, was already beginning to function somewhat as a manager/agent, leaving Wells free to write. This was one of the most intensive periods of work in his lifetime.

260. To J. M. Dent

Illinois, ADL

Lynton
Maybury Road
Woking   Sep 17. [1896]

Dent

Hope reconsider about illus. Reasons. 'Silly clowning'. others admirable.[1]

Nothing 'sordid' in requiring a reasonable guarantee, that the Heinemann business will not be repeated. I ask only that your promise shall be formally guaranteed. Moreau still in 1st ed. want of advert. & gen. neglect. That he was going to do his best for. "Is it so vy sordid to refuse to admit the possibility of that again?" H went abroad & left it to junior partners. Suppose you abroad in 1898?

I believe you <u>will</u> do your best for the W. of C. Other things approx equal, I prefer you to publish my books. "But it's not nice to go calling me sordid after - as Pinker will tell you - I refused a much better offer from Hutch. in order to give you the W of C. - solely because I felt bound by your enterprise with the W. Visit.

Unlikely, unless Pinker is approached, that business will be done with L & Mr. L. till after Xmas.

---

[1] This sentence, although elliptic, probably refers to the publication in *Pearson's Magazine* of 'In the Abyss', July 1896, and 'The Rajah's Treasure', August 1896, pp. 155–6. These same pieces also appeared in the *New York Times* 6, 7, 8 July 1896 and 7, 8, 10 August 1896 in reverse order. Both versions were lightly illustrated. 'The Rajah's Treasure' is a rarity as it was published in boards only once, in the United States in *Thirty Strange Stories* (New York: Edward Arnold, 1897). It has also been reprinted in a facsimile edition (New York: Causeway Books, 1974).

261. To the Editor, *Saturday Review*[1]

PLS

[London]　　　　　　　　　　　　　　　　　　　　　　　　22 September 1896

Dear Sir, It seems I have been wrong all along, and if I was only a manufacturer with thirty-six years of experience I might have known that fully seven years ago there was an efficient London microscope to be got at less than five guineas. I am bound to take the word of Mr. Crouch for that, and gladly assume that the high power was a really serviceable sixth. Only being merely a possible purchaser, at the very centre of the market, I sought it unavailingly, and so did my students, until the German instrument came along. For all practical purposes, it did not exist. No doubt the British merchant is, with characteristic modesty, even now concealing from sale that cheap balance I asked for, and that intelligently arranged set of chemical apparatus. If so, and he is simply waiting for his would-be customers to find him out, he is even a worse business man than I gave him credit for.

Mr. Crouch may take my word for it that the students' microscope trade is an altogether different market from that which the splendid work of Carl Zeiss won for Germany.[2] It was not "fashion", but necessity drove the English students to German makers. I doubt if the ordinary elementary science student who seeks a microscope has ever heard of Zeiss. But Mr. Crouch, being a British merchant, is scarcely to be taught by a mere consumer. No doubt he will rest satisfied with his own theory in spite of my assurance. "Gratuitous trumpetings" of German goods indeed! My article was an embittered lament.

When will our merchants and manufacturers learn the obvious lesson that the discovery of a customer's means and what he wants, and what he thinks he wants, and the conscientious satisfaction of these conditions, is of far more importance than even a couple of centuries of "experience" and old-fashioned "take-it-or-leave-it" routine? Mr. Crouch, still unaware that there are two points of view in every market, still satisfied that only the merchant can understand the trade, is evidently not grateful for my article - and so he proves my case against the British merchant in his own person up to the hilt.

H.G. Wells

---

[1] A letter in response to the instrument maker Crouch's criticism of Wells's article on cheap microscopes. It appeared in the issue of 26 September 1896, p. 344, under the title 'Cheap Microscopes'. The original was entitled, 'Cheap Microscopes and a Moral', 12 September 1896 pp. 277–9. This long article is important both from the point of view of knowledge of English-German competition in skilled scientific machinery, but also because it provides several anecdotes of Wells's teaching.

[2] Carl Zeiss (1816–88) was a noted manufacturer of optical instruments in Germany.

262. To the Editor, *Saturday Review*[1]

PLS

[London]   [c. 20 October 1896]

Sir, I need only say in reply to the further communication of Mr. Crouch that I have received several letters from various parts of the country asking for the address of the German firm whose microscopes I recommended. The writers are still not aware of the existence of such instruments. As I am not an agent for the German firm, and write simply to stimulate British makers, I have been a little troubled how to answer these communications. I presume you will have no objection to any British maker who will supply for three and a half guineas or less an efficient microscope in a stout box, with a low-power objective and good high power of 1/6 inch, for which he will pledge himself, briefly signifying as much (and his address) in this column. Otherwise my article will simply have advertised German goods.

Yours, etc.,
H.G. Wells

---

[1] Crouch continued to complain to the editor about Wells's charge concerning the lack of inexpensive microscopes. Wells responded once again with this brief letter, in the issue of 24 October 1896, p. 444, 'Cheap Microscopes'.

263. To J. M. Dent

Illinois, ADL

Lynton
Maybury Road
Woking   [*c*. October 1896]

£150 on a/c
25% at 6/-
2½ per copy
in colonials is
in Dent's offer

Dear Mr. Dent

Thanks for your letter. Did I not know that your zeal for humanity is indubitably real, I might think your last two letters a veiled threat to wreck the Wheels of Chance unless you get 'Love & Mr. Lewisham' on favourable terms. As I said in my previous letter I can consider no offer that does not <u>guarantee</u> a sale of the <u>Wheels of Chance</u> that will satisfy me. It might be done in this way - if the Wheels of Chance payments up to the end of 1897 (including ch. on account) exceed £330 - then the ch. on a/c of the new book might be a certain sum - say £ §[1], but that if the payments fall below £330 then the cheque on account of the new book shall be increased to compensate me.

P.S. Reminder of C.T.C. Gazette[2] & sent a para for insertion in local papers.

---

[1] Wells uses this symbol to indicate an unknown quantity.

[2] A newspaper with news from the cycling associations.

264. To Mr Sergeant[1]

Illinois, ALS

Lynton
Maybury Road
Woking   [late Autumn 1896]

Dear Mr. Sergeant.

Thanks for your letter. By all means cut the 'contents' if you think proper.

Of light sketches I can promise nothing, though if ever I do anything more for an Ed paper I shall probably send it to you.[2] What terms would you offer? Just now for the ordinary trade goods[?] I'm raising my price from £3 a thousand to £4 for English serial rights. I've a novel to finish, another to write & about a dozen short stories agreed for. But it's simply a little boom I think & I daresay I shall be at peace again by 1898 to gibe at things scholastic.

That man A.M. Davies would do you some readable articles, I think - only you must warn him to be as light as possible. He has a cautious conscientiousness like a garden roller & flattens all the vigour out of his work in revision.

Yours very faithfully
H. G. Wells

---

[1] Sergeant was apparently an editor for a magazine. However he is unknown beyond that inference. Later evidence, letter 271, suggests that Sergeant may have been the new editor of *The Educational Times*, which Wells had once edited.

[2] This is the transition period of Wells's writing. In 1896 he produced several pieces for *The Educational Times* early in the year, and in 1897 he wrote his series on teaching for the *Daily Mail*. Although he continued to think of himself as a teacher and a writer on educational matters, this content was increasingly a lesser theme in his writing.

265. To Grant Allen

Illinois, ACCS[1]

Lynton
Maybury Road
Woking   [1896]

My dear Grant Allen,

     On Wednesday next we move to Heatherlea, Worcester Park, a picturesque and unsanitary house in the early Victorian style standing in its own grounds of a half a quarter of an acre on the London clay. Worcester Park is conveniently situated on the high road to Epsom and has an excellent but infrequent service of trains to Waterloo. It is inhabited by amateur poultry fanciers and dog lovers with occasional literary men and there is a well built church with three bells and an attractive service within five minutes walk of the house. The name of the house refers to the oak trees which grow so luxuriantly in the district.[2] I do not know if you and Mrs. Grant Allen ever penetrate into this region, but if so no human being can be possibly be so glad to see you as we shall be. On Saturday we are always at home, and the other days we shall always be glad to stop at home if we hear you are coming.

    I got a <u>Strand Magazine</u> with your diamond story and it seemed to me that you kept off that X-L story very neatly. But the thing I am looking forward to is that third novel of yours - of the Hill Top strain. I shan't be happy until I get that - and Le Gallienne's novel.[3]

    The great advantage of correspondence cards is that they set a limit to lengthy letters, which might otherwise become tedious. One can be concise on a correspondence card without seeming to be uncivil, whereas there is something a little too suggestive of the business man (to my mind) in a letter which can not carry its signature over the sheet. I strongly recommend this useful little invention to you, as an excellent method of economizing time at the writing desk. The only drawback is when by any chance your communication overflows to a second or third card in which case not a little annoyance is caused your correspondents (unless you number and arrange the cards neatly and systematically in his (or her) endeavours to find which comes after which.

    Our joint regards to you both.
        Yours very faithfully
        H.G. Wells

---

[1] This letter exists in the correspondence card from which this transcription was taken, but it

was also published in Grant Richards, *Memoirs of a Misspent Youth* (London: Heinemann, 1923), pp. 329–31. A correspondence card was slightly larger than a visiting card, about two by three inches, and could be inserted in an envelope for use in the mail. Wells, as his comments suggest, liked the cards and continued to use them for some time before he began to use the more conventional postcard and smaller note paper stationery.

² Heatherlea would normally be thought of as a meadow with small shrubs such as broom and heather. Perhaps Wells is referring to small pin oaks, or perhaps he is making a small joke about developer's and builder's names.

³ Grant Allen's first two novels were *The Woman Who Did* and *The British Barbarians* and were called the Hill Top novels. If a third volume was written, it was not published apparently. Wells had reviewed both of those which did appear, the first rather harshly, and the second one only slightly less so. Grant Allen knew that, but pursued the relationship just the same. Le Gallienne's book, also reviewed by Wells was *The Quest for the Golden Girl*.

266. To the Editor, *Saturday Review*[1]

PLS

[London] [*c.* 1 November 1896]

Sir, In a special article in the "Saturday Review" of 11 April, 1896, reviewing my "Island of Dr. Moreau", Mr. Chalmers Mitchell, in addition to certain literary criticisms, which rest upon their merits, gave the lie direct to a statement of mine that the grafting of tissues between animals of different species is possible. This was repeated more elaborately in "Natural Science", and from these centres of distribution passed into the provincial press, where it was amplified to my discredit in various, animated, but to me, invariably painful phrasing. And the contradiction, with implication of headlong ignorance it conveys, is now traversing the continent of America (where phrasing is often very vivid indeed) in the wake of the review copies Mr. Stone is distributing.

I was aware at the time that Mr. Chalmers Mitchell was mistaken in relying upon Oscar Hertwig as his final authority upon this business, that he was making the rash assertion and not I, but for a while I was unable to replace the stigma of ignorance he had given me, for the simple reason that I knew of no published results of the kind I needed. But the "British Medical Journal" for 31 October, 1896, contains the report of a successful graft, by Mr. Mayo Robson, not merely of connective tissue between rabbit and man. I trust, therefore, that "Natural Science" will now modify its statement concerning my book, and the gentlemen of the provincial press who waxed scornful, and even abusive, on Mr. Chalmer Mitchell's authority, will now wax apologetic. There is quite enough to misunderstand and abuse in the story without any further application of this little mistake of Mr. Chalmers Mitchell's. -

Yours, very truly,
H.G. Wells

---

[1] This belated response to a review of his novel, *The Island of Doctor Moreau*, came about because newly published evidence supported his point of view. His letter appeared on 7 November 1896, p. 497 under the title 'The Island of Doctor Moreau'. Chalmers Mitchell responded with an apology the next week, although he did point out that he had liked the book and that he had given Wells good publicity with his review.

267. To J. M. Dent

Illinois, ADL[1]   Nov. 10 - 96

<u>Dent</u>

Your letter destroys my last hope for the <u>W. of C</u>. Do you really think there are no bk advt in the Queen? I take it I may consider all negoc. at an end for <u>L & Mr. L</u>. Now as it's not much good for you to go on with these 2 bks of mine I'm afraid, wd you care to sell the entire stock of them to me, cancel our existing agreements & have done with the whole business. If so please let me know forthwith. I will see if something may not be arranged.

Dec. 15 1896. <u>Re</u> comparison of the 2 accounts for W. Visit. 1895 1st half 1896. I find that on Dec. 31/95 you state you have 78 copies in stock - On Jan 1st/96 you have 234. Cannot understand that. Also in first a/c 150 copies stated to be on sale with Smith & in 2cd, no sales are given thr. Smith but unsold amount to 156. Of course I cannot go on doing business on these lines. There is absolutely no account of American sales. If only <u>one</u> copy sold in Am. I am entitled to 10 % thereon. Frankly I must ask you to let a business man acting on my behalf square up these accounts.

D. 17. I insist on Am. royalties. Neither do I see why I wait till Feb. There is no provision for any delay. I am in no mood to make you concessions over & above the agreement. I must also ask that colonial edit. appears in our accounts.

---

[1] This letter and the two following appear on the same sheet of paper, in holograph draft, unsigned.

268. To George Gissing[1]

Illinois, ALS

Heatherlea
Worcester Park
Surrey [30 November 1896]

My dear Gissing,

(The beast grows familiar.)[2] I want to see you now much more than I did, and I hope this clear dry weather will do its duty by your cold. And as for bronchitis and so forth, if you want to meet a man of extraordinary gifts in this way, you cannot do better than to meet me. You could not possibly waste my time, but it will be wiser all the same to warn me of your advent lest you find me away on some fool's business or other. Besides walking it is possible to reach this place by passenger train to Worcester Park.

Take care of yourself, there's a good chap! because now I've written you so impudently - after a struggle with my natural shyness if you'll believe me - and you've answered so kindly, I've a sort of feeling that this should have happened before.

Yours ever,
H.G. Wells

[A sketch map of directions was appended to this letter.]

---

[1] As stated in the Introduction letters from Wells to other people, which are published elsewhere in virtually complete form, have received only token notice in this collection. Such a person is George Gissing. In 1961, Royal A. Gettmann produced *George Gissing and H. G. Wells: Their Friendship and Correspondence* (London and Urbana: Hart Davis and University of Illinois, 1961), which was the standard edition. However, scholars today will also want to use *The Collected Letters of George Gissing* edited by Paul F. Mattheisen, Arthur C. Young and Pierre Coustillas (Athens, Ohio: Ohio University Press, currently 9 volumes). New letters from both sides, as well as new interpretations, make this a very useful edition. The placing of the Wells correspondence in the context of Gissing's life is of great importance. Three letters are included in this collection, all from 1896-7, which are to be found, along with others from this period, in volume 6 of *The Collected Letters of George Gissing*.

[2] Wells and Gissing had recently met at a dinner party at the Omar Khayyam Club, a literary dining association. Gissing describes the scene very well, both in his diary and in other letters, as Wells rushed boldly up to him, taking Gissing by surprise. He and Wells became instant friends.

269. To Elizabeth Healey

Illinois, Typed Transcription, Extract [November 1896]

[Dear Miss Healey,]

[...] T.P. is certainly being very good to me, is he not? And likewise the great Pearson is perceptible here, and there [they're?] industriously spreading my fame - I'm very glad indeed you liked the S.K. story.[1] Even now I'm engaged on the same (or similar) stuff, but this time it is to be an ample novel, and the museum and the schools and the streets, Clapham and Chelsea and so forth, are all to come in. Heaven knows when it will get done, for writing fantastic romance is one thing, and writing a novel is quite another. Have you read of the worthy Hoopdriver?[2] I hope you will, and I hope you will like him -

---

[1] 'A Slip Under the Microscope', a story set at the Royal College of Science, South Kensington, had been published in *The Yellow Book*, January 1896.
[2] J. E. Hoopdriver is the leading male character in Wells's comic novel about bicycling, *The Wheels of Chance* (London: Dent, 1896).

270. To A. T. Simmons

Illinois, AL

Heatherlea
Worcester Park, Surrey [late 1896]

Mr. H.G. Wells presents his compliments to Mr. A.T. Simmonds & begs to return him a card which Mr. A.T. Simmonds has presumed to address to Mrs. H.G. Wells. He will be obliged if Mr. A. T. Simmonds will explain the word underlined on the said card. At present Mr. H.G. Wells can only regard it as an insult, as gross as it is unwarranted. Pending such explanation, Mr. H.G. Wells must decline to regard Mr. A.T. Simmings as the friend he has previously professed himself to be. And he would further ask Mr. A.T. Simmerings who the 'El 'e is to talk about honesty?

271. To Mr Sergeant

Illinois, ALS

Heatherlea
Worcester Park

October 1896
[*in another hand*]

My dear Sergeant

I'm glad you liked the article, & D.V. I will write for the 'Eddie' someday to refresh the meaning of such friends as I have among its readers. But if you really want my memory to be kept green among your readers why wait for that. There are books I'm publishing & many such fanciful occasions.

Yours ever

H. G.

P.S. Lloyd Morgan has a book called "Habit & Instinct" coming out; It is right down on my subject & is sure to be good. I should very much like to do a signed review of it for you if you will let me.[1]

---

[1] Wells reviewed Morgan's book in the *Academy* 9 January 1897, p. 37. He liked the book which he saw as a follow-up to Huxley's later writing on the role of habit in possibly enhancing and influencing instinct.

272. To an unknown recipient

Illinois, ACCS

Heatherlea
Worcester Park
Surrey

[17 December 1896]

Dear Sir

I'm very glad to find anyone who thinks well of my Moreau. The book was unlucky at the outset, but I think it has the vitality to live through its troubles. My warmest thanks to you for backing my opinion. Voluntary appreciations such as yours are one of the pleasant things in authorship.

                      Yours very faithfully
                      H. G. Wells

273. To Henry Hick[1]

Bromley (photocopy), ALS

Worcester Park   [late 1896 - early 1897]

My dear Hick,

    "The Disappearance of the G.P." is a little off my line. But, I tell what I think might be done. You go & get the stuff & write the blessed article, let me as an expert see the article & give me the right of offering a suggestion or so where it is needful, & then let me try & place it. Mind you I don't say I <u>can</u> place it; only I think very likely (my standing in the trade) I might.

                      Yours very faithfully,
                      H. G. Wells

---

[1] Hick was Wells's physician at this time of severe illness, which was complicated by a damaged kidney. Hick was recommended by George Gissing whom he had known since schooldays. These letters were provided in photocopy to the Bromley archive by Dr Barbara Hick, Henry Hick's daughter, at the time of the centenary of Wells's birth (1966). At that time they were in the personal possession of the Hick family.

274. To Fred Wells[1]

Illinois, ALS

Heatherlea
Worcester Park   New Year's Eve, 1896

My dear little Bruzzer Freddy,

    I had your funny card for which, Bruzzer Freddy, there was one and a penny to pay! but I would have cheerfully paid much more than that rather than not have had it. And as it is New Year's Eve and I have been thinking over the past year and all that has happened, I don't think I can do better than write this

letter to you before the New Year begins. And to begin with myself, I have been still on the rise of fortune's wave this year, and it seems as though I must certainly go on to still larger successes and gains next for my name still spreads abroad, and people I have never ever seen, some from Chicago, one from Cape Town, and one from far up the Yung T'se Kiang in China, write and tell me they find my books pleasant. So far it has meant more fame than money to me, but I hope next year that the gilt edge will come to my successes. This year I have made between eight hundred and a thousand and next year it will be more and after that still more, and then I hope to put in operation little plans I have. You know the old people are now pretty comfortable at Liss, and Frank's business really seems on the move. There were two packing cases of clocks and things in the passage of the house when I went down there yesterday. And next year I hope to be able (although I don't want him to know yet for fear of disappointment) to put him firmly on his legs. I think it will be possible to get him into a shop in a good position in Liss, and to let the old folks have a better cottage than they are in at present. But you know the old maxim - hasten slowly. I want everything safe and straight first. Then when Frank is a really efficient citizen again - we shall be seeing you back I expect, brown and strong I hope and with a little something in your pocket, and then we must see whether at Wokingham or Petersfield or some such place, it won't be possible for you to start with fair prospects. Eigh? The little old lady is rosy and active - fit for twenty years I shouldn't wonder, and before that time perhaps she will see all three of us flourishing in our own homes, and as cheerful as can be. The old man too is none so dusty a chap when you get him on the right side - and he seems hale enough for a century. So that this New Year's Eve I feel uncommonly cheerful and hopeful, not only for myself but for the whole blessed family of us.
    Good luck Bruzzer Freddy
        Yours ever,
            H. G. Busswhacker

I don't know if you see Pearson's Magazine out there – in April next a long story of mine will begin and go on until December, and I expect great things for it. Pearson's Magazine mind! – not Pearson's Weekly.

Remember me kindly to Johnston who's a nice old chap isn't he? When is he coming over? If ever he comes I shall expect him to come and stop here for a time to gossip about old times.

Look out for the Saturday Review if you get a chance of seeing it. You will see among the reviews every week now H.G.W. which is me.

And don't forget to write to a chap and tell him all about yourself.

---

[1] Also appears in *ExA*, ch. 6 §7.

275. To Fred Wells

Illinois, ALS

Heatherlea
Worcester Park
Surrey [February 1897]

Dear little Afrikander,

    Just a line to remind you I live. Everything going well. Have sold another story & book for £550 - so the family's safe for a time. You've got to invest in the academic periodicals - order them at your newspaper shop if necessary. <u>Pearson's Magazine</u> for March - & on to the end of the year. <u>Pearson's Weekly</u> for June & July. And keep your eye on the <u>Idler</u> if you see it about anywhere.

Let's hear from you & all about you.

                Yours ever
                The Busswhacker

276. To Henry Hick

Bromley (photocopy), AL

[Probably Worcester Park,
although another hand has
annotated this as Arnold
House, Sandgate, which seems
improbable.] [c. 1897]

Dear Hick,

    I want things thus in a story.

A "man of pleasure" is in pursuit of a young person of beauty & virtue to her & the sympathetic heroes misery. The man of pleasure feels ill & consults a doctor who tells him either that he is within §[1] days of death or that he will be in excessive pain in § or an undefined number of days.

He determines to commit suicide & desists from this pursuit.

Thinking over things he perceives fresh aspects of the case, interviews the young people in a vein of enormous magnaminity & departs to commit suicide as if it were on the girl's account.

They treasure his memory for ever after. [2]

? What might the disease be to satisfy the conditions of this story?

? Some pending news terrible that arises from excess would be good. - But N.B. diseases in magazine stories must be decent.[3]

---

[1] This symbol was used by Wells to indicate that he required a specific number of days from Hick.
[2] This outline plot becomes Wells's unjustly forgotten story, 'A Story of the Days to Come', which appeared in five parts in the *Pall Mall Magazine* in 1897.
[3] This letter is signed with a big flourish of the pen rather than a signature.

277. To Henry Hick

Bromley (photocopy). ALS

[Address unknown]   [c. 1897]

My dear Hick,

  May I give the gentleman angina pectoris with the other things? On the other hand, I've thought simply of giving him "beans" without explanation. Like God a novelist must supply phenomena - not explain, 'em.
      Yours ever
      H.G.

278. To Henry Hick

Bromley (photocopy), ALS

Worcester Park
Surrey   [1897]

My dear Hick,

  Could you not come down here for Monday or Tuesday night dining with us, sleeping here & going on to Charing X next day? Then I might persuade Gissing along again to dinner. I am in your hands in this matter. If you can continue it I should greatly prefer you should come here. See Hamlet Monday night - come here Tuesday afternoon. Eh? If you send a tannergram[1] to that effect, I'll immediately write Gissing.

              Yours ever,
              H. G. Wells

---

[1] Not in the Oxford English Dictionary in this form, but it apparently meant a telegram which cost six pence, as an analogy to 'tannercab' which is cited as a use at about this same time. The word is clearly tannergram, not telegram.

279. To the Editor, *Pearson's Magazine*[1]

PLS

[London]   [March 1897]

[Sir,]

    Heaven alone knows how much I write on an average, but on an average I burn half at least of what I write - the net product is not more than 1000 words a day.

    I like thinking out my stories but I hate writing them; the only things that are pleasant to write are essays (but they are not nearly so pleasant to sell) and malignant criticisms of my contemporaries. For six months or more when I was scrambling for a footing among novelists, I must have turned out, Heaven forgive me! about 7000 words each working day, "Moreau" and "The Wonderful Visit" came in that feverish time and then were theatrical criticisms and book reviews, and copious articles and the beginning of a novel that was a bother even to burn.

    I hope some day to give two years to a book and to be able to burn it at the end if I do not like it. No novelist can do his best work until he feels free to do that.

              H. G. Wells

---

[1] The April 1897 issue of *Pearson's Magazine* carried a feature, 'The Output of Authors', pp. 456–63. Many authors provided brief letters about their working habits. Wells's appeared on p. 460, illustrated with a photograph. His serial, *The War of the Worlds*, began in the same issue pp. 363–73.

THE LETTERS: 1880-1903

280. To George Gissing

Illinois, ALS

Heatherlea
Worcester Park
Surrey   Bank Holiday [19 April 1897]

Dear Gissing,

On Wednesday at latest Madame and I will D.V. start for Petersfield in Hampshire - on our way to you. We shall reach Budleigh Salterton on Monday or Tuesday evening so that rooms might be taken for us (if you have not repented over your promise) for Monday onward. I have just been reading 'The Whirlpool' - but I am not going to waste conversation in letters. I had set my heart on reviewing the book for the Saturday. And so had Harold Frederic.[1] And as he was the more alert he bagged it. Damn him!

I had a letter from Hick and he tells me you are very much better. Go on doing that.

        Our warmest regards
                Yours ever,
                H.G. Wells

A Frenchman named Davray [2] who was here on Saturday came hither fresh from George Meredith, who had the Whirlpool in hand & expounded it to him. Meredith was all for praise.

Madame says I have given no indication of the sort of rooms we want. But any sort will do, provided they are clean and the people of the house not so genteel as to shame two dirty cyclists[3] - one bed room and one sitting room is the technical things she says.

---

[1] Harold Frederic (1859-98), an American novelist who moved to England in the 1880s; he is probably best remembered for *The Damnation of Theron Ware* (1896). He did review the Gissing novel in the *Saturday Review*, 10 April 1897.

[2] Henri Davray was one of the foremost translators from English into French at this time. He translated much of Wells's work as well as Gissing's, and he also translated Meredith's *An Essay on Comedy and the Use of the Comic Spirit* for the *Mercure de France*.

[3] Few roads were paved at this time and cyclists raised thick clouds of dust in the country. This accounts for the fashions in large hats, veils and dustcoats, often called 'dusters' (the very word conveys the ambience).

281. To A. M. Davies

Illinois, AL

Heatherlea
Worcester Park
Surrey[1]   Spring [1897]

Having a look at the Machine.
By the Bye, where are those maps you had last year? Whenwegettem.

Yours

HG

Directions for descending from bicycle on left side.

Observe when your left [pedal] is descending and about 30° from the nadir.

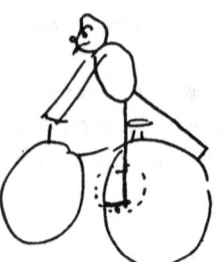

Stand on left pedal throwing up right leg.

Bring this in a graceful curve of the hind mud guard &

leap lightly to the ground.

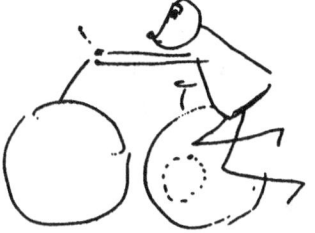

The treadle moves against your weight & assists the leap.

Then smile   Thus.

The method for the right side is right for left the same.

---

[1] This three page letter is located in the A. M. Davies outgoing file at Illinois. It has no salutation, but is a lovely example of Wells enjoying his talents as he instructs Davies on how to ride a bicycle.

282. To Henry Hick

Bromley (photocopy), ALS

c/o Mrs. [*illegible word*]
Spa Cottage
Budleigh Salterton   May 2 1897

My dear Hick,

    I am a wanderer - a vagabond - a sorefooted idler this spring. I had a letter from you somewhen somehow in which you said kind things. I fancy to come to Lulworth Cove when we are there. Did I answer it? If not, call me a hog. I definitely remember intending to answer it, & that is all. We shall perhaps be cycling into Kent this summer. If so we will very gladly avail ourselves of your invitation to come to Romney. Gissing is here. He has been doing well, but has caught a cold this last day or so. Last night he resumed tobacco after seven days.

Yours ever,
H.G.W.

283. To William Heinemann

Illinois, ACCS[1]

Heatherlea
Worcester Park
Surrey [7 August 1897]

Dear Mr. Heinemann,

You not only bother an author to ask for what is due to him but you are uncivil over the payment. You say you overpaid me for Moreau (that agreement also covered the War of the Worlds). I am prepared to do this in order that you may not complain to that effect further. <u>I will pay back every penny I have ever had from you for the book rights of Time Machine & Moreau, buy all stereo plates, copies & so forth at the valuation of any independent & competent person</u> on condition that all existing agreements between us are cancelled. Do you really think you lose by me? If so I think that is a fairly generous offer of release to you. If you don't accept it I hope you will at least have the grace to apologize for that "overpaid".

Yours very truely
H. G. Wells

---

[1] Although this letter starts out as a holograph business letter, and is signed by Wells, the number of erasures, cross-outs, and balloon additions to the text on the second and third correspondence card, may mean that the letter actually sent was reworked from this draft.

284. To George Gissing

Illinois, ALS

Heatherlea
Worcester Park
Surrey [c. 9 August 1897]

Dear Gissing,

I've had a sort of nervous period since that article appeared & your letter was a very welcome termination thereunto.[1] The stuff was criticism of a sort, & by no means an appreciation, which from me would have been a little impertinent, quite graceless & (as some people know I know you personally) of no benefit to either of us. I think I see your point re Rolfe & Morton - but I always give myself the benefit of a delay before I admit an error. There's a trickle of little mentions like the enclosed - one in <u>Daily Chronicle</u> of a brief but friendly sort. Where there is more than mention there is misconception (naturally) as in the <u>Speaker</u>. I envy your moorland. We are very hot and close here, & I have been very much worried by a commission for two short stories & an inability to get up to the mark with them - a consequent disorganization - nervous worry - sleeplessness, swearing, weeping. I've resigned myself not to do the things this morning rather than do them badly & am resuming my notional idea of mind. Funny beasts we are! Give Walter our warmest regards.
                                                  Yours ever,
                                                  H.G. Wells
Have you heard from that man Hick - brevity remarkable.

---

[1] Wells's important article on Gissing had just appeared. 'Novels of Mr. George Gissing', *Contemporary Review*, vol. 72 (August 1897), pp. 192–201. This piece, one of the earliest critical commentaries on Gissing, dealt with his fiction in a formal discussion of style and content.

285. To Henry Hick

Bromley (photocopy), ACCS

Worcester Park [c. Summer 1897]

My dear Hick,

Just now I'm halfway to brain fever with a damned story but very likely in September we shall take a snatch of holiday. If so, we may descend. But meanwhile - where is that article on the G.P.? [1]

Yours ever,
H.G.W.

---

[1] The proposed discussion of the decline of the general practitioner doctor was apparently never written.

286. To Edmund Gosse[1]

Leeds, ALS

[Worcester Park
Surrey] Oct. 2nd/97

My dear Mr. Gosse,

I am delighted to find that you think well of my story & that you read my work of the <u>Invisible Man</u>. I've had the gravest doubts. I've scarcely any facility in story building and simple as the thing seems it cost me a vast deal of labour. After it was sold & within three weeks of its serial printing I discovered so much clumsiness that I had to take it all to pieces & reconstruct it. Since which I have funked reading it. So that your good opinion is an immense relief to me. But quite apart from that I was glad of your letter. It introduces a personal element & an incentive to literary virtue. The temptations besetting the young man of illiterate origins who has the type of gift I possess are very great. There is the persuasion that one might be slap-dash & still effective enough or even more effective with the Great Heart.[2] There is the still more immediate smear of sentimentality of a popular sort. One says, "I know I could

make this shine & glow, and the rewards as Sir Walter[3] points out are desirable & increasing, & after all why not?" To which it is a saving antidote to think that this will be a matter of interest to Gosse who has also edited Bjornsen.[4]
My warmest thanks.
Yours faithfully
H.G. Wells

---

[1] Sir Edmund Gosse (1849–1928) was one of the foremost editors and critics of the late Victorian and Edwardian periods. His imprimatur helped make reputations. Wells had clearly achieved recognition when such correspondence came to him unsolicited.
[2] The book buying public
[3] Sir Walter Besant (1836–1901), a founder of the Society of Authors, who wrote a regular book review column in the 1890s. Wells did not like Besant's views, nor his use of the phrase 'The Great Heart' to mean the reading public. He satirised Besant several times in the *Saturday Review*, and writes disparagingly to Gissing about him as well.
[3] Bjornsterne Bjornson (1832–1910) a playwright, statesman, and Nobel Laureate in Literature in 1903. He and Gosse were good friends.

287. To an unknown correspondent

Illinois, ALS

Heatherlea
Worcester Park
Surrey [Oct. 18, 1897][1]

Dear Sir,

I'm glad to learn you still read me, & I think your point about the engine business decidedly good. I can only plead that he was already more than half mad. But to be truthful - I overlooked that probability.[2]
Yours very faithfully
H. G. Wells

---

[1] Date supplied by another hand.
[2] Perhaps a reference to the plot structure of *The Invisible Man* (London: Pearson, 1897) or to 'The Lord of the Dynamos', which appeared in the *Pall Mall Gazette*, 6 September 1894 and in *The Stolen Bacillus, and Other Incidents* (London: Methuen, 1895).

288. To the Editor, *Academy*[1]

PLS

Heatherlea
Worcester Park
Surrey [c. 10 November 1897]

Sir, As a parlour game there's no greater fun than Academy picking for those who practise, or think they practise, letters. I have read your list with immense interest. It is an Academy of (respectable) letters. Who is Mr. W.P. Ker, and who is the Rev. Aidan Gasquet? And why does the Duke of Argyll[2] always figure in this sort of thing? His name has been before me from my earliest years, and from my earliest years I have been trying in vain to discover his connexion with literature! And Mr. Aubrey De Vere - ? A charming poet, I am told; but would he be on your list if the <u>Reminiscences</u> had not been recently published? It is curious to see the "scholar" and the minor poet filling up the gap left by Huxley and Tyndall. Your list contains quite a crowd of respectable scholars, but no "scientific" literary men. Surely Lloyd Morgan, say, might weigh against Jebb or Salmon. Is Skeat really a "literary" name. If philology is "Literature", then so are astronomy and biology, and you must consider Norman Lockyer, Ball, and Ray Lankester. Grant Allen, it is true, wrote the <u>Woman Who Did</u>; but that he is an indifferent novelist does not conceal his other very considerable work. And is Gladstone included by virtue of his translations or his <u>Impregnable Rock of Holy Scripture</u>, or his brief, but effective, contributions to the criticism of contemporary works? Of omissions there are Gissing and Moore and Bernard Shaw and Oscar Wilde. There is a lot of overdone Heine about Shaw; but eliminate that and there is sufficient literary residuum to put beside, or even a little above, Bryce or Trevelyan. Moore's <u>Esther Waters</u> is an unweeded garden; but weight a book like that against — . But this sort of gossip is interminable.. -

Yours very truly,

H.G. Wells

---

[1] The editor of the *Academy* put forward the idea of an English Academy similar to the French Académie in its issue of 3 November 1897. The response was very large and very varied. The magazine gave a list of forty names whom they thought might be elected. The editors also offered a prize of a hundred guineas for the book deemed best of the year by nominations from readers, and fifty guineas for the one voted second. The wide-ranging discussion appeared in the issues of 6, 13, 20, 27 November and 3 December. Wells's comments appeared on

pp. 401–2, 13 November 1897. Shaw's contribution to this debate appeared in the same week, p. 402.
[2] More readers objected to the inclusion of the Duke of Argyll than that of any other individual. He was, in truth, not a writer, being included because of his support for letters.

289. Alfred C. Harmsworth to H. G. Wells

Illinois, ALS

36, Berkeley Square, W.   18 . N. 1897

My Dear Sir,

Will you allow me to say how much I appreciated the spirit of your article in my "Daily Mail" to-day.[1] I am giving it as a text to all my young men.
Faithfully yours,
Alfred C. Harmsworth[2]

[*Wells wrote this barely legible note on the letter*]:

There are two lines almost equally important. Reorganize and expand London & provincial Universities. - & reorganize of secdy education. And, - though its still to be made manifest - immensely interesting subjects of knowledge in the right way.
Yours very sincerely
H.G. Wells[3]

---

[1] Alfred Harmsworth (later Lord Northcliffe) (1865–1922) was complimenting Wells on the piece in the *Daily Mail*, 18 November 1897, the first of Wells's new series, 'The Root of the Matter – Some Reflections on the British Schoolmaster'.
[2] Wells had known Harmsworth since his days at Henley House School, and was to write a number of useful articles for Harmsworth publications throughout his life. The two men were associated with the War Aims campaign during the First World War at Crewe House, see volume 2. Still later Wells was to use aspects of Harmsworth's career to write a major piece, 'What is Success?,' *T.P's Weekly* and *Cassell's Weekly*, 24 November; 1, 8 December 1923. It was published in the United States in *The American Magazine*, December 1923.
[3] Reacting to Harmsworth, the managing editor for the *Daily Mail*, S. J. Prior, also wrote to Wells telling him of Harmsworth's interest, and asked Wells to extend his series to include an article on 'The Ideal School Board'. Wells commented on the margin of this second letter, 'Thank you, I will write on the school board if I understand the issues. But, it is really too late with the election occurring today. I can write on my creed. Perhaps it is better to write on what a proper

school should be'. On another part of the letter Wells also wrote the following note, and eventually all of his comments appeared in a formal letter to Harmsworth, see letter 291. 'The Daily Mail is an immense temptation to any opinionated man. That column is, just at present, the most efficient position in the press. My article was the result of an impulse and I'm better at an outburst like this than a sustained attack. Moreover, I have set myself at the things. But I would rejoice indeed to see you using your immense influence to my ideas. In effect reorganization of the highest education. There are almost equally (unfinished – responsibility and expense of London and financial (university – unity – and [*illegible word*] of the Secretary of Education. And – through the skills to be made manifest immensely interesting subjects of Howlett[?] in the right way.

290. To J. M. Dent

George Locke, ALS

Heatherlea
Worcester Park
Surrey   Nov. 19, 1897

Dear Mr Dent,

Certainly that new reprint of the 'Wheels of Chance' may go. But we won't do anything to remind people of it, & someday I will make it practically a new book.

For the Wonderful Visit in addition to certain verbal changes, I want to take out the Athenaeum allusion, & a totally unnecessary chapter which describes the recovery of Gotch & breaks that effect. A line in the epilogue replaces that. I also want a quotation on the title page, a cut in the violin playing - & a few other such things.[1]

As for that great novel. All great & complete work is leisurely work. For a man of my turn of mind and ample solvency is a necessary preliminary to accomplishment. Until the summer of 1896 I never was £100 ahead of the gulf - & that with a considerable group of dependents is no great sum. Since then - thanks chiefly to Pearson's high cheques & liberal advertisement of me - I have come upon better conditions.[2] And now - a thing by no means obvious - All my published work up to now & all appearing in 1898, except revisions of the Invisible Man[3] six short stories (Stone Age)[4] & the revision of the War of the Worlds was finished before August 1896. And from then to now - fourteen months of work. All that time I have worked to & fro on two books & on nothing else. And neither of those books is nearly finished yet. "Love and Mr Lewisham" is as yet not half complete & "When the Sleeper Wakes" is a pile of big fragments. The price of either - will be I hope in accordance with those facts.

Yours very faithfully
H.G. Wells

---

[1] These are changes from the first edition of the *Wonderful Visit*.
[2] Wells's work had been promoted fairly heavily in this period as the weekly magazine *Pearson's* had published several of his pieces. Dent also published *The Invisible Man* and promoted it quite hard for this period of usually quiet and conservative advertisement.
[3] Wells reworked this book fairly substantially for the American edition, which appeared with an epilogue. Since that time the epilogue has usually, but not always, been included as part of the English editions as well.
[4] *Tales of Space and Time*, again rewritten, was published in 1899 from Harper and Brothers, in both England and the United States.

291. To Alfred Harmsworth

Hofstra, ALS

Heatherlea
Worcester Park
Surrey [end November 1897][1]

My dear Sir,

I'm glad you liked the article. The Daily Mail is an immense temptation to an opinionated man. That column is just at present the most efficient position in the press. My article was the result of an impulse. I'm better at an outbreak like this than at a sustained attack.

Moreover I have set myself at other things. But I would rejoice indeed to see you using your immense influence to bring about an efficient reorganization of our higher education. There are two lines of work in this direction almost equally important - the reorganisation & expansion of the London & provincial Universities, & the reorganisation of secondary education. And -

though its still to be made manifest - these could be made immensely interesting subjects, I believe, if handled in the right way -
> Yours very truly,
> H.G. Wells

P.S. I've no objection to Le Gallienne seeing this letter. In fact, I'd like him to.[2]
> Yours ever,
> H.G.

---

[1] This letter is the final form of the drafts which appear in letter 289.
[2] Wells eventually wrote five major articles and two longish letters to the *Daily Mail*, 18 November; 4, 17, 23, 24, 28 December 1897.

292. To the Editor, *Daily Mail*[1]

PLS

Heatherlea
Worcester Park　　　　　　　　　　　　　　　　[*c.* 14 December 1897]

[Dear Sir,]

Professor Sylvanus Thompson, taking a text from my first article upon education in the '"Daily Mail", draws an obvious conclusion, and asks why London waits for an efficient modern university.

The answer is quite short and simple. Because the friends of a number of second rate or quite ineffective teaching institutions in London appear resolute to utilize the widespread feeling in favour of such a university for the financial benefit of some of these institutions, and to sacrifice the most important natural interests in the job. These intrigues and able misstatements of the question at issue confuse the public mind and divide the forces of reform. The sham London University Reformer is the reason why London waits.
> H. G. Wells

---

[1] Wells was quick to pick up more evidence to support his proposed curriculum and administrative reforms. This letter appeared on 16 December 1897, p. 4, under the title 'Why London Waits'.

293. To the Editor, *Academy*[1]

PL

[Heatherlea,
Worcester Park] [*c.* 1 January 1898]

[Dear Sir,]

Henley and Henderson's edition of Burns is the sort of book that particularly deserves "crowning" - A magnificent performance of the utmost value to English literature, and not a very remunerative one to its authors. Mr. Henry James's What Maisie Knew ranks next, perhaps. The Nigger of the "Narcissus" is, to my mind, the [most] striking piece of imaginative work, in prose, this year has produced. Captain's Courageous I couldn't read because of the illustrations; so I know nothing thereof.

[1] The *Academy* gave an annual prize of 150 guineas for the best book of the year and 50 guineas for the second best. This letter includes Wells's nominations for 1897. Others responded to the call as well and the nominations were published in the issue of 8 January 1898, p. 34.

294. To Elizabeth Healey

Texas, ACCS

[Heatherlea] [4 January 1898]

Dear Miss Healey,

I'm sorry I discontinued my zoo subscription three years ago or more in a season of great financial stress - & have never renewed it. How goes the world with you? With me it travels at a ghastly pace. I finished the War of the Worlds in the summer of 1896. Then, said I, let me do something worthy to prove I'm no charlatan. And here we are Jan 4 1898 & though something is done, nothing is finished. At that pace it's a dozen good novels at the utmost between me & the grave. Ars longa, sic transit, & so forth. My good Simmons calls for a day or so - with a touch & more of middle age. Eheu fugaces.[1]

Burton I heard is grey. I labour under suspension of a liver - though I did 90 miles in 7 hours this autumn, & I find myself deploring the virtues of my youth, & attending to the factors of my demands. What will become of us all? This is an outbreak of the personal. My philosophical cold heart is above these things. But how do you see all these things.? Don't you occasionally want to vividly go it. Haven't you good moments - I have - when in the middle of an eminently useful & decorous career, you would like to go a bust for all you are worth? Don't say I presume on an ancient friendship? These are earnest & fundamental questions. What is the good of living if we don't sometimes interchange experiences in really important things.

       Yours ever,
       H.G. Wells

---

[1] 'Eheu fugaces ... labuntur anni.' Alas! the fleeting years slip away (Horace).

295. To 'Pinnie' Robbins[1]

Illinois, ALS

Heatherlea
Worcester Park
Surrey   [c. 1897-8]

My dear Pinnie,

  I've been thinking over your financial position. I don't think £75 a year is enough for you nor do I think it fair that you should not have more. Amy's idea is that you should sell <u>Branscombe</u> and blue[2] the money in an annuity. That's not an unfair idea, but I gather you don't like it. But it's not fair to you that you should have so small an income simply because you want to leave her the house - I suppose you do want to leave her the house. I think under the circumstances it is only right that I should make up something at least of the deposit, of the difference, i.e., between the income you get & the annuity you would get. Now I've been computing & I think I can do this much in safety at present; pay you £35 a year on condition that you make a proper will leaving the home to Amy. I expect that condition is already satisfied. This will give you a present income of £110 beginning as soon as you leave Heatherlea. I don't think it is as much as you would get on the house as an annuity (by a long way), but that I will calculate out later, & so soon as I can get settled & am satisfied that my plan of work is not too greatly impaired & so on - in a year say - I will revise this and see if I cannot better it. I'm very anxious that you may be comfortable, & the idea of you pinching on £75 gives me the horrors. I'm really getting better. But for a year at least my nerves & my power of locomotion will be those of an old man.[3]

Yours very faithfully,
Bertie

---

[1] The name 'Pinnie' was the nick-name of Amy Catherine Wells's mother. There are a few letters to her in this collection, but basically she is a shadowy figure. Her given names are unknown. Branscombe must have been another house owned by Pinnie Robbins.

[2] 'Blue' is slang for to spend extravagantly.

[3] Wells is legitimately concerned about the state of his health, and even his prospective life span. Hick, his physician, had prescribed a move to the seashore for the clear air. Another relapse was still to occur. Eventually the couple built a house, Spade House, in Sandgate.

296. To Edmund Gosse

Leeds, ALS

[London]   [date unknown, but in 1898]

Dear Mr. Gosse,

By the same post came your letter with your good opinion of the 'War of the Worlds' & a cutting from the American <u>Bookman</u> in which you say all sorts of kind things about the 'Invisible Man'. I am very greatly obliged to you & I shall look for the <u>Saturday</u> with very pleasant anticipations.

Yours very faithfully,
H.G. Wells[1]

---

[1] Gosse very probably had been reading *The War of the Worlds* in serial form. It appeared in *Pearson's Magazine*, April–December 1897.

297. To the Editor, *Critic*[1]

ALS

Heatherlea
Worcester Park
Surrey, England   21st January, 1898

I have received a rather startling cutting from the Boston <u>Post</u> through the Author's Clipping Bureau. The cutting is dated 27 November, the accompanying invoice is dated 31st December, the Boston post-mark is 7th January and it has reached me here today. From it I learn that my story <u>The War of the Worlds</u> "as applied to New England, showing how the strange voyagers from Mars visited Boston and vicinity", is now appearing in the <u>Post.</u> This adaptation is a serious infringement of my copyright and has been made altogether without my participation or consent. I feel bound to protest in the most emphatic way against this manipulation of my work in order to fit it to the requirements of the local geography.

Yet it is possible that this affair is not so much downright wickedness as a terrible mistake. The story originally appeared simultaneously in the American <u>Cosmopolitan</u> and the British <u>Pearson's Magazine.</u> Mr. Dewey of the New York <u>Journal</u> called upon me in November last and arranged for its serial republication in the evening edition of that paper. In our agreement (of which I have his signed memorandum) it was stipulated that the publication should be with the consent of the American publishers and that no alteration in the text of the story should be made without my consent. On 26th December I received a cablegram from the Boston <u>Post</u> making an offer for the serial republication of <u>The War of the Worlds</u> "as New York <u>Journal</u>". To this I cabled "Agreed". And now I find too late that my story has been flaunted before the cultivated public of Boston disguised and disarrayed beyond my imagining. What has been done to it? I fail to see how a rag of conviction can remain in it after this outrage. I do not know what a remote Englishman may do in such a matter. At any rate I beg you will give me the opportunity of disavowing any share in this novel development of the local colour business.

H.G. Wells

---

[1] This is a very elusive piece. In late 1897 and early 1898, *The War of the Worlds* was serialised in both *The New York Evening Journal* and *The Boston Post*. These were bowdlerised versions using New England and New York locales, in an eerie forerunner to the 1938 radio production. Wells was informed that the pirate editions had occurred under the name of H. C. Wells.

The American Critic was a relatively short-lived effort to produce fair reviews and commentary. Wells wrote to them complaining of his treatment. I have never seen the original letter, but it was reprinted in *The Wellsian*, vol. 2, no. 3 (1968), p. 24.

298. Isabel Fowler-Smith to H. G. Wells

Illinois, ALS

Thornwood
Knowle Hill
Twyford, Berks [February 1898]

My dear Bertie,

I should have written before but I thought I would not bother you with a letter until I could tell you the result of my first hatching.[1]

I have twenty four healthy little chicks in the Foster Mother. Unfortunately we had to buy a lot of eggs as sixteen have proved infertile. I have fifty of our own eggs in now & hope for better luck next hatching time. The Incubator is quite easy to work & keeps a wonderfully even temperature. I am so very sorry you have been seedy, don't get influenza or don't overwork yourself will you? What has been the matter, nothing serious I hope. At the rate that your work is published I am afraid you put the greatest strain on yourself. Don't overdo it, will you?

Thanks very much for the 'War of the Worlds'. I read it in Pearson's & see you have altered the end somewhat. If I might venture to pass an opinion, I think the alteration is a great improvement. Where in the world of all that's wonderful do you get your ideas from? And you make them so terribly realistic too. It is marvellous.

If you have a moment let me know as how you are. Thanks for the cheque.

I had a letter from your mother yesterday. The good little woman remembered my birthday. It was kind of her.

Do let me know how you are.
Yours very sincerely
Isabel

---

[1] Isabel Wells married a man named Fowler-Smith with whom she set up a chicken farm in Berkshire. Although Wells was relieved from the payment of alimony, he contributed to the purchase of the farm, as he was to do with other ventures later. This letter and letters 316 and 317 are the only ones remaining from this period. Others appear in volume 2. Unfortunately Wells's responses have not survived.

299. To the Editor, *Saturday Review*

PLS

[Heatherlea,
Worcester Park] [*c.* 20 February 1898]

Sir, - The retort of the author of "The Canon"[1] has called my attention to the fact that a sentence indiscreetly inserted in the proof of my review of the remarkable book suffered in the hands of the printers, and "nephridia" twice became "neplividia". I suppose my handwriting was to blame. The rest of the retort scarcely matters.

H.G. Wells

---

[1] On 12 February 1898, in the *Saturday Review*, vol. 85, pp. 211–13, Wells had reviewed Grant Allen's *Evolution of the Idea of God* which he rather liked. He also noticed a book on the development of canon law which he found arcane.

300. To Miss Charton

Hofstra, ALS

Beach Cottage
Granville Road
Sandgate Feb. 15th [1898?]

Dear Madam,

As I am now living so far from London, it will not be worth your while I am sure to come so far for the short interview you require. I have therefore pencilled you a few notes about my first literary successes, which I hope is the kind of thing you want.
Yours very faithfully,
H.G. Wells (ACW)[1]

Miss Charton.

---

[1] This letter is in Amy Catherine Wells's hand, although Wells signed it. The interview/story may be the one which appeared in the *Bromley Record* in February 1898. By this time, of course, Wells's native town was beginning to be interested in his career.

THE LETTERS: 1880-1903

301. To A. T. Simmons

Illinois, ALS

Beach Cottage
Granville Rd.
Sandgate[1]   [early 1898]

Old Simmons, Damned old Publisher Simmons.

We've had such a damned house-hunt. Lord! Not a home to be got - not what's fit for me to live in nowadays - not one. So we've took a blarsted little furnished house for the winter, we have! Heatherlea's got let & we have to live somewhere, See? Damned old blooming old Drunkard, <u>you</u> are. We're going to store the Heatherlea furniture all excepting some books, & the blooming pianner, & Mrs. Robbins is off on her own. I was going to buy a house on the landslip but a blessed surveyer chap put the 'utter' kybosh on that. See? (You're a nice old cup of tea, <u>you</u> are.) So now I'm thinking of building a nice little 'ouse with a tower. My health continues to mend, it does. The Picturesque Person called God is evidently giving someone else a turn. Give my love to old Gregory (bless his heart) and pray God night & Morning to change the nasty expression of your face.

Yours ever,
H.G.

---

[1] The heading of this letter is in ink and Heatherlea, Worcester Park, Surrey, has been cancelled by a pen stroke. The letter must have been written soon after Wells moved to Beach Cottage.

302. To A. T. Simmons

Illinois, ACCS

Beach Cottage
Granville Rd
Sandgate [1898?]

Dear Mr. Editor,

State briefly the behaviour of glass, rocksalt & metal to radiant energy & name some substance solid in liquid which is opaque but diathermanous.

                         & oblige
                               The Paraclete[1]

---

[1] A Wellsian religious joke; 'The Paraclete' is the Holy Ghost as comforter or advocate.

303. To Harry Quilter

Hofstra, ALS

Hotel Alibert
Roma, Italy[1] [end February 1898]

Dear Mr. Quilter,

Heavens defend me! But have I given you offence with my confounded way of saying things? It's not a question of "worth-while" but the limitations of capacities. I have a dread of doing many things very badly instead of one thing passably well. And I have always set myself to do things that will tax my utmost capacity. Think how short life is. If you do indeed see your way to make a play of that book it will be altogether wrong for me to come in for half, for you will add something that is not there at present — the drama. I am absolutely certain there is no play, not even a one act play in the story as it stands & that the dialogue save for a few lines is not suitable for dramatic use - it does not develop into "situations" with sufficient rapidity. Consequently any play that results will be yours. Tax yourself ten per cent if you will, on my behalf, but for the rest - I decline that unearned increment. Only on such conditions am I a consenting party to this enterprise. Else I will annoy you with copyright & all sorts of disagreeable things.

Rome is changed indeed, Gissing says - iron railings all about the forum is the least of it & the beastliest houses of this sort

[drawing of a house]

full of a Saffron Hill population[2] & the smell of onion cookies. Fine red electric trams everywhere, and the Corso speaks English from end to end. But the wolves[3] are back in the cage in the capitol. For all that it has been a time of wonderful sensations to me - for I have never even crossed the channel before.
Our kindest regards to yourself & Mrs. Quilter.
Yours faithfully,
H.G. Wells

---

[1] This was the first visit that the Wellses paid to the Continent. They had a wonderful time, staying with Gissing and meeting other English friends. The Wells family were fairly close to the family of Henry Quilter at the time. Quilter, a theatrical impresario and would-be author, was interested in dramatising Wells's fiction. They were both in Florence during part of this trip, but were unable to meet as letters 305 and 306 indicate.

[2] Saffron Hill is a street and area in Southwark, London. I presume that Wells is referring to the predominately Italian section of London in 1898.

[3] The wolves probably refers to the famous statue representing the legend of Rome's founding by Romulus and Remus, supposedly saved by being suckled by wolves.

304. To Percy Redfern[1]

Manchester, ALS
Local Studies Unit
MSF O91.5 Rel.

Hotel Aliberti
Roma, <u>Italy</u> [end February 1898]

My dear Sir,

At last I can find a little time to write in answer to your interesting letter, particularly interesting to me since I was apprenticed to a draper for a couple of years. The copies of the 'Shop Assistant' have not arrived here - possibly they will await me in England as I am likely to be moving about from place to place - but I shall look forward to reading your contributions not least with considerable curiosity. Until I see it, I am of course, quite in the dark as to your literary possibilities, but your position & ambitions I can understand well enough. I know that to be an assistant in a shop is not a pleasing way of life, very irksome in a hundred ways, very hopeless for a man without command or hope of capital, & socially not very useful, or at least not obviously very useful. And I know that itch to write & how attractive the freedom & repute of writing must seem to you. But the transition means a perilous journey - make no mistake about that. It is not like changing your trade. A draper may be a second rate hand or a third rate hand, and still find a place in the world for him. But for the man from below, there is no place in the world of journalism & literature unlesss he is an exceptional man.. And there is no more pitiful lot in the world than the man who moved by literary ambitions or the still more potent fascination of the drama, has come out of his proper sphere & failed. Of such are the shirtless peasants[?] of the British Museum, the begging letter writers, the rabble of Fleet Street loafers, terrible figures of futility. Before you make any irrevocable step weigh yourself - are you sure enough of your ability to stake your life on it? And next, are you sure of your character; can you stand ten years of disappointment without growing bitter or will you hesitate & repent? The ability is only one side of this question - given that, you want doggedness & industry beyond the common lot. Then are there any people dependent or likely to be dependent upon you? This is an important consideration. And again, are you sure of freedom from the snare of romance & sexual attraction that may suddenly turn your dearest ambitions to empty vanities? It goes without saying you must if you start to be an author stay celibate until you succeed.

Suppose all these things you answer in the affirmative, even then I counsel no such departure. Get the shortest hours you can, live on as little as possible, read hard & work hard & do nothing else. For reading do not read novels in the ordinary way, but take a few that shall be your model & read & read them & see how the passages that startle you are done, read good criticisms of books you know, work to enlarge your choice of words, work at a dictionary, drill yourself at formal verse, rondeaux, ballades, sonnets & so forth, & do not try to write a novel or anything longer than 5000 words for six years time. For writing, write articles & short stories about the life you know & never write anything you do not feel to be real & true. N.B. Kipling revises his work for three hours & reads it aloud to hear how it sounds. A pithy series of short stories or sketchy stories of the every day life of the shop should be your most possible enterprise. The penny evening papers, Globe, P.M.G., & St James's Gazette.

pay from one guinea to three for such things. The clever work of Ansley & Pett Ridge would give you a model. You must also have a very fair chance with <u>To-Day</u>, the <u>Idler</u>, & <u>Black & White</u> for such writing.

When you have made £50 in one year at that sort of thing, then, if you think you can live on £70 a year, leave the counter & take your chance, & if I am alive then, let me know.

Lord! You've got a heavy thing in front of you. Don't dream of waking to find yourself famous or any such damned nonsense as that - sheer, <u>hard</u> good work is the only thing, & courage.

With best wishes
Yours very faithfully
H.G. Wells

There are at least ten who fail to one who succeeds.

---

[1] Redfern became a very well known follower of Tolstoy and was one of the leading figures in England interpreting his political views. He wrote a biography of Tolstoy and is best known for his *The New History of the C.W.S.* (London: Dent, 1938). This work is a major work on Cooperatives in England and is the formal account of the first seventy-five years of the Cooperative Wholesale Society.

305. To Harry Quilter

Hofstra, ALS

Hotel Alibert
Roma <u>Italy</u>   <u>March 20</u> [1898]

My dear Mr. Quilter,

I've been doing complicated calculations with a calendar & a book of tickets & my promises, & I am afraid, much as we regret it, that we cannot come to Florence. (Our heartiest good wishes to Mrs. Quilter & that young gentleman come herewith.) I would have carved a fortnight from the time devoted to Rome only we are not alone here but in the company of that man Gissing and when our stay in Rome is over he will go north and we south and Heaven knows when we shall meet again. I must go south because my journeyings have been previously arranged even to the steamboat here on May

6th.[1] And then work awaits me. And I must confess I dread the distraction of my attentions a little. I have attempted in my own mind to give all the rest of the year to that novel I spoke of. Heaven knows what would become of me if I went astray after this fascinating Fata Morgana of the stage. The prizes are great but the worries are many. So I take it you must do that play, of your own right. But possibly in the scenario stage I might see it, and give a suggestion or so to the enterprise. What do you say to that? At the same time this is only a temporary suspension of your invitation mind. We hope to come into North Italy next year - we've seen nothing of it yet, and see you both & that young gentleman a truely polyglot by that time. Our kindest regards to you both.

Yours very faithfully
H.G. Wells

---

[1] The visit to Italy has been well treated by Patrick Parrinder in *The Gissing Newsletter*, 'The Roman Spring of George Gissing and H. G. Wells', vol. 21, no. 3 (July 1985), pp. 1–12.

306. To Harry Quilter

Hofstra, ALS

Going on to
Hotel Genève,
Napoli
(for the next month)   [*c.* late March 1898.]

Dear Mr. Quilter,

       How goes the play? You know I am sceptical of the dramatic quality of the book & I'm wondering very much how many things you have been forced to alter & add. A case of flint soup — very good in the end, with a little stock, salt, vegetables & wine added to the original infusion of flint.

       Our days in Rome are at an end but it's been a wonderful time for our untravelled eyes.

Yours faithfully,
H.G. Wells

307. To Fred Wells

Illinois, APCS

[The postcard has etchings of the Colisseum, St Peter's and the Temple of Castor and Pollux, with the words, 'Saluti da Roma'.]

Rome, Italy[1] [25? April 1898]

Very many thanks for your letter. I've written to Mr. Leatherby. But I can't get you the right glasses unless you send me one of the old lenses. - Send the unbroken glass.

Yours ever
H.G.

---

[1] It is remarkable that this card survives since it was sent from Rome to Fred Wells, c/o Messrs Pudden & Luck, Johannesburg, S. A. R., Transvaal, in parenthesis: 'nella Africa meridionale'. It cost 10 lire (two 5-lire stamps) for its carriage.

308. To Mr Draper

Trinity College, Cambridge, ALS
[From Cullom Collection Q96][1]

[Address unknown] May 13th 1898

Dear Sir,

The details concerning me for which you ask are these: —
 <u>1.</u> I was born Sept 21 1866 at Bromley Kent. My father is Joseph Wells, who used to play cricket for Kent. My education began at a private school in Bromley, then I was at Midhurst Grammar School & afterwards at the Royal College of Science London. Degrees B.Sc. London, first class honours in Zoology, & F.C.P. / Fellow of the College of Preceptors
 <u>2.</u> The following are my published books.
>Textbook of Biology 2 vols 1892-93
>Select Conversations with an Uncle 1895
>The Time Machine 1895

The Stolen Bacillus 1895
The Wonderful Visit 1895
The Island of Doctor Moreau 1896
The Wheels of Chance 1896
The Plattner Story & Others 1897
The War of the Worlds 1898
When the Sleeper Wakes 1899

3. My permanent address is this one that I write from.

                        Yours very faithfully
                              H. G. Wells

---

[1] This letter is located in a collection of autographed letters obtained by a former student at Trinity College, who willed them to the College and its Faculty, to whom I am very grateful for permission to print the letter. Draper may have been a journalist.

309. To William Briggs[1]

Illinois, ADLS

Heatherlea
Worcester Park
Surrey   [1 June 1898]

My dear Mr. Briggs,

    I'm greatly obliged to you for the copy of the book, though for several reasons I am not particularly delighted with the alterations made. Naturally one has a tenderness for one's first book, and I think Davies should have done me the civility to consult me in the matter. [*Four lines are blackened to illegibility.*] ~~Note, speaking generally, I do not approve of his changes.~~.

    My book was, no doubt, open to considerable criticisms; it was done in haste & the haste showed. But, I think the zoological part at any rate had vigor and the botanical part ~~to put it mildly defective~~ was erected on an insufficient basis of 'knowledge'. To use a journalistic vulgarism, I did tear out the "guts" of the subject I presented them ragged and bleeding. But Davies has not ~~I consider~~ trimmed & clarified he has defaced & overlaid. Every paragraph has been changed almost ~~messed about~~ often in the most trivial way. ~~& even the concluding statement has been emasculated~~. He has ransacked almost like a personal enemy, counting any change ~~as~~ a gain. And if you will reread the preface you will see his claims amount to the book, ~~He claims every change in the new edition of the book.~~ (The only chapter he has left me any credit for, the chapter on the skull, ~~is grossly made ridiculous deliberately by the representations of and unintelligent copying of my Diagrams~~ has been & still is damaged by his mention of errors in my diagrams. ~~I refute strongly the views as central to the otiscapula otic in the back area of the skull.~~

"Enlarged & revised" will I think make the case. In no sense has there been joint authorship. The preface must I suppose stand. But I certainly think that before Davies was permitted finally to apportion the credit for the revised work a proof ~~of his~~ should have been submitted to me. His claim to have rewritten is quite misleading. ~~He cannot write.~~ He has taken out words, replaced words & phrases, added words phrases & figures from other text books but there is no [word blacked out] lucid explanation in the book, no passage of exposition as distinguished from flat statement that is still not essentially mine. In the embryological section for example where my facts have suffered most by the passage of time, his interpretations lie almost across my arranged explanations like luggage in a hall.

But enough of ~~this bitterness~~ criticism! I am very greatly obliged to you for your willingness to meet me in this matter.

Yours faithfully,
H.G. Wells

~~In the making of the botanical textbook by him I should imagine there is no need to elaborate its relationship to the biological textbook it supercedes.~~

---

[1] This letter was written in anger, but also in sorrow, to his former employer at the Correspondence College, William Briggs, who owned the rights to the *Textbook of Zoology*. Briggs had had the book revised by Wells's friend and classmate, A. M. Davies. Wells resented this appropriation of his book, although in fact he had sold up all rights. Other letters in this collection also show Wells's feelings about Briggs, and about Davies. The draft which appears here is heavily interleaved with corrections, crossings out and other revisions. I have retained the crossings out in this and in the subsequent letter to A. M. Davies to give a sense of how difficult the letters were to write. The letters, for which these are the drafts, do not exist as far as I can determine. Wells's name remained on all revisions of the book until the 7th edition in 1934, even though he received no money from the sales and had no input into the text beyond the first two editions.

310. To A.M. Davies

Illinois, ADLS

Heatherlea
Worcester Park
Surrey   [c. June 1898]

My dear Davies,[1]

Briggs has sent me the textbook. I am not surprised that I have had to get it from him, instead of receiving it from you. ~~Of course it should have come from you with a decent apology instead of as foolish and impertinent a note as you have written. And even if we were personal enemies instead of two persons with a sort of faded sham of friendship between us, a proof of the preface at least if not a scheme of the alterations should have been surely submitted to me. Not that you have failed consulting me so far from submitting proof to me in accordance with the obvious courtesy of the case.~~
No one but you among all the people I know could have been quite so oblivious of an author's natural tenderness for his first work, or so deliberately antagonistic to all the associations of the book. The preface ~~is a pitiful~~ had clearly been edited at Cambridge but there is still matter enough for ~~performance~~ complaint. ~~You claim all your dark claims~~ after having spoilt one of my best diagrams ~~my chapter~~ on the skull by drawing the mucus as a sort of nucleus to the capsula you pretend I am responsible for that - ~~naurally claiming~~ & you practically claim all else. Your claim to have rewritten the book is absurd. ~~& I cannot believe that you are unaware of that you cannot write~~ You have revised things whose bearing on the general effect of the book you do not appreciate ~~are too dull to understand,~~ you have rewritten words & phrases for the most part capping my points, & you have added things from other textbooks. But where there is still lucid explanation in the book, wherever statements are timeless, the spirit of generalization, there the treatment remains mine. ~~You know it is mine, & you are too mean, too greedy of petty repute to admit as much even of the turn of a phrase.~~ In the embryological chapter, for example, in spite of the new facts that have come in, my prepondency will be manifest to anyone capable of criticism who compares the two versions.
~~And when you are not trying hard to believe that my writing is yours by notice of an added [dot?] appearing over i, you are trying hard to win a little credit for your wife's very admirable copies of other peoples illustrations. I tell you these things plainly now, because I do not suppose I shall ever write to~~

~~you again and I do not want you to be in any error as to my opinions of you in this affair~~

I have written to Briggs complaining of the implicit injustice of the preface & pointing out how baseless is your claim to have "rewritten" the book, & I am also asking him to restore the proper title of the book, ~~which is~~ "A Textbook of Zoology by H. G. Wells". (revised ~~& edited~~ by A.M. Davies) - ~~if you like~~). In that way my paternity in the book will be indicated, & at the same time the tinkering it has undergone will be properly ascribed.

Yours faithfully,
H.G. Wells

~~And so we go our several ways. I shall call your name with considerable vehemence in private for some time for indeed you have been pitifully secretive, disloyal & shabby to me, but in the end I shall bear you no ill will. You have no originality & little courage but you are highly intelligent and & our wife is an industrious helper. . In the end you will probably be a successful & useful man.~~
~~Yours ever sincerely~~
H. G. Wells[2]

---

[1] What follows is a seven-page draft of a letter to Davies about the *Textbook of Zoology*. It is a remarkably disorganised mass of notes. Whether it or another version went to Davies is not known. This draft appears in the Davies papers from Wells, but it might have been placed there later by others; see Wells's letter to Elizabeth Healey, letter 352 and the letters to and from Briggs on this subject, letters 309, 311 and 312. Wells also drafted a letter to *Nature* discussing the new edition of his book. However he apparently thought better of it, and that letter was not sent. Parts of the latter draft are in the Illinois archives. In the draft, after disavowing Davies's efforts to revise his book, which he described as 'a queer volume [written] to facilitate the operation of passing candidates through the rather peculiar biological examinations of London University,' he remarked that it was too bad that Davies had wasted his time. The introduction of the new edition carried the following remarks, 'The general plan of the work belongs to the well-known author H. G. Wells, B.Sc. but little of the first edition remains unaltered. The book has been thoroughly revised and largely rewritten in the light of present knowledge by others who hold themselves entirely responsible for the present issue'. The 6th edition, of 1915 was revised by J. T. Cunningham; W. H. Leigh-Sharpe edited the 7th. Davies's wife redrew the illustrations for the 3rd edition. Later editions have new and anonymous illustrators. Wells had, of course, sold his rights to Briggs, and so the book, which was a money spinner for the publishers, returned no funds to Wells. One can easily believe that his name helped sell the work. It was a good 'standard' text in its time. Wells and Davies, old friends from college days, were estranged by this episode.

[2] There are two more pages of phrases, sentences, cross outs and trial balloons which do not appear in the letter, but are filed with it. What is interesting is that Wells deliberately plays down his feelings from the draft form of the letter to the one which I presume went to Davies. There was a brief reconciliation late in their lives, see volume 4.

311. William Briggs to H. G. Wells

Illinois, TLS

[Cambridge]   8 June 1898

Dear Mr. Wells,

In reply to yours,[1] part of the book is from your old book and some is original matter by Davies. The preface contains a full account of what is due to you and what to Davies.

I am perfectly willing to consult your wishes in the matter and should be glad to hear what you suggest, although as the purchaser of the copyright I am at liberty to do as I think right.

                                  Yours Sincerely,
                                      W. Briggs

---

[1] This is Briggs's response to Wells's letter 309.

312. William Briggs to H.G. Wells[1]

Illinois, TLS

12 Queen Anne Terrace
Cambridge   14 June 1898

Dear Mr. Wells,

I instructed that a copy of the text-book of Zoology should be sent you. You may remember that some time ago you gave your permission for Davies to revise[2] the book. It seems now that Davies has put in a good deal more original matter than I expected.

I should be glad, after you have seen the book and especially the preface, for you to write me stating your wishes and we can put in new titles in the next binding.

I quite endorse your statement of your position that the book is a text-book of biology by H. G. Wells edited, enlarged, or revised by A. M. Davies; if his work has gone beyond this it was not at my instruction. Certainly I gave him a free hand but it was intended to be within these limits.

Perhaps "enlarge and revised" would meet the case?

                                  Yours sincerely,
                                      Wm. Briggs

---

[1] This is an interesting letter which may have been a letter written 'for the files', so to speak. It may also indicate that Briggs took some of Wells's strictures and changed the text of the revised edition. If this is so, no evidence of an intermediate text is available. It probably is simply a

case of Briggs setting the record straight, but done in a kinder spirit than their earlier exchanges.

[2] The word 'write' is crossed out.

313. To William Heinemann

Illinois, Typed Transcription[1]

Heatherlea   July 8, 1898

My dear Heinemann,

If you don't feel sure you could do <u>much</u> better with '<u>When the Sleeper Wakes</u>' than with '<u>The War of the Worlds</u>' there's an end to the matter. I'm sick of seeing my good honest work fizzle in obscure corners. It's absurd to talk of dealing with the book upon the basis of previous sales. At that rate I might live & die, a sort of literary page in the train of Caine Zangwill[2] & so forth. It's £750 or nothing. If you don't intend to publish the book on that scale you are no good to me as a publisher. Indeed why should I have a publisher for the certain sales? For an edition of 4000 copies it must pay me far better to print & bind myself & sell directly to the book sellers.

I have been told once or twice that publishing is not philanthropy. But authorship is not solely for the support of the class of publisher.

Practically then this negociation is at an end.
Yours ever faithfully,
H.G. Wells

---

[1] In the early days of the creation of the Wells archives in Illinois, transcriptions were provided to Illinois by various sources. They were filmed in an early version of microfilm, now severely faded, which are called in Illinois, 'the Lazarus files'. The film is essentially unusable now, but typed copies of its contents appear in the standard files. Such is this letter whose provenance is unknown otherwise.

[2] Wells is referring to Hall Caine, and Israel Zangwill who wrote *The Children of the Ghetto* (1892) and the play, *The Melting Pot* (1908). Zangwill and Wells exchanged letters which appear towards the end of this volume and in volume 2.

314. To Henry Hick

Bromley (photocopy), ALS

Worcester Park   July 16, 1898

My dear Hick,

      I'm working up to a holiday bust, but not this week. One of these days I think I shall rise & gnawing my breakfast (in one hand) pack a holdall with the other and start - you ward. I shan't get to you that night, I expect, but I shall wire to acquaint you with my movement. Meanwhile Mrs. Wells will be jamming a portmanteau together. You begin to see the proposed plot. A simultaneous attack on this man Hick & his unfortunate wife & household. Attention concentrated on the Rye road & suddenly Mrs. Wells descends detraining in their rear. Eh?

Yours ever,
H.G. Wells

[*On the verso of this sheet, written as an afterthought and at a slant appear these words: 'Gissing writes to say that he can ride without his hands, that a fly in his eye rather pleases him than not. Pleases him that now, that his difficulty in breathing has disappeared, Gissing's on his bicycle - all's right with the world.'*][1]

---

[1] Some of these letters to Hick are virtually indecipherable and my readings are somewhat problematic. Gissing was learning to ride a bicycle, although he never really mastered the machine.

315. To Henry Hick

Bromley (photocopy), AL

Worcester Park
[*Letter written at
Seaford, en route*]   [August 1898]

Expedition to Romney[1]

———

Bulletin

———

The expedition of the Wellses to Romney has now passed its more acute phase. It began suddenly a fortnight ago, the onset coming on July 19th. There were markedly feverish symptoms and a tumorous swelling containing night dresses

& other matters on the frame of the gentleman's bicycle. The expedition travelled rapidly to Pugsley where winding up of the lady's dress took place & a severe fall. The expedition, nothing daunted, broke itself in two. The lady took her contusions to Lewes by train & the gentleman (so to speak) followed by high road. Night prevails. The next morning (July 20th) the expedition resumed & reached Seaford in Sussex - 12½ miles from Eastbourne & about 30/40 from Romney. There the expedition passed a tranquil night, & instead of taking the turning to Eastbourne next morning, found itself presently near Uckfield. Interruption of the expedition occurred & it went home, after a peaceful night at Nutley in Ashdown Forest. For some days there was absolute tranquillity, succeeded on Thursday July 28th by packing & general inflammation. A trunk & lady's hat box & other matter was exuded & on July 29th the expediton violently discharged itself to Seaford again. <u>Why</u> Seaford? Why not direct to Romney? Because it would seem we are not dealing with a simple case of expedition here, but with expedition complicated by unfinished novels or at least one unfinished novel. The Roentgen ray[2] apparatus has revealed a dark disorderly mess in the trunk, (crushing one of the lady's blouses which is very probably the irritant body in question.) It is proposed that the patients shall remain in absolute seclusion at Seaford for the next three weeks undergoing daily operations for the removal of this complication. That disposed of, the expedition to Romney will be a comparatively simple matter.

---

[1] Wells was writing *Love and Mr. Lewisham* at this time. Hick had prescribed exercise, especially bicycling, and so the letter is by way of reporting results. The extent of Jane's contusions and the problem with the trunk are not alluded to again.

[2] Original name of the X-ray

316. Isabel Fowler-Smith to H. G. Wells

Illinois, ALS

Thornwood
Knowle Hill
Twyford, Berks   Aug. 11 1898

Dear Bertie,

    Thank you very much for the cheque. I am sorry to hear you are seedy again, why don't you try a more bracing place than Worcester Park, but it's such a bother to move isn't it?

    Things are going very quietly with me. Bertie Williams[1] was staying with me last week but she went off home in a hurry to do some work that was wanted. I am very fond of her & often ride over to Windsor on my bike & see them.

I wanted your mother to come up to see me this summer, but she does not seem inclined, I wish she would. I should very much like to see her again. I don't hear much news of you. How are things going with you?

Yours sincerely
Isabel

---

[1] Bertha Williams was a second cousin to both Wells and Isabel. She was one of the children from Surly Hall whom Wells had known from childhood.

317. Isabel Fowler-Smith to H. G. Wells

Illinois, ALS[1], Extract

[Summer 1898]

[...] better & stronger.

Did you get my last letter. I see you haven't taken any notice of a little suggestion that was in it, why not?

I shall expect a longer letter next time with more news about yourself & other things. You know I am interested, don't you?

Can I send you anything in the way of country produce. I mean chickens or eggs. Of course I don't know how you are situated in your present abode. Perhaps you would rather wait until you are settled again.

Nell is staying with me for a few days just now & I am teaching her to ride my bike. Now go on getting better, won't you & keep ever so cheerful & hopeful & write again soon please.

Yours sincerely
Isabel

Thanks for the Cheque.

---

[1] The upper right corner of this four folded letter is cut away, so that the place of writing, date and opening paragraph are missing.

318. To an unknown correspondent

Illinois, ACCS

Worcester Park [1898?]

Dear Sir,

I'm delighted to find such a constant reader. I think you've read me all - bar a little book of dialogues 'Select Conversations with an Uncle' published by Lane & of no great merit - the least despicable being one about an egg & two at the end.

Yours very faithfully
H. G. Wells

The story you want is the 'Plattner Story' of a bookful and published by Methuen.

319. To Sarah Wells

Illinois, ALS

The Swan, Hythe
[*Worcester Park stationery
letterhead crossed through here.*] [September 1898]

My dear Mother,

I hope there has been no anxiety because of the cessation of postcards. I have been so very busy thinking over houses that I really forgot them - shocking as it is. We have found nothing that suits us & we are both very tired & miserable. - for Amy who is not very well just now. One house in this town might do but the owner wants an impossible lease. Amy has gone again into Folkestone this morning. I am afraid we may have to take a small cheap house for six months & then try again. You see I cannot possibly get through the winter at Worcester Park, lodgings & boarding houses are too uncomfortable for anyone who is not well, & altogether we're in a fix. It serves me right for taking that home in Worcester Park. Apart from the house difficulty Diss &

Sandgate & Folkestone are pleasant & convenient places, warm & sheltered & very dry.

There are convenient houses & houses along the sea front, theatres & reading rooms so that it is possible for a man who can hardly walk 2 miles & who cannot cycle or anything of that sort, to get along without being dull.

We are going back to New Romney tomorrow & then I don't know where we shall go. Possibly to Hastings or St. Leonards to look about there. Amy's a little brick or I don't know what would become of me. With love from us both to you all.

Yours ever
Bertie

320. To A. T. Simmons and Richard A. Gregory

Illinois, ANS

[Sandgate] [September 1898]

Dear Tommy, or Gregory, or both,

Here's something I want badly; what is used to <u>fake</u> the CO_2 & lime water experiment.

What other fakes of this sort are in use?

Someone wrote to <u>Nature</u> once to recommend a <u>fake</u> for Linconet's[?] experiment. - who & when?

Yours ever,
H.G.

P.S. I'm getting on tremendous - vast eating - a walk yesterday - drives. The kidney evidently healing fast.

321. Joseph Conrad to H. G. Wells[1]

Illinois, ALS, Extract

September 6, 1898

[...] It saddened me the more because for the last two years your review of the <u>Outcast</u> in the <u>S.R.</u> compelled me to think of many things till then unseen. I have lived on terms of close intimacy with you, referring to you many a page of my work, and continuing many sentences by the light of your criticism. You are responsible for many sheets torn up and also for those that remained untorn and presently meeting your eye has given me the reward of your generous appreciation.

It has been treasured and if two letters that I wrote you in that time were never sent it is only a further proof of our intimacy. I had obtained so much from you - that it was unnecessary to presume further. And, indeed, there was perhaps a deficiency of courage. I am no more valorous than the rest of us. We all have, in our audacities, to feel something solid at our back. Such a feeling is unknown to me. This confession is induced by honesty which you will take for what it is worth. To be dishonest is a dangerous luxury for most of us, I fancy, and I am sure it is so for me.[. .]

I felt what you say myself in a way. The feeling, however, which induced me to write that story was genuine (for once) and so strong that it poked its way through the narrative (which it certainly defaces) in a good many places. I tell you this in the way of explanation simply. Otherwise, the thing is unjustifiable.[2]

[...] When are you going back to work. May it be soon.! I, for me, can not have enough of your work. You have done me good. You have done me good every day for many months past. Some day you will perhaps ring me - [*illegible word*] me out - but it will be too late, I shall always be yours.

Joseph Conrad

---

[1] In this extract from another letter from Joseph Conrad to Wells, Conrad is touched by Wells's letter to him and expresses concern at Wells's illness.

[2] A long paragraph follows on meeting with men from the voyage later in the United States.

322. To Richard A. Gregory

Illinois, ALS

Reply to
The Homestead
Sandgate [22 September 1898]

Dear old Gregory,

My offer of generalities[?] for Heatherlea was mostly by way of a jest. I expect that the incoming people will take the fittings & the rest I shall move here. But if there's anything you fancy, what we don't fancy so much, I'm ready to deal at most reasonable rates - "below store prices". My bicycle I've given away to the Doctor[1] chap here in a sort of "appreciation" over & above his fees. He's a fine hand at diagnosis. I forgot about that proposal to sell to you, and I saw he wanted the machine. Am I a scoundrel?

And now for an exorbitant request. There was a land slip at Sandgate[2] Hooray, got the date! <u>Spring 1893.</u> I want to mug that up at once as I am going to buy a little home in the affected region. Can you put me on to that information? I know its a big order, I'm asking. If there's anything in <u>Nature</u>, could you tell 'em to send me the number, or numbers (with a bill) and if there's anything in any learned societies proceedings, could you do ditto for me? And I'm keen to know soon.

I'm getting efficient again but still very easily fatigued & quite unable to travel or walk far because of the risk [of] reopening my healing abscess (damn it!) But if this little house turns up trumps, I may be settled in a month now.

Lord! It's lucky this didn't happen three years ago. Give my love to Tommy.[3] You might delegate him to hunt up the learned society part of the business. He's an F.G.S., isn't he? Cheer up, both of you & keep your respective peckers soaring.

Yours ever,
H.G.

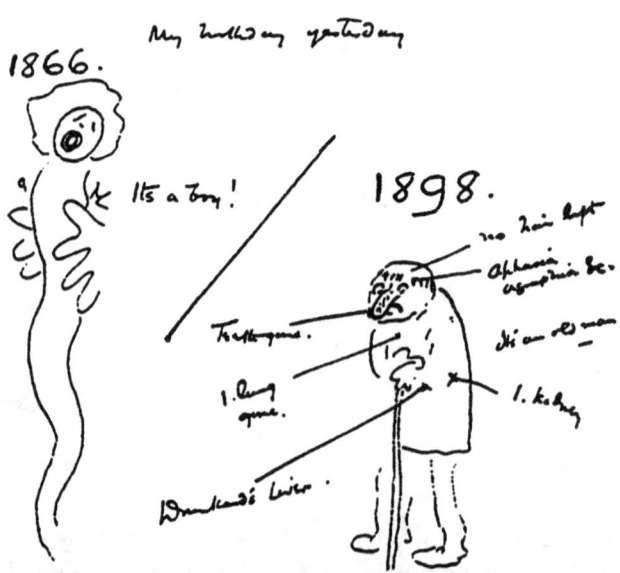

[1] The doctor referred to here is Henry Hick. Hick put Wells on complete bed rest in Hick's own home, forced him to modify his diet and eventually stopped the bleeding which had reoccurred, for the third and perhaps most dangerous time. Whether it was ulcers, tuberculosis, or the result of the kick at Holt Academy, we do not know.

[2] Wells and Jane did not buy the little house in Sandgate mentioned here, but their pleasure in the location and Wells's recovery led them to have a house built for them by the famous architect C. F. A. Voysey. The house was called 'Spade House', because the playing card spade motif was used as decoration.

[3] Simmons was acting as a part-time assistant to R. A. Gregory at *Nature* as well as working on other publications.

323. To Elizabeth Healey

Illinois, TCC, Extract

Beach Cottage
Sandgate   [late in 1898]

[...] This vast silence has contained memorable things - I have been very ill. ... Henceforth I must go gently, no violent exercise and an austere regimen, such is the doctor's prescription. I am giving up the Worcester Park house for some obscure geological reason and I have to live here. ... We are in a furnished house wth a back door slap upon the sea. ... The shrimps will come in and whack about on the dining room oil-cloth.

324. To Richard A. Gregory

Illinois, ALS

Arnold House[1]
Sandgate   [Autumn 1898?]

My dear Gregs,

    Here is a fable.
  The blacksmith went to the cobbler & watched him make a pair of shoes. "You humiliate me", he said. "Such shoes I have never thought of. Uppers &

lace holes! Lord! When I look at the simple heavy things I make, & call shoes, it makes me grovel."

Now really he was a first class blacksmith & the shoes he made were perfect & the cobbler was in good truth a butcher, & the real difference between them was this, the blacksmith was a modest man.

Yours ever,
H.G.

---

[1] Arnold House was the place rented by the Wellses until their own home was built.

325. To Henry Hick

Bromley (photocopy), AN

Worcester Park
(probably written from
Beach Cottage, Sandgate) [October 1898]

I write, honey handed & with a honey smeared face, resting halfway through, to thank the good Doctor Hick who has done this thing to me.[1]

---

[1] Wells had suffered a relapse, due primarily to overwork, and Hick had prescribed rest at the seaside. The letter is written from the boarding house and it may be incomplete.

326. To Henry Hick

Bromley (photocopy), AN

[Beach Cottage,
Sandgate] [late October 1898]

[Two messages are scrawled on a single sheet of paper, without salutation or close. The first request probably relates to the beginning of work on Mr. Waddy; the second refers to Wells himself.][1]

[1] An old gentleman living at Folkestone, helpless about the lower limbs &

amazingly irascible, has to have every disease that is compatible with reasonable mental vigour. Please give me a complete list.

[2] Treatment of complaint absolutely successful. You have established me on firm foundation once more.

---

[1] Whether these were hand-delivered or posted, is not known. There is no salutation, or closing, but they were written by Wells and they are to Hick.

327. To Sidney Low

Illinois, Typed Transcription

Beach Cottage
Granville Road
Sandgate   [November 1898]

My dear Low,

What horrible thing have you done us? Here am I a wreck and got to call on this literary lodestone. Doesn't Lady Jeune know everybody personally?[1] I shall spill my tea and be upset for weeks. Sir Francis I shall of course be a better man at home with - we've had business relations in the past. But the whole affair puts you in the light of a treacherous betrayer of innocent invalids. God forgive you.

                                    Yours ever,
                                    H.G. Wells

---

[1] Low had written to Wells asking him to take tea at Lady Jeune's, later Lady St Helier, author of *Memories of Fifty Years* (1909), who wished to meet him. Sir Francis Jeune was president of the Divorce Court which accounts for Wells's reference to business in the past.

328. To Sidney Low

Illinois, Typed Transcription

Beach Cottage
Granville Road
Sandgate   [November 1898]

My dear Low,

When I wrote in protest I had not seen Lady Jeune. I had heard legends of her collecting habits. I feared a sort of higher Sladenism.[1] But she is all the more dangerous - because she is really charming. She intimates social developments. Before God I do not want them. I want to do my work in quiet. I have only these poor rags of physique and an easily tired brain. What is pleasure to healthy people is almost intolerable stress for me - a dinner bought chatter. I want to pile a little cairn of books and die in peace. But indisputably she is a charming person. I have given up my home in Worcester Park and strangers possess it. London clay - unfit for me.[2] I am building a little cottage here and meanwhile we are in a draughty little furnished house with the spray at the back door. Our united regards to Mrs. Low.
                                          Yours ever,
                                          H.G. Wells
(Damn all architects.)

---

[1] What the 'higher Sladenism' was is obscure. However, it may refer to Douglas Brooke Wheelton Sladen (1856–1947) who became editor of *Who's Who* from 1897 to 1899. Under his editorial lead the annual publication, which had first appeared in 1849, was heavily advertised as in 1898 as '2cd year of the new issue' and Sladen apparently cast a wider net for subjects than had been the norm.

[2] Wells was still recovering from his various illnesses. He had been told that he must go to the seaside for its bracing air, and he had also been told to restrict his activities very severely.

329. To Frank Wells

Illinois, ALS

Heatherlea
Worcester Park
Surrey[1]   [November 1898?][2]

[*sketch of Catherine and Wells meeting Sir Francis and Lady Jeune*]

Little Bertie All right. Father prostrated Saturday by his venture but recovering slowly. Don't forget - Sir Francis Jeune - the Eminent Judge. Father will know his line of business.
  Hope you all keep well.
    Love to all from us both
      Bertie

---

[1] Address crossed out
[2] After Wells and Catherine had attended the party where the judge on Wells's divorce court, Sir Francis Jeune, was in attendance. Wells is also telling his brother Frank, to whom this was certainly sent, although it is filed with Fred Wells's letters, that he had survived the ordeal without much damage to his health.

330. To the Editor, *Literature*

PLS

[Sandgate?]   [early December 1898]

Sir, - An unhappy coincidence is annoying Mr. R.H. Vincent, the physiological psychologist. To my shame I must confess that I did not know of his work until quite recently. And before that knowledge came to me there appeared in the Strand Magazine, a story about "spirits" and things, suggested by Mrs. Piper's performances, in which a psychologist named Vincent takes a prominent part. If I had known there was a psychologist of that name I should not have done such a thing of course. People are bothering Mr. Vincent to know if there is "anything in it" and whether the story is based on something he has communicated to me. I can only offer him my sincerest apologies. Of course there is nothing to it.[1]
    H.G. Wells

[1] This apology appeared in *Literature*, 10 December 1898, p. 556. Wells changed the character's name to Vincey in later printings of 'The Stolen Body'.

331. To Joseph Wells[1]

Illinois, ALS

Beach Cottage
Granville Road
[Sandgate]   December 18th, 98.

My dear Father,

I've been meaning to write to you all this past week and tell you about the work in hand. I don't know anything about the Bookman paragraph of which you speak - could I see it? Possibly Nicol got hold of something through Barrie (who came to see us). But the paragraphs in the Academy were written by Hind the editor after a visit here in which we talked about our work. The serial about the year 2100 will appear very soon now in the Graphic with coloured illustrations. I've altered it a good deal for the book, which will be published in April or May by Harper Bros., and then this long silence of a year and more will be over. It's rather in the vein of the Time Machine but ever so much larger in every way. I don't think people will have forgotten me in the interval. The old books keep on selling - each at the rate of four to six copies a week bringing in little cheques for five pounds or so for the half year. The other book the Academy spoke of is now being put on the market by Pinker, it's a sentimental story in rather a new style, and I think he has offered it to Harper's Magazine. It's called Love and Mr. Lewisham. I'm also under a contract to do stories for the Strand Magazine but I don't like the job. It's like talking to fools, you can't let yourself go or they won't understand. If you send them anything a bit novel they are afraid their readers won't understand. Two stories they have had, I consider bosh, but they liked them tremendously. Another I have recently done they don't like although it is an admirable story. So that will go elsewhere. Just now I am writing rather hard - though this is between ourselves - at a comic novel rather on the old-fashioned Dickens line, a lot of entertaining characters doing ordinary things. I keep better here than I've been since I was at South Kensington and get good work out of myself every day. There are more ideas in a day here than in a week of Worcester Park.[2]

Amy wishes me to say there is a Turkey at Shoolbreds simply gobbling to get at you, and it has some minor luggage under its wing. Our love to you all. Perhaps we may travel your way next Spring. It seems ages since I saw you. Best wishes for a Merry Christmas.

Yours ever,
Bertie

Our Fat Cat has fled. Break it gently to Frank.
No colds I hope?
No trouble with that liver?

[A little sketch shows a turkey <u>en route</u> to Nyewood.]

---

[1] Also appears in *ExA*, ch. 6 §7.
[2] The new book was *When the Sleeper Wakes* which was serialised in *The Graphic* from November 1898 to February 1899. *Harper's Magazine* serialized it in the United States. *Love and Mr. Lewisham* was serialised in the *Weekly Times* from November 1899 to February 1900. Harper and Brothers published the book. His *Strand* pieces about which he was so severe, were 'Mr. Ledbetter's Vacation' (October 1898), 'The Stolen Body' (November 1898) and 'Mr. Brisher's Treasure' (April 1899). The one they did not like is probably either 'Jimmy Goggles the God', published in the *Graphic* (November 1898) or more likely, 'Miss Winchelsea's Heart' (October, 1898) in *Queen*. All three of these stories appeared in the United States in *McClure's Magazine*.

332. To Henry Hick

Bromley (photocopy), ALS

[Beach Cottage
Sandgate]   [late December 1898]

A Happy New Year to you all

My dear Hick,

I haven't written to thank you yet for the good Charron. It's replete with the very wisest sort of wisdom & when at last I let it go from table to the bookshelves it shall shoulder Richard Burton (for whom God be praised.)

Professor York Powell was here today & I showed him the book. He knew Charron he said very well in the original French.[1]

I hope that all little people & Mrs. Hick are well & with my utmost blessing for this New Year season.

Yours ever,
H.G Wells

---

[1] Comparing this book with Robert Burton (1577–1640) is Wells's highest praise. *The Anatomy of Melancholy* (1621) remained one of his best-loved books, and later the model for his own, *The Anatomy of Frustration*.

York Powell, who died in 1904, was a friend and mentor of Wells. When Wells wrote *First and Last Things* (1908) he wrote movingly, in the section on death, of his feeling of being bereft when Powell, 'Bob' Stevenson and W. E. Henley died. There is a brief biography of Powell in Elton Powell, ed., *Frederick York Powell: A Life and Selections from His Letters* (Oxford, 1905).

333. To Harry Quilter

Hofstra, ALS

Beach Cottage
Granville Road
Sandgate   [late 1898?]

My Dear Quilter,

Thanks for your letter. I hope you'll soon be out of bed again. Bed is a bore. I also am there today with a cold. I'd rather you *not* read that serial. It's a little more finished in the book (which I will send.)

Yours very faithfully
H.G. Wells

334. To Harry Quilter

Hofstra, ALS

Beach Cottage
Granville Rd.
Sandgate [date unknown]

My dear Quilter,

We have been sitting here two days, so to speak, with our little hands nice & clean, waiting for the book — which I will confess I am exceedingly curious to see. But thus far nothing has come & I have unpleasant visions of a misdirected packet, & the like. Did you direct it to Worcester Park?

The idea at least is noble. I have often thought that with lithography & photo procedures this sort of thing must come. I treated the idea facetiously in an occasional article reprinted in Certain Personal Matters.[1] For many essays of the more personal sort - Lamb's for example, & such whimsical stuff as Sterne gives me - a quirky variable script would be infinitely preferable to print.

Yours ever
H.G. Wells

---

[1] Several of Wells's pieces in *Certain Personal Matters* (London: Lawrence & Bullen, 1897) deal humorously with the issues of composition, dedications and other publishing matters.

335. To Harry Quilter

Hofstra, ALS

Beach Cottage
Granville Rd.
Sandgate [December 1898]

My dear Quilter,

I've been through the book with vast interest. It's certainly a most remarkable production & the general idea & many of the ideas in the detail I like extremely. The lettering too is often very charming. But some of the drawing seems to me abominably bad, not bad in a quaint or amusing way, but bad simply by reason of hurry, avoidance of model or lay figures & lack of anatomical feeling.[1] I would try to avoid this dispraise if I could, but it can do no good to conceal from you the effect these illustrations of yours have on me. The great joy a book of this sort should give, is in the delightful turning over & over of the pages, the discovery of fresh subtleties, little nooks & corners of beauty, here & there. It should reek of study & thoughtful elaboration. Of all things that it should <u>not</u> have, the most disastrous is surely the flavour of haste. Now the illustrations (not the borders) are [needling?] They distract one from the borders altogether. And the left handed reduplication of each border instead of the witty variation of theme the ideal book should have is a perpetually reoccurring disappointment. As a matter of fact, ten years of devotion would not suffice to do this book properly - & that only after years of preparatory study. And it is the sort of thing that ought not to be done, if it is not done with elaborate leisurely pleasure.

I would not write with this atrocious plainness if I thought this was really your best work. Taking it as a sketch, as a project, it is the most hopeful & brilliant production I have seen for many days. The page of preface is charming altogether, the lettering of that is simply beautiful. Here & there are flashes of witty delight - the rats going into the Weser water, for example, & many very pleasing pages, the rat town, the piper's score (but you did not want for any idea from the twining flowers) the heralds, the Piper's Sheet & the Farewell. But these things only accentuate the wickedness of the haste that has marred this bright undertaking. The whole thing is amateur & a beginning. The apparent versatility is simply that you have not found yourself yet in this work. But were you now to take something half the length of this, give it twice the time & keep your limitation as to the human figure <u>& face</u>, a very pleasant book indeed, would, I feel sure, ensue. Or, if you were to limit yourself to suggestion (the admission of limitation is the secret of living) and direct instead of drawing another volume of this sort, availing yourself of the many able youngsters who have had that training in drawing you so evidently have not had (impecunious youngsters who might find a glorious blend of patron & publisher in your energetic person) then we might have a triumph. (And how he will take all this the Lord knows!)

Our kindest regards to Mrs. Quilter & our warmest wishes for the New Year.

    Yours ever
    H.G. Wells

[1] In Wells's preparation as a teacher he received formal instruction in several aspects of drawing, and received certificates and prizes for his work. This is the information he draws upon to criticize Quilter's work.

336. To Harry Quilter

Hofstra, ALS

Beach Cottage
Granville Rd
Sandgate [December 1898?]

My dear Quilter,

There's not an atom of offence. I was only glad you weren't hostile & sorry I'd been so tactless. I know I'm a brute with other people's work but then I'm a bit of a brute with my own. I will show you someday certain private copies of my "works". They are black with revision & remorse. I've spent weeks over the penmarked book of the Wheels of Chance & given it up at last. That young woman is a dummy of wood, & the construction reeks of the amateur. It's beyond repair. And the War of the Worlds is a clotted mass of fine things spoilt. The serial that's beginning in the Graphic[1] is almost intolerably wrong & I am rewriting & cutting whole chapters from the book. Is it any wonder that I found my own qualities in other men's work? It isn't as if I assumed for myself or anyone any sort of perfection. Then - you might smart. And I've a tremendous dread of the exchange of admiration & of burying my own talent under a heap of friendly appreciation. The ways of art are lengthy & austere. I know better than you do what a beginner I am. It's just because I am a beginner & because I believe that the laws of effect hold good unusually that I went through your work as I did & contrasted what you have done with what I consider you ought to have done to get what you sought. I own that to tell you what I thought was a breach of good manners, cheeky & quite uncalled for. But thought is free, & thought about art singularly free. And now is your humbled spirit at rest? As for my retiring on my dignity, I don't do it Sir.[2]

Yours ever
H.G. Wells

[1] The *Graphic* began its serialisation of 'When the Sleeper Wakes' in November 1898.

² An indication of the accuracy of Wells's observations is borne out by the publishing history of this work. It was revised in book form, and then, some years later, revised as to title, with the rejection of much material of what was an unnecessary and weakly drawn romance. The second version, *The Sleeper Wakes*, is a better volume, although both bear reading. Both have been reprinted within the decade in the United States.

337. To Harry Quilter

Hofstra, ALS

Beach Cottage
Granville Rd.
Sandgate [date unknown]

Mr dear Quilter,

Thanks very much for your letter — your request for privacy shall be punctiliously observed. I fancied you invited my opinions - hence my unhappy error. I don't know whether I quite agree with you in your imputation of seniority into the question of criticism but I believe I shall come round to that in time. And anyhow I am tremendously glad to find you are not really offended at my crude uncultured honesty. The authoritative critics will make up for my deficiencies.
                    Yours very faithfully
                    H.G. Wells

338. To Harry Quilter

Hofstra, ALS

Beach Cottage
Granville Rd.
Sandgate [end December 1898]

My dear Quilter,

Happy is the couple that has no history. I am better & keep getting better under a strictly hygienic regime. Jaëger wrappings enswathe me, alcohol & tobacco pass my lips no more, no violent exercise is permitted me, I keep hours & Mrs. Wells rules me with a rod of iron. Under these conditions I understand I may go on indefinitely but the kidney of my youth will return to me no more. So much for myself & Madam. The work is happily part of the regimen. I have at last finished <u>Love & Mr. Lewisham</u> & it is to be disposed of. But there is a short Philistine called Pinker (J.B. are his low initials & Effringham House Arundel Street his lair) who has taken it from me to chaffer with publishers. There are things called serial rights & America which he understands & I do not & for English book rights he gets me about ten times what I used to get for myself. Yet I would be heartily glad if you would publish the book. I loathe the brainless production of the common publisher intensely. I dislike the shape & size of his books & particularly his dream of a "series" — the most incongruous authors all jammed into it — & his sheep like advertisement. What could be more curse-worthy than the "Fourteen Good Novels" idea of advertisement. The way Dent turned out <u>The Wonderful Visit</u> & <u>The Wheels of Chance</u> is horrible. On the former he has an old block of <u>Cupid</u>, he has spread the book to the utmost limit to make 5/- nett, and he reprints it with all its original errors because he is too mean to let me rectify them. <u>The Wheels of Chance</u> is detestably illustrated, the pictures mere stuff thrown in to satisfy the greed for quantity, (an insurance ticket might have been better) & of that too a carefully revised version waits (for ever) on my shelves. That too he reprints with things that make me lie awake of nights. And if you talk to him, you might think his one object in life was to publish beautiful books. He never advertises either book, & they sell about five a week each. I haven't the slightest doubt the books would sell briskly if he would only deal with them proper. And Heinemann again. Look at my unfortunate <u>Moreau</u> done up in a sort of blood-stained mustard. I could weep to see my works dressed like charity children, if it wasn't for rage. But you have got at a sore point & I rave. If only you will introduce intelligence into publishing you will have my unstinted blessings.

Pinker I believe has <u>Love & Mr. Lewisham</u> in offer to Blackwoods.[1] I'm not sure. He doesn't repeat things to me until they are settled because they upset work so much. But if you will write to him, he will tell you all these complicated things.

Our best wishes for a Happy New Year to you both.
Yours very faithfully
H.G. Wells

---

[1] Harper and Brothers published *Love and Mr. Lewisham* in both London and New York. It was serialised in England in *The Weekly Times* beginning in November 1899 until 1 February 1900. There is a contract for an American serial, supposedly in *Ainslee's Magazine*, but a search of that journal from February 1898 to January 1901 did not reveal it. Perhaps it was resold or published in a second magazine.

339. To H. B.

Boston, ALS

Beach Cottage
Granville Rd
Sandgate[1]
[date unknown; end 1898, beginning 1899?]

The Lord has been hard upon us H.B, the Lord has borne very hardly upon us. You know he has taken my left kidney now, as well as my right lung, & all the hair from a square inch on my head top & several of my back teeth. He is taking me in parts is the Lord he is not waiting for the publication in volume form & I wonder which he will make the next instalment with all my little mind. And the Lord will not let me have a house here, though in heaven there are many mansions standing simply against the Judgment. He tried to make me buy Varne [?] View but the surveyer told me otherwise & I did not & now the Lord is wroth. I am homeless and Heatherlea has got let and I have to have that furniture removed and stored and I am here in a furnished house and such furniture you never saw. Such being the Will of the Lord. And whether I shall buy a house or build a house or fly, into the uttermost parts of the earth & howl <u>Damn</u>, no man can tell. But the Lord being so bent on keeping me homeless has forgot to stir up my insides as usual, and <u>I am getting better.</u> And this place is a lovely place & everybody ought to live here. So that if nothing prevents I will get a man to build me a house here pretending it is for someone else & saying as much in his prayers. And when the lightning conductor is on the house the Lord will not be able to prevent my going into it & I will go into it blaspheming & the Lord may go & fry cheese for all I care. So much for the Lord. May he bless you & keep you all together not taking one part of you before the other into his Rest. And so putting the Lord aside, how are you all there? It is shameful my not having written before but the Lord has pestered me greatly. And for a long season there has been a beautiful hat done up and waiting to be sent to you and why it was not sent the Lord only knows. But this place is a lovely place & everyone ought to live here. There are views of wooded hill & sea that make you, in a weak depleted state, come near to weeping. And at Thorncliffe camp are recruit [*illegible word*] a drilling & cavalrymen learning to ride & suchlike pleasant sights to see. And in Folkestone many bright people going to & fro. And on the beach below the Leas the excursionists like little ants in great multitudes going to & fro. And all the big ships going everywhere & smacks & cutters, brigs & brigantines, ironclads & white steamers going by for ever to all the world. And white birds. Indeed it is a lovely place & pleasant at all times. And when the wind blows & the tide is high the spray raps our dining room window & when the sun shines Madam bathes from the back door. And at low tide there are starfish in great quantity. So that I am glad I am not dead but alive to see all these pleasant things.

    Our love to you all.
      Yours ever,
       H.G. Wells

---

[1] This eight-page hand written letter has no addressee. One possibility might be Richard Gregory, for it is written to someone close, but not in his immediate family. The mention of furniture might indicate Gregory as Wells had promised him the pick of the Heatherlea furniture, but he had to renege on his offer when the move to Sandgate became permanent. Another possibility is his friend Burton, who is still a feature in Wells's and Healey's correspondence, see letter 342. There are many mentions of Burton in Wells's correspondence, but no extant letters to him as far as one can tell. This is a useful letter and one simply wishes that the recipient were known. Burton's first name was William. A third possibility might be H. B. Marriott-Watson.

340. To Harry Quilter

Hofstra, ALS

Arnold House
Sandgate   Jan 2/99.

My dear Quilter,

  I was very glad to find your friendly letter awaiting me here yesterday when I returned from a little excursion. I still think, as I said before, that the Wonderful Visit [1] can not be dramatized and anyhow I would not care to participate at all in the attempt. But if you care to base a play on the book there is nothing to prevent your doing so and it is entirely open to you, so far as I am concerned, to use some portion of the dialogue on the bills or anything of that sort if you think proper. I think I told you that Boucher has a feeling for the book.

  Our very kindest regards & good wishes to Mrs. Quilter and yourself for the new year.
      Yours very faithfully,
       H.G. Wells

[1] The novel did attract prospective playwrights and producers. Boucher wrote a version which had at least one copyright performance. Another (perhaps the same) was produced by a person called Charlotte Bouchier and in the 1920s a version by St John Irvine was tried twice in the West End. The latter version was panned because of a religious tableau and Wells, although he had discussed the play with Irvine, disclaimed any part of it after these attacks. Apparently he did not like the tableau either. There is some evidence that Wells met Quilter through his wish to use the play, although they also shared the interest we have seen in well-made well-illustrated books, see letter 367 and others in volumes 2, 3, and 4.

341. To A. T. Simmons

Illinois, ANS

Beach Cottage
Granville Rd. [Feb. 1899]

Dear old Thomas,

Damn letters! On or after Saturday week we shall be in Arnold House Sandgate with a visitors room proper vacant. Come down for a week.
Yours ever
H.G.

342. To Elizabeth Healey

Illinois, ALS

[Stoke on Trent] The Universe
Germinal [March] 11, 99[1]

Dear Miss Healey,

I am profusely apologetic. In the simple simile of the Sierras, you appear to have been "ryled" by the artless contrariness of my last. It *was* wrong to abuse Radicals when you had just declared yourself one, rude it was. But your correspondent didn't mean you. He regards you as the One Good

Radical, the Redeeming Feature of the Cities of the Plain. Come out of <u>that</u> lot - he would say to you, you are a lot too good for them. You appreciate the spirit of the Radical Abuse now.

Considerable misapprehension exists as to Burton. He <u>is</u> a Radical (Etymologically) a thirster & hungerer after a Radical Revolution. He <u>does</u> hate Radicals (currently) of the Land Allotment, Heaven's Revelation of Free Competition, Individual Liberty type, which is also the type of the Star and the Daily News, I believe. This reconciles all I said about him & Radicals.

About you & him. You are wrong to hate him simply because he was once loud against you. There are a few things I would invite you to consider in this matter. One, that he never had an opportunity of knowing you personally before he expressed "disapproval". I <u>know</u>, though I don't know precisely who did it, that he was furnished with a sort of 'character' of you or rather caricature which he had sufficient confidence in his informant, to let guide him into a position of antagonism. We are all martyrs to that sort of thing. I hated Burton quietly but firmly for a year on the strength of such a sketch, but it did not prevent our being very good friends at last.

Secondly, I must tell you that when I was ill among very unsympathetic strangers at Holt, Burton came with his wife to see me, in a spirit that was more than brotherly - for I have brothers - that since, he has done more for me than any of my blood relations & that now his resources are between me & death in the wretchedest poverty. And this is not the only instance of Burton's unselfishness.

Thirdly, as a final to that Miss Wallace business. I know that Burton, all the while he was in London, wrote every day to his wife, & that he spent a great deal more than he could afford in all sorts of dainty books & so forth for her. I knew a good deal of Burton's conscience in those days, and I do not know a man who has as clean hands as he in such matters; which in the presence of Galahad Clarkson, Innocency Jennings, Saved from fire Card, & others of the spotless robe is saying a great deal.

The weather here is vile. Trusting to see you with a recovered throat next Saturday.

Believe me to remain
Yours very sincerely
H.G. Wells

---

[1] Despite the reference to '99', this letter belongs to March 1888. Wells is using the French Revolutionary calendar: 1789 + 99.

343 . To William Heinemann

Illinois, ALS

Arnold House
Sandgate, Kent   April 19th,/99

Dear Mr. Heinemann,

Your accounts to me of the three books you published for me is unsatisfactory in several respects & I shall be obliged to you for further details & for a proper authentication of some of the figures you give. In the first place you have failed to bring the accounts of the American <u>Time Machine</u> & <u>Dr. Moreau</u> up to date. There must of course be a balance due to me in regard to these either in your hands or in the hands of your American agents.

Then there are certain items ascribed to the sale of "serial rights" in France of these three books. I understand you had sold the translation rights outright. If you have not done so, what have you done?

Then I do not accept your figures of the sales of my three books. All three have been printed in unusually heavy editions and the customary printed ones (which are not allowed for) must amount to a heavy picking. I want an account of the actual as distinguished from the nominal printing and also the binders account. The proportion between the sales alleged to be colonial & the English sales does not tally with my experience[1] with other publishers & I shall be obliged for some proofs, in that respect also.

Finally there is no statement of copies sold of <u>The War of the Worlds</u> as between Harpers & Arnold & yourself. As Mr. Arnold has already made an arithmetical error to my disadvantage in rendering an account to me I think I am entitled to insist upon having any figures you submit properly charged at Messrs. Harper's account.

       Yours faithfully,
       H.G. Wells

---

[1] Up to this point, the letter appears to be the original holograph copy. After this it appears to be a draft, in the form we have. Along with this letter there are a number of very heavily worked other drafts, dated 'Apr 22'. Wells says in this draft (perhaps not sent) 'I *do* object most strenuously to exerting myself in these affairs because you fall short & your clerks make "mistakes".' Heinemann apparently suggested that Wells could examine his books, and went on to say that clerks had made mistakes, and that the sub-ordinate USA publishers had not rendered their accounts to Heinemann in very good shape. Wells was convinced that his publishers, for whatever reason, did not keep very good books. The draft is filled with crossings-out which are not reproduced here.

344. To William Heinemann

Illinois, ALS

Arnold House
Sandgate, Kent   May 22 [1899]

Dear Mr. Heinemann,

  I have carefully considered your proposal with regard to 'Moreau' & the American royalties & I think that it will be fair to do as you propose & take the mean of the anterior & following years for the missing years.
  With regards to the account of English royalties, I am undecided. I shrink from the bother of litigation & on the other hand I don't care to let the matter pass simply because you are defiant & troublesome. It's rather a case for the Author's Society than for me as it affects the general body of authors. I'm busy now but I will consider the whole question at my leisure & let you know then what line I take. In one of your letters you say that when the Editions are cleared up you will be able to put any error about "overs" right. I don't see how that is to be done - unless you then do the dissecting that ought to be done as an ordinary thing before the author's accounts are sent out.
      Yours very faithfully,
        H.G. Wells

345. To Elizabeth Healey

Texas, ALS

Sandgate [from postmark]   25/5/99

My dear Miss Healey,

  I am sorry indeed to hear that you have been having bronchitis and I can assure you that you have my keenest sympathy. These lung things have only one redeeming feature - they do **not** produce the horrible depression of profounder disorders - they leave the mind clear & flippant. Whereas, for example, drunkard's liver colours the mind a sort of muddy blue and produces the most infernal sensations on the top of the head. At least I am told so. For my own part I do not care into what affliction the effete monarchy of the universe plunges me nor how deep, so long as my heart sticks out.

We shall both be very glad to see you in July. This place gets as black with excursionists as a blighted tree, then, I am told, but we do chance to have a sort of little corner of beach of our own on which the visitor from London is placed for the day.

Our best wishes for your lungs & you
Very faithfully yours,
H.G. Wells

346. Richard Gregory to H. G. Wells

Bromley (photocopy), ALS

19 Western Rd.
Wandsworth Common   22 June /99

My Dear H.G,[1]

Your fundamental question does not admit of an exact solution unless you know what impression the falling man makes in the ground, or the time every part of his body takes to come to rest after the impact. F. Castle has sent me the enclosed answer to the question, which you will remember was, 'A man weighing 7 stone jumps vertically down 12 feet on earth. With what force do his feet strike the ground?' Castle's answer may be summarized as follows: He reaches the ground with a velocity of 27.7 feet per second. If every part of his body were brought to rest in 1/1000th of a second, as if he were inanimate, the force of the impact would be 34.4 tons.

The force of gravity at the surface of any planet is directly proportional, by the law of gravitation, to mass & velocity proportional to the square of the radius, that is, it is mass/radius^2. Taking the mass of the man as 0.012 the earth's mass & the radius as 0.273 the Earth's radius, the surface gravity at moon = $0.012/(0.273)^2$ = 0.18, that is, 18 per cent, of about ⅙ of what it is on the Earth. If, therefore, 34.4 tons be taken as the force with which the man struck the earth, the force with which he would strike the moon would be about 5.7 tons.

A man who can step two feet here could with the same exertion step 12 feet on the moon, but I don't see how he would do it unless he had very long legs.

Do you know Percival Lowell's book on 'Mars'? You ought to see it, as the whole question of what a man could do on another planet is there considered in detail.

I have finished your "Sleeper" and became much excited over the latter half. This appeared to me to be full of forcible writing but I am afraid I got a little mixed in some of the detailed descriptions preceding it.

Yours as always,
R.A.G.

---

[1] This letter from R. A. Gregory, a close friend throughout his life, illustrates how Wells's friends often provided sources for the materials used in his novels. Here Gregory is answering a query from Wells with the kind of information which gave *The First Men in the Moon* (1901) such verisimilitude. Percival Lowell was the leading astronomer of this time, and the man who was most responsible for the idea that some intelligent species had lived on Mars. Wells used this idea in *The War of the Worlds* (1898), and Gregory's question to Wells suggests that he had either not read it or had forgotten some of the premises in that book. Castle was another well-known astronomer and physicist of the period. His mathematics of the relative gravities were the standard figures in school text books in the 1930s.

347. To Sidney Low

Illinois, Typed Transcription

Arnold House
Sandgate   June 23, 1899.

My dear Low,

    Do not imagine I have taken to the typewriter or anything of that sort. I could no more bring myself to write on one of these infernal implements than I could wear tin underclothing. But the fact is my wife (Bless her) with a view to assisting me in my literary avocations has decided to practise the art. This little machine came yesterday and since then I have been just looking over it preparatory to placing it in her hands. Whether I shall ever resume my literary avocations is now extremely doubtful. She, after a regrettable exhibition of impatience and ill temper has gone out for a walk.

But this is by the way; the thing I have been meaning to write to you about for weeks - only it has always be so difficult to find the letter-writing materials - is, when are you coming down for a week-end to us. We are now in an elegantly appointed villa residence with a visitor's room, accommodation for bicycles and access to the beach. We shall both be delighted if you will choose your dates and come. If possible soon.

       Yours ever,
       H.G.

348. To Fred Wells

Illinois, TLS

Arnold House
Sandgate   Friday June 23, 1899

My dear Freddie,[1]

  Behold! thy brother has bought a typewriter and is writing to you there upon,the practice of the profession of letters having reduced his proper handwriting to a state unfit for the human eye to look upon. He is still anything but expert upon the blessed instrument and every now and then figures turn up instead of let5ers and capitals %_&'°*£ and so on. However we must all live and lear%.

I wrote to the Jeffries[2] and I expect they will come and stop here a few days on their way to the continent. We are you close to France;-we can get across to Boulogne in two hours . The other day Frank was here and we ran over and stopped the night, Frank's first night out of his native land.

How are things going with you? With me everything is very uneventful , I am building my house and writing hard and learning to swim You will have received my last book some weeks ago, the next will be out in October I expect.

    MY wife joins in love and good wishes,
        THE bBusswhacker

---
[1] This is an exact transcription of the letter
[2] The Jeffries are unknown.

349. To Grant Allen

Yale, TLS

ARNOLD HOUSE
SANDGATE

JULY 13th, 1899

MY DEAR GRANT ALLEN,

I was tremendously glad to get your letter. I was beginning to be afraid that you were going to treat my clownish little allusion as it deserved, - which wouldn't have been like you. But I'm immensely impressed by this question of marriage so far as it affects children. (Getting people born and educating them are after all the real human concerns - all other things are secondary.) I don't agree with your views but I think you have set a host of people thinking about these matters who otherwise would not have thought at all and the temptation is strong to keep the discussion round you. It is quite possible that illegitimate children are as a class more spirited than legitimate but this may very possibly be because the people who under existing conditions produce them are as a class more adventurous than the average. And, after all getting the children is only the beginning of the business. I really don't see how apart from the salaried official you are going to rear and educate the offspring of people who don't stick together. But some day I hope I may have a chance of a good long wrangle with you over all these things. Life is too short for argument by post.

We are very sorry indeed to hear you have malarial fever. Did you bring it from the tropics? My friend and neighbour Conrad has a very fine thing in that line that he brought from the Congo. On this topic of health I incline to the garrulous. Since this time last year I have had revolutionary experiences; ten years ago I had a kidney smashed at football, the silly viscus went and healed itself in a jimcrack fashion and last summer, annoyed by some gleams of prosperity that had come to me, blew out its stopping and starting off suppurating in the most imposing style. I've had to give up the house I had at Worcester Park and do my best to settle here following a regimen of restrictions that makes me envy every tomb I see. I musn't smoke or drink the good alcohol God sends, I mustn't ride a bicycle or take any exercise. I am a mere sink into which Contrexeville is poured. . . . Enough of these things!

How is Mrs. Allen? We often think of you both now for we are trying most desperately to build a house here. We are still after a year's effort negotiating for a site. Remember us both to her and believe me,

> Yours very faithfully,
> H.G. Wells

It will be observed the young man has a typewriter! It was bought for Mrs. H.G. a month or more ago but so far she hasn't been allowed within a yard of it. It's magnetic.

350. To an unknown correspondent

Illinois, ACCS

Arnold House
Sandgate\
Kent

Sept. 19, 1899
[*in another hand*]

My dear Sir,

I'm not at all ill, but my last illness leaves me very unstable - hence the abandoned lecture. It's very good of you to take the interest you do in my health & work. The Stone Age stories (with others) will be published by Messrs. Harper under the title of "Tales of Space & Time"[1] next autumn. Messrs. Harper will also publish Love & Mr. Lewisham, but I do not know whether that will be next spring or next autumn.

I'm afraid Ostrog isn't killable, at least by Graham.[2]

> Yours very faithfully,
> H. G. Wells

---

[1] *Tales of Space and Time*, consisting of 'The Crystal Egg', *New Review* (1897), 'The Star' *Graphic*, 22 March 1897, 'A Story of the Stone Age', *Idler* (May–September 1897), 'A Story of the Days to Come', *Pall Mall Magazine* (June–October 1899), and 'The Man Who Could Work Miracles, *Illustrated London Weekly* (July 1898) was published in late 1899. *Love and Mr Lewisham* appeared in the Spring of 1900.

[2] Ostrog and Graham were characters in *When the Sleeper Wakes* which Harper brought out in early 1899.

351. To Harold Guest[1]

Boston, ALS

Arnold House
Sandgate, Kent   Nov. 27th 99

My dear Sir,
  All my fiction is handled by Mr. J. B. Pinker & usually at prices rather higher than those you propose. Moreover I have not been writing short stories recently & I have consequently little disposition to 'chill' anyone's mind. And really when I said I was not doing very much it meant that I was not doing very much. It was not my coy way of getting higher prices.
                              Yours very faithfully
                                 H.G. Wells

---
[1] Guest is not known.

352. To Elizabeth Healey

Illinois, ALS

Beach Cottage
Granville Road
Sandgate   [December 1899]

My dear Miss Healey,

     I have been having most awful times with solicitors and such like beasts trying to get land to build me a house in this Paradise. I have had days of incapable rage with these sinuous tricky creatures and at last I have cast these cares upon the good Pinker who does all my publisher hunting and my mind is comparatively at peace again.[1] Also I have been beginning to work. I have managed to finish a moral novel about South Kensington and such which I've had in hand two years and the Pinker is trying to sell it. When it will appear Heaven knows. It has the seductive title of Love and Mr. Lewisham, and its up to your neck in sentiment and emotion and such. Then there is a story to begin as a serial in the Graphic after Christmas. It is lunatick stuff and I do not clearly remember what it is about. But as it is to be illustrated in colour, that scarcely matters, does it! This place (plus Folkestone) is the most habitable place I've ever been in. For an elderly invalid (as I am practically) it is incomparable.

Did I tell you I have formally dropped Davies (intimating as much to him in an agreeable letter) on account of his impertinent revision of my biology & his mean & greedy preface? I commended him to God's mercy. He's the only friend I ever had to dismiss. Thank God. Burton ignominiously chucked (for levity, most unjustly) years ago. Against Davies I have smouldered for some years & the book affair was not so much the cause as the last straw.[2]

The Rev. A.T. Simmings grows in grace & dignity & is now about to edit (with Gregory) a paper for Macmillans called The School World. I notice with pleasure an article by that eminent educationalist Mr. H.G. Wells is promised for the first number. I have also seen with pleasure and interest portraits of him at various phases of his development in the Strand. (He must have been a nice child.)

How do you face the intricate problems, the warring desires, the tragic circumstances of life? Let me know how things go with you.

    And believe me always,
     Yours faithfully,
      H.G. Wells

---

[1] Wells's illness prevented him from undertaking small tasks in furthering his career which he had enjoyed. He was forced to rely on Pinker who did an excellent job, even down to the details of house construction. This however brought him closer to Wells than the author wished and eventually would be part of the reason Wells dropped him. Catherine increasingly took over these details until the early 1920s, when her own health began to fail. Marjorie Craig, who married their first child George Philip, took over Catherine's role in these matters until the end of Wells's life. He was well served by these faithful companions.

[2] See letters 309–12

353. To Elizabeth Healey

Texas, ANS

Beach Cottage
Granville Rd.
Sandgate [end 1899]

Dear Miss Healey,

My wife and I will be glad to see you if you should come down some day this winter. Our station is Shorecliffe - but you must let us know when you are coming.

Yours ever,
H.G. Wells

354. To the Editor, *Grocer's Assistant*[1]

PLS

Arnold House
Sandgate, Kent January 3rd, 1900

My Dear Sir,

Last August the neglected state of my correspondence led to good resolutions, and I purchased a small but convenient letter file, in which to place letters requiring an answer at an early date. I then lost the letter file. The systematic rearrangement of my books natural to the New Year has now restored me to your communication, and I find your stamped, addressed envelope not a little reproachful.

Certainly I have every reason to sympathise with grocers' assistants, for though I was not one myself, I was for some time apprentice to a draper, and I had the pleasure and benefit of the friendship of several assistants in the grocery trade. I knew the pinch of it all; the intolerable hours, the brutal competition, the many petty tyrannies of retail trade, and I only wish I could see my way to suggest drastic reforms that would at one blow remove all these evils. But I cannot. Two things I would counsel. One is that the grocer's assistant should set before his eyes, and keep before his eyes, the supreme duty of kindliness, help and charity towards his fellow assistants, and especially towards his juniors; and secondly, that he should endeavour to expend every bit of energy he can, and honestly avoid expanding upon his master's business *in increasing his own efficiency.* Let him learn French, read sedulously the trade organs, master business correspondence, and eschew all frivolous pursuits. Above all let him avoid dancing classes, Sunday-Schools, the society of condescending persons of a superior class, the banjo, fiction, and the feminine sex. And cultivate orderly habits.

Yours very faithfully,
H. G. Wells

---

[1] This letter appeared in *The Grocer's Assistant*, vol. 1, no. 6 (February 1900), p.154.

355. To Mr Connell

Boston, ALS

Arnold House
Sandgate, Kent   Jan. 28th, 1900

My dear Connell,[1]

I am tremendously glad you like that experiment of mine. It's not much altogether, I'm afraid, but Lord! the trouble it was to prevent it being even less than it is. I started that thing when I went into that house at Worcester Park 1896 and was at it off & on until last September. So I'm particularly tender & grateful of your praising it.

What are you doing at my birth place?

Yours very faithfully,
H. G. Wells

---

[1] This letter probably responds to a congratulatory letter on *When The Sleeper Wakes*. Who Connell, if that is the name – it is extremely difficult to read – was is unknown. He may have been a former schoolmate or acquaintance from Wells's youth.

356. To W. E. Henley

Illinois, ALS

Arnold House
Sandgate Feb. 4th, already 1900

My dear Henley,[1]

    The Lord God bless & keep you & make you forgive me for not writing before. Excuses I have none. My head is mud & my bowels immobile. Why should I go about pretending to be a Decent Person? I have no excuse whatever. I didn't write. V'la tout an R.A.M.S.[2] He's not a decent person either. He goes & has things that are strokes and ought to be treated as such. Only in some subtle way they are not. They [found] something wrong with his veins & that is practically the same thing. He lies in bed & he cannot talk & I'm damned if I see how it is going to go on. The thing has no point at all. It is one of these disastrous messy affairs that you cannot take hold of anywhere. It makes one think there is something confoundedly George Gissingish about Almighty God. It's grey & dismal & that's all the point it has. There's nothing to be done. It all rests with R.A.M. The doctors say he has his prospects of getting in a sort of way better. He will not be able to work much again so be very loving. The best chance for him is to get out to Capri & settle down in a way of life there - - - It's the worst thing I've seen for some time. We are dark of mind. I don't see where the daughter & the small boy are going to be in fifteen years time. I could digest all that Steevens business but this beats me altogether.

    Schrundhand[?] got the N.A.R[3] for November a few days ago. I like that year all round & some of it is altogether quality. You say things I feel & understand & you say them better than I could imagine them said. There's IV, V, IX, X, XIV, XIX, XXI, XXIII, & XXIV, all to my mind simply & actually beautiful. There's just a few other [*illegible words*] dead. Come to think of it - dead all of them. But then I have deficiency of appreciation. I understand there are points in this game of poetry, I haven't mastered. Blether being truthful is still Blether to me. Most poetry strikes me as unnecessary blethering. I class it with lace at its best - the common poetry. You are in some ways out of that trade. This of yours is organic. It is life, surging..

    Why don't you do some impressions of the war?
      Our love to you both,
        Yours ever,
          H.G. Wells

[1] Of all the letters written by Wells this may be the most difficult to decipher properly. The writing is microscopic as it often was, under stress, from early in his career. Henley had backed him, when he needed it, over *The Time Machine*, and Wells knew how much he owed him. In this time of great physical weakness, coupled with the Boer War and anxiety over his brother, and perhaps with not too long to live, Wells was appealing to Henley again. In this letter Wells is also praising Henley's new book of poems, *Hawthorn and Lavender*, which was being serialised. Wells later described this book as one of the best books published in 1900, *Academy*, 7 December 1901.

[2] This obscure reference probably refers to R. A. M. Stevenson (Bob), R. L. Stevenson's cousin. He was a well known conversationalist and, along with Professor York Powell, is remembered with Henley in a chapter on death in Wells's book of personal philosophy, *First and Last Things* (1908). These three people were important older men who provided a philosophical stability to Wells.

[3] *North American Review*

357. To the Editor, *Morning Post*

Illinois, PLS

Arnold House
Sandgate   Feb. 9th 1900

Dear Sir,

  I want to strongly express my sympathy with your crusade against the present administration of the Patriotic Fund. But I think it is a particularly painful thing that it should be necessary for a lady of 'gentle birth' to suffer, before the brutal incivility that some people habitually receive in this country not only from the official class but indeed from all the more prosperous classes in this country, and it should in this particular instance have been mitigated. I can assure you that there is nothing very exceptional about the methods of the Patriotic Fund. The circumstance that the men whose widows are being patronized, snubbed, shamed & insulted have in many cases manifestly been killed through the flippancy & incapacity of officers & administrators of the "Charity" dispensing classes, simply gives point to one particular instance of a universal evil.

          Yours very truly
          H. G. Wells

358. To Fred Wells

Illinois, ALS

Arnold House
Sandgate England

Feb. 13th, 1900

My dear Fred,

I'm trying to send this letter to you <u>via</u> Paris,[1] and I enclose with it a letter from Mother. She has been writing every fortnight since the war began and all her poor little letters are stuck at Cape Town I suppose and will be for a year or more. She keeps well, although it has been a trying winter and indeed we all keep well. There is very little news to tell you now that I am writing. Scatterly[2] is in London & I hear from him at times, but I have not seen him this visit. He has taken a furnished house until the war is over. I am just beginning to build my house at this place. The contract was signed yesterday and today they are cutting out the turf to dig foundations. I have had a book delayed by the war excitement but it will probably come out before the spring is over. It is queer how the country has settled down to a state of war. At first everyone was tremendously excited & every little bit of fighting produced an uproar in the papers. Now people are getting stolid. The troops come to Shorecliffe here for rifle practice at the Hythe ranges & then go on. Just now we have a volunteer regiment, tremendously fine men they look beside the militia boys in garrison here. Everyone is surprised by the stand the Boers are making but everyone seems absolutely set upon fighting to an end. I think too that everyone is heartily sorry the war ever began. But there is no going back.

Let me know if this letter reaches you, and if it does and you want to write to me, address, M. H.G. Wells

chez M.H.D. Davray[3]
38 Avenue d'Orleans
<u>Paris France</u>

And if you want to write to Mother
Madame Wells
chez M. H. D. Davray
and the same address.

Your letters are a great comfort to her.
By the bye, if this war goes on for a year or more will you still stop at

Johannesburg? If not, and you care to come home, you will be very welcome indeed both here & at Liss.

> Your very affectionate Brother
> Bertie

---

[1] The circuituous route was caused by the Boer War.

[2] Unknown, but perhaps a mutual friend from South Africa.

[3] Davray was Wells's chief translator at this time. He was the perfect choice according to Gide. In fact Davray later produced a book with a long chapter on translating Wells, giving his favourite passages from Wells's books, Henri Davray, *Pages Choisies* (Paris: Albin Michel, 1931). There is an interesting preface (pp. 7–18), in which Davray described his translation methods. He portrayed Wells as 'formidable et étonnement variée', which might be rendered as 'wonderful and astonishingly varied'. Davray went on to discuss others with whom he had worked in the translation of Wells's books.

359. To James Nicol Dunn[1]

Hofstra, ALS

Arnold House
Sandgate, Kent   16/2/1900

My dear Dunn,

It's kind of a busy man like you to find time to write me a note. I'd like that Educational labour tremendously. I don't think that it is so much jobbing - though no doubt that beautiful word flounder should be seen[?] in the edifice - as that sort of indolence that irritates men in secure positions, that is doing so much evil everywhere just now. And conceit! If I still had the self confidence & temper of a few years ago I would be writing you partly illegible, bitter, overreaching and at times many spiteful letters for publication on Educational questions until you sickened of the very name of Wells. But as it is I send you my schemes & earnest prayers to get things done.

I am very much better again, indeed I am well, if only I can keep well, and we are living a very pleasant life in this place with a study window that looks upon the channel & a small garden bounded on the South thereby. It has been borne in upon me - in the small hours chiefly - that the life I was getting into was prideful & competitive, & the work I had done & was doing, was crude & cheap & so far as work goes I have been so to speak 'in retreat'. Chiefly abstinence from Vagabond Dreams & press cuttings - mostly peacefully austere. I don't know how far that sort of thing can be avoided. In the first place one must live, I suppose, but there is no doubt the conditions of the 'literary life' - one calls it that - are just as demanding & cheapening as this life can be. (All the same, when at last I do publish that work I have been writing for a little eternity I shall send you a copy & ask quite shamelessly for a handsome length of review.) But I do think at last that I have got it out of my head that the paragraph concerns me.[2]

Do you ever do 'week-ends'? I have long cherished an idea that someday we might talk a day away. I have a fancy we might get on rather well - you know we really don't know each other - and if someday you could run down here and stop Saturday night say it might be pleasant for us both. This is a very ageeable little place in sunshine, there are pleasant walks out by the downs, & almost always our spare bedroom is at your service. My time has a fine uniformity & if you thought fit to come, I would leave the choice of a date to you. When there are thick fogs in London there is blue sky here and you can decide to come as late as Saturday morning. I have a telephone (How's that for 'retreat'?) And you can always call me up & find if I am at home. Telephone <u>Sandgate 031 031</u>

     Yours ever,
     H.G. Wells

---

[1] Dunn (1865–1919) was editor of the *Morning Post* from 1897 to 1905. Dunn may have responded to Wells's letter 357 which had recently appeared in the *Post*.

[2] Wells may be talking of *Love and Mr. Lewisham*, *The Wealth of Mr. Waddy* or perhaps the abandoned novel about Esau Common. This letter is six pages long in Wells's most minute script. Wells was active in the New Vagabond Club at this time, which is referred to in the text. The addressee is unknown to me. This is a period in which Wells is seeking, rather desultorily, an academic post, see the letters in volume 2 to A. J. Balfour.

360. To Elizabeth Healey

Illinois, Typed Transcription, Extract   May 24, 1900

[...] I have been prowling about the North of France on a bicycle and paying a visit to the Exposition and having influenza and so forth. Uneventful events constitute my days, I have got to the middle period of life,[1] I think, the beginning of the middle at any rate, 'ammer, 'ammer, 'ammer on the 'ard, 'igh road - the first excitement of the start into "literature" is over and I am working, I hope with an increasing strength and quality - at certain projected things.

The first excitement of the start is <u>quite</u> over. We never see a press cutting, insult interviewers, avoid literary dinners, pursuing our exalted way towards a goal of our own. Also we are building ourselves a home. Every symptom in fact of incipient Middle Age.

[1] Wells was thirty-four years old in the autumn of the year this letter was written.

361. To Fred Wells

Illinois, ALS

[Arnold House
Sandgate, Kent]   May 27th, 1900

Mother's had no news of you since December. A telegram "all's well" to her would be a great relief.

My dear Fred

      Just a line in the chance of its reaching you soon. How's business & what are you going to do? If you like to run home there will be a welcome for you here & at Liss, as you may well imagine.
                Yours ever
                  H.G.

362. To Elizabeth Healey

Illinois, Typed Transcription, Extract   June 22, 1900

[...] I am glad indeed to find you like "Love and Mr. Lewisham" so much. So far as labour and thought count in these things, writing it was an altogether more serious undertaking than anything I have ever done before. I suppose I have torn up and shied away about twice as much stuff as still stands in the story. But it really seems this time as though I am to be even more than fairly paid for the trouble and toil I have had. You know there is really more work in that book than there is in many a first class F.R.S. research, and stagnant days and desert journeys beyond describing. But don't imagine there are any portraits in the volume.

363. To Sarah Wells[1]

Illinois, ALS

Arnold House
Sandgate, Kent   June 7th, 1900

My Dear Little Mother,

As it is so near quarter day I am sending you on £15 and I hope that in another week I shall see you. It was very jolly was it not? getting that letter from Fred and by this time I daresay he is reading all the letters you have been writing him since the war began. What a budget it will be for him!

But I don't like to hear you have 'put by' £5. I don't want you to go pinching and saving out of the money I send you. It isn't any too much anyhow and you ought to spend it all upon things to make life pleasant.

I am sending you a first review of <u>Love and Mr. Lewisham</u>. They have sold 1,600 copies in England and 2,500 in the colonies before publication, and I think the book is almost certain to beat any previous book I have written in the matter of sales.

Give my love to Father and Frank. And believe me
              Your very affectionate son,
                          Bertie

---

[1] Also appears in *ExA*, ch. 6 §7.

364. To Edmund Gosse

Leeds, ALS

[Arnold House
Sandgate, Kent]   June 10 1900

Dear Mr. Gosse,

    It was the publisher who sent you "Love & Mr. Lewisham" but it was done, I can tell you now, at my request & most certainly but for a kind of shyness I feel about this sort of thing, I would have sent it to you myself. I was very anxious for you to read the book because of the kind things you have said of my work before, but on the other hand, there is a sort of compulsion about the book for the author, a sort of "R.S.V.P" planned that I hoped wouldn't come in to bother you if you were busy or not interested. I am very glad indeed & proud that you have read it and that you think so well of it. Indeed I am personally grateful for I toiled & attempted more in writing this book than I have ever done before and it has become at last something organic & personal in a way that my books certainly haven't been before.

I recommend your visit to New Romney very readily[?]. Since then I have become altogether healthy & active again. We are camped here in a narrow ignoble little house with a little garden that runs down to the sea - & if only we could keep on bathing we should be very comfortable - and we are waiting for a house to get itself built close by to which we shall presently remove ourselves. And I spend my days studying Whittaker's Almanac & the Times atlas & proposing presently, interesting in fact quite distinctly each day, to write.
Yours very faithfully
H. G. Wells

365. To Edward Garnett[1]

Texas, ALS

[Address unknown] June 26, 1900

Dear Mr. Garnett,

I am really immensely obliged to you for reading & then telling me what you think of what is practically my first novel. I did indeed very much want you to do it. And if I may criticise a critic I would like to say how much I appreciate the acute distinctions you draw between the two methods of literature that interweave in my work. I had no idea how strong the touch of 'demonstration' came in at times, nor quite where the tendency to 'asides' interferes in the effect. It is the sort of thing that a man is almost unable to discover for himself, - it is a matter of bad habits - and in making it suddenly clear to me you have done me a service for which I can scarcely thank you enough. You are right, or at any rate, you ought to be right in missing the sweep, the unity, the presence of the end in the opening, which is a condition, if not the condition of beauty of form. The first chapter was designed of course to balance against the last, with the business of the shadows & the girl inside (in chapter 1) & inside the window (in the last chapter), but it misses the real presence, the presence of racial destiny in Nature overwhelming the individuality.[2] I perceive I was timid with that & shirked it. I admit there is nowhere that effect of his little life circles with the arc of the huge circle of the common life sweeping through them & in a sort of unfavourable mysterious way locking them together in a scheme outside his personal schemes altogether.

But I don't quite see your statement that I proffer an 'explanation' of life in the book & that my 'art' gets the bulk of that explanation. I offer nothing more than the imagine - I should be even myself damned uneasy[?] if I did. I offer the image - not I had to offer that image of the outer sweeping force. Whether the themes of life are those of Lewisham or Chaffery - the last thing of Lewisham is obviously only a reproduction of Chaffery's teachings.

I do hope I may meet you soon. Intelligent talk about the work which is practically the substance of my existence now does not come in my way - ever. Conrad is good but his temperament is utterly different from mine - we speak a different language. Don't you come sometimes to see him? If you do cannot we get him to bring you here or cannot I come on to the Pent?

Yours very faithfully
H. G. Wells

---

[1] The literary critic, Edward Garnett (1868–1937) had the power to make an author with favourable comments, and a number of Wells's contemporaries benefitted from this attention, as did Wells himself. The extent of the criticism, and Wells's response, indicate how important a writer he was becoming. They are discussing *Love and Mr. Lewisham* which had recently been published. Further letters to Garnett appear in volumes 2 and 3.

[2] This letter exists in a very faint form, so some of the readings are conjectural. Garnett apparently raised both questions of style and meaning in his comment, which has not survived. Wells had deliberately created opening and closing mirror chapters. His overall theme – a discussion of the impact of class relations on ideas and personality – is less obvious, but nevertheless present in this work, as well as in many others which Wells had written or would write in the future. Lewisham is a young idealistic teacher, but he gets involved in rescuing a young woman, whom he marries, from Chaffery, a medium who made his living through conducting false seances.

366. To the Editor, *Queen*

Illinois, Typed Transcription

[Sandgate?] July 6th, 1900

Sir.

There runs through your review of my 'Love and Mr. Lewisham' an insinuation that the book is a thinly veiled autobiography, an insinuation which rises at last to positive statements, to this sort of thing for example: 'Mr. Wells' extremely amusing and graphic account of the various educational agencies to which he applied when, owing to the distractions he had failed in his career at South Kensington'.

I must protest that this is intolerable and I shall be obliged if you will permit me to deny as publicly as Mr. Douglas Sladen has been permitted to state, that 'Love and Mr. Lewisham' is, in any sense, autobiography. Not only is this not so, but there is no sort of parallelism or coincidence between my private life and the story I have invented. Mr. Sladen writes with such a convincing air of really knowing all about me, that this emphatic denial is absolutely forced upon me.[1]

Yours very truly
H.G. Wells

---

[1] Whether this letter was published is not known. For another view of Douglas Sladen by Wells see letter 328.

367. To Charlotte Boucher[1]

Illinois, ALS

[London?]   July 11, 1900

Dear Miss Boucher,

I have read the play with very great interest and amusement & I quite agree with Mr. Coope's opinion - though I am afraid my opinion is only a very outside one. I see nothing in the play to which I can reasonably take exception but I sh. be greatly obliged if you wd change Mr. Mendham's christian name. If you should read my <u>Certain Personal Matters</u> someday you will see why.

For the use of my idea & for such lines of my dialogue as you have used I think an acknowledgement* on the programme will be quite a sufficient return. With best wishes for your success

Yours vy truly
H.G. Wells

* This play is based on The Wonderful Visit by H.G. Wells.

---

[1] Despite the similarity in names, Charlotte Boucher is a different person than the individual,

Bouchier, who was also attempting to write a play based on *The Wonderful Visit*, see letter 340 and others in volumes 2, 3 and 4.

368. To the Editor, *New Magazine*

Illinois, ALS

[Sandgate] July 21, 1900

Dear Sir,

It is highly probable that I shall alter the concluding chapter of <u>The First Men in The Moon</u> very considerably in the next month & I shall be glad if the alterations can appear in the serial.[1] The story will certainly remain as it is as far as chapter XVIII. Beyond that point I should be very glad if you would delay printing & illustrating as long as you conscientiously can. I have an impression that I can see my way to a more effective conclusion. Of course this may not come off but in that case the original M.S will stand.

Yours very faithfully,
H.G. Wells

---

[1] Of all Wells's novels *The First Men in the Moon* underwent the most extensive alteration. It was originally intended to be five linked short stories but gradually the plot linkage became stronger and public reception of the work was sufficiently enthusiastic to add the equivalent of two more stories. The various serial productions were hastily put together to meet the demand, but very faulty texts resulted, some of which continue to be printed. For an explication of the development of the novel, see David Lake's introduction to the OUP World's Classics edition (1995).

369. To an unknown admirer

Illinois, APC

[Sandgate?] [date unknown]

Dear Sir,

I am taking a holiday - I've been wandering & I hope you will excuse post card.[1] I don't trust my own memory because I believe much more in hallucination of memory than in hallucination of sense but my mind is perhaps abnormally analytical & the educated person may be as you say. I don't know when I will publish another volume of [stories.]

---

[1] This message appears on the bottom of a very small postcard in tiny letters. The card has a view of the Vallée de la Meuse, L'Abbaye de Maredsous.

370. To the Editor, *The Morning Post*[1]

PLS

[Spade House,
Sandgate, Kent]   Oct. 12, 1900

Sir, There is surely a limit to the permissible oddness of a review, and surely that limit is passed in your treatment of 'The Soft Side', the new collection of stories by Henry James. Your reviewer's case seems to be that the stories would puzzle Civil Service candidates if they had to make a *précis* of them, but why your reviewer got on that tack only Heaven and your reviewer know. It is perfectly true, of course, but then it is true that you could not use them for election addresses nor copy them out as your own original love-letters nor find your way about Italy with them if you took them instead of a Baedeker. But no one, except possibly your reviewer, would ever try to do so. One gathers that he has 'searched for a plot and found only prattle'. I like the suggestion of that conscientious search. First find your plot - the 'plot' of a short story! 'Where the devil is the plot?' He turns at last to the only apparent substitute, 'the prattle', or mere writing, in despair. 'The prattle is highly polished and pleasant, but it is 'decidedly thin', he writes, too evidently with a natural sympathy for thickness. Imagine a comparison on these lines between 'Tristam Shandy' and 'Called Back'. Imagine your reviewer transferring his natural gift to the treatment of a kindred art, and comparing a portrait by Rembrandt with Frith's 'Derby Day', all to the advantage of the latter. 'The copyist of Mr Rembrandt', he would say, 'searches for a good hard, definite outline in vain. Over great spaces there is nothing painted - absolutely nothing but prattling colour - 'incoherent' brush marks and their 'drift quite unascertainable'.

His review cuts me the more keenly because 'The Great Good Place', concerning which story he uses this phrase, 'a succession of incoherent remarks and its drift quite unascertainable', has been a source of particular delight to me. I have read and re-read it many times. It seems to me to be just one of those happy, perfect things that come to reward the good artist for many laborious, not quite perfect, days. And then - your reviewer's voice is heard. I cannot imagine the lack of imagination that fails to see that restful place Mr James has so happily invented.

That 'Europe', which your reviewer calls 'heavy talk', is really a quite amazing story of a dreadful old woman, and the cousin in 'Paste', the widow in 'The Real Right Thing', and that delightful magazine editor in 'John Delavoy' live and entertain - as very few figures in fiction do entertain. Even the larking in 'Maud Evelyn' and 'The Third Person' struck me as exceptionally good fun.

And the word 'prattle' in connection with Mr Henry James, and the length and position of the review, and generally the whole thing, are matters that stir me to protest. I suppose that no one who has given a year's serious thought to the art of English fiction will dispute that Mr James is one of the three living great masters of that art, as an art, that with Mr George Meredith and (conceivably) Mr Hardy he forms a group of seniors that the younger writers ripen only to respect, and that so soon as the market bawling of these present times has died away he will come to his own place. Evidently there is a section of the public to whom the qualities of his work are 'quite unascertainable', and, though I should doubt whether they form a large portion of Morning Post readers, I can understand that it is reasonable for a daily paper to give a warning that for the after-dinner reading of dull people Mr James will not do. But it seems to me to be considering and indulging that sort of person altogether too much to present Mr James in the manner of your review. Surely in the past Mr James has undergone a sufficiently ample amount of the sort of punishment a reviewer may inflict for the perplexing distinction of his work. What harm can there be, and who is going to suffer to any appreciable extent, if, temperately and modestly, and without any attempt to direct the natural direction of the 'boom' current, the indisputable fact that Mr James is, after all, no mere obscure novelist in a crowd, but a very considerable Literary Swell indeed, is permitted occasionally to appear?

Yours, etc., H.G. Wells

---

[1] This important letter was first noticed by Bernard Bergonzi. It was printed in *The Wellsian* NS no. 4 (Summer 1981), pp. 36–8.

371. To George Gissing

Illinois, ALS

Arnold House
Sandgate, Kent   19 October 1900

My dear Gissing,

    The days slip by and there being no specific thing to write about there comes with none of them the now-or-never that stirs to the act of correspondence. Just where are we? Just as we were when you were with us - except that the <u>Fortnightly</u> will cease to interest me after this month.[1] I do really admire & delight in your <u>By the Ionian Sea</u> which seemst not only to me but to almost all the people I have spoken of such things, by far the finest work you have done - in conception & in quality alike. Popham that good man next door gets the <u>Fortnightly</u> from me & after that Joseph Conrad bears it off & then it goes to Hick. And it promises well for the book when it comes that James has just made a success with some French travel impressions.[2]

    Our home is now very nearly done indeed and we hope in another month to be up there. The plumber draws near the end of his labours, the last grate was being fixed today, every day I get paint on my clothes from some pleasingly unexpected quarter, there is glass in the verandah door & the scraper has come. Also there is a man a planting trees. Up & down the pergola (which isn't a pergola at all that being merely its name) we have stuck ∞00 daffodils - or 800 - there is room for a dispute how many bulbs were in a bag. but anyhow a marvellous number.

    Let us know how you are and when you are coming this way to England again. And if you should come why should not Madame Gissing come also - at least thus far into England - while you wander further into Pinkerdom and so forth?

    And with our kindest regards to you both
        Believe me ever my dear Gissing,
            Yours very sincerely
              H.G. Wells

---

[1] Gissings's *By the Ionian Sea* was being serialized in the *Fortnightly*, and the last instalment was in the October issue. Gissing never received this letter as it was unclaimed at the Poste Restante in Valais, Switzerland, and was returned to Wells. This is the primary reason why we have it at all, as relatively few of Wells's letters to Gissing were preserved.

[2] *A Little Tour in France* (London, 1900), actually published at about the time this letter was written.

372. To Fred Wells

Illinois, ALS

Arnold House
Sandgate, Kent   25 - 10 - 00

My dear Fred,

How are you getting on under the British flag? All right I hope, & stock coming to hand and business looking up. We all keep our eyes on the papers & now & then I get a chat with some returned soldier & hear what a fine place Johannesburg is. I hope before long the Peace will have come and that you will be able to take your long deferred holiday & see us all once more. You must come & stop a good long time with me & mother must come to be with you, in the family mansion that is now almost finished. They are putting in the casements now & the electric light & the plumbing & it will all be finished & spick & span for you to see. And its all my own, - since you didn't see fit to invest your savings in such a perilous enterprise as house-property-in the best part of England - and its all paid for & its worth £2000.

The old man I am sorry to say is suffering very much from a sore foot - so that he isn't able to get about & enjoy life very much. Mother & Frank keep well. Frank is becoming a bit of a furniture dealer & seems happy enough in his way. He was up here a month ago and did some bathing.

And My dinner bell has just gone, so that I must pull up short.

A Merry Christmas, if I do not write again before then & with kind regards from Amy.

Your affectionate Brother
The Busswhacker

373. To Arthur Conan Doyle[1]

PL

[Arnold House]
Sandgate, Kent   [1900]

My wife, for whose verdict I waited, has just finished the <u>Duet</u>. And, as I chanced on a sort of "slate" of the book last week, it occurred to me you'd not be offended if I wrote and told you we both like it extremely. It seems to me you have the shape and the flavour (or the texture or quality or atmosphere or whatever term you like) just as rightly done as it can be. They're a middle class couple and simple at that; but the ass of a critic seemed to think that this somehow condemned the book.

I've spent a year out of the last three at a similarly "commonplace" story.[2] (Still at it.) So I'm not altogether outside my province in judging your book.

---

[1] This letter was written as a sort of fan letter after Wells and Catherine had read Conan Doyle's novel, *A Duet, With An Occasional Chorus*, published in the autumn of 1899. The letter appears in John Dickson Carr, *The Life of Arthur Conan Doyle* (New York: Vintage, 1975), pp. 166–7.
[2] Wells's book was *Love and Mr. Lewisham*, which was published later in the year. The critic in question was probably Dr Robertson Nicholl, who reviewed the book at least six times under various *noms de plume*. Wells had his own difficulties with this peripatetic reviewer. He wrote to Conan Doyle, in a fragment quoted in the Conan Doyle biography, on the occasion of Doyle's being knighted on 9 August 1902, saying, 'I think the congratulations should go to those who have honoured themselves by honouring you.'

374. To John Galsworthy

PLS

Arnold House,
Sandgate, Kent   Nov. 16, 1900

My Dear Galsworthy,

It was kind indeed of you to send me your book[1] and I have read it with very keen interest and pleasure. I think it shows a really fine sense of effect and the figures (of the older men especially) finely modelled and drawn. I don't know whether I quite fall in with the central antithesis. You see I'm an extensive skeptic, no God, no King, no nationality — and among other things I don't believe in is this 'Artistic Temperament'. I've never met it to recognize it — conceivably because I haven't the necessary ingredients for its sympathetic recognition. I've a strong belief that the artist is just one sort of practical man and differs — if he differs at all — from other sorts of employed preoccupied men in his relations to women only in the fact that his work frequently stimulates his imagination in that direction. This does not lead as a rule to maiden passions for maids.

Yours ever,
H.G. Wells.

[1] Galsworthy had sent Wells a copy of *Villa Rubein* (London, 1900). The novel, later revised, was a closely drawn picture of Galsworthy's sister and his brother-in-law. This letter appears in H. V. Marrot, *The Life and Letters of John Galsworthy* (New York: Scribner, 1930), pp.120-21. F. M. Hueffer's comments on the novel appear immediately after it and make an interesting comparative critique. Wells and Galsworthy had a long, but not always harmonious relationship, as co-founders and early presidents of PEN. In the late 1920s Galsworthy and his wife often visited Wells at Lou Pidou. Relationships were strained somewhat after Galsworthy did not support Wells in the controversy over the 'Troublesome Collaborator', for which see below volumes 3 and 4.

375. To Max Judge[1]

Milwaukee, ALS

Arnold House
Sandgate, Kent   Nov. 16, 1900

Dear Sir,

I am greatly obliged to you for the copy of the Bungalow with your very interesting account of Lympne. We have described the same view though your account is fuller than mine and also - since you were not hampered by the necessity of making a Mr. Bedford's residence a little vague in position - much more accurate. Since I wrote that, I have discovered an even finer sunset on this marsh from Aldington Knoll.[2] If ever you revisit that hill coast, I think you will find it worth your while to travel on to Aldington & see it.[3]

Yours very faithfully,
H.G. Wells

[1] The addressee is unknown to me.
[2] A handwritten copy of this letter by another hand accompanies it. At this point the text varies from the handwritten letter 'The reason I'm not a draper's assistant now is simply because I could not pack parcels properly nor fold cloth. My mother's housekeeping was shocking[?] Her cooking especially. Still I find a large proportion of truth in what you say, You have got [*missing words*] a bit through hearing too much of the "All men are born equal" stuff and you are beginning to see subnormalcy everywhere. Do you think Winston Churchill normal or a criminal defective? He has genius, I admit.' The copyist has conflated two letters.
[3] The area of the Channel coast under discussion is the scene of the opening of *The First Men in the Moon*. Bedford, unhappy because his play is failing, describes the marsh at Lympne. There are several sites along this coast which are very reminiscent of the opening of the novel.

376. To Graham Wallas[1]

LSE, ALS

Arnold House
Sandgate   Nov. 27. 1900

My dear Wallas,

      I am very glad indeed (& rather proud) to be given your book by you and I know I shall find it very interesting so soon as our present agonies (the birth pangs of a home) are over. But now we neither read nor [think] beyond such questions as whether the pot board be blackened & why the casements are being painted green when we understood black it was - I think. But beyond such cumulative[?] reasons as that, it is a frequent matter of abundant thought to me just how the great Liberal party arose, just why it was so profoundly right, & issue a movement from certain points of view & why it was so amazingly shallow & zealously ignorant of the most patent facts in many of its generalisations, nevertheless. Of these matters, D.V. & unless I see you beforehand, & can talk it all, I will write further when I have read the book.

      Please remember us both very cordially to Mrs. Wallas, & believe me,

                              Yours ever,
                              H.G. Wells

---

[1] This letter marks the first epistolary exchange between Wells and Wallas (1858–1932) who were to have a long friendship, with peaks over the next half dozen years, and which was renewed later in the early thirties. Wallas was a social and political theorist, one of the founders of the Fabian Society, on the faculty at the London School of Economics and author of several books. Walter Lippmann regarded Wallas as a mentor from Wallas's years at Harvard, and this led to Wells's acquaintance with Lippmann, see letters in this volume and in volumes 2 and 3.

THE LETTERS: 1880-1903

377. To E. V. Lucas[1]

Boston, ALS

[Spade House
Sandgate, Kent]   Monday [date unknown]

Dear Mr. Lucas,

    The trains are usually pretty punctual here and I think we shall have long enough (two hours & a half), to get everything done if you come by the later train. You will find a small yellow omnibus which will bring you to the door for sixpence, at the station.

                      Yours very faithfully
                      H. G. Wells

---

[1] E. V. Lucas (1868–1938) essayist, poet, biographer and publisher. He wrote more than thirty volumes of light essays and was an authority on Charles Lamb.

378. To Mr Stirling[1]

Texas, ALS

Spade House
Sandgate   [date unknown]

Dear Mr. Stirling,

       The wolfs eyes reflected the fire & so fear more the corruption of man. That is why they "gleamed redly". A dog looking out of a dark place at the light will often (& sometimes men's eyes also will) reflect a luminous red. I've seen it. It isn't the green of a cat at all.

                      Yours very sincerely
                      H.G. Wells

---

[1] Who Stirling was is not known. Another Stirling, or perhaps the same one, exchanged a letter or two over socialism later, see volume 2. The latter Stirling was from California. The date of this letter is also something of a mystery; it is written on Spade House letter paper, but discusses matters which probably arise out of *The Island of Doctor Moreau*.

379. To the Editor, *Grocer's Assistant Year Book*[1]

Boston, ADLS

[London] [date unknown]

Dear Sir,

I am keenly in sympathy with those who find themselves caught in the meshes of a shop assistant's life. It is no abstract sympathy. I was in the net myself; for two years - the most miserable years of my life - I was behind the counter of a draper's shop. The peculiar wretchedness lay in the hopeless want of time to think or act for oneself. I felt even then and I feel even the more distinctly today that the life then offered me was a hideous insult to my possibilities, and had I not been able to believe that there was a way out of the systematized drudgery that forced itself upon me I must quite deliberately have 'got out' of a world that could misuse me so.

You will know, if you have read my '<u>Anticipations</u>' that I am entirely out of sympathy with the Trade Union point of view, which accepts current conditions & current appliances as final & seeks to make life tolerable for the meaner & the less capable members of a trade as the price of crippled efficiency for the trade as a whole. The grocery trade is as much a public service as the army - in England it is probably the more efficient of the two - and, as in the army, the ideal should be to keep in & keep on working for the maximum efficiency & the maximum economy. For a grocer's assistant who is satisfied with what he does & with his life generally & things as they are, who simply wants a little more leisure to play bagatelle & a little more money to pay for admission to a cricket ground in order to watch someone else play cricket, for the unambitious wasters of the gift of life, I have no sympathy whatever. For such, I wish nothing but fourteen hours a day work, meat at 4 [*an illegible symbol*] a pound & paper blankets. It is for the self respecting, ambitious 'white men' of the trade that I am concerned. For the sake of the nation & race & for their own sake such men must be given opportunity. The first element in opportunity is time. I am in favour of early closing, therefore, - compulsory early closing, because it is, I am convinced, absolutely impossible to make the shopping class understand what a serious matter late shopping is. And next cheap books & cheap classes within the reach of a grocer's assistant. And thirdly a raising of the age at which boys may leave school to be "caught" by grocers. I rejoice at any labour saving appliance & every feat of business organization that reduces the number of persons whom it is necessary to employ in this limited life & increases the personal value & efficiency of those that remain. And with my best wishes for luck & an ampler life to every subordinate & progressive assistant in the Grocery Provisions & Allied Trades.

> I am Dear Sir
> Very sincerely yours
> H.G. Wells

---

[1] I do not know whether this was published. When I was writing my Wells biography, the tone and words of the letter were close enough for me to consider it a draft of his letter to their magazine of 1899 (see letter 354). It is a draft of a similar letter, but not that one. He used several of the phrases found here, or variants of them, in a number of related articles. This *could* have been as late as a speech given in 1922 when he spoke to a similar group but which was never published. I think this unlikely. The citation of *Anticipations* argues for a pre-First World War time frame.

380. E. Ray Lankester to H. G. Wells

Illinois, AL

[London]   Jan. 5 01 [?]

[Dear Mr. Wells,][1]

[...] I fear that a great catastrophe must come up in England - an utter defeat and breakup - before the rotten crusts of conceit, imbecility, and self-indulgence which dominate us, will be got rid of, and the rottenness may have spread too far below the crust before that happens.

---

[1] E. Ray Lankester, who was reviewing *Anticipations* for *Nature,* invited Wells to a private tour of the Natural History Museum followed by dinner. Lankester was about to be named Director of the famous London landmark. This occasion marked the beginning of their long and fruitful relationship in the areas of scientific education. Lankester went on in this letter to remark that he was not as sanguine as Wells about the possibility of a new Republic coming to England. This extract is worth reprinting as an indication of the state of mind among many English intellectual leaders, which also helps to explain the tremendous success which Wells's book enjoyed. The two men had a strong relationship, but unfortunately I have been unable to locate the Wells side of the correspondence. The Lankester side is located at Illinois.

381. To the Editor, *Fortnightly Review*

PLS

[Spade House] [February 1901]

Dear Sir:

When I wrote the obvious concerning the current Cyclists' Drill of the War Office, for the December issue of The Fortnightly Review, it did not occur to me that any serious attempt to answer my criticisms would be made.[1] But I gather from his article in the February Fortnightly that Lt.-Col. Balfour does propose that a case can be made for that remarkable little pink book. The case, it seems, consists very largely in the unsparing denunciation of myself, and in an interesting, but irrelevant, history of military cycling in this country. If this were a merely personal matter I should be willing to leave things at this, but in an issue of such grave public importance as I hold this to be, I am forced, quite against my inclination, to deal in a hostile and destructive spirit, - no longer with the Unknown Entity responsible for that Drill-Book, but with that Entity revealed- as an interesting (and quite naturally extremely irritated) individual.

A certain flavour of personality in this discussion is, unhappily, quite unavoidable. I alleged - it may be a little vehemently - that those who were concerned in the production of the War Office Cyclist Drill Book, had neither "imagination nor the intelligence necessary for their task." And Lt.-Col. Balfour now avows himself the principal author of that work. I trust, however, that it will be possible to touch the unavoidable essential of this question without further unreasonable offence, and to distinguish between Lt.-Col. Balfour's very considerable exertions and very high and patriotic views on the one hand, and his capacity for creative organization on the other.

Before coming to the more serious matter of this dispute, I must point out that Lt.-Col. Balfour scores almost his solitary effective point against me by a docked quotation. This is a controversial expedient of doubtful value. I objected that a sleeping sack, and "perhaps a blanket", would be better than the heavy overcoat which is included in the regulation equipment. Lt.-Col. Balfour rather boldly omits my "perhaps a blanket", and points out what a very bad time an outpost of cyclists provided only with sleeping sacks would have on a cold night. He makes such excellent use of this solitary opportunity, his suggestion of a patrol going their rounds sack-race fashion is so divertingly made, that I could find it in my heart, having regard to the annoyance my previous article had evidently given him, to wish the point legitimate. But I am warned by a cutting from a newspaper recently sent on to me, that it will be unwise to let judgment go by default on this, and so I must insist that this, the only really effective point Lt.-Col. Balfour has made, is, according to all the accepted methods of controversy, in effect if not in intention, a foul.

Upon most other points at issue, Lt.-Col. Balfour's method is not so much to reply to my objection to his drill-book as to mingle with his denunciations of me as "an arm-chair, ignorant person", and so forth, the most astounding and incredible admissions. Of our two papers in the <u>Fortnightly</u>, I must confess that, with all the will in the world, mine does very much the least to demonstrate the need of drastic War Office reform, Consider this passage:

> Mr. Wells then proceeds to make a fundamental misstatement, and one which unfortunately vitiates every argument he uses that has been done in the past. He says: "The pink book ...frankly admits itself an exposition of 'Cyclist Drill' as evolved by the War Office *after the quickening experience of the year 1900*" (the italics are mine). It is the third edition of a drill-book written by me in 1889 ...The pink book of 1900 differs only from that of 1897 in some minor points, and in the addition of Appendix A and B. The pink book of 1897 only differs from that of 1889 in certain amplifications, owing to the elimination of tandems, tricycles, and multicycles.

In other words, the War Office after the quickening experiences of 1900, serenely printed and put forth the twelve-year-old projects, practically unmodified, of a man who boasts of forming his conception of cycling on an old-fashioned ordinary, with a seven foot wheel, and whose "practical experiments of the movement of cyclists in considerable bodies", date from the days of the diamond frame safety, when the pneumatic tyre had still to convince, and the giant, unstable "ordinary" machine, useless across country and incapable of luggage, was indeed as well as in name the ordinary machine.

Lt.-Col. Balfour's long account of the numerous extensive manoeuvres in which he has participated since the book was done, simply intensifies my case that the War Office has been dull and negligent in the matter to a scandalous degree. For if nothing else was learnt in these manoeuvres the conduct of them must have been remarkably bad, and, on the other hand, if anything was learnt it ought to have been incorporated in the drill-book.

A second admission destroys, or goes very far towards destroying, the fundamental dogma of the War Office that cyclists are infantry. Lt.-Col. Balfour begins quite impenitently: "Now, as the cyclist is a foot soldier ... he must of necessity know military drill." But he ends: "I could scarcely ask the Adjutant General to re-write the Infantry Drill because I thought that a simpler one would be more easily adapted to movements of cyclists." If that is not a complete recognition of my startling proposal that cyclists are, after all, neither cavalry nor infantry but cyclists, it is, at any rate, a very considerable inkling.

There is a further passage to the same effect. "Does Mr. Wells", asks Lt.-Col. Balfour, "seriously imagine that, when I am drilling my battalion in Wellington Barracks....I am keeping my cyclists trailing at its heels? On the contrary, they will have ridden miles out of London, and will be practicing one of the many tactical execises especially suited to their characterisitics." He omits, however, any reference that enables me to find these special tactical exercises in the drill-book he is defending. It is just my case that such exercises do not exist, that they ought to exist,[2] and they are not likely to exist until the War Office develops quite unprecedented inventiveness. And incidentally, we get this stupendous admission of cyclists manoeuvring on the remote outskirts of London while their colonel manoevres in Wellington Barracks! What possible good is this practically sessile colonel miles away? Does he heliograph instructions when the sun shines and subside when the weather is dull? Or do they use the telephone system, such as it is, of this unhappy land? Or is he really no good at all, and this metaphorical connection between him and these cyclists, just folly and no more?

Apropos of that great-coat question, Lt.-Col. Balfour lapses still further and describes an operation conducted by "battalions" of cyclists. But under the system he is defending, battalions of cyclists are just what is impossible. My case was that this system gives us no organized cyclist force at all, but a miscellany of odd companies differing in uniform and equipment, under different miles-away Colonels, and practically incapable of efficient co-operation. Now Lt.-Col. Balfour descends upon my statement that these cyclists are inseparably linked to infantry battalions with particular vigour. He describes this organization as a "plum". "I have", he says, "hopelessly confused peace administration with war organization", and he makes it clear that the national danger of a War Office, should war break upon us and a cyclist force be needed, [he] proposes to draw the men *"from the various companies"* of the battalions to which they belong - every company in the battalion may be depleted - and [then] to dispatch these shreds and patches of the British Army against a conceivably efficient enemy as a cyclist force. This scheme to commit manslaughter might be set working to-morrow. And here, at any rate, I will plead guilty to the charge of "ignorance". Lt.-Col. Balfour rails against me. I did not know. I did not guess the depths to which the War Office might sink. I jumped to the conclusion that the cyclist company was at least a separate company, because there are a thousand reasons why it should be so, and none why it should not. But you see!

Finally, to show "what results our early efforts to train cyclists can produce", Lt.-Col. Balfour positively prints a letter in which the extreme misery of a cyclist outpost cut off from its kit by that "carted baggage" folly, is very vividly described. Although I knew him to be the author of this drill-book by the time I reached this passage, I could scarcely believe my eyes. But there the thing stands in his paper. And this little tale of quite unavoidable hardship is just one small example, a hand specimen as it were, of the realities this drill-book may bring out.

By virtue of this harmless-looking little pink pamphlet, unless some grievous outrage to Lt.-Col. Balfour's pride of authorship is speedily done, I am convinced that men of my blood and class will be brought to intolerable hardships, to shame and surrender, to useless struggles, and wounds and death.

Faithfully yours,
H.G. Wells

---

[1] Wells is referring to his piece 'The Cyclist Soldier', in the *Fortnightly Review*, vol. 74 (December 1900), pp. 914–28. The piece was a longish review/article on soldier cyclists and especially their drill manual. Wells was in the midst of a novel which was later abandoned, 'The Loyalty of Esau Common', dealing with some aspects of modern warfare, one part of which appeared in *The Contemporary Review*. Lt.-Col. Arthur Balfour, as the author of the drill manual, responded in the February issue of the *Fortnightly Review*.

[2] There is an explanatory footnote at this location in the original: 'In this connection, Lt.-Col. Balfour says, "I gather that Mr. Wells does not see the necessity of a drill at all, and belabours me almost as though I was responsible for the great 'Rifle Club' project. But that was the Prime Minister, not me; and I take no share in these intestine feuds. I specifically insisted that my ideal soldier cyclists were to be *soldiers* (I italicized that), not haphazard levies." Because I assert that this drill, for which Lt.-Col. Balfour claims the responsibility, is absurd and useless, I no more repudiate "drill" than a person would repudiate food by insisting upon the low nutritive value of mud pies.'

382. To Joseph Wells[1]

Korn, APC

[Italy]   Feb. 2. 01.

No letters today or yesterday. Send me a list or copies of any telegrams in packet. How's the weather? Love from us both.

---
[1] Joseph Wells mounted postcards sent to him in the first decade of the twentieth century, using adhesive paper. The scrap book, originally a large antique copy of Parkhurst's *Greek Lexicon*, is now in the collection of Eric Korn. He graciously allowed me to use the postcards for this collection. These postcards were sent to Spade House as Joseph Wells apparently acted as caretaker while the younger Wellses took their holidays. Some of the postmarks are conjectural as they have become smudged over the years.

383. To Joseph Wells

Korn, APC

[Italy]   13 Feb. 01.

Here we are. Lemons on trees & sun <u>hot</u>. We had one packet of letters dispatched Friday. Hope your foot [mends]. Love from us both.

384. To Joseph Wells

Korn, APC

Genoa, Italy   3. 4. 01.

Please show this to Jessie. I fancy she thinks the Italians are not a clean people.[1]

---
[1] This card has a scene of clothing hung out to dry across two narrow streets in the city of Genoa. Jessie may have been a servant at Spade House or a cousin of Wells.

385. To A. T. Simmons

Illinois, AN

Spade House
Sandgate   24 - 4 - 01

Mr. H. G. Wells presents his compliments to Mr. A. T. Simmons & begs to inform him that his current weight is now
<u>10 stone 7 pounds</u>
For the most part muscular matter.

386. To Sidney Low

Illinois, Typed Transcription

Spade House
Sandgate, Kent   5.5.01.

My dear Low,

      I'm glad you like Anticipations I, but how about Anticipations II and the Census returns?[1] Yesterday I was modest and to-morrow also I will be, but to-day! Can I spot you a winner? Want to know a good Investment? Size (and colour) of majority at new Election? Anything? The horrible thing is that no one will realize that article was written before the Census began.

We are very jolly - we have been to Italy and came back much exhilarated and how about a week end soon? Can you get away?

Do you know those very cheerful young people the Guests were here recently? Guest is the first young man that ever brought it home to me another generation has arisen.[2]

                        Yours ever,
                        H.G.

(Special to Mrs. Low)   [*A drawing of Arnold House, where the Wellses lived while Spade House was under construction, marked, 'To let Furnished' appeared in the original.*]

                Our warmest regards to you both.

[1] The serial version of *Anticipations* was appearing in the *Fortnightly Review*. Low had congratulated Wells on the first selection on 'Locomotion', and he was particularly pleased that his second section, on urban life, had been authenticated by the first published census returns.
[2] Haden Guest and his wife were members of the Fabian Society, see letters in volume 2.

387. To Sidney Low

Illinois, Typed Transcription

Spade House
Sandgate, Kent   30. 5. 01.

My dear Low,

I'm tremendously sorry to have gone over some of your work without a decent acknowledgement and I hope to be able to read "The Rise of the Suburbs" and admit your priority in the book. We hold you for that week-end some time <u>after</u> August. Until then from now onward the Acting Manager of the establishment will I am afraid not be very fit for social duties. There is to be a New Century generation of Wells's and the eldest is now imminent.[1]

Yours ever,
H.G. Wells

Our warmest regards to you both.

[1] George Philip Wells was born 17 July 1901. He was known as 'Gip' virtually all of his life.

388. To Elizabeth Healey

Illinois, ALS

Spade House
Sandgate, Kent   2 - 7 - 01

My dear Miss Healey,

There comes a letter from Miss Liveless[?] to remind me incidentally that the Lord God has for some reason failed to move me to write to you for ever so. How - as offensive people say - ARE you? What are you doing and what are you hoping and (among other things) why haven't you written to me? I, you know, have been going on & going on. You cannot imagine just how rapidly & sensibly one does go on in this sort of place & this sort of way. Last December I was writing some ambitious stuff called <u>Anticipations</u> for the <u>Fortnightly Review</u> & I am writing it still - & it is July! Little things have happened by the way but that is the essential history. I had about a month in Italy I seem to remember & I fancy I have done a short story. "Anticipations" is designed to undermine and destroy the monarch, monogamy, faith in God & respectability & the British Empire, all under the guise of a speculation about motor cars & electrical heating. One has to go gently in the earlier pages but D.V. the last will be a beauty.

I have little news of any old Kensington people except Jennings & that is bad news. He was here for a time this spring, ill, broken in body & spirit, a beaten man and I fear an utterly hopeless one. I fear on the whole I am getting more of my share of the wounded & fallen this way. In the last three years, Nisbet, & Stevenson, Stephen Crane & Steevens[1] have made my acquaintance for the sole purpose of collapsing in conspicuous distressing ways before my eyes so to speak. Gissing came here six weeks ago palpably dying but at that I rebelled & he has just gone away again mentally aggrieved and weighing 10 lbs more than when he came. When I make a new acquaintance, I hasten to give him fattening food and I take him for walks. But these anxieties age & wear - I am not the man you knew - a sort of dontcareadamndishness fades & fades. Also I shall presently be a father - in two weeks time - & it makes me feel that youth is very nearly over. I weigh ten stone seven - at <u>one</u> time it was never over seven stone two. This is a sad letter.

When Miss Liveless [?] comes to England won't you bring her to see me. This house will be infested with doctors & nurses in a week or so & until the end of August very probably. But I do feel you ought to see me again before prosperity & respectability & all the cares of this world inflate & sober me beyond your recognition.

Do you realize we have not seen each other since A.D. 1893? I don't realize it a bit - but there the thing is as a statistical fact anyhow.

Yours ever,
H.G. Wells

---

[1] J. F. Nisbet was a psychologist.

Bob Stevenson was a cousin of R. L. Stevenson, and a very dear friend of Wells.

Stephen Crane, the American writer had died in 1900. Wells was able to advance his reputation.

George Steevens was a writer who covered the Boer War and wrote one of the best travel books on the United States in this period, *The Land of the Dollar*, a book which Wells admired very much. It served as a sort of Baedeker for the USA.

389. To Rudolf Cyrian[1]

Illinois, ALS

Spade House
Sandgate   9 - 7 - 01

My dear Sir,

I am very greatly obliged to you for your very valuable observations on my first <u>Anticipations</u>. I hope to be able to embody your remarks in a qualifiying footnote for the book.[2]

Yours very sincerely,
H.G. Wells

Rudolf Cyrian, Esq.

---

[1] Cyrian is unknown to me.
[2] At this time Wells was able to add footnotes to the various printings of the text, which went through eight impressions in a very short time. The book varies from copy to copy, with the Tauchnitz edition of late 1902, and the cheap edition of 1914, closest to the author's last revisions, prior to the Atlantic edition, which appeared in the mid-twenties.

390. Elizabeth Pinker to Amy Catherine Wells[1]

Illinois, ALS

[London]   July 19, 1901

My <u>dear</u> Euphemia,[2]

You have behaved nobly! The glorious 17th of July! I do hope you and Master Wells are both as well as you can be. But, I say, Euphemia, how about those 2 ozs over 9 lbs. Are your scales absolutely reliable? While you were about it, you might have beaten Elizabeth by more than a miserable 2 ozs. Pooh! I tell Ralph now he <u>has</u> got a friend even though it won't count a bit presently.

Don't I see in my mind's eye those two making us sit up. I am sorry it is so hot for you. When the time comes I shall run down on the day, as I shall be simply dying to see you all.

Take care of yourself,
Elizabeth [3]

---

[1] This letter commemorates the birth of the Wellses first child, George Philip.

[2] 'Euphemia' was the name of a character in several stories in Wells's short fiction of the 1890s. Some of the characteristics were based on 'Jane' and for a period, Amy Catherine was called 'Euphemia'. At about this time, she and Wells adopted 'Jane' as her name. When Wells selected twenty-two examples of this shorter fiction for the Atlantic Edition in the mid-1920s, he entitled that part of volume 6, 'The Euphemia Papers'.

[3] Elizabeth Pinker was the wife of James Pinker, Wells's agent at this time. Ralph Pinker was their child. He eventually took over the Pinker agency, but Wells had by that time long since moved to A. P. Watt as his representative.

391. To Edith May Nesbit (E. Nesbit)[1]

Bromley (photocopy), ALS

Spade House
Sandgate, Kent   5 - 8 - 01

Dear little May,

I'm just back from my wanderings and I find a letter here from Miss Kendon[?] who would like you to come about the 3rd of September. I'll write to tell her you will come on that day if it is convenient to you. Your machine still hangs fire as those Scoundrels at the shop want to make out you had some accident with it and that the collapse isn't their fault. You never <u>did</u> have any accident with it, did you? But we'll soon get all that settled.

How are you getting on? Are you having a good time? Tell me all (or most of all) you are doing.

I had very good riding all the time I was away & I have found my farm house room. It's whereabouts is a dark secret to be confided to no human being. I shall go there tomorrow & work. The address (if you tell anyone you incur my unrelenting animosity) is at Mr Banks, Ruffans[?] Hill Farm, Aldington, Kent.[2]

I really had a good time, except that for some reason when one rides alone one gets so abominably hungry. I went through Tenterden, Bodiam, Brighton, Worthing to Petersfield & came back by Brighton, Hastings & Winchelsea.[3]

My dear girl I hope you are being happy & good. Let me know just how life is going with you & with love from us both.

Believe me yours ever,
H.G. Wells

Kind regards to Mrs. Coperman[?] G.P. flourishes.

---

[1] E. Nesbit was the pen-name of Edith May Bland, née Nesbit, the author of many famous children's books, including such famous titles as the *Would-be-Goods*, *Five Children and It* and *The Railway Children*, see letters 447 and 454.

[2] Just how long Wells used this *pied-a-terre* for a writing sanctuary is not known, but the location was in use for up to a year after George Philip Wells was born.

[3] Wells thought nothing of riding fifty miles a day on his bicycle. The circuit he describes was a popular ride before the First World War.

392. To W. E. Henley

Boston, ALS

Spade House
Sandgate   31 - 10 - 01

Dear 'Man of Letters',[1]

I have seen the Wonderful, the Glorious, the Incredible, the Dazzling, the Simply & Altogether True, the Final & Only Possible Portrait of yourself. It is given to few to be Immortal, but to be doubly Immortal, to be not only a Master but the material of a masterpiece, this God has kept for you! We shall die, we shall fade, we shall be obliterated by bloody photographs and hated & forgotten, and you, you know, you will shine in a gallery, you will look with an eye of undimmed blue, with your living expression of a kindly truculence, over the easels of the poor little copyists year after year, year after year - until every prophecy I ever made has come & gone. But they will call you "Henley" like sensible people. "A man of letters" indeed! Are you ashamed of yourself, or who is ashamed of you? What the Ell!

Our love to you both,
H.G.[2]

[1] W. E. Henley was Wells's mentor for his writing.
[2] The story of their relationships is well told in John Connell, *W. E. Henley* (London, 1949), where this letter is also reprinted, in a slightly different form. The portrait was by William Nicholson, (1872–1949), see letter 453. Henley died soon after the exhibition.

393. To Joseph Edwards

Texas, ALS

Spade House
Sandgate, Kent   7. 11. 01

My dear Sir,

Do you mind sending me a copy of the Year Book. I enclose 1/3-. This happens to be my year. I am publishing in a week or so (Chapman & Hall) a book called Anticipations, which is in effect the prospectus of a new revolutionary movement, and I should very much like to blow a little in your annual if it is what I imagine it to be. My revolutionary movement is new I think in some points, and if you know Blatchford I would be tremendously glad if you could suggest to him that the Clarion ought to secure a copy of the book for review. I badger my publisher to send out copies intelligently - but you know what publishers are!

Yours very faithfully,
H.G. Wells

Joseph Edwards, Esq.[1]

[1] A holograph response to Wells's letter from Joseph Edwards appears on the verso of this letter, as well as a note signed 'A. C. W.' giving Edwards's address.

394. To Joseph Wells

Korn, APC

Basle, Switzerland   8. 11. [01?]

We came straight here, travelling all the night. Very cold in the small hours. We shall be at Lugano tomorrow. Remember me to Jessie & [*illegible*].

395. To an unknown correspondent

Illinois, ACCS

Spade House
Sandgate
Kent   15 - 11 - 01

Dear Sir,

For Text Book read 'Principles'. The publisher is Macmillan. By the bye I have made a footnote of your letter in <u>Anticipations</u>[?].
[Sincerely yours]
H.G. Wells[1]

---

[1] The edge of this correspondence card is illegible in my copy.

396. To A. T. Simmons

Illinois, ALS

Spade House
Sandgate   22. 11. 01

My dear Tommy,

<u>That's</u> awright. But don't you go sinking the Old Friend in the Disciple too much, because the latter may be not yet the former - you lose sometimes but you don't get no more of 'em. We really have, I think, done something with this <u>Anticipations</u> & I suppose we've got to stick the angular points into people's stummicks as much as possible & give 'em to think. <u>You</u> see the <u>School World</u> does its jooty in getting the book read, see? And if you happen to be about the country & get a chance at a booksellers or anything of that sort, do. I really don't want showing or puffing with my other stuff, but for <u>Anticipations</u> I'm disposed rather to <u>claim</u> help in propaganda.

Your letter has really put it into my head that there are people in the world who would stand a whole book of me, pungent, detailed, elaborate & complete, on Education - not merely generalities but the things to do, how (rather precisely) to do them & all the rest. It would be a year of pretty steady work for me - I shall think that over a lot. The devil is, to make it pay. I will not do work for nothing if I can help it.

Yours ever
H.G.

397. To Mr Courtney[1]

Illinois, ALS

Spade House
Sandgate   24 - 11 - 01

Dear Mr. Courtney,

If <u>Anticipations</u> should go on to another printing would it be possible to make a few alterations & additions? I know nothing of the cost of such changes, but as I have made notes of all of the points with a mind to such an eventuality, I am appending them & you will therefore be able to make an exact estimate of what might be done. The edition so treated must of course be advertised by <u>Revised & Corrected</u>.[2]

Yours very faithfully,
H.G. Wells

---

[1] Courtney is unknown. He may have been an editor at Chapman and Hall.
[2] As the book was such a good seller, the publishers were happy to accommodate Wells. As a result there are several states of the book.

398. To T. L. Humberstone[1]

Illinois, ALS

Spade House
Sandgate   25. 11. 01

Dear Mr. Humberstone,

I am doubtful if mine would be considered a desirable name for that governing body. I don't think I should resist being put upon it or refuse to play my part, but I don't care to be put forward & declined.
                            Yours very sincerely,
                            H. G. Wells

---

[1] T. L. Humberstone was a writer and editor in educational journals of this period. He supported Wells when he stood for Parliament later, and their somewhat limited relationship continued until the 1940s. Humberstone occasionally sought small funds from Wells in much of the latter parts of the relationship. The date is somewhat problematic. There is some blotching of the legend; it could be ii rather than 11, and it could be 07 rather than 01, but I believe the dates assigned to be correct.

399. To the Advertising Manager, Chapman & Hall

Illinois, ALS

Spade House
Sandgate   28. 11. 01

Dear Sir,

I'm very glad indeed to see you advertise <u>Anticipations</u> as a second edition. I am taking a far keener interest, I think in the advertisement of the book than I am even of my earliest ones. I do not know if you intend to advertise at all in the clerical & medical papers. I have an idea that such papers reach a different constituency and that each reader almost is a possible centre of talks in a new district. I have a passing fancy at any rate that a specially angled advertisement for these channels might be of service & there can be no harm I think in telling you as much. The phases I think that would attract the ministers of religion most is "A Compedium of Unorthodox Faith" followed by not too explicit

press notices, & for the married man, "A Scientific Restatement of Political & Moral Ideals". But, really you know, whether such special advertisements do naturally advance a book is not my department of the business at all.
      Yours very sincerely,
      H. G. Wells

400. To Graham Wallas

LSE, ACCS[1]

Sandgate   13/12/01

My dear Wallas,

  I am (by your grace) a National Liberal (? a new variety or perhaps even a sub species?) Since I last saw you a certain Dobbs led me within the camp of the true basis of a sound Political Economy & I am going to pour it out on Webb shortly.
 Sandgate is light & sunny - pleasant change from Barnes (q.v.)
      Yours ever,
        H. G. Wells

---

[1] A draft of the letter exists in Illinois as well.

401. To Arnold Bennett [1]

Texas, ALS

Spade House
Sandgate   20. 12. 01

Why should Chesterton flourish while Whitten[2] is a violet? Tell Whitten to wake up & and be a little pushful & tell people things.

My dear Bennett,

  I've just read this new light Chesterton on ME in the Pall Mall Magazine & Really, you know, he's an ass. 'The most polished and futile of centuries', i.e., Either the century of Cromwell or the century of the French

Revolution. His judgement does not penetrate, it's smarm. On me, anyhow he is no better than Lewis Hind.[3] I am confirmed in the opinion I derived from Zangwill's[4] appraisal that Chesterton must be an imposter.[5]

No further light on "The Crime"[6] so far, but I hope.

Yours,
H.G.

---

[1] The letters to Arnold Bennett that appear in this collection do not appear in the Harris Wilson ed. *Arnold Bennett and H. G. Wells* (Urbana: University of Illinois Press; London: Hart-Davis, 1960). Many of them are in Texas, and these were reprinted by John R. Harrison, 'Yours, H. G.: Some Missing Letters to Arnold Bennett', *English Literature in Transition*, XXV (1982), pp. 10–20.

[2] Wilfred Whitten conducted book review columns in a variety of journals.

[3] Lewis C. Hind was a literary critic and editor. He had given Wells space in the *Pall Mall Budget* in the 1890s.

[4] Israel Zangwill (1864–1926) was a novelist and essayist of the late Victorian era. He was one of the foremost Zionists of this time; see letters in volumes 2 and 3.

[5] Wells had not yet met G. K. Chesterton (1874–1936) when he wrote this and would never have allowed himself such remarks *after* their meeting.

[6] 'The Crime' was a play that Wells and Bennett were writing. It was never staged as the play called for a corpse on stage at the first curtain. Superstition concerning such a beginning could not be overcome, to say nothing of the merits of the play. The evidence from Bennet's letters suggests that the play was mainly talk, and outlines. Chesterton's most telling comment about Wells's writing at that time appears in his collection, *Heretics*, in which he wrote a serious analysis of *The Food of the Gods*. Wells and G. K. Chesterton were good friends, see letters in volumes 2 and 3. It is possible that this Chesterton could have even been Cecil, the brother of G.K.

402. To A. T. Simmons

Illinois, ALS

Spade House
Sandgate   22. 12. 01

My dear Tommy,

The School World article was most helpful - just the very thing to set the Vacillating Nix at the book.[1] Smith & Mudie's[2] continue to repeat & there is repeat for Colonial copies.[3] Fourth edition in the press and I am a very grateful man to all my fellow creatures.

Yours ever
H.G.

Why don't you take a week off? We've got no room to spare in the house but if you'll occupy a bedroom in Sandgate this house will be your day-hotel.

---

[1] Who Nix was is not known. However one of the letters in the Sotheby sale, described in the appendix, was from this period and was signed by James Nix as well as by Wells. He must have been a casual literary acquaintance interested in educational matters from the context. The only James T. Nix (1852–1912) traced was an American lawyer and bibliophile who lived in New Orleans at this time. He was a much sought after dinner speaker on the subject of books.
[2] W. H. Smith and Mudie operated circulating libraries in the latter part of the Victorian and the Edwardian era, where one could borrow popular books for a small daily fee.
[3] Colonial editions were more cheaply bound and sold for a lower cost outside the United Kingdom. Royalty payments were less. A third method of selling books was in the North American market, where often royalties were as high as in the UK Bindings and paper often differ, as does the text occasionally.

403. To W. H. Henley

Illinois, ALS

Spade House
Sandgate   24 - 12 - 01

My dear Henley,[1]

I find myself reading your <u>Hawthorn & Lavender</u> & reading it <u>again</u> as one looks at a picture or calls again for music & it came upon me that if you had never done another book you might be a great poet for me; in my world where poets are looked at or thought of with more enquiry than welcome, & a suspicious steadiness to ride them down to small dimensions on the slightest symptom of essential littleness [is always present.]. Indeed just now I would almost argue the new Henley a better man than the old, but I know how soon the flames of literary passions light, & I will not split the camp of your friends by going on with that comparison. What takes me overwhelmingly is the sort of concentrated sublimated & altogether beautiful seasoning of the year you have done. I didn't get that at all at the N.A.R. & not at first from the book. At first I went through it as one goes through one's real springs, remarking that here is greenness of germination, here a red leaf & there a fine show of dry ripe seed heads. Then reflecting at a little distance came the bigger thing - the secular effect. Whereupon one gets the book & has it all over again. I am a hard man to please, easier for carping & explanation than for submissive appreciation & it is rare [that] I am satisfied & rare indeed that I get the complete satisfying sense of a beautiful thing that I get from Hawthorn & Lavender. The black boat comes in imaginatively laying in the grand space of the general effect with the Japanese quality of being put there & no possible where else, & how the devil? Not that it has anything but an artist's relation to you, for as far as I can discover from Hawthorn & Lavender you are about five years younger than I am and about as much played out as George Philip Wells.[2] Give us some more. And I take it ill of you that we who are in everything but chronological accident your seniors, should have to go & slavishly work away for the New Republic while you sit tight on the lyrical secret.

Our warmest wishes to you both anyhow.[3]

Yours ever

H.G.

---

[1] This is one of the most difficult letters to decipher of any I have seen. However the contents are worth the effort. Wells is able to pay his mentor his highest compliments. The wording is slightly problematical, as indicated.

[2] Wells's new-born son

[3] On the verso of the last page is a note in Henley's hand to an unknown person. It reads: '5/11/01. This, my dear young friend, is a letter from the author of *The Time Machine* & *The Martians*. When you have finished[?] please send it back. What price that [*illegible word*]? Yours ever, W. E. H.'

404. To Cosmo Rowe

Korn, ALS

Spade House
Sandgate   27. 12. 01

My dear Rowe,

I'm glad indeed to think of you so congenially employed & I like that [hoss?].[1]

We are jolly & I don't know if you've heard it, but we've got the Best Baby in the World - just five months old now & a fine manly tenor.

I hope you'll not miss calling here if ever you come within 20 miles of us. The house is rather a lark. Everything goes well with us & Anticipations my magnum opus is in its fourth edition.

Our best wishes to you both for a Happy New Year

Yours ever,

H.G.

[1] This word is illegible; it may be a joking American-style reference to a horse or even 'boss', see letters 89, 92–3 for other letters to Rowe.

405. To Richard A. Gregory

Illinois, ALS

Spade House
Sandgate   29. 12. 01.

My dear RAG,

We'll have a Republic in twelve years - or at any rate we may have if only everyone will buck up. The amount of latent treason I am discovering is amazing. I shall talk treason at the R.I. I am going to write, talk & preach revolution for the next five years. If I had enough money believe me to keep me off the need of earning a living I would do the job myself.

I'm afraid we can't dine with anyone. Little author has to be kept steady.[1] But I may come and gossip this afternoon.

Yours ever,
H.G.

By the bye, I shall be up Jan 7th. Come and have an eighteen penny lunch with Simmings & me & perhaps the missis & May Nisbet.

[1] This is the occasion of the remarkable talk, 'The Discovery of the Future', at the Royal Institution. It is his first and, in some ways, most analytical attempt to explain his thinking, especially in the matter of the impact of evolutionary thought on possible futures.

406. To Clement Shorter[1]

Illinois, ALS

[London]   1 - 1 - 02

My dear Mr. Shorter,

I am amazed and disgusted to think that no copy of <u>Anticipations</u> has reached you. <u>Chapman & Hall</u> publish in a manner quite beyond my maddest imaginings. If ever a book needed the stimulus of presentation copies &

something of the nature of an explanatory introduction in the press it is <u>Anticipations</u>. I rarely intervene at all in the prospects of my books, but in this case, where I am exceptionally keen to get read, I sent in a list of men who I knew could & probably would, read, understand, and help the book. And these imbeciles neither sent out these copies nor let me know they had not done so. The consequence is that I have imagined myself the victim of snubs & slights from perfectly innocent men, & no doubt many of these men are feeling very natural resentment with me for my neglect.

If I let myself loose upon the topic of publishers who in this big world, with a book like <u>Anticipations</u>, will deliberately plan that enterprise to a probable sale of 7,000 copies, I should defile this letter with horrid blasphemies. I could have published the book infinitely better myself.

    Accept my sincere apologies
     & believe me
      Very sincerely yours,
       H.G. Wells

---

[1] Shorter (1857–1926) was an author and critic. His notices often ensured the success or failure of books, so Wells's concern that no review copy had been forwarded was a legitimate worry. He edited the *Sphere* for many years.

407. To Harry Quilter

Hofstra, ALS

Spade House
Sandgate   17-1-02

My dear Quilter,

  Very glad of your letter. The S.J.G.[1] review did me no end of good. I've just seen <u>W.</u> & <u>W.</u> & I'd be delighted to have a copy from you.

We send our very warmest regards to you both. (which won't be affected in the slightest by anything you say in <u>W.</u> & <u>W.</u> I'm certain)
      Yours ever
       H.G. Wells

---

[1] *St James's Gazette*

408. To A. H. Wilkerson

Hofstra, ALS

Spade House
Sandgate   17 - 1 - 02.

My dear Sir,

    I'm not in need of secretarial help at present but if I am you might be the sort of helper for me. Please let me know of your change of address.
                              Yours very sincerely,
                              H. G. Wells

A.H. Wilkerson, Esq.

409. To Mrs H. B.

Texas, ALS

Spade House
Sandgate   27 . 2 . 02

Dear Mrs. H.B.[1]

    I send you pamphlets & you return me masterpieces of gracious & wonderful praise, so subtly & ingeniously done that for a space I sit in reverence at my own feet marvelling that I have so long slighted my own greatness.

    It may not have been good for me but your letter was very nice & I am greatly grateful to you therefore.
                          Our warmest regards,
                          Yours ever,
                            H.G. Wells

[The opposite page has a sketch of a tiny Wells sitting at the feet of a large Wells, captioned, 'The Birth of Self Respect'.]

---

[1] This letter may have been addressed to E. Nesbit (Mrs Hubert Bland).

410. To the Editor, *Nature*

PLS

[Spade House] [mid-February, 1902]

"T.B.S." is quite right. I regret very much that I did not verify my quotation. A confusion of Og's bed and the lopping propensities of Adoni-Bezek seems to have decayed to the likeness of Procrustes. I have lived in this error for years. I have often used the image of King Og's bed in conversation, and, I think, in published matter. No one has ever detected my slip, and it is by no means impossible that I am the centre of propagation of a mistake that will turn up again.[1]

    H.G.Wells

---

[1] This letter refers to Wells's famous lecture at the Royal Institution on 24 January 1902 on 'The Discovery of the Future'. It was published soon after the talk, in *Nature*, the *Proceedings of the Smithsonian Institution* and many years later, in *The New York Times*, in book form by Fisher Unwin in 1902, Fifield in 1913, and Jonathan Cape in 1921 and 1925. It also appeared, with the error corrected, in the Atlantic Edition of Wells's writings, and has recently been republished by the H. G. Wells Society, annotated and edited by Patrick Parrinder. Wells used the biblical metaphor of King Og's bed, rather than Procrustes. Og, who appears in Numbers 21: 33–5 did have an iron bedstead, but Procrustes was the person who lopped or stretched people to fit his bed. This letter, which appeared in *Nature* on 20 February 1902, p. 360, immediately follows the letter of T.B.S., who wrote from Edinburgh. I do not think Wells used the Og reference anywhere else in his writing. Adoni-Bezek was a king of Bezek, captured by the men of Judah and Simeon, taken to Jerusalem where he was mutilated and died in 1449 B.C. (Judges I: 5–7). The Wellses continued attempting to correct the error, as when Catherine Wells wrote to Fifield on 31 October 1917 asking him to correct this 'tiresome letter'. This latter letter is in the Jonathan Cape archives located in the University of Reading.

411. To Albert Wilkerson

Hofstra, ACCS

Spade House
Sandgate   1. 3. 02

Dear Sir,
      I regret that I cannot attend your meeting. But I shall be glad to hear when the Young Britons[1] have formulated themselves a little more definitely. How are you going to reach them & how do you propose to do it?
                  Yours very sincerely,
                  H.G. Wells
Albert Wilkerson, Esq.

---

[1] The Young Britons are unknown to me. Wilkerson and Wells had had a correspondence concerning possible secretarial work, see letter 408.

412. To Sarah Wells

Korn, APCS

Ostend   31 March 1902

We have both been rather seedy & have fled to Belgium for a change. Good crossing this afternoon.
                  Busswhacker

413. To Graham Wallas [1]

LSE, AL

Spade House
Sandgate, Kent   19 . 3. - 02

Dear Wallas

When I don't send off my articles, I feel, "Here am I seeming to slight my Uncle Wallas!" and contrition is my portion, but when I do they come back with 1000 words missing[?] from a better man than myself, much improved[?], contrition is my all. However, there it is, and you are a good New Republic man.

I won't use the L.S.E. experiences of money collecting because I want simply to get the principle driven home & not to follow details of administration too far.

I think I am clear enough that the wastrel (bless his heart!) may have his simple or complicated pleasures so far as I'm concerned, so long as he doesn't have children. But it really isn't my affair whether he practises - not temperance because temperance is the <u>optimum</u> amount of physical pleasure - but either abstinence or indulgence.

Year by year my Christian training scales off me and I get more and more purely physiological with regard to sexual intercourse. A man or woman ought to have sexual intercourse. Few people are mentally, or morally or physically in health without it. For everyone there is a minimum and maximum below which lies complete efficiency. Find out your equation, say I, and then keep efficient.

Since it became clear to me that reproduction and sexual activity can be disconnected, the whole human not [*two illegible words*]. The ungovernable complication is venereal disease. Over and above sensations there are of course emotions in these affairs but the emotions can be controlled by suggestion & interpretations in a thousand different ways. Our system focuses all the emotions into jealousy. A Maori is proud to marry a girl who has had numerous lovers.

We've got to rationalize the sentiment in these affairs. But that's a matter for morals, I submit. Anyhow, I don't intend to raise the flames of public sexuality by specifically recommending preventions now. One thing at a time.

From first blast the public is going to swallow a lot from me and my affair as a good monarch is to make it all go over easy.

I loathe systematic education and medicine.
[...]I'm extremely doubtful whether children should be taught kindness & I don't think a child needs other children until 4 or 5, but my reason I shall keep till we get a chance to talk together.

---

[1] Both the original at the LSE and the copy in Illinois are difficult to read in several places because of paper creases. Wells was writing, and Wallas was criticising his manuscript, which would become *Mankind in The Making* in 1903.

414. To Joseph Wells

Korn, APCS

Dinant, Belgium   8 April 02

We shall be back in Sandgate on Friday night. I have had a good rest & I am now quite fit for work again. <u>Love from us both to all.</u>
                                   Bertie

415. To A. T. Simmons

Illinois, ANS

Spade House
Sandgate   11. 4. 02

My dear A.T.S.

    Permeate.[1] There is no reason why a salutary time should not be given to the R.P.A. I've given 5/- on the N. Study Ex$^{m.}$
                         Yours
                          H.G.

---

[1] Wells is urging Simmons to become active in what is probably a teachers' group.

416. To Rudolf Cyrian[1]

Illinois, ACCS

Spade House
Sandgate   15. 4. 02

Dear Sir.

Thank you very much indeed for your good wishes (I am very much better & back at work again) and for the very suggestive news about the noiseless rifle.
                             Yours very sincerely,
                             H. G. Wells

---
[1] See letter 389

417. To Fred Wells

Illinois, ALS

Spade House
Sandgate   5. 5. 02

Dear old Fred,

    It is this sort of thing.

[*a sketch of two standards with a banner reading 'Welcome' hung between them*]

I hope you are coming home resolved to have a good time.[1]
I shall keep a bedroom disengaged in this house for you for all the time until you go again & you must consider this your headquarters. It is a very pleasant place here, bands, promenades, pier & all that sort of thing - sea bathing if you like. I'm laying in cigars at Liss & here and if I can get my work done in time I shall cycle to Southampton & meet you when you land. I suppose you will take a day or so at Liss & then I hope you will come on here with mother. I think of taking a three week walk in the Alps with the missis after June 10th

and I thought that you & the mater might like to have a quiet time here. Unless you would like to come over the Alps with us? But of all these things we will talk more when we meet.

    Yours ever
    Bertie

---

[1] Fred was about to arrive home for a holiday from South Africa where he had been living for several years.

418. To Fred Wells

Illinois, ALS

Spade House
Sandgate   [? May 1902]

Dear old Fred,

  Life is too short for long letters. You'd better come right home & have a pick up at Liss & here. Warmest good wishes & hoping to see you.
    Yours ever
    H.G.
    The only original Busswhacker

419. To Sidney Low

ALS[1]

Spade House
Sandgate   7. 5. 02

My dear Low,

  I have read and reread your impressions of Rhodes[2]. I've never come across you upon that sort of thing before. The thing strikes me as being quite tremendously good - if you'll stand my telling so. Have you done any other impressions at any time? If so I'd very much like to read 'em. I think it's a first class portrait, critical, wide, concrete and vivid. A dozen or so like that (with good photographs) would make a most remarkable and desirable book.

Yours ever,
H.G. Wells

---

[1] I did not see this transcript at Illinois, but as with letter 453, I found it in Chapman-Huston's *Lost Historian* (London, 1936), p. 90.

[2] Wells is referring to Low's obituary notice on Cecil Rhodes, who died March 1902. It appeared in the *Nineteenth Century*, May 1902.

420. To Sidney Low

Illinois, Typed Transcription

Spade House
Sandgate   10. 5. 02

My dear Low,

I shall look for those other Epitaphs and I'll keep the <u>Standard</u> Rhodes[1] for a day or so as I want to show it to that scoundrel Popham here![2] Some day the industrious historian will dig out these descriptions of yours and make pleasant and picturesque quotes (anonymous) in his vivid volumes. Why not quarry for him?

Yours ever,
H.G.

P.S. Where I find this Rhodes different from much of what people might call "this sort of thing" - impressions by G.W. Steevens or the young Kipling, e.g. - is that it comes from a man who really knows and who has a system of proportions, while these others they're (damn) clever and well informed and vivid and striking and picturesque and all that, but they really, you know, <u>don't know</u>. They love effect, pure and simple. Your effect is all right, but it isn't the thing.

---

[1] This letter also refers to Low's article on Cecil Rhodes. Steevens (1869–1900) was an acquaintance of Wells and wrote books on travel, including an especially good one on the United States. He was also a war correspondent and died while reporting on the siege of Ladysmith in 1900.

[2] This must be the same elusive Popham who was close to Wells, see the Introduction for an account of the Popham correspondence.

421. To Sidney Low

Illinois, Typed Transcription

Spade House
Sandgate   26. 5. 02.

My dear Low,

I have read all these articles with interest and admiration. They are good but variegated - as good as the run of your talk - but not quite in the vein of happy portraiture you have struck in the Rhodes. Mostly they work an aspect, they are observations. What took me about the Rhodes was that it was a complete exhaustive impression. There was really nothing left to do with Rhodes one felt after that but to fill in dates and statistics and much of that sort. You play the artist to get at the bowels of the thing. For the most part with these other articles you don't do that. One feels reserves - as one often does with you. The real thing in your mind you not only haven't cared to express but you haven't even very much troubled to look at. Judging by that Rhodes I should say if it wasn't for those reserves of your being a man of the world, you'd be a most amazing Goddy person with a pew. I hope to goodness you'll let yourself out again soon.

                                                Yours ever,
                                                H.G. Wells

422. To Sidney Low

Illinois, Typed Transcription

Spade House,
Sandgate   29. 5. 02.

My dear Low,

It's good of you to say such things of "Anticipations" and Kidd.[1] If I may fling my cloak of modesty over my shoulder for a moment - I could eat Kidd. But as you see, every damned half crown review, one after the other, blazes off at him, and Frederic Harrison[2] and Crozier[3] and all that sort. Oh, well —. I am torturing finishing the first three of a new set of articles for the F.R. and then we are going off to place my heated brow against the Alps. And we shall be back when the bloody Coronation is over.[4]

Yours ever,
H.G.

---

[1] Benjamin Kidd (1858–1916) was a social psychologist of considerable note. He spent much of his life attempting to reconcile biological evolution with social change. His most famous book was *Social Evolution* (London, 1895), which Wells reviewed in *Pall Mall Gazette*, 24 May 1895, under the title 'A Touchstone for Mr. Kidd's Prognostics'.

[2] Frederic Harrison (1831–1923) famous English positivist. He wrote the replacement introduction to George Gissing's *Veranilda* after Wells's efforts were found unusable by the family. His *Autobiographic Memoirs* appeared in 1911.

[3] John Beattie Crozier was a philosopher and historian. He and Wells clashed on several occasions, especially in the *Fortnightly Review*.

[4] King Edward VII had an emergency operation for appendicitis on 24 June 1902 and his coronation in fact was postponed until 9 August.

423. To Joseph Wells

Korn, APCS

Airolo   18 vi 02

My dear Dad,

We are having a very jolly time. We have just walked 12 miles right to the summit of the St. Gothard. The last two miles in snow up to our knees. We sleep here tonight & go down into the Italian valley tomorrow. We have had a splendid time. Love to you both from us both.

Bertie

424. To T. L. Humberstone

Illinois, ALS

Hotel Faido
Route de Gothard   18. June 02

[*A nice etching of the hotel, located on the St Gothard Passat at 800 metres of altitude, appears at the top of the page. According to the caption, the hotel was three hours by train from either Lucerne or Milan.*]

Mr dear Sir,

I'm delighted to find another of the old R.C.S. men at this sort of thing. Simmons & Gregory whom I mentioned in my last are both R.C.S.s, but I didn't get the assemblage. I was a teacher in training & never did either chemistry or mechanics. The parallelism of our luck is perhaps closer than you suppose. - I had three or four years when I could get nothing printed at all except in the educational monthlies - save for a Globe [*illegible word*] or so. I think that there must be some necessary drilling one gets in this period of dreaming - bee fashion - at short paras. I should have thought the '<u>Speaker</u>' a great score in those days.

Don't count on that article of mine, but count on my sincere good wishes for the S.Y.A. and believe me,

       Yours ever
       H.G. Wells

By the bye, <u>Dr. J. Miller Maguire</u> of 9 Earl's Court might give you something on education for the army if you asked him. or Capt. Nash of Surbiton. (details of address unknown to me.)

[*in pencil in Catherine Wells's hand*]- I find I've got my address book with me. Nash is 7 Berkeley Place, Wimbledon, S.W.

425. To Arnold Bennett

Texas, ALS

Spade House
Sandgate   July 4, 1902

Dear Bennett,

I think J.B. P[inker][1] is rather unwise in not checking Walker in his design for something 'personal'. You might do a pseudo- "impression" of the man's argumentative side.

                                      Yours,
                                      H. G.

---

[1] Pinker, who was at this time acting as agent for both authors, liked the idea of having one of his authors write about another, feeling that one would get paid in cash, and the other in publicity. A few of Wells's letters to Pinker appear in this collection. The Bennett-Pinker correspondence, which was very detailed, appears in volume one in the four-volume Bennett letters, edited by James Hepburn, *Letters to J. B. Pinker* (London: Oxford University Press, 1966).

426. To Graham Wallas

LSE, ALS

Spade House
Sandgate   12. 8. 02

My dear Wallas,

I'm just off to Paris but thanks stupendously for your letter. Do you mind the enclosed footnote? If not please return it to me & I will tack it on to my finish.

                                      Yours ever,
                                      H.G.

427. To Graham Wallas

LSE, ACCS

Spade House
Sandgate   16. 8. 02

My dear Wallas,

I shall stick in the footnote and unless you telegraph your disapproval[1] I shall use your name. It's more interesting like that, I think. The paper hangs up for a space, I've written up to November & there's no hurry to provide any more, but I shall go on again soon & I will certainly send you copies - though it's a shame to prey on your brains in this way. Our love to you both.

Yours ever,
H.G.

---

[1] Wells's book *Mankind in the Making* was being serialised, although not as rapidly as Wells had expected. Wallas provided some material for him.

428. To T. L. Humberstone

Illinois, ACCS

Spade House
Sandgate   4 - 9 - 02

My dear Humberstone

I read your letter in the Wishart[?] with very great interest. I am impressed with the idea that you will succeed as a journalist.

Yours ever,
H.G. Wells

429. To Elizabeth Healey

Illinois, ALS

Spade House
Sandgate, Kent   6. 10. 02

My dear Miss Healey,

What you tell me of Miss Calvert is very distressing & it fills me with a sort of shameful congratulations to think she should cherish such dellusions about my health & make out of my sleek prosperity a tale of martyrdom to comfort herself withal. I was at the opening of the R.C.S. a day or so ago & saw your father & the Roses & one or two other old students of our time. Judd mistaking me for some respectable person shook hands effusively. I went with Simmons who said he had met you.

I have been working my hand with the new <u>Fortnightly</u> stuff this summer - so hard indeed have we both been at it that photography & such relaxations have vanished out of our crowded lives.[1] Miss Levitas[?] plays like summer lightning in our horizon but comes no nearer.

Yours ever,
H.G.

---

[1] Wells is referring to the serialisation of *Mankind in the Making*. Neither Miss Calvert or Miss Levitas is known – Levitas may have been a journalist. Judd was a professor of geology at the Royal College of Science.

430. To Mrs Rook[1]

Illinois, ALS

Spade House
Sandgate   8. 10. 02

Dear Mrs. Rook,

I've just thought of summat. You propose to ride part of the way from London to S'gate. Well - look at a map of Kent before you decide where to alight. There is no high road along the S.E. route. I'm writing from Tunbridge Wells (where we are spending a night for the sake of a walk) & I've no map by me but I think you will find that to strike the straight high road you must come by the L. C. D. Ry. to Maidstone or Chatham. The roads from Tunbridge to Sandgate are just rectangular corners the whole way. [*A sketch of abrupt connected angles occurs in the text at this point, with an arrow pointing to them.*] This sort of thing.

Straight road from Ashford.

Yours ever,
H.G.

[1] She may be the wife of Clarence Rook, an author who wrote fairly extensively on Bernard Shaw.

431. To an unknown correspondent

Hofstra, ALS

Spade House
Sandgate   9.11.02

My dear Sir,

I am greatly obliged to you for your interesting letter. I doubt your theory of procreation though. In Shakespeare's time men believed just the other way about & thought the club of hot desire better than the fruits of cold habit. 'Bastard' was sometimes heard as a compliment in the middle ages.

It would be interesting if someone would set to work upon the point you raise and find what proportion of, say, the best thousand Englishmen were first, second or third sons. Even then if you found an inferiority in the first sons it might be due to the inexperience of the mother in nursing & so on, quite apart from essential difference in quality - or to the want of childish companions in infancy.

There's a vast amount of research of this sort crying aloud to be done. — by anyone with time to spare.

Yours very sincerely,
H.G. Wells [1]

[1] Wells's correspondent was commenting on serialised portions of what would become *Mankind in the Making* (London: Chapman and Hall, 1903).

432. To Beatrice Webb[1]

LSE, ALS

Spade House
Sandgate   28. 11. 02

Dear Mrs. Webb,

We didn't come. Disaster overtook us. The flat which was to be 'quite ready' by 4:30 yesterday afternoon, was simply packing cases jellied in chaos at six. It became evident we could never dress & extremely doubtful if we should ever wash again. Mrs. Wells did in the most pathetic manner attempt to disinter clean things. (Her hands were like this

& Time advanced relentlessly thus.

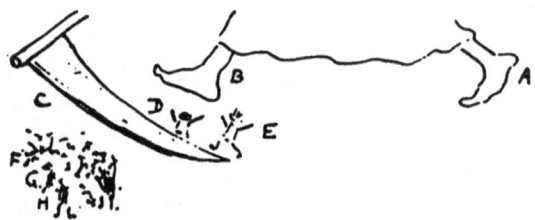

Explanation of the Diagram
A & B The Feet of time; The Best Foot is forward.
C. The Scythe of Time.
D. Jane and E. Herbert George Wells,
F.G. H &c. A Brilliant Assembly from which they are relentlessly cut off.

We are going down tomorrow.

Yours very sincerely,
H. G. Wells

<u>Aras - Sane Aras - Scientific Frontiers.</u>

---

[1] Beatrice Webb (1858–1943) was married to Sidney Webb (1859–1947) with whom she conducted a life devoted to the attainment of Socialism and to a study of the working class and trade unionism. They were founders of the Fabian Society and helped to establish the *New Statesman*. Together they wrote many books. Wells and the Webbs maintained cordial, occasionally close relations; however they had many disagreements over the means to their generally identical ends.

433. To Louis Barron[1]

Illinois, ADLS[2]

[Spade House
Sandgate]   9 / [12] 1902

Dear Sir,

     I can give you the translation rights of the 'Wonderful Visit' for £10 on the condition that the translation shall be made & published before the end of 1903. The £10 to be paid £5 now and £5 on publication & the rights to revert to me if you fail to publish within the specified time.[3]
                                       Yours very sincerely,
                                       H.G. Wells

[The following is a draft comment on Barron's final letter]:

I have written to the Director of the Figaro & Mercure pointing out that Barron has no authorization from me until the £10 has been paid & I have written a curt notice to him asking him to pay £10 & saying that I believe what Davray says of his translation is quite correct.[4]

---

[1] Although Wells settled on translators whom he trusted and whom he thought sympathetic to his style of writing and his thought patterns, early in his career he was prepared to experiment with translations, and in this case, it led to a small problem. On 11 November 1902 one Louis Barron wrote to him offering to translate *The Wonderful Visit* for £10. Wells had written to him first, apparently thinking that he was a publisher, hoping to have the book made available in French. Wells responded with this letter.

[2] This letter and the following one were written on the reverse sides of the letters Wells had received. There was a third Wells letter also, but only a fragment remains.

[3] There was confusion about this offer. Barron did not pay the fees set by Wells, but he did translate the first edition of the novel, without the brief epilogue. He offered it to *Mercure de France* and perhaps *Figaro*, but when Henri Davray, Wells's regular French translator heard about it, he approached Barron, pointing out that the translation he was offering needed redoing as there were two different editions. *Figaro* may even have published parts of it. Barron appealed to Wells, saying that the book without the epilogue was a better book, and that Voltaire, Heine and Swift would not have added the epilogue. In addition he asked Wells to forgo the £10 fee. Wells was the loser in the transaction, and it therefore came to an end.

[4] When one reads Barron's letters, it is quite evident that his translation would not have been adequate for Wells's purposes. It was events like this, however, which indicated to Wells that he needed more real help from his agents and secretaries. He could no longer conduct his business

alone and still do his writing. Catherine would do her part, of course, but their family was very young. Wells began to farm out work, first to his cousins, and then he engaged a part time secretary, Horace Horsnell. From this time, a professional secretary-cum-manager was part of his entourage.

434. To Israel Zangwill[1]

Central Zionist Archives,
Jerusalem, ACCS
File A120/614.

Spade House,
Sandgate   22. 12. 02

My dear Sir,

    Do you take any interest in this possible election for London University? If so, I presume you would incline to support Collins. Your name would certainly be of very great service to his need.[2] London University - politics are all too political just now - mean little committees in funny little rooms seem to do the whole business & the whole thing is now in the convention that L.U. is just like any other constituency. It would be much more interesting & instructive if we made these candidates aware that they really proposed to represent us & if we, at least, brought our beautiful large intelligent eyes palpably to bear on them.

Yours very sincerely
H.G. Wells

---

[1] Zangwill (1864–1926), one of the foremost Zionists of his time, he wrote *Children of the Ghetto* (1892) and *Ghetto Tragedies* (1894). He and Wells carried on a dialogue and occasionally wrote to each other on the general subject of Zionism. These letters are the best refutation for recent attacks on Wells as being anti-Semitic.

[2] Wells's physician from the late 1880s was standing for the London Universities seat in the next parliamentary election. Wells and Zangwill both had votes in this election.

435. To the Editor, *The Young Man*[1]

PL

[Spade House
Sandgate, Kent] [late December, early January 1902/3]

I regret very much that the pressure on my time prevents my giving the attention I would like to do to your very interesting question. Mr. Swift impresses me as having on the whole correct but fragmentary views of the present state of affairs. Its title, however, 'The Decay of the Novel' is mere nonsense, and worthier of Sir Edward Clarke than of a man of literary education. The novel has altered its form. It is shorter, has fewer "characters" and more shape, symmetry and directness than it had in the sixties. The Titanotherium has given place to the horse in this field. But for the life of me I can't see any decay in its quality. Consider - taking instances haphazard - the character-drawing and the texture of Mr. Joseph Conrad, the painstaking neatness of Mr. Jacobs (who is nevertheless popular), the quality of 'Anthony Hope', the artistic care of E.A. Bennett. I believe Paul Kelver,[2] for example, would have stood as high among its contemporaries if it had been published in the fifties, or higher, than it goes today. How good was Gissing's Charlatan again! How altogether magnificent was all that was not altogether bad in Kim! Think, too, of the vigour of Mr. Morley Roberts, the tapestry weavings of Mr. Maurice Hewlett, the writing of Mr. Pugh's Tony Diver and Mr. Arthur Morrison's work. And what is wrong with Mr. Marriott-Watson's Godfrey Merrivale? Other names come crowding to my mind. Decay of the novel indeed!

Mr. Swift's idea that a literary academy in England at the present time would be anything but the last experiment(?) of vulgarity suggests an ignorance of human nature quite surprising in a novelist of Mr. Swift's respectability.

---

[1] This piece appeared in *The Young Man*, vol. 17, January 1903, pp. 22–4, and is a response by Wells to a question concerning 'The Decay of the Novel'. Others who responded included Thomas Hardy. Patrick Parrinder kindly provided me with a copy of this item. Swift was a journalist and literary editor of the magazine.
[2] Jerome K. Jerome, *Paul Kelver* (London, 1902)

436. To an unknown correspondent

Illinois, ALS

Spade House
Sandgate [c. 1902-4][1]

The Stevenson article is Golly. You are the greatest innovater in the world. Success in criticism. Third[?] part. O my bloody eyes & britches! Go on! Write a history of late literature of the Reign of Q Victoria the good. O my guts & Liver! Go it! Put em all down - just as they was & are. Bathing dresses prohibited. I get a little innovative I know, but the idea of putting down just what you thought of a writing life never entered my head. I'm making notes now for Gissing & Henry James & Conrad. That Stevenson article will simply ravish every High School in the country. O they will be pleased! And the British Weekly! It's only beginning.

Yours ever,
H.G.

---

[1] This letter, on four correspondence cards, has no addressee and no date. It could have been addressed to a number of people, such as W. E. Henley, or Sidney Low, but we have no exact information.

437. To Edmund Gosse

Leeds, ACCS

[London] 20 - 1 - 03

[*At the top of this letter is the legend: 'Temporary Premises - The G.A. (English Branch)*]

My Dear Gosse,

I am a little giddy from my sudden amazing ascent, & a little scared. But, I thank you with all my heart for the honour you have done me.

Yours ever,
H. G. Wells

President of the Goncourt Academy (English Branch).[1]

---

[1] Although Wells had belonged to the Omar Khayyam, a dining club, and had recently joined

the White Friars Club, this new election honour provided him with an entry to the highest literary circles. How much he used this facility and entrée is difficult to know. By 1907 he had settled down in the Reform Club, his haven for the remainder of his life. Gosse (1849–1928) was the pre-eminent literary critic of this time and a letter from him simply indicated that the recipient had 'made it'. By a quite extraordinary coincidence Gosse was living at 17, Hanover Terrace, Regent's Park, just a few doors from where Wells would live the last decade of his life. Gosse held a number of significant positions in the British Library, the Board of Trade, and later was Librarian of the House of Lords. He was instrumental in bringing Henrik Ibsen (1828–1906), the Norwegian poet and playwright, to the notice of English critics. His most famous book, *Father and Son* appeared in 1907, see letters in volumes 2 and 3.

438. To T. L. Humberstone

Illinois, ACCS

Spade House
Sandgate [probably 1903]

Dear Sir,

I very much regret missing your letter. Did you send it to that hotel? I regret still more I cannot write that article.

Yours very faithfully
H. G. Wells

439. To T. L. Humberstone

Illinois, ACCS

Spade House
Sandgate 16 ii - 03.

My dear Humberstone,

I haven't seen the S.Y.G. yet.[1] Simmonds should be enterprising and send me a copy.

Yours ever,
H.G. Wells

[1] Humblestone edited several school magazine annuals and this is probably one of them.

440. To Methuen

Illinois, ALS

Spade House
Sandgate   9 - iii - 03

My dear Methuen

    I think the agreement is vague & dangerously worded rather than bad in intention & I think instead of waiting to talk, I will send you a revised version. I want the document to cover all books between us & to have a uniform system of settlement.

                              Yours very sincerely
                                  H. G Wells

I shall post the revised agreement tomorrow.[1]

[On the opposite page is another part of this letter, crossed out by another hand.]

I find in going through these things that accounts have not been rendered me for the six penny Stolen Bacillus since 1901. Could you let them send from the office a memorandum of that editions' sales?

[1] Methuen had published *The Sea Lady* in 1902. Apparently the firm was attempting to develop an agreement with Wells to publish most or all of his books. In the event, Macmillan became that publisher for a time.

441. To E. C. Bentley[1]

Hofstra, ALS

National Liberal Club
Whitehall Place, S.W. 18. iii. 03

Dear Sir,

Your letter has just followed me from Sandgate and I am greatly obliged to you for your very flattering allusions to my work. This question of disarmament is one in which I am keenly interested but upon which I have arrived at no conclusions of a sufficiently definite sort for expression at the present time.

Yours very sincerely
H.G. Wells

---

[1] Probably Edmund Clerihew Bentley (1875–1956), a journalist and novelist, most famous for inventing the verse form, the clerihew, and for his detective fiction, especially *Trent's Last Case* (1913).

442. To Mr Vallardo[1]

Illinois, ALS

Spade House
Sandgate 31. iii. 03

Cher Monsieur,

J'ai vu aujourdhui Messieurs Kozakewicz (de 2. Place de Baleguilles Paris) et Davray qui sont en train de publier un traduction de l'ouvrage de lequel je vous avais ecrit. "Place aux giantes" ou "Eue[?] i Gigante." Ils croirent qu'il sera plus avantageux pour eux qu'ils auront beaucoup d'avantage s'ils publient leur traduction un neuds[?] au moins ou plus. Eu avance giudre[?] du version Italien. Ils ont dessireent l'intention de publie ce livre dans le printemps de 1904 apres [avoir] vu publication en feuillton. J'ai sipre[?] faite un traite avec M. Kozakewicz pour quelques de mes ouvrages et si vous voulez lui ecrire il soit/sera possible d'arranger pour le publication de la version Italiene en bon temps suivant a version Francais, traduit de Francais. Mais si vous pouvez trouver une bon traduction pour traduire directement de la version Anglaise il sera possible peut etre de faire cela independement de la version Francaise.

Je suis Monseiur &e
H.G. Wells

N.B. Je tiens qui une bonne traduction de l'anglais. Je peut ecrire des lettres longues en Anglais sans reprise.

[Dear Sir,

I met today with Mr Kozakewicz, of 2 Place Baleguilles, Paris and Mr Davray, who are planning to publish a translation of the work I have recently written about to you, The Land of the Giants or The Huge Ones. [i.e. The Food of the Gods]. They think that it will be more advantageous for them and that the advantage will be considerable if they publish their translation more or less simultaneously. Their appearance should precede the Italian version. They expect to publish in the spring of 1904 after seeing the serial publication. I have signed an agreement with Mr Kozakewicz for several of my works, and if you wrote to him, it should be possible to arrange for publication of the Italian version in due course following the French version, translated from the French. But if you are able to find a good translator[2] who translates directly from the English version, it would perhaps be possible to proceed independently from the French version.

I am, sir, etc.
H.G. Wells

N.B. I hope you are able to read English, for then I would write this long letter to you in English without the need for summary.[3]]

---

[1] Mr Vallardo later translated Wells's novels into Italian for many years. Although signed, the letter is certainly the draft from which a fair copy was to be made for Vallardo. No diacritical marks appear on this copy, and the French is as it appears in Wells's hand. Wells had a grasp of French with which he could conduct conversations, but his written French was somewhat sparse. These matters improved somewhat as he spent much time in France, but his accent never improved to any great extent, a fact which he understood and for which he was apologetic. A few other letters appear in French in volume 4, but they appear to be reworked into a more formal presentation, and appear as typed copies. For translations I wish to acknowledge the aid of the copy editor of this work and my colleague, Professor Jacques Ferland.

[2] Wells's French says translation, but the sense of the sentence seems to call for translator.

[3] Wells may be referring to the tradition that English people cannot write in French, or he may simply be trying to provide an opportunity for Vallardo to respond in English, which Wells probably preferred.

443. To W. E. Henley

Korn, ALS

Spade House
Sandgate   10. iv. 03.

My dear Henley,

I am confirmed in a belief that G. K. Chesterton is a damned ass.[1] He is this shape [*a grotesque sketch with rather a large stomach*]. A tallowy lump of young man with a silly laugh & no neck & <u>Please</u> God I will someday suddenly I will carve his guts out - his vital organs.

Yours ever,
H.G.

When are you coming back to your flat?

---

[1] I am not sure whether Wells and Chesterton had yet met, nor do I know the reason for the letter. This must have been about the last letter Henley received, see an earlier Wells complaint to Arnold Bennett, letter 401, dated 20 December 1901.

444. To Alex M. Thompson[1]

Illinois, Typed Transcription

[Spade House]   15. 4. 03[?]

I want to do a little as well as I can - I think it's bad for a man and his subject and a sort of blacklegging to be all over the place and doing everything in a hurry.

---

[1] Thompson was editor of the Socialist magazine *Clarion* and he hoped Wells could write a regular column for the journal.

445. To Mrs Sitwell

Boston, ALS

Spade House
Sandgate   17 - v - 03

Dear Mrs. Sitwell

I found your note on my return to London & I can assure you that in the first place I took no trouble at all save to vary my daily walk with a land lady or so, and in the second [place]. that before all things we want you to give us the same trouble again at no distant date. But we have the consolation that had you come, you would have found us a brace of the most detestable sick people imaginable, whereas now perhaps when at last you meet us it may be — as Henry James might say - we shall be up to our poor little par.
                                                    Yours very sincerely
                                                    H.G. Wells

446. To E. Nesbit[1]

Illinois, ALS

Spade House
Sandgate, Kent   3. VIII. 03

Dear Lady,

                    A roofer !
The thing cannot be written! Time, I think, must take on the task[?] of dreading the departure of a fellow, embittered & thoroughly damned man on one Thursday & he returns on the next, pink - partly his own & partly reflection from Enid[2] - brilliant, with a beautiful hand resting in one pocket & a programme in the other & his manner full of the next speeches. I've - as I have already said - the gratitude of a lifetime....

Remember me to Bland[3] whose state seems better than it was, to Iris - I think repeatedly of these last beautiful moments. - and to the charming lady whose name I have never been able to grasp but whose mind I dread & admire - to Miss Hintson[?] & the lady I universally beat at Badminton. I've sent <u>The Country of the Blind</u> to Rosamund & my respect to Enid enclosed. Paul (who is [*illegible word*]) greet for me & Jimmy (who is [*illegible word*]) Remember me to Reynolds[?], my fortunate suppliants[?] and there as it is clicking among you all! Remember me to Eric as was John. Yale I know is too light minded to teach me & the older dog too old. (The jackdaw never liked me.) [4]

Fine impalpable threads of speech & associations wail from having to stay away, hold me to your upstairs[?] & you, I maintain bedrooms, take me under the trees of your lawn, and to your garden paths, to the [*illegible word*] seats in the garden & all about you.

It's been a bright clear time.
Yours ever
H G Wells

---

[1] This rather incoherent and hurried letter thanks E. Nesbit, while describing in a surreal way, a significant weekend in Wells's life. He was apparently having some domestic problems, and this weekend enabled him to calm his nerves. Other oblique references to this weekend occur in biographies of E. Nesbit. The holograph is tiny, and the copy from which I worked was extremely difficult to read. Some of the reading is, therefore, conjectural.

[2] Wells, in a slip, called Edith by the name Enid.

[3] Hubert Bland, a Fabian, a writer, and the male head of this remarkable menage. Bland conducted a love affair with the housekeeper in the house, from which union Rosamund Bland was born, while maintaining his relationship with Edith Nesbit. Wells was said to have remarked that this was a household where they needed to choose their beds early. As the letter suggests guests came and went all the time. There are only a few letters to Nesbit from Wells but they all have a certain air of personal interest which is not present in many of his letters. When Doris Langley Moore came to write her *E. Nesbit: A Biography* (London, 1932, revised edition 1966) she visited Wells who read the draft pages dealing with this time, gave her parts of letters to use and read, and withheld others from her, while generally vetting her treatment. Although the revised edition was supposed to restore this material and others, it is a very circumspect work still.

[4] It is difficult to tell whose names are real as in the list of those he mentions are dogs, birds, and humans. Some of the names apparently refer to amateur theatricals which played a part in the weekend. Although the last paragraph is suggestive, it may simply reflect Wells's exuberance as much as his romantic nature. Rosamund Bland is still a girl at this time, but a few years later, she and Wells had a brief affair. There are a few letters which are part of this aspect of Wells life, see volumes 2 and 4.

447. To James B. Pinker

Hofstra, ALS

[Sandgate] Aug 4 '03

My dear Pinker,

I doubt the wisdom of offering the reluctant Brett[1] four books for £1200. I mean I don't think he'd accept. You'd better write at other Americans for offers.

What news of Bertram Walker?

Yours ever,
H.G. Wells

---

[1] The persons mentioned are otherwise unknown American publishers or editors. This Brett, or another of the same name, later worked for Doubleday.

448. To Graham Wallas[1]

LSE, ALS

[Spade House
Sandgate] Aug. 23. 03.

My dear Wallas,

Sep. 1st is Tuesday week. How are we going to fix up things? Will you come along Monday to dinner & shall we start on the 4 boat on Tuesday for Bâle. My times are entirely free just now, there is no work on hand & two or three days earlier or later is all the same to me. I have got all the needed maps.

I suggest the following directions for posting letters. Assume we start on the afternoon of the 1st.

All letters up to & including
First post on the 2cd - to Poste Restante, Saas im Grund
          6th ditto Ariolo
——————— 9th - Illanz
——————— 11th - Ragatz
          All in Switzerland.

Telegrams before these dates to The Hotel, Tosa Falls, <u>Italy.</u>
                              Yours ever,
                                H.G.
These are the only places we are certain of touching.

---

[1] This is the first of several letters concerning the Alpine trek which Wells and Wallas made in 1903. Wells had done the trek before, but Wallas was an inexperienced walker. The two men used the journey to think through several political matters then current, talk about their books and prospects, rest and relax. Both men produced significant works which were influenced by this journey. Fictional versions of it also appear in *A Modern Utopia* (London, 1905) and *The New Machiavelli* (London, 1911).

449. To T. L. Humberstone

Illinois, ANS

Spade House
Sandgate
24. 8. 03

My dear Humberstone,

      Lanterns don't come in for my article.
                              Yours ever,
                                H.G. W.

450. To Graham Wallas

LSE, ALS

Spade House
Sandgate   Aug. 28. 03

If you could come Monday morning, we could start that afternoon. - - or if you could catch the 2:20 I could join you at the boat. In that case book second return to Bâle at Charing Cross.

Dear Wallas,

        Come earlier if you possibly can. Every day counts. Don't bring a second suit, or anything inconvenient to carry. If your mackintosh covers your knees & you have a change of stockings what more <u>can</u> you want?

  I'll get all necessary maps.

  Quinine, cascara, insect powder, sticking plaster.

      Sticks are best bought out there.

There's no means of taking our gear about but our backs.

                      Yours ever,
                        H.G.

You'll find a portable pair of slippers a great comfort in the evening.

451. To Graham Wallas

LSE, ALS

Spade House
Sandgate   [c. 29 August 1903]

Come as early as possible. If possible to catch the 4 boat Sunday. H.G.

Dear Mr. Wallas,

        H.G. wears on the tour Tweed Knickerbocker suit. Flannel shirt Brown boots (string). Hobnails. Tweed cap.

He will take a Knapsack containing
  Slippers
  Blue glasses —
  1 pair stockings —
  waterproof cape
  Panama hat
  Hanckerchief [her spelling]
  Flannel shirt
  Collars
  brush & comb - toilet trifles, bits of sticking plaster etc.   - <u>Flask with brandy</u>.
  Some milk chocolate

Change of underclothes
Medium thick - which can be worn as pyjamas at night.
Carbolic soap, & vaseline for blisters feet advisable - effectual Mackintosh advisable
[*this last sentence in Wells's hand*]

The blue glasses are really necessary. Your letters have crossed evidently - He has written you suggesting you should come here on Monday & set off together. Boat goes at 4 p.m. [*Wells's hand for this last sentence*]
on Tuesday. this day [*these last two words in Wells's hand*]
He will take his ticket at Folkestone Harbour on starting - 2cd class. & 1st on boat.
Give my love to Mrs. Wallas who I hope is making you solemnly promise to walk through Switzerland roped to something safe. Tell [her] S'zerland is a horrid dangerous place - & she is to make you promise to be <u>extremely cautious</u>.
Very sincerely yours,
Catherine Wells.[1]

---

[1] Although these letters may sound a bit like outfitting Tenzing and Hillary for the last stretch of their Mount Everest ascent, Wallas had never done anything like this before and he needed the help of the experienced mountain hand, Wells, who was familiar with the walk.

452. To Catherine Wells

Illinois, ALS

Hotels Glacier de Rhone &
Belvedere
Canton du Valois
Suisse [nr. Grinset]   [? September 1903]

[*The letter masthead has a tiny comment, 'Bins en route for Hospenthal', with a mark high on a map of the valley glacial moraines.*]

D'st Lady Dear,

As we think it will clear up & W. is a little indisposed to start, I have conceded an hour though there you are d lady at Hospenthal waiting to be read - & to fill up what is there to do, of the slightest sense except d lady to write to you. I haven't had a bad time altogether & most instructive. W. is a great cowardly calf full of queer base ways & that sort of thing & going about with him like this one gets to know him to the marrow. The intimacy of travel together helps one to value the sort of thing a wife has to stand, & when I listen to his twaddle (he has about 50 Pilgrim's Way things in constant circulation) or observe his constant lapses into petty selfishness or mark the queer curiosities that have arisen between him and Audrey, to learn his appropriations & shortcomings, I fink ——.[1] It is heart searchings. I fink of all the moments of silence, you, poor dear, must have had. Please God there may be a blessing upon this Journey, & that I may be a more eloquent husband to you for all the rest of my life. (I shall use W. freely in the next novel.) [2]

And dear Bits, these poor creatures do not depend on each other as we do. W. is in no hurry to arrive at Hospenthal, & I - I haven't 'ad a touch of you & nothing of you since we got your little postcard at Saas - um - Grund.[3] Nothing of you at all! But all [missing word] I have been making the journey the better by noting half way & things so that the most dear lady will be able to look over it all when we do it really next year without our fatigue. All sorts of things I've noted down & gone past. I wouldn't go up the Eggishorn, & wouldst to go up the glacier to the C[?] Hut or anything like that because they meant extra days, I can do them just as well with you. D. Bits it's very lovely here in lots of places, & I only in a sort of intellectual way perceive it, but some day next year I shall come with my real organ of aesthetic enjoyment & watch it while it considers things too lovely for words. D'old freckled little face. The only value of a fing like the glaciers hard by is just to make your d'old freckled face look pleased. Outside just now was a thing you would have liked ever so - a rainbow.

[Wells provides a little sketch of the Rhone valley, as it appeared with misty rain, & heavy clouds over the glacier.]

(Also I have drunk lots of beer. But all the time I couldn't stop finking 'ow you would have 'njoyed seeing me drink that beer.)

I shall come home close after this letter.

Dearest love to you, Mater Bits. Dear Bits.

---

[1] Wells often reverted to a sort of baby talk, or to a Cockney accent, when writing to his wives and sweethearts. This is an example. Apparently Wallas had wanted to talk about his relationship with Audrey, his wife.

[2] Wallas appears in *A Modern Utopia* (1905) as the botanist and in *The New Machiavelli* (1911) as Willersley.

[3] This was a planned postal stop for the trip, as were Ariolla, Illanz and Ragatz.

453. To Sidney Low[1]

PLS

Spade House
Sandgate   15. 9. 03.

My dear Low,

I have just read your "Henley" on my return from a tramp in Switzerland and really you know it takes me even more than your "Rhodes"! - partly because I knew the sitter. I am not a cultured gent and without authority but it seems to me that your opening four pages and the pictorial touches throughout couldn't possibly have been better written anyhow and that the passages about Stevenson and the N.O. are a little grey only by comparison. But I hesitate to praise where frankly I feel outclassed. There you are! I perceive a book now quite clearly. For my own taste I would have it illustrated. Nicholson's Rhodes might do and Rothenstein's[2] and Nicholson's Henley.[3]

Yours ever,
H.G.

---

[1] Another letter from Chapman-Huston's biography of Low, p. 93, see letter 419. The article on Henley (1849–1903) appeared in the *Cornhill* in September 1903.
[2] William Rothenstein (1872–1945), a neighbour of Wells, was an important portrait artist. Wells wrote an introduction to an exhibit of his work focusing on India in 1911, *Catalogue of Drawings Made in India*. For letters to him see volumes 2 and 3.
[3] Nicholson (1872–1949) did the 'Henley' which hangs in the National Portrait Gallery, see Wells's letter to Henley 392 on his views of the portrait.

454. To E. Nesbit[1]

ALS

[Spade House
Sandgate, Kent]   September 17, 1903

Dear Mrs. Bland,

The stories are good and gay and I've liked the book immensely. They are a game and a very pretty game and all sorts of people will do their little talks more carefully on account of them, and with little plagiarisms more or less carefully handled. They hang queerly and pleasantly between the blood and racket of this sensual life. They are not the heady stuff of Romance nor that reality that cuts to the bone, but they are quite delightful Young Fancies.

Yours ever,
H.G. Wells

---

[1] From Doris Langley Moore, *E. Nesbit: A Biography* (London, 1932, rev. ed, 1966), pp. 102–4. I am quoting this letter exactly as it appears in this biography, but all details may not be as in the original. Wells chose the letters to appear in this book and vetted the pages which concerned him and his relationships with members of the Bland entourage. This letter concerns a collection of children's stories oddly entitled *The Literary Scene* (London: Methuen, 1903).

455. To Rudolf Cyrian[1]

Illinois, ALS

Spade House
Sandgate   19. 9. 03

Dear Sir,

I know that about the P.O. guide — but test it!
Yours sincerely,
H.G. Wells

Rudolf Cyrian, Esq.

---

[1] Wells exchanged letters with this unknown person on several occasions in these years, see letters 389 and 416. The spelling of his name seems to vary in Wells's writing.

456. To T. L. Humberstone

Illinois, ALS

National Liberal Club
Whitehall Place, S.W.   Sep. 22. 03

Dr. Mr. Humberstone,

    I'm sorry to say I've no money to invest. And had I, with Consols going begging at 88 3/4 & everything in proportion - you know, you're coming on the market at the wrong time.

                                                Yours very sincerely,
                                                     H.G. Wells

457. To the Editor, *Daily Chronicle*[1]

PLS

[Spade House
Sandgate]   [mid-September 1903]

    Sir, It is an excellent general rule that an author should not reply to a review of his work, however unfavourable and unfair, but in the case of your notice of my "Mankind in the Making", it seems to me that the limits of endurance are passed. Your reviewer leaves me sore and exasperated, and I will not deprive him of the little personal triumph of that admission; my motive in writing is to point out that to attain this end he has found it necessary to depart with vigour and freedom from the truth about the book. It is one that has been written with seriousness and sincerity; it appeals, very particularly, to that section of the public touched by "The Daily Chronicle", and to let judgment go by default in this instance would be to carry the dignity of authorship altogether too far.

    When a man discusses, as I have done in this book, the grounds of his general attitude towards social and political questions, he must necessarily touch on many divergent issues, and I suppose it is legitimate for your reviewer to gather together this allusion and that illustration, cutting out the explanatory bridges between them, in order to convey the impression that the book is a disorderly gabble at large. But, it is not legitimate, however anxious he may be to discredit me as a flightly inconsequent creature, to quote half a sentence from p. 102, to raise an objection to answer, "Pooh! the objection is dismissed in a sentence", and then to misquote one sentence extracted from the discussion of a quite different issue altogether on p. 176, as though I had indeed dismissed this objection in this manner. After which your reviewer, with an irresistible escape of taunting bitterness, breaks out into "It's as easy as inventing the Invisible Man! Weave 'em all into the complex!"

Nor is it legitimate to give with a fine air of summary projects that I sketch out simply to illustrate how little we have exhausted political possibilities, to stifle my repudiations and qualifications, and to present me as in a mood of glib finality expounding these as a gospel. He quotes the rawest looking package from a sort of stamped tin model of a system of jury election I propound and writes: "For him there are no dilemmas. He has a beautiful scheme ready to his hand." Now how are your readers to know that I write: "This suggestion is advanced here in this concrete form merely to show the sort of thing that might be done ... But even in this state of crude suggestion, it is submitted that it does serve to show the practicability of a method of election more deliberate and thorough," etc.?

Throughout his review, your reviewer, pursuing his unknown ends, plays me this trick of deliberate misrepresentation. He declares I have a "nice little plan for remodelling the House of Lords. County councils are to elect earls, doctors and engineers are to create dukes." One must question whether he belongs to that class that cannot justly apprehend or to that which cannot securely convey. The book runs: "Let us simply for tangibleness put the thing in a concrete plan." and in what follows there is no mention of country councils and of doctors and engineers, thus, "There is no reason why certain great constituencies, the medical calling, the engineers, should not specifiy one or two of their professional leaders, their 'dukes.'" From which your reviewer emerges with this poor bent jest: "When your doctor is called in to feel your pulse he will tell you whether you are a suitable candidate for a dukedom."

And so on down the column runs this strain of falsification ... I have thought my best and done what I can to set it forth, and I want my book to be read. It is intolerable that I should submit to the injury in the eyes of your readers an unchallenged acceptance of this review entails.

Yours very sincerely,
H.G. Wells

---

[1] When Wells returned from his walking tour of the Alps with Graham Wallas he found that his new book of philosophical analysis, *Mankind in the Making*, had been treated in the *Daily Chronicle* in a frivolous way – that is by a critic who called for Wells to return to fiction, and leave this kind of writing to others. He responded to the review on 21 September 1903 under the title 'The New Utopia'. His reviewer countered in the same column, essentially unrepentant, as when he remarked, 'In my presumptive judgment, Mr. Wells is a better romancer than sociologist.'

THE LETTERS: 1880-1903

458. To Israel Zangwill

Central Zionist Archives,
Jerusalem, Typed Transcription
File A420/614

Spade House,
Sandgate   24 - 9. 03

Dear Mr. Zangwill,

Very many thanks for your New Year Greeting. I would very greatly like to meet you. Would you come to lunch with me at the National Liberal Club on Oct. 6th at one?

Yours sincerely,
H.G. Wells

459. To Israel Zangwill

Central Zionist Archives,
Jerusalem, Typed Transcription
File A420/614

Spade House,   Sep 28/03
Sandgate

Dear Mr. Zangwill,

I'm sorry indeed to miss meeting you but a time will come - and sorrier even though it's nothing serious for the reason. I can't believe it's absolute levity takes you into that nursing home.

Excuse this pencil, but my fountain pen is in hospital and I can't write with the other pen that's about.

With my best wishes to you,
Yours ever sincerely,
H.G Wells.

460. To George Trevelyan[1]

Illinois, ALS

Spade House
Sandgate   Oct. 9. 03

Dear Mr. Trevelyan

That series of articles has quite definitely shaped and I can tell you all about it now. They will run from 8 to 10 in number & with an average length of five or six thousand words. But I'll tell you these things when I see you. I've waved a hand at prices, if you remember & you said I think that £400 would not overwhelm you. I'm quite willing to settle at that.

I shall be in London on the 16th & my lunch time is free - can you lunch at the N.L.C. that day?

Yours very sincerely
H.G. Wells

---

[1] Probably the senior Trevelyan, George Otto (1838–1928). He was a politician, member of Parliament, holding several Cabinet offices and, in later life, a historian. They may be discussing the serialization of *A Modern Utopia*, although it is also possible that this refers to a series of articles, 'From A Study Fireside', which appeared from March to May 1904. There is an outside chance that this refers to *Mankind in the Making*, but the timing seems too late for that.

461. To J. Treat[1]

Illinois, ALS

Spade House
Sandgate   Oct. 14. 03

Dear Sir,

I know little of publishers - dealing with them mostly through an agent - but if you'd like to send that chapter you speak of I will ask someone who knows better than I what he thinks of its possibilities.

Yours very sincerely,
H. G. Wells

---

[1] Treat is unknown.

THE LETTERS: 1880-1903

462. To Graham Wallas

LSE, ALS

National Liberal Club
Whitehall Place, S.W.   Oct. 15/03

My dear Wallas,

    I didn't intend that nomination to take effect before the new year but I'll write the Sec'y to that effect & head it off. The books testify to a most excellent excursion - & Jane shall return them before Monday. Everything goes well with us. The same to you.

                          Yours ever,
                          H.G.

463. To Graham Wallas

LSE, AL

Spade House
Sandgate   [date unknown]

To Graham Wallas, Esq.

Move on Sir? But there was a gentleman Sir, said I should be let in Sir, if I'd wait a minute Sir. Seemingly I went to sleep Sir.

464. To Ralph Mudie-Smith[1]

Hofstra, ALS

[Sandgate] Oct. 17. 03

Dear Sir,

I am really very greatly obliged to you for the manuscript of Dr. Clifford's sermon. I find it difficult to express [the] interest and in effect the intense gratification it is for me to find my book so generously entertained. Few people have had as much reason as I have had lately, to appreciate the fine & fearless catholicity of the modern nonconformity.

Yours very sincerely,
H.G. Wells

---

[1] This letter is barely legible. Dr John Clifford, whose sermon Wells was reading, was a leading London nonconformist minister who refused to pay his school board rates, used in part to support Anglican schools. This created a serious problem for the Fabians, who had made gains in the school board elections, for Clifford was a Fabian. Eventually Stuart Headlam, also a Fabian, resigned his school board position. Later Wallas, who was opposed to religiously supported education for public schools, resigned from the Fabian Society, as they sided with Clifford, urging continued partial funding of religious education. Mudie-Smith was a collaborator, adviser and confidant of Wells at the time of the imbroglio in the Fabian Society. He and Wells met often to discuss sociological ideas and strategy.

465. To Ralph Mudie-Smith

Hofstra, ALS

Spade House
Sandgate Oct. 23. 03

Dear Sir,

I should very greatly appreciate an opportunity of meeting Dr. Clifford, but I hope you will not think me ungracious if I tell you I would rather it happened somewhen after the second week in November. My wife is not in very good health just now & I want to be home with her as much as I possibly can & I cut my time in London just now as closely as possible.

Yours very sincerely
H.G. Wells

R. Mudie-Smith, Esq.

466. To Sarah Wells

Illinois, ALS

Spade House
Sandgate   Oct. 31, 03

My dear little Mother,

The new little boy seems to be a great success.[1] He weighed ten pounds at birth, which is nearly a pound more than Gip, did and he has I think a more powerful howl. We think of calling him Frank after his uncle. He is at present interesting rather than beautiful & with a lot of very fair hair. Amy is doing very well. We have Mrs. Corcoran, the same nurse as before & an Irishwoman. She has come to us from the Harmsworth household - the Harmsworths who own so many papers.

We got the workmen, who have been making a nursery in the roof, out of the house a week ago. None too soon!

You must come along and see your two grandchildren as soon as the spring gets warm. Frank is welcome any time he likes to come and now the rooms are in the roof there is always room for him.

Love from us all to all of you,
Yr. Affectionate Son
Bertie

---

[1] Wells's and Catherine's second child, Frank, was born on 31 October 1903.

467. To J. B. Pinker

Hofstra, ADL [early November 1903]

[On a letter, located at Hofstra, dated 28 October 1903 from E. L. Ross, editor of a magazine called The Traveller *published both in America and England, asking Wells to write an article which would deal with the matters discussed in* Mankind in the Making, *Wells wrote]*:

Dear J.B. If this came to you, [ask] £50 per thousand for an article not less than 2500 words.[1]

---
[1] If he wrote this article, it has not been located.

468. To C. W. Adams[1]

Boston, ALS

Spade House
Sandgate   2 - 11 - 03

My Dear Sir,

     You ask just the question I find most difficulty in answering. The eighth paper in Mankind in the Making[2] will shape my ignorance. I don't think there is a general rule to go upon. Knowledge the natural way is for knowledge to grow step by step between thirteen & eighteen in the case of western whites. In a complex growth nothing can make simple. If you have any views or ideas I'd be glad to know them.

Yours sincerely
H. G. Wells
Novelist

---
[1] Who Adams was is not known.
[2] This chapter, entitled 'The Cultivation of the Imagination', is Wells's effort to understand and describe the first phases of cognitive learning.

469. To Ralph Mudie-Smith

Hofstra, ALS

[Sandgate] Nov. 5. 03

Dear Sir,

  I shall be in London on Tuesday next and if it is possible for me to meet Dr. Clifford then I shall be very glad to do so. I shall be dining in London on Monday night & other things being equal I should like to leave London by the 9 p.m. from Charing X on Tuesday at latest, but I have no other engagements yet for that day. If, however, Dr. Clifford is not available on Tuesday I could stop overnight for Wednesday. (I have a room in Clement's Inn) and I expect now to be coming to London fairly frequently for a time - if neither Tuesday nor Wednesday will suit your convenience.
        Yours very sincerely,
        H. G. Wells

470. To Henry Newbolt[1]

Hofstra, ALS

Union Society
Oxford   Nov. 9. 03

My Dear Newbolt,

  I have just read to the Philosophical Society of this most amiable & hospitable place a little paper called '<u>Skepticism of the Instrument</u>' which they seem to think rather a lark. It's a little in the way of 'Pragmatism' the new doctrine expounded by Schiller & Co., sometimes with them & sometimes joggling them in their stomachs if you follow me. Would you care to have it for the <u>New Review</u>?[2] It is about 3000 words & no Pinker intervenes. It's in the lecture form of course, with apologies & an allusion or so.
        Yours ever,
        H. G. Wells

[1] Henry Newbolt was editor of the *Monthly Review*.
[2] In the event, the piece did not appear in *The New Review*, but in *Mind*, July 1904, pp 379–93. A slightly abridged version appeared as an appendix to *A Modern Utopia*. as well as another shortened version in *First and Last Things*. Pinker was still his agent at this time, but Wells was soon to go to A. P. Watt for these services.

471. To H. A. Jones[1]

Texas, Typed Transcription

Spade House
Sandgate   Nov. 10. 03.

Dear Mr. Jones,

     I am unhappily unable to get to Shaw's on Friday to meet you at lunch (though I hope it will not be long before I do meet you again) and in his letter I learn for the first time that he has intercepted and kept a copy of Metchnikoff, you meant me to read. That's your Socialist all over! Meanwhile I have read and re-read the English translation.
          My sincere & belated thanks to you,
              Yours very sincerely,
                 H.G. Wells

[1] This is the first letter I have seen addressed to H. A. Jones, (1851–1929) a playwright, author and friend of Bernard Shaw's. He and Wells had a long relationship which ranged through different degrees of friendship, see letters in volumes 3 and 4.

472. To H. A. Jones

Texas, Typed Transcription

The Reform Club   [c. 1903]

My dear Jones,

     I haven't written plays for a number of reasons, but one of the chief of these was the persuasion that my work might in the end be made abortive by the incalculable whim of the Censor. His recent obstinate campaign against Shaw does, I think, justify my discretion.

          Yours very sincerely,
          H.G. Wells

[*On the bottom of this transcript is a Wells holograph letter to Jones's daughter which appears in volume 4 of this edition. A second copy of the transcription is annotated by Wells as the transcriber had had a difficult time reading his writing.*]

473. To the Librarian, Zoological Society

Korn, APCS

[London - prepaid
postcard]   [*c.* 1903]

Regret I was prevented from coming up today with <u>Saunder's British Birds</u>, but it shall be sent tomorrow (Thursday, i.e.). I have not sent it by post as bindings sometimes get hurt that way.

          Faithfully yours,
          H.G.W.

474. To Henry Newbolt

Hofstra, ALS

Spade House
Sandgate   Nov. 14, 03

My dear Newbolt,

  I'm sorry I wrote '<u>New Review</u>' for 'Monthly' but then I knew you were going to say I was indistinguishable from Kidd[1]- & I am sorry now that I did not put '<u>Review of Reviews</u>'.
 I won't risk a rejected communication.
         Yours ever,
         H.G Wells

[1] Wells was influenced by the work of Benjamin Kidd, especially his book *Social Evolution* and frequently recommended his work to others. The journals that he mentions do not contain anything written by Wells at this time. Wells had offered Newbolt the piece read before the Oxford Philosophical Society, but either Newbolt rejected it or the Society, which published *Mind*, may have had a first refusal on the piece. This also may, however, simply be a piece of Wellsian humour.

475. To Ralph Mudie-Smith

Hofstra, ACCS

Spade House
Sandgate   Nov. 14. 03

Dear Mr. Mudie-Smith,

I am now very much freer than I was, and entirely at your disposal for a meeting with Dr. Clifford, but if you can fix it up so as to save me a special journey to London I shall be glad. I have to come up for a dinner on the 19th, & a lunch, afternoon meeting & dinner on the 20th. & I shall also be up for the Royal Soc'y dinner on the 30th.
                    Yours sincerely
                    H.G. Wells
Also up for dinner on Dec. 14th.

[*On the verso of the card, in another hand are the words '1 o'clock Wednesday'*]

476. To Edward Garnett

Texas, ALS

Sandgate   Begun somewhen three
                            weeks ago or so - &
                            then lost owing to
                            domestic crisis,
                            finished Nov. 19th 1903

My dear Garnett,

I'm just through with 'Light & Shadow' & I found it altogether a most interesting & curious book. I'm in pain tonight & it's kept me reading all the time up to midnight. It's curiously ill done at places, reads like a very literal & conscientious translation of something extraordinarily good. The miracles for example were never done with the telling epithet, the mere glancing deflection of the phrase, always with 'like a ——'. To me the vein of feeling - which is the essential of the book - is foreign. I've imagined such phases in my adolescence, but never to the pitch of really having them. I know they are had. A negro, a Revivalist, certain sorts of Germans, would resonate to the pitch of it all perfectly. It's, as I think you told me, a complete temperamental picture. It's curious how entirely I haven't 'been there', & how entirely I believe what you tell me of emotion in the book. I've lived & lusted, been jealous, with & without cause, done I think most of the things & all on a different palette of colours, on a largely different instrument with a different Klang-tint, (I think they call it) The thing most remote from me is Driscoll's rebound from a sense of personal worry to a sense of unusual injustice.

This aversion to the women after achievement is also simply not to my pattern - Bernard Shaw evidently has it. And finally the book dates. Altogether it's a most interesting document and one I'm extremely glad you 've let me see. Why afterwards didn't you go on? You must have been young enough when you did it, not to have thought it a final test.

When am I to have that primer letter from Mrs. Garnett? We have added a son to the world since this letter was begun & he, poor little chap, has done his best to get out of things again, but I think we have him now all right. He went & got his intestines blocked with some curded milk. Mrs. Wells is doing well, and we shall probably be in London together for a few days in the first or second week in December. How is Mrs. Garnett now? We think very often of her & her threatened sight & hope against the threat.[1]

Yours ever,
H. G. Wells

[1] The bottom of the second page of this letter is filled with smudged pencilled comments on Wells's remarks by Garnett.

477. To an unknown addressee

Editor's collection, ALS

Spade House   20 - 11 - 03

Dear Sir:

    I took my degree at the London University in 1890. I like less & less to give biographical details as I grow older and if you will forgive me I will not answer your other questions.

                    Yours Sincerely,
                    H.G. Wells.

478. To James Welch[1]

Illinois, ALS

G.W.R.[2]   Saturday
                                                                  [date unknown, postmarked
                                                                  Nov 21, 03.]

Mr. James Welch, Esq. of 4 Verulam, [?] Grey's Inn.

Dear Mr. Welch,

    I suppose you are still glowing luminously from that transplant drink[?] of yours.

    Can I trouble you to send me your copy of that scenario we made? I want to show it to a cousin of mine next week.

                    Yours ever,
                    H.G. Wells

Homage to Mrs. Welch.

[1] Welch (1865–1917) was an actor who was strongly identified with the Stage Society, where he was one of three persons on the Executive Committee. The Stage Society produced many plays for one or two performances as a test for the play, and whether the censor might intervene. Welch played in *Arms and the Man* and other plays by Shaw. His interpretations of Ibsen characters were significant as well.

[2] Possibly 'Great Western Railway' and the letter was written on the train.

479. To Edmund Gosse

Leeds, ACCS

Spade House
Sandgate   Nov. 26. 03

My dear Gosse,

    I am in a state of vehement discontent with all my American publishers, agents, reviewers, critics. Do you know anything of that marvelous disorderly continent? Are there any respectable people there at all, over & above Howells & William James? I want to get in touch with the American library world, if any. I want an intelligent American publisher as a final outcome of these inquiries. I want to be done properly. Who is it knows all about these things? To whom ought I to go? I've left these things to Pinker too long & I perceive something has to be done. I think even of going to America. But who are the people I ought to see?

                                    Yours ever,
                                    H.G. Wells

I hurl these impassioned inquiries with a sort of abandoned confidence in your good nature.

480. To Theodore Bartholomew[1]

Boston, ALS

Spade House
Sandgate   Dec. 2. 03

Dear Sir,
 I am very greatly obliged to you for your useful note upon my book. I am sometimes inclined to think that the difficulties I have tried to meet in my book by suggesting multiplicate library copies may be met in the future rather by expanding cheap book production & by everyone owning the books they read.
                                    Yours sincerely,
                                    H.G. Wells

---

[1] Bartholomew is not known. He had written to Wells about chapter 9 in *Mankind in the Making* on 'Higher Education', which is a long disquisition on delivery of knowledge, and the possibility of inexpensive paper backed editions of books for everyday use.

481. To Edmund Gosse[1]

Leeds, ALS

[London]   Dec. 3, 03

My dear Gosse,

 I've heard no more of Algernon Gissing[2] but I fancy it was a case of chronic financial debility & that the ambition was a sinecure. But I will try & get discreetly into touch with the case & let you know. I have someone else on my mind in the shape of Mrs. Cobban. She's a plucky and capable woman, a good housewife, & a laundress and cook & I think she will be able to get along reasonably well, if only she can get a clear start. I went through a domestic budget with her, & I think from £100 to £150 would do much there. Dunn has raised about £30 in & about the M.P. & I've beaten up a few people & have got from five of them £19 with a hope of more from some still silent. I believe this case has already been before the R.L.F., [3] but if Pugh deserved £75, she ought to have £7500.

I answer this at length to your interrogations, but now let me thank you most warmly for your advice about America. I just know Appletons - I don't know any American publisher because I'm Pinkered. I find Pinker pays excellently as a means of serializing things & selling stories, but books is different. For books you must have good publishers & stick to your publishers. I've got that settled on here & if any American problems of a grave & respectable sort would come directly to me with grave & respectable proposals to do me outright I'd be as open to them as a paddock to the light of day. And if you know the Appletons & would give them a hint of as much, you would do me the greatest of services.

I'm so glad you like my stories.

Yours ever,
H.G. Wells

---

[1] Portions of this letter, especially the first page, are written very faintly and are virtually unreadable. It is an important letter however as it not only shows how widely the Gissing situation was an issue, but it also sheds light on the relationship of authors, editors and agents in this period, and the significant role played by critics such as Edmund Gosse.

[2] Brother of George Gissing, and virtually unknown today, although he wrote a dozen novels about the lower middle class in England in this period. The issue is the creation of a pension for Gissing's children from the Royal Literary Fund. Gosse essentially made these decisions, although he was responsible to a supervisory body.

[3] Royal Literary Fund, which granted pensions to authors and their heirs who were in financial straits. Gosse had much to do with it, as did Edward Clodd, both of whom knew Gissing, and were well aware of the needs, and Wells's efforts to solve the problems of the estate.

482. To Mr Everett

Hofstra, ALS

Spade House
Sandgate   Dec. 4. 03.

My dear Everett,[1]

    My face is at your service. Can your man bring his own light & do the trick at my room (6 Clements Inn) on Wednesday, 16th Dec. at 5?
                          Yours ever,
                          H.G.

---

[1] A photographer no doubt.

483. To Catherine Wells

Illinois, ALS

The Playgoers Club
6, Clement's Inn
The Strand, W.C.   Dec. 16, 03

Dst Person,

    I'm a remorseful & sad Binder this morning, with a general feeling of 'aving frown fings[1] at the only person worth loving in the world. But I was piled up on to yesterday & reely that wasn't quite workable that scheme of yours, though I can quite understand it looked a lovely solution (& may do so still to you) but it isn't & wasn't & won't reely if you'll take my poor word for it & forgive any injustice I've done to that excellent (but entirely different from us, Thank God!), Burkes. I'd rather get the thing absolutely off my mind, but I'll go over it with you, rather than have a little sore place left. But even this morning I feel as though the top of my head might blow out at any moment if I go on with this, & that might be bad manners even in the Playgoers Club. The Blind story has vanished under a turbid flow but I'm trying to hold to a project (still inchoate) for getting hold of Houghton Mifflin or the <u>Atlantic Monthly</u> for the N. Utopia. I want any poor workable scrap of cerebral lobe to go on with that - which is after all the most important thing. We've quite got the upper hand of the Windsor party, I'm sure we could squeeze them very tight if we choose, but it is not worth while & I'm still a little against extreme measures & I shall go the £450 for peace - an absolute finish & peace. Phew! That's off - anyhow. I was fotographed by an ass of a photographer at 5 yesterday & afterward bathed & lightened up for Webbs. Came off better there than I expected & I think talked well. Walked across St James's Park to Savile with MacKinder talking fiscalities, meant to write to you & fell in with that Oxford Hegelian Webb & talked myself blind & deaf - & clean forgot your letter. Spent the night in imaginary conversations & have just breakfasted (about 11 a.m.) Why in God's name do I accept the invitation of that ass Fenn? That dear Cartie[?] is my principal trouble now.

The Lewisham & Dulwich election have amazed everyone. I shall write a Martian sort of story for the express purpose of settling accounts with L & D.[2]

My warmest love to you, P.C.B.[3] & don't think me an outrageous squasher of Hopes. But what we want before all things is a household we can leave with a tranquil mind, at any time, without any <u>chance</u> of explosive or disrupting elements. I don't think it have proved to be that. If that Mee creature is suitable and quite trustworthy, I think he'd be less irritating & more calculable than a brisk young German. You can have him in the house half the time. I really don't see why, too, we shouldn't wait on ourselves at table, but of course you know better than I do about these things. I don't see why we shouldn't be a little original in our table methods, but perhaps that wouldn't work. It would free our table talk from a certain restraint, if we did wait on ourselves. And cooks I know are hard to get, but don't you think that for an extra £5 a year, you might get something more helpful & intelligent than Bessie? And with respect to all these things, we want <u>not perfection</u> but a working compromise. We want perfection in my work (& we don't get it), but for these incidental things, peace & good humour & a controlled expenditure & a feeling of confidence that there will be no surprises. Model housekeeping isn't our business, but model literary production. We want good understandable contented servants who will do the work reasonably well, & a home that nods along. You put a sort of artistic anxiety into your home management, a constructive & reconstructive solicitude that keeps the home far too sharply focussed. Provide against disaster, of course, but for the rest, keep on shifting control & responsibility on to your servants, pay 'em well if they take it on. & don't worry - don't worry. What the Devil does it matter if Mrs. Sidney Buxton, for example, has a house & household in perfect working order?

Probably she has. But I'm not Sidney Buxton, ('orrible idea.). What does it matter if Newton Abbey does miracles of domestic economy? I don't want to slave for Harmsworth and die in Ladysmith. The Webb household outshines yours - it does. Simply because the Webbs are compared with us limited & stupid & vulgar people. My house is not made with hands, my success, our success is not to be measured by material things, our reality is dreamland & the unseen. My dear, dear wife & helper, do keep in mind, say it over to yourself night & morning like a prayer, that whatever you do or fail to do, in the housekeeping & house managing line, or whatever we fail to do, or succeed in doing in financial affairs, clever house management & all the things of the manor, in reality these are incidental & secondary things. They don't deserve to break your rest of nights, there's a waste & tax of heart & brain that are made for better things. They signify a little more than patience or chess (which we abandoned cheerfully some years ago) but not so very much more.

Yours ever - very tenderly reely, my dear

Bins

Don't lets be like wasted champagne.
Keep cool & keep your cork in, & think silly little things.

Keep this beast for a week & then I'll amuse him. He's the brother of Jamie Alsung & no more my first cousin than —— Fenn. Harrison's badinage about our address has reminded me of T.E.B. Oakley, at his best'. [4]

---

[1] As is often the case Wells reverts to a sort of baby talk when writing to his wife and sweethearts. This usually occurs when relationships are strained, as in this letter. There is a Wells essay in *Pall Mall Gazette*, 4 December 1894 entitled 'In the Library: Some Reflections on a Married Couple', which is a discussion of baby talk between husbands and wives.
[2] It is not clear whether Wells ever followed up on this idea.
[3] He frequently uses this as a pet name for her. No meaning has been elucidated. The first letter could stand for 'Poor' as he was very apt to use 'poor' and 'little' as adjectives when addressing

women, such as his mother, his wives or his lovers. He also uses 'poor' for men occasionally, but almost always when they were dependent on him, or when he is discussing them with someone else. This last use is less frequent.

[4] Fenn, Oakley and Alsung are unknown persons, but apparently individuals Wells saw at his club or elsewhere. Readers of this letter will want to compare its contents with another letter from 1914 which has a somewhat different sense of household, see volume 2. This letter was addressed to 'Jane' at Spade House, while the other, eleven years later, was addressed to Easton Glebe, which is also of some importance in the equation. With its eight pages in his tiny script, this letter is one of the longest holograph letters still extant. Under the mental anxieties, of course, lie the sexual anxieties, for both persons. The script is minuscule, as it often became when he was under personal stress. It is a letter best read with a magnifying glass, and one wonders how Catherine read it. It is very significant, I believe, that although there are letters from Wells to Catherine while he was travelling, these powerful and extremely personal discussions also took place through letters although they were seeing each other much of the time; apparently the letters, not face-to-face meetings, were the only way he could gauge the strength of their feelings. Some of her letters to him are similar, filled with a restrained intensity. They appear in the Appendix. It seems remarkable that these two, so open in so many ways, still found it difficult to be direct, and chose to discuss such matters by post.

484. To Frank C. Wells[1]

Illinois, ALS

Spade House
Sandgate

[not known, but probably 1903]

My dear Frank,

The missis wants to come home because

(i) Her <u>Churchman's Magazine</u> hasn't come & there is the next quarter to pay. Do you mind sending the obscene rag on & paying for it & telling her you have done so.

(ii) She wants warmer underclothing & neither Daddy nor Frank could find it. Dare you find it & send it on.

(iii) There is a winter dress wants trimming. Can you send that too, <u>stylishly packed</u>?

Love to you both,
Bertie

[*in Catherine Wells's hand*]:

I send this note of your own, just to remind H.G. Esq. how impossible it is to get any workable ideas into Mrs. Joseph's noddle. The G.V. has explained [in his] last letter to her respecting joint ownership & she thinks it much better to "stay quiet" until the spring. G.V. very cleverly set before her the enormous - cost to you - of Frank's mad ideas - of course nothing at all will be done. Ask yourself how a business idea would work with Joseph Sarah & Bert. There would be a grey deed - and don't forget it - about the first 10 minutes. Can't you put the question to Mrs S. yourself. Just enquire if she will sell. On terms of last spring. It's quite useless our writing. Hope all is well. Missus for a pail & happy.

---

[1] This letter concerning Sarah Wells's visit to Spade House comprises four pages, two by Wells and two in Catherine Wells's hand. I date it 1903 because I believe this is the last visit she paid to her son before she died in early 1904. The next letter is probably related to this one as well. Sarah was able to visit her grandsons, and there are several photographs of her and Wells from the visit.

485. To Sarah Wells

Illinois, ACCS

Spade House
Sandgate   [probably late 1903]

My dear little Mother,

    It's all right - cheer up. I'm in no hurry if you are not.
                Yours ever lovingly,
                    Bertie

486. To Edmund Gosse[1]

Leeds, ALS

[London] [probably 1903]

My Dear Gosse,

I've been extravagantly delighted by some praise I've found over your signature. I do really value your good opinion of my work.
Very many thanks
Yours ever
H.G. Wells

---

[1] This letter could have been written earlier than 1903, but the location of its filing and the use of 'yours ever' suggest 1903 rather than 1898–1901.

487. To Israel Zangwill

Central Zionist Archives,
Jerusalem, ALS
File A420/614.

[London] [perhaps 1903?]

My dear Zangwill,

Yes, I admit the Darkest Russia paper does not confine its list of Russian wickedness to the grievances of the Jews. But do grasp one idea about me. I am not a Christian. I am a gentile which is a purely negative expression but I am not a Christian. I hate Christian partisanship quite as much as I hate Jewish partisanship. Hits at Christians fly rather wide of me.[1]
Yours ever,
H.G.

---

[1] Wells was careful to make this distinction between his own beliefs and those of Christians all his life. In addition he disliked aggressive nationalisms of any kind, including Zionism. He exchanged letters with both Zangwill and Chaim Weizmann on these topics later; see letters in volume 4. Wells had apparently made a comment on Zangwill's book, *Darkest Russia* (London: Macmillan, 1902) to which Zangwill took some exception.

488. To Henry Newbolt

Hofstra, AL

The Mermaid
Rye   4:30 p.m. [Sometime between 1903-6][1]

Reeves the good & Wells the witty,
Safely come to Rye, (how pretty!)
Wretched Newbolt greatly
                      pity,
Cornered in that damned
                      Committee
Cursing it and London City.
Serve him right!!
  So ends the ditty   p.t.o.

[*Page two*]

[*Page three*]

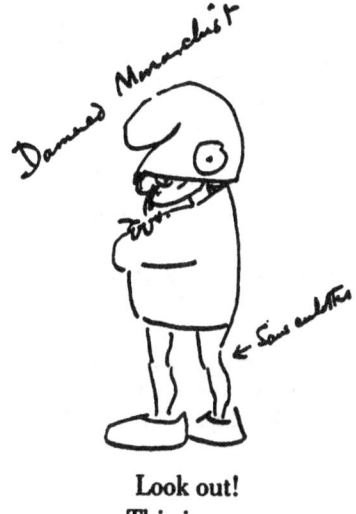

Look out!
<u>This is me</u>.

[*Page four has a small sketch which is entitled: A Lanterne So Perish all <u>Monarchists</u>*]

[*Page five has another small sketch: 'I'm not the only one'*]

[*Page six*]   Wells the good & Reeves the poet
tired, jolly — and don't they know it!

---

[1] The first page of this letter is not in Wells's hand, so what we are probably looking at is a joint effort of Wells and Pember Reeves.

489. To an unknown addressee[1]

Illinois, ADLS

[London] [c. December 1903]

Dear Sir,[2]

    I'm glad you liked the article. It was an impulse. I would certainly quote[?] your shift about the S[chool] B[oard] - if I understood the issues. But,

I don't beyond a column of scolding for [what] has happened & Creed was [illegible word]. I could do so nobly. And its too late to restate the principles of the contest. Besides - I've my own all too difficult work. That article was a lapse not a central point. The B[oard] schools are our most efficient schools. If I do get loose again I much prefer to get loose with secondary and higher teachers.

Yours faithfully,
H.G.Wells

---

[1] Wells was good about responding to people who commented on his social and political work, unless the volume of correspondence was overwhelming. I have included some of his responses as further evidence of his thinking and his personality.

[2] This letter is a handwritten draft written across a letter from the *Daily Mail* of 18 November 1903. It refers to a series which Wells wrote entitled 'From a Study Fireside', which discusses the content of religious education in board schools, among other matters.

490. To an unknown correspondent[1]

Illinois, AL

[Address unknown] [*c.* 1902-3]

I thought it would cheer you up a bit to know I've got this influenza Something aweful. I'm incapable of anything but this. I torment[?] you because it only became better on today. As I can think of nothing to do I draw portrait of my wife. [*an arrow leads to his usual sketch of Catherine*]
who is writing to you -

---

[1] Although there is no addressee on this letter, it does have a sketch of a person in a chair at the top, and it may have been a second sheet of a letter to W. E. Henley.

THE LETTERS: 1880-1903

APPENDIX

In nearly forty years of thinking about H. G. Wells, his life and his work, many of my ideas have changed, by long thought, conversation, or the simple erosion of jejune ideas and attitudes by both time and evidence.

One of the more telling changes came when I began to think of Catherine Wells as she really was, as Catherine, not 'Jane'. Why she agreed to the name change, or why Wells proposed it is simply something we will never know. I have described her as elusive, diaphanous, painted in pastels, but also as a tough business person, a protector of her own and other's rights and a dynamic intellectual. But, she still does not speak to us enough. (To rectify this fault, I am currently working on a biography of Catherine Wells, which will be presented with some unpublished work of hers.)

I am convinced that truly to understand H. G. Wells, one must also begin to understand Amy Catherine Robbins Wells. To that end, I include here five letters from Catherine to Wells to allow the reader a further glimpse into her character.

Letters A6-A8 cover correspondence with Winston Churchill which I tracked down on a visit to Churchill College at Cambridge after the pagination of the text had been completed. I consider they are of sufficient importance to warrant inclusion in this volume.

A1. Catherine Wells to H. G. Wells

Illinois, AL

Spade House,
Sandgate [c. 1900-1901]

Dearest, dearest, dearest, dearest – do not forget me – do not fail me. My dear love do not doubt. Do believe in me a little – till I make you quite believe – till I can show you. Oh, but I love you and I am just longing, longing for the time to come. My very very dear.
Your (shameless) wife in love

A2. Catherine Wells to H. G. Wells

Illinois, AL

Spade House
Sandgate

Tuesday night
[1901–1902]

My <u>Dearest</u> (<u>Still</u>!)

It is half past nine & no boddy to come & gossip stoopid rubbidge in its ear at all! And <u>where</u> are you? I don't know where you are laying your homeless fuff. Perhaps under the stars – unable to find a roof.

Dear one, I am very sorry, I was all silly old crying when you went. I didn't really feel a bit dismal, only somehow I think you reduce me to a sort of dewpoint – & the foolish thing is always being tearful and doesn't want to be.

Ever since you went G.P. hasn't uttered a sound – not finding it any fun to squeak when "farger" wasn't about. Ah! I called up my address book & found all sorts of amoosin' fings which was a most nice 'sprise. Also I have gained possession of the cheque book! The window & the hill have been most amoosing all day, & I am staying in the same room. Pinnie cannot come till tomorrow – she says she saw May off all right. Only one letter for you – request for subscription to memorial to Charlotte Yonge – shall I send £50?

My dearest – my dearest – good night.

My love to the Henley's & to Mrs. Maitbryde. –

A3. Catherine Wells to H. G. Wells

Illinois, ALS

Spade House
Sandgate

[September 1903]

My dearest, dearest.

I had your letter this morning, & darling one, you write me letters full of tender, sweet things, & they make me cry, & they are sweeter to have than you can possibly think. And I laughed a great deal over your 'scription of poor Wallas' boots, & altogether it was well that I had taken the letter, being a letter from my very dear one, away to a quiet corner of the garden to read. Oh! you dearest thing in the world. I can fink of you & I know just how your dear hair feels when I ruffle it up & every fing about you.

I am really not feeling any blues at all. I have embarked on vast seas of silly needle-work things & I take an outing every day; this evening I walked into Folkestone, & that makes me sleep well & not be frightened in the least. And it only seems dull when I call to mind what a difference it is when you are old at mome.[1]

A characteristic letter from Gissing isn't it? His remarks about benefit to his poor health from the recent [departure] from St. Jean de Luz (wh. used to be absolute perfection for him) & his note about Henley's wealth are particularly fine. Waugh writes he will wait to hear from you before venturing to publish M. in M.

No Thomases come yet. Perhaps tomorrow. Gip has been in hysterics of rapture all day because there is a circus here, & he saw the procession. Also stray elephants & such like from early morning, & the universe has been a rapturous feast of Jumbos & camels & everything he likes best. Take care of yourself, though I know you will. It's very queer that I always regard myself as afraid in this world up to a ripe age, quite solidly, & you you seem to hang beside me by the slenderest thread of chance, that at any instant may snap. (Silly old Bitz).

My dear, dear, dear,
your Bitz

---

[1] I believe this is a piece of personal vocabulary, perhaps, 'hold at home'.

A4. Catherine Wells to H. G. Wells

Illinois, ALS

Spade House Wednesday
Sandgate Apr. 4th 1906.

<u>Dearest</u> Bins.

Please Bins, would like you to come nome how. Just – for an hour or two, then go back! Becos the nome is not a nice nome, but very whitewashy, & the garden not sutch a nice garden as some day when I have put in more flowers. It was fine, & Gip & I had dinner together on the verandah. There was Canary pudding, which he ate immediately, & then remarked, "Mrs. Kemp's canary is dead." (Profound pause) "I spose this <u>is</u> Mrs. Kemp's canary." He also came & was a dear old noosance while I gardened. He thinks the new steps quite agreeable to glide about on & climb over the side of, & I gardened little fings into that wall, & put in nasturtium seeds all ready, for dear Bins. I picture you, dearest, just arriving at the Stature of Liberty this vey minnit. & having all your nice luggage upset on the quay by customs house. & then you sobbing becos you can't pack it again. Presshus dear! Well, I gardened. & then went to see Lady Chichester, who tells me that holy terror Lady Jane Taylor is in Folkstone. I hope she won't come after poor Bitz (picshur wanted here) [*a sketch of Lady Taylor chasing Catherine*] Dear lady Chichester was wearing a skirt all bunched up with straps – a real German one. & she took one all round the garden, gave me a large bunch of cammelias & showed me all her china too. Old ladies fink I am such a nice little meek fing, Bins. Mrs. Gaylady Wilshire & sister come tomorrow. She said she knew when she saw me that we should have a <u>great</u> deal to say to one another. I'm rather skeered, fearing she is a little bit Soulful. But I will do my best dear Bins. I kiss you dearest. dearest. Oh! you must love old Bitz! Old Bitz luvs nuffin s'cept you.

Gettin some captivatin costumes to kill you wiv.
Your evr own
Bitz.

A5. Catherine Wells to H. G. Wells

Illinois, ALS

Spade House
Sandgate

Thursday
Ap. 26th [1906]

My dearest, very dear love.

Writing in pencil in my bedder room, the house being rather pervaded by hammering & so on. Beryl Reeves to lunch, who made it evident she thought it an enormous treat to come to lunch with me – tea to Mrs. Croker, who went on talking in one solid flow for two hours & a half. I getting away at last by a determined & plucky effort. Poor old Croker doddering in & out – he has had a brain 'Illness' & it doesn't seem to have improved that article very much.

Dear love, dear love, is it all well with you? This is the last letter for Chicago, after this they shall go to Washington, which will make another stage in this long long, oh you don't know how long time.

I feel tonight so tired of playing wiv' making the home comfy, & do if there was only one dear rest place in the world. & that was in the arms & heart of you.

There is the only place I shall ever find in this world when one has some times peace from the silly, wasteful muddle of one's life. Think. I am thinking continually of the disappointing mess of it. The high bright ambitions one begins with, the dismal concessions – the growth, like a clogging hard crust over one of house & furniture & a lot of clothes & books & gardens, a load dragging one down. If I set out to make a comfortable home for you to do work in, I merely succeed in contriving a place where you are bored to death. I make love to you & have you for my friend to the exclusion of plenty of people who would be infinitely more satisfying to you. Well, dear, I don't think I ought to send you such a letter. It's only a mood you know, but theres no time to write another & I have been letting myself go in a foolish fashion. It's all right, you know, really, only you see I've had so much of my own society now, & I am very naturally getting of such a person as I am. How you can ever stand it! Well.

Your very loving CB.

Praps its Mrs. Croker has depressed me. Yes! Yes it is him. Croker. She is so frivolous!

A6. To Winston Churchill[1]

Churchill, ALS

Spade House, Sandgate   19-11-01

To Winston Churchill, Esq.

Dear Sir

I am greatly flattered & interested by your letter and glad indeed that my publishers have done me the kindness to send you a copy. But you bring home to me very clearly that – very probably because my desire to win some scientific & medical people to my view – I have failed to give the proper value to one very important point. My predominating people to come are to be "educated not trained" (see pages 84 & 140) and in your litany where it came to "from the drum of all specialists" I too will most heartily join in the "god [illegible word] delivers us" with you. Indeed, in another book, The First Men in the Moon, which ___[2] is publishing, I have been giving the specializer sort to the best of my ability.

That you should find my estimate of the rapidity of development excessive is simply due to the difference in our social circumstances. You belong to a class that has scarcely altered internally in a hundred years. If you could be transported by some magic into the household of your ancestors of 1800, a week would make you at home with them. In that time the tailor, hairdresser & the atmosphere of different manners would have done all that was needed. But of the great grandparents who [illegible word] me in 1800 it's highly probable they could not read & that any of them would find me & that I should find them as alien as contemporary Chinese. I really do not think that you people who gather in great country homes realize the pace of things.

I must repeat my gratification to find you have read my book & I have had an immediate aim in writing it. I do sincerely believe that Liberalism (as Gladstone knew it) is as dead as Adam and that there is an urgent need for an ordered body of doctrine that will secure for the scattered good intentions that are the soul of Liberalism to come together upon. I have prepared an ordered body of doctrine. Take it or leave it, it is a more coherent & constant thing than any political leader can produce today.

Yours sincerely
H. G. Wells

[1] Churchill had received a copy of *Anticipation* from Wells's publishers. He liked the book and wrote a very long (nine pages) analysis of it for Wells. This letter is Wells's rejoinder.
[2] A contract had not yet been signed. Two publishers had offered to publish the book.

A7. To Winston Churchill

Churchill, ALS   21 11 01

My dear Sir

   I should certainly like the discussion you suggest and I hope you will remember your suggestion when Parliament is sitting. It will interest me tremendously to make your acquaintance. To me you are a particularly interesting & rather terrible figure. Believing as I do that big slides & new fissures are bound to come in the next few years, I fancy at times that you are a little too inclined towards the Old Game. More than anything else I speculate whether you anticipate that when you are sixty you will be in or upon a Conservative Party with a Liberal opposition & an Irish corner in a British or Imperial Parliament & if not where you expect to be.

                                                    Yours very faithfully
                                                    H. G. Wells

A8. To Winston Churchill

Churchill, ALS

                                                                                                  March 5th 02

Winston Churchill, Esq.

My dear Sir
   I shall be in the outer lobby of the House of Commons at 8 tomorrow.

                                                    Yours very sincerely
                                                    H. G. Wells

For Product Safety Concerns and Information please contact our EU
representative GPSR@taylorandfrancis.com
Taylor & Francis Verlag GmbH, Kaufingerstraße 24, 80331 München, Germany

www.ingramcontent.com/pod-product-compliance
Lightning Source LLC
Chambersburg PA
CBHW071220290426
44108CB00013B/1237